ATTACKING AFRICA'S POVERTY

ATTACKING AFRICA'S POVERTY

Experience from the Ground

EDITORS
Louise Fox and Robert Liebenthal

THE WORLD BANK
Washington, D.C.

ISBN-10: 0-8213-6322-0
ISBN-13: 978-0-8213-6322-5
eISBNs: 0-8213-6323-9/978-0-8213-6323-2
DOI: 10.1596/978-0-8213-6322-5

Library of Congress Cataloging-in-Publication Data

Attacking Africa's poverty: experience from the ground / edited by Louise Fox, Robert Liebenthal.
   p. cm.
 Includes bibliographical references and index.
 ISBN-13: 978-0-8213-6322-5
 ISBN-10: 0-8213-6322-0
Economic assistance—Africa—Case studies. 2. Poverty—Africa—Case studies.
   3. Economic development projects—Africa—Case studies. I. Fox, M. Louise. II. Liebenthal, Robert. III. World Bank.

HC800.Z9P6318 2005
339.4'6'096—dc22

2005043453

Cover photo: Primary school, Kampala, Uganda (2003); Arne Hoel/The World Bank.

Contents

I

ATTACKING POVERTY IN AFRICA

II

IMPROVING THE INVESTMENT CLIMATE

v

III

DELIVERING SERVICES TO POOR PEOPLE

Figures

Boxes

Contents   ix

Tables

Foreword

Reducing poverty in Africa might appear to be an elusive, even quixotic, goal, and a book about Africa's successes in reducing poverty might also seem at variance with conventional wisdom about Africa. By all measures, poverty in Africa as a whole has increased and deepened; and the prospect of meeting the Millennium Development Goals seems to be receding.

World Bank forecasts anticipate per capita growth averaging 1.6 percent over the 2006–15 period—a reversal of the region's long-term historical decline. But even this is far short of the growth needed to reduce poverty to half the 1990 level. In fact the number of poor in Sub-Saharan Africa is expected to rise from 314 million in 2001 to 366 million people in 2015. Only one African country, Uganda, has seen a steady, decade-long decline in poverty. In this respect, Africa stands in sharp contrast with the rest of the developing world, especially East Asia, where poverty is being reduced consistently across countries and over time. Why then another book about reducing poverty in Africa, especially since so much has been written, not least in the World Bank, about what is needed to reduce poverty?

There are two reasons. The first is to document experience of successful efforts to reduce poverty in Africa, even if they have not been of sufficient scale, or have been offset by policy failures, conflict, and adverse global conditions, so that we can all learn from this experience. Second, much of what has been said about reducing poverty in Africa either concerns broad policies—macroeconomic stability, structural reform, public expenditure reallocation, and the like—or small islands of success whose larger relevance is often hard to distill. This book attempts to bridge that gap between "big picture" trends and experience and those isolated examples by documenting cases where significant numbers of people were affected.

What emerges is an impressive range of cases. They give grounds for some real hope, and they provide useful learning for all of us—policymakers, governments, businesses, service providers, NGOs, and donors. We learn, for example, how Ghana has been transforming its basic institutions dealing with water and sanitation from bankruptcy and ineffectiveness to financial viability and decent basic service. We learn about Rwanda's efforts to introduce a basic justice system in the wake of one of history's worst episodes of genocide, as the basis for peace and development. We learn how mechanisms to empower communities for basic social infrastructure provision have been developed and scaled up in Malawi and Zambia, two countries whose poverty levels overall have remained obstinately high. We learn how four countries introduced free primary education in the 1990s, despite high poverty levels, immense resource constraints, and huge skepticism from the professionals. Finally, we learn how Kenya grew its horticulture industry to become its second largest export industry—and how it scaled up microfinance institutions, despite corruption and the loss of much external aid.

We learn not only what was done—we learn how. What were the political circumstances? What role did political leaders play? How were institutions changed? How was technology introduced? How did innovation happen? How was information and learning disseminated? Did outside forces, such as donors and trade, help or hinder?

The cases in this book are not a scientific sample. We cannot draw continentwide lessons from them. However, they do tend to confirm much that we already know. In particular, their messages resonate with those from African leaders, through the new mandate of the African Union and its New Partnership for Africa's Development (NEPAD)—especially those of good governance. In a synthesis chapter, the cases are located within the context of Africa's political history, for it is above all in the realm of politics that good governance must be installed and maintained; and it is in the realm of politics that real priority, and not just lip service, is given to poverty reduction and social justice.

Callisto Madavo
Former Vice-President, Africa Region, World Bank and
Visiting Professor, School of Foreign Service,
Georgetown University

Preface

How, in practice, has poverty in Africa been reduced? What have been the factors that have made it happen? Where has poverty actually been reduced? What are some of the successful experiences? These were the main questions that inspired this book and the collection of case studies that it contains.

The cases were developed for the "Scaling Up Poverty Reduction" global learning process, which culminated in the Global Learning Conference in Shanghai, China, from May 25 to 27, 2004, hosted by the government of China and the World Bank. That conference, which brought together more than 600 high-level participants from all over the world, including Presidents Benjamin Mkapa of Tanzania and Yoweri Museveni of Uganda, discussed more than 70 cases from across the developing world, to take stock of the current state of poverty reduction. The purpose was to share insights on the key factors underlying successful experiences in the case studies and to identify practical measures required to accelerate growth and poverty reduction.

Before the conference, 20 global videoconferences brought together several hundred development practitioners to compare and contrast their experiences around these same case studies. In addition, there were seven field visits to review cases on the ground. Now the World Bank is publishing some of the African cases presented at the Shanghai conference to open them up to a wide audience and to focus on Africa-specific lessons from Shanghai.

The framework[1] for the Shanghai case studies emerged directly from *World Development Report 2000/2001: Attacking Poverty*, which set out two strategic pillars as the basis for poverty reduction:

- The investment climate—creating the conditions for markets to operate effectively (good governance and the rule of law, openness to trade and investment, and improved infrastructure).
- Social inclusion—ensuring that poor people have equitable access to assets, services, and markets.

In addition, the "Shanghai framework"[2] suggested four implementation factors that serve as drivers of pro-poor change:

- Commitment and political economy for change—the political will of decisionmakers to undertake the necessary reforms.
- Institutional innovation—building the institutional capacity for innovative solutions.
- Learning and experimentation—the process whereby successful approaches are discovered and applied.
- External catalysts—the role of exogenous factors in stimulating and reinforcing pro-poor changes.

To identify African examples that fit this framework, advice was sought from African governments. There is no pretense that the 12 cases in this book come close to exhausting the possible cases that could have been presented, or that they represent all the best experience in Africa. Among the cases with clear, documented evidence of success, these were selected to be broadly representative of the continent as a whole, and such that the lessons of experience—both success and failure—could be told as candidly as possible.

For each case study, an African presenter with direct experience of the case, generally as a leader or manager, was identified to present the case in the global video dialogues and at Shanghai. Supporting the presenter, consultants were identified to prepare the case studies. The consultants' role was to be the hand that held the pen for the presenters: to collect the relevant facts, present available analysis, and help "tell the

---

1. Scaling Up Poverty Reduction Conceptual Framework, www.worldbank.org/wbi/reducingpoverty/docs/conceptual.pdf
2. See "Conceptual Framework" at www.worldbank.org/wbi/reducingpoverty

story." Presenters and consultants were invited to consider the implementation factors set out above, but were encouraged to tell the story in their own way, with whatever framework they found most illustrative.

The cases are not intended to tell the whole story of poverty in Africa. That has been done in several places.[3] They are intended as part of a learning experience in which events are set out as graphically as possible, including frankly personal anecdotes about how obstacles were overcome. They are not intended to be examples to be replicated uncritically, or stamped out by a machine. Instead, they are intended to stimulate thought and experiment. In addition, given Africa's poor experience overall in poverty reduction, they are intended to demonstrate that there have been and are success stories on the continent.

The Shanghai conference resulted in an Agenda for Poverty Reduction, which summarized the key lessons from the case studies and drew implications for international action.[4] For this book, a synthesis chapter was also prepared to take a little further the thought behind the first implementation factor, political economy for pro-poor change, and relate the experience of the cases to recent African political history.

The book is organized in three parts. Part One contains the synthesis chapter, followed by the country case study of Uganda (Sustaining Growth and Achieving Deep Reductions in Poverty), an integrated view of Uganda's experience over roughly the last decade. At the time of writing, Uganda is the only low-income African country to have reduced poverty steadily for more than one decade. However, Burkina Faso, Ghana, Mozambique, and Tanzania are showing signs of more consistent performance, while Botswana and Mauritius have remained good performers throughout.

Part Two groups the cases related to the investment climate (Ensuring Security and Justice in Rwanda; Fueling Cooperation in the Senegal River Basin; The Kenya Horticulture Success Story; and Harnessing Information and Communications Technologies in Botswana, Mauritius, and Tanzania). Part Three dwells on social inclusion and presents the remaining cases: the Kenya Equity Building Society and the Kenya Rural Enterprise Programme; Free Primary Education in Kenya, Lesotho,

---

3. *World Development Report 2000/2001: Attacking Poverty.* United Nations Human Development Reports.
4. See www.worldbank.org/wbi/reducingpoverty/docs/confDocs/ShanghaiAgenda-FinalVersion.pdf

Malawi, and Uganda; Improving Water and Sanitation Services in Ghana, Lesotho, and South Africa; Defeating Riverblindness; Social Investment Funds in Malawi and Zambia; and Stemming the Spread of HIV/AIDS in Uganda.

The Africa Region team preparing the Africa papers was led by Louise Fox, under the general direction of Paula Donovan, with assistance from Robert Liebenthal. The presenters, consultants, and task managers for the individual case studies are acknowledged throughout the book. Administrative support was provided by Jeannette Kah le Guil and Bona Kim. The case studies were reviewed by Alan Gelb, Sudhir Shetty, and David Dollar. Editorial assistance was provided by Bruce Ross-Larson and Meta de Coquereaumont, with Thomas Roncoli, Christopher Trott, and Timothy Walker.

Abbreviations and Acronyms

ACP	Africa, Caribbean, Pacific
AfDB	African Development Bank
AGOA	African Growth and Opportunity Act
APOC	African Programme for Onchocerciasis Control
ART	antiretroviral therapy
CIE	Interstate Committee (for Management of the Senegal River Basin)
COMESA	Common Market for Eastern and Southern Africa
CWSA	Community Water and Sanitation Agency
CWSP-1	First Community Water and Sanitation Project
Danida	Danish International Development Agency
DCK	Dansk Chrysanthemum and Kultur
DFID	Department for International Development, United Kingdom
DWAF	Department of Water Affairs and Forestry
EAC	East African Community
ECOWAS	Economic Community of West African States
EDG	Guinea Electric (utility)
EDM	Mali Energy (utility)
ESOP	Employee Stock Ownership Program
EU	European Union
FAO	Food and Agriculture Organization of the United Nations
FOB	free on board
FPEAK	Fresh Produce Exporters Association of Kenya

GATT	General Agreement on Tariffs and Trade
GDP	gross domestic product
GEF	Global Environment Facility
GNP	gross national product
GTZ	Deutsche Gesellschaft für Technische Zusammenarbeit (German Technical Cooperation)
GWh	gigawatt-hours
GWSC	Ghana Water and Sewerage Corporation
HIPC	Heavily Indebted Poor Countries
ICT	Information and Communications Technology
ICTR	International Criminal Tribunal for Rwanda
IFC	International Finance Corporation
IMF	International Monetary Fund
ITU	International Telecommunication Union
KANU	Kenya African National Union
KAS	K-Rep Advisory Services (Africa) Ltd.
KDA	K-Rep Development Agency
K-Rep	Kenya Rural Enterprise Programme
KWA	K-Rep Welfare Association
MASAF	Malawi Social Action Fund
MRND	Mouvement Révolutionnaire National pour le Développement
MW	megawatts
NEPAD	New Partnership for Africa's Development
NGDO	nongovernmental development organization
NGO	nongovernmental organization
NRM	National Resistance Movement, Uganda
OCCGE	West African Epidemic Disease Control Organization
OCP	Onchocerciasis Control Programme of West Africa
OERS	Organization for the Coastal States of the Senegal River
OMVS	Senegal River Development Organization
PAPSCA	Program for the Alleviation of the Social Costs of Adjustments
RDP	Reconstruction and Development Programme
RIPA	Rwandan Investment Promotion Authority
RPF	Rwandan Patriotic Front
RRA	Rwanda Revenue Authority
SADC	Southern African Development Community
SAED	Senegal River Development Agency
SENELEC	Senegal National Electric Company
SOGED	Diama Dam Management Company
SOGEM	Manantali Dam Management Company
SONEES	Senegal National Water Company

SRP	Social Recovery Project, Zambia
STD	sexually transmitted disease
TASO	The AIDS Support Organization
TCRA	Tanzania Communications Regulatory Authority
TDR	United Nations Development Programme/World Bank/ World Health Organization Special Program for Research and Training in Tropical Diseases
THETA	Traditional and Modern Health Practitioners Together against AIDS
TRASA	Telecommunications Regulatory Authority of Southern Africa
TTCL	Tanzania Telecommunications Company, Ltd.
UIA	Uganda Investment Authority
UN	United Nations
UNCDF	United Nations Capital Development Fund
UNDP	United Nations Development Programme
UNESCO	United Nations Educational, Scientific and Cultural Organization
UNHCR	United Nations High Commissioner for Refugees
UNICEF	United Nations Children's Fund
UPOV	International Convention for the Protection of New Plant Varieties
USAID	United States Agency for International Development
VCT	voluntary counseling and testing
WHO	World Health Organization
WTO	World Trade Organization
ZAMSIF	Zambia Social Investment Fund

PART One

Attacking Poverty
in Africa

1

The Political Economy of Pro-Poor Policies in Africa
Lessons from the Shanghai Conference Case Studies

RWEKAZA MUKANDALA, LOUISE FOX,
AND ROBERT LIEBENTHAL

As Africa enters the twenty-first century, it is clear that Kwame Nkrumah's prophecy to Africans in the late 1950s—"seek ye first the political kingdom, and all shall be added unto ye"—has not come to pass. The political kingdom was secured with the gaining of political independence, but it remains fractured, fragile, dependent, and weak. The realization of other benefits, especially economic development, has remained elusive. During an era of unprecedented global economic growth, Africa seems to be a continent left behind. While other regions increased per capita income, raised literacy rates, and improved health care, per capita income in Africa was roughly the same in the 1990s as it was at independence in the 1960s. During the 1990s nearly half of all Africans lived on $1 a day or less, and 30 percent of the world's poor lived in Africa—a higher share than at independence. (All monetary amounts are in U.S. dollars.)

Africa also ranks at or near the bottom in global comparisons of social indicators of development such as literacy, life expectancy, and health care. In many African countries

Rwekaza Mukandala can be contacted at redet@udsm.ac.tz, Louise Fox at lfox@worldbank.org, and Robert Liebenthal at rliebenthal@worldbank.org. The authors thank Alan Gelb, Sudhir Shetty, and Joel Barkan for extensive comments.

one in five children dies before the age of five. Across the continent 250 million people lack access to safe water, more than 200 million have no access to health services, more than 140 million young people are illiterate, and less than a quarter of poor rural girls attend primary school. HIV/AIDS is reducing life expectancy by up to 20 years, more than erasing the gains made since the 1950s, and orphans make up almost 15 percent of the population in the most severely affected countries. While developing countries in other regions are exporting a higher proportion of manufactured goods, African economies remain heavily dependent on exports of primary products, unable to diversify their economies or industrialize (Hoekman and Kostecki 2001), leaving Africa with less than a 2 percent share in world trade (World Bank 2000a).

This failure to develop and to eliminate poverty is especially hard to understand given Africa's endowments at independence. Carol Lancaster (1999), for example, speaks for many in the introduction to her book, *Aid to Africa*, when she poses the question: Why, after four decades and billions of dollars in foreign aid, has Africa failed to develop? How is it that Africa has not effectively tackled the problem of poverty despite immense natural resources, including oil, diamonds, gold and other base metals, and agricultural and tourism potential; a declared commitment to development; and the talent of its people?

One way to find an answer is to turn the question on its head. This was the approach used in the Shanghai conference of May 2004, which asked: How can *successful* experiences of poverty reduction be reproduced or scaled up? Surprisingly, despite Africa's overall poor performance, there are many success stories of poverty reduction—some documented in this volume.

In this chapter, we approach the Lancaster question in two ways. First we review the broad internal and international forces that have influenced Africa's political economy of poverty reduction. This is important because the development of society does not occur in a vacuum, nor is it turned on and off like a switch. It is the result of historical forces in both the external and internal environments. These sections look at the political and economic environment outside and inside Africa, analyzing the factors that influenced the adoption and successes of pro-poor policies and programs. They explore the political reasons why overall poverty has not been reduced despite the pockets of success described in the case studies, and suggest ways to create a more conducive political environment.

Next we turn to the lessons from the pockets of success and present nine lessons from the case studies. Eight of these are directly related to some aspect of governance, especially the role of political factors. The ninth is related to the role of innovation, piloting, evaluation, and replication. The case studies suggest that poverty reduction occurs only when it is a high priority for decisionmakers and when they focus on the institutional, technical, economic, and social changes needed to bring it about. References to political will, political commitment, leadership, and political support occur frequently in the case studies—and tend to be present in the successful ones. The case studies also show the importance of learning, adapting, and scaling up; taking advantage of good development; and working together to prosper in favorable times and to find opportunities in unfavorable times. The conclusion draws together lessons from the historical overview and the specific cases on what has driven successful poverty reduction scale-ups in Africa. These drivers include having government leadership that is committed to both democracy and development and that bases its decisions on a rational assessment of realities and the values of inclusiveness and justice. The survey also highlights the importance of a conducive external environment, including an expanding and accessible international trading environment.

Despite the dismal track record of recent history, there are indications that conditions are better for positive change to take place. Since the late 1980s Africa has entered a new era in which most states accept a liberal political order, a market-oriented economy supported by an efficient state, and a commitment to reducing poverty. At the very least, this has reduced the ideological barriers between African countries and donors as well as among African states, raising hopes that more functional partnerships can be forged with external actors and within the continent to address the problem of poverty. Perhaps Kwame Nkrumah's prophecy was correct after all: it was the political kingdom that came first, and only now is Africa finding the right political formula.

The Global Context for Scale-up: External Political Cycles

Multiple factors in the external political environment of Africa worked against successful economic policy and poverty reduction, helping to explain why poverty remained entrenched in much of Africa. However, many other factors were neutral or even positive.

The Cold War and Preferential Trade Arrangements: 1960–80

At independence African countries joined a world divided into two spheres of influence. One centered on the Soviet Union and the centrally planned economies of Eastern Europe, China, and Cuba. The Soviet Union shared an anticolonial and anti-imperialist perspective with the African states, but it was unable to transfer the substantial resources needed by the fragile new states to keep their political and economic systems functioning and to fulfill independence-era promises of development. The limitations of the socialist alternative to the Western-oriented international economy were evidenced by the inability of Mozambique to join the Soviet-dominated Council for Mutual Economic Assistance in 1980. With no realistic options available, African countries were left—and actually encouraged by the Soviet Union—to participate in the Western-dominated international economy (Clapham 1996).

The ground rules for the Western international economy laid after World War II aimed to create an open international trading regime. The main international institutions shaping the Western global economy were the International Monetary Fund (IMF), the World Bank, and the General Agreement on Tariffs and Trade (GATT), whose overriding purposes were to rebuild Europe and ensure that international trade would not be constricted by balance of payments problems, lack of suitable infrastructure, or protectionist policies.

While the wartime experience taught the Western industrial states that an open trading system is the key to global prosperity and security, African countries learned a different lesson, influenced as well by dependence, structuralist thinkers such as Raul Prebisch and Andre Gundre Frank, and the Soviet prewar experience. They concluded that protectionism was needed to spur industrialization and that as primary product producers they would never achieve societal development under an open trading system (Rapley 2002). While the West was working to create an open trading system that reduced trade barriers by extending the most favored nation principle to all trading partners, African and other developing countries pushed for the acceptance of the principle of special and differential treatment in the GATT negotiations. They sought nonreciprocal access to industrial country markets so that they could embark on a policy of import-substitution industrialization within protected domestic markets (Hoekman and Kostecki 2001).

The notion of special and differential treatment underpinned the way African states sought integration with the international economy. As part of the call for a new international economic order, African governments, riding to power on the backs of populist anticolonial movements, demanded that the right to development accompany independence. African and other developing countries argued that their poverty entitled them to a transfer of resources, with as few conditions as possible, from the richer countries (Brown 2000).

The United Nations created benchmarks for the amount of official development assistance that rich countries should provide. Developing countries demanded special loans from the international financial institutions, with low interest rates and long repayment periods. Commodity price support mechanisms were written into international trade agreements such as the 1975 Lome Agreement. U.S. concerns about cold war geopolitics and European desires to protect economic interests in their former colonies facilitated the acceptance of the principle of the right to external assistance (Brown 2000). The rise of the welfare state after World War II and the widespread acceptance of Keynesian economics and other statist models of economic development in the West pointed to the acceptance of an international welfare system and statist economic policies among the poorer "development partner states."

While industrial countries accepted this principle of entitlements, they never fully embraced the large-scale transfer of resources. Very few countries outside Northern Europe met international benchmarks for official development assistance. Preferential access agreements to industrial country markets invariably left out products and commodities that would harm key domestic constituencies, and the burden of debt repayment fell squarely on developing countries until the late 1990s.

African countries actively sought to reduce their dependence on the West and were early rhetorical supporters of regionalism as a path to economic development. The East African Community (EAC) was created in 1967, the Economic Community of West African States (ECOWAS) in 1975, and the Southern African Development Community (SADC) in 1980. But before the 1990s, none of these regional organizations made much progress toward integrating national economies, creating common currencies, or establishing customs unions. During the 1970s and 1980s these efforts at regional integration were hampered by colonial legacies, different development strategies, protectionism, an inability to ensure fair benefits, and national rivalries and personal animosity between leaders. By 1977 the EAC had collapsed, and the other regional organizations were unable to overcome the practical hurdles hindering economic integration. They also failed to achieve their political goal of reorienting the nature of the relationship between African countries and Western donors.

The nature of relations between African countries and advanced industrial countries during this era is perhaps best typified by the Lome Agreements between the 15 countries of the European Union and the 71-nation-strong ACP (Africa, Caribbean, Pacific), the first of which was signed in 1975. Lome gave former European colonies nonreciprocal special access to European markets, and it provided for payments to ACP countries that suffered from lower than expected earnings from their primary commodity exports (Gibb 2000). The original Lome Agreement stressed that Europe and ACP were equal partners, meaning that ACP countries had the sovereign right to choose their own development strategies. Negotiated at the height of developing country "commodity power" in the mid-1970s, the Lome Agreement represented the high-water mark of developing countries' ability to make demands on their industrial country partners (Brown 2000).

During this period the West allowed aid recipient nations considerable discretion in organizing their domestic economic and political systems as they saw fit (Brown 2000). Foreign assistance was provided mainly in the form of project financing, mostly for infrastructure but also for technical assistance. Local "ownership" was not a major concern, and projects were usually run by a cadre of expatriates (sometimes the same ones who had managed the colonial infrastructure). Thanks to buoyant prices for commodity exports, African countries during this period were not as dependent on Western assistance as they became in the years that followed.

For the United States economic assistance was determined largely by cold war geopolitics, while for Europe the main consideration was maintaining influence in former colonies (Clapham 1996). Both emphasized political stability and promotion of overall economic growth; poverty reduction strategies consisted primarily of benefits from a growing economy trickling down to all levels of society. Both self-declared socialist states such as Tanzania and Zambia and nonsocialist states such as Kenya and Côte d'Ivoire tried to greatly expand subsidized and free social services.

The external environment for Africa during this period was not a hindrance to development. Until the oil shocks, the terms of trade were not unfavorable, capital flows were maintained, and the global economic environment was expansionist.

Debt and Adjustment: 1980–90

At the beginning of the 1980s, it was already clear that Africa's performance was lagging badly, and that the gap in performance between Africa and the rest of the developing world was opening up. Between 1960 and 1979 per capita income in 19 African countries grew less than 1 percent, and 15 countries recorded negative per capita growth. By comparison, annual per capita income in all low-income developing countries grew 1.7 percent, and even South Asia registered annual per capita increases of 1.5 percent. In some countries—Côte d'Ivoire, Kenya, Malawi—per capita GNP growth during this period was much more rapid (2.7 percent a year), but these countries, too, fell victim to the terms of the trade shocks of the late 1970s, and they made few inroads against poverty even when growth was strong (World Bank 1981).

At the beginning of the 1980s, the search began for a diagnosis of Africa's poor performance and for strategies to address it. The Organization of African Unity published the Lagos Plan of Action in 1980, calling for a more self-reliant and economically integrated African continent by 2000. The World Bank conducted a series of studies, starting with the Berg Report of 1981. Partly because of growing disillusionment with Africa's economic performance and increasing doubts about the effectiveness of aid, within a decade of the signing of the Lome Agreement the idea that developing countries were entitled to aid from industrial countries came under serious challenge from the industrial countries. In 1979 and 1980 conservative governments took power under Margaret Thatcher in the United Kingdom and Ronald Reagan in the United States. These leaders advanced a neoliberal agenda that was hostile to state involvement in the economy and the notion of entitlements, both domestically and internationally.

This ideological shift to a neoliberal agenda was bolstered by a drastic change in power relations between donor and recipient countries ushered in by the debt crises that began in the late 1970s and assumed dramatic proportions in 1982, when Mexico announced that it was unable to make its foreign loan payments. The debt crisis in Africa was brought about by the fragility of African economies, which could not cope with the spike in import costs due to the oil price shocks of 1973 and 1979 and the subsequent increases in interest rates and drying up of commercial lending.

The emergence of debt problems tipped the balance of power in favor of donor countries and international financial institutions, ushering in what Clapham (1996) calls the era of "externalization of African economic management." To access loans from the IMF and World Bank, African countries were required to restructure their economies. Structural adjustment was a direct attack on the right claimed by African countries to determine their own development strategies because they had to institute market-friendly economic reforms or face the prospect of being cut off from external financial resources. Whatever the merits of the reforms proposed by Africa's donors, most notably the World Bank, their effectiveness was vitiated by their association with the apparent assault on sovereignty represented by the "reform or else" approach. African countries often agreed to conditions only to receive aid, implementing as few of the reforms as they could get away with (Clapham 1996). Half-hearted government commitment led to problematic results. Within Europe and the World Bank there were growing concerns about the costs of structural adjustment for the poor. Declining social indicators spurred the World Bank to focus on the social dimensions of adjustment, while activists pressured for debt forgiveness for African and other poor countries.

Poverty reduction was in general subordinated to concerns over macroeconomic imbalances and the need for reform of the domestic economic environment. The prevailing economic model was "trickle down": the notion that macroeconomic stability plus structural reform to improve the efficiency of resource allocation would, without other interventions, reduce poverty. The assumption was that the smaller the role of the state, the better. Privatization was encouraged, regardless of whether there was a competitive environment to support it. The subsequent failure in the 1990s to improve African economic performance—whether because the diagnosis and policy package was incomplete or because of poor implementation or lack of resources—led to the recognition that a different approach, emphasizing concern about poverty and "ownership," eventually coupled with debt relief, was needed.

The End of the Cold War, the Growth of Global Trade, and the Movement for Debt Forgiveness: 1990–2000

The collapse of the Soviet Union brought about for the first time a truly global economy; with the rise of the World Trade Organization (WTO), a standard set of rules was developed to structure transnational economic relations. Africa's relations with external benefactors also changed as donors introduced overt political conditionality in determining the allocation of aid. By the mid-1990s, donors had recognized the need for debt relief and grants to support poverty reduction programs.

The growth of the WTO and globalization have marked a continuation in the trend of increasing global integration and interdependence, but African countries have largely been left out of this process. Africa's share in global trade has declined since independence, and levels of foreign direct investment are low. Moreover, with the institutionalization of the WTO after 1995, the idea that all countries should be bound by the same rules has replaced the notion of special and differential treatment, which had been a hallmark of Africa's demands in global trade talks.

To win the assent of developing countries to the WTO process, however, the notion that poor countries deserve special treatment has managed to linger on. The European Union's Everything But Arms initiative, adopted in 2001, offers low-income developing countries special access to European markets (except for certain products, such as bananas and sugar, which are to be phased in). The rationale behind Everything But Arms was the same as that underpinning the global trading regime under GATT, namely, that low-income countries were not in a position to compete with industrial countries (or even other more economically advanced developing countries) in an open market and were entitled to special and differential treatment due to their poverty (EU 2001a). A similar rationale motivated the U.S. African Growth and Opportunity Act (AGOA) described below.

The rise of globalization has also sparked renewed interest in regional economic integration in Africa. In the late 1990s, for example, the EAC was revived, and slow but steady progress is being made in West Africa under ECOWAS. New initiatives were launched in southern Africa under SADC, and in southern and eastern Africa under the Common Market for Eastern and Southern Africa (COMESA). With globalization and the rise of regional trading blocks around the world, African leaders are eager to ensure that their continent is able to keep pace with economic change and are taking regional economic integration more seriously. The move to a more liberal order has also removed some of the earlier ideological and economic stumbling blocks to integrating national economies, leaving a favorable external environment for regionalism.

Freed from the constraints of cold war rivalry and disappointed by years of economic stagnation, donors were presented with the opportunity to reduce their commitments to African countries that either did not share their political values or did not offer positive returns on investments. While strategic and national considerations (such as the United States' desire to create alternative sources to Middle East oil) remained a major concern for bilateral donors, there was less urgency to support corrupt and authoritarian regimes. French President François Mitterrand announced the new era in donor-African relations at the Franco-African Summit Meeting in June 1990, when he warned African heads of state that they could no longer count on French support if they undermined popular participation in their countries' politics (Clapham 1996). Soon major donors, including the United States, the United Kingdom, the European Union, and Japan, began to consider democracy and human rights as criteria for distributing aid.

The failed state was as much a part of the 1990s in Africa as was liberalization (Reno 1998). Shorn of external patronage, the state collapsed in Liberia, Sierra Leone, Somalia, and Zaire. The instability caused by civil war adversely affected not only the countries in which the conflicts took place but in their neighbors as well. The economies of Burkina Faso and Mali have been adversely affected by the political instability in Côte d'Ivoire. The whole Great Lakes region of Central and Eastern Africa has paid a price for the political instability in Rwanda, Burundi, Uganda, and the Peoples Democratic Republic of Congo. Instability in Liberia spilled over into Sierra Leone and Guinea. The civil war in Sudan has run on for years and fueled a brutal insurgency in northern Uganda.

On a more positive note, the end of the cold war has allowed many long-standing conflicts that were closely linked to the global superpower competition between the United States and the Soviet Union to end. With the United States no longer fixated on containing communism, conflicts, especially in Southern Africa, were resolved through independence for Namibia, majority rule in South Africa, and the end of insurgencies in Mozambique and Angola.

The end of the cold war also marked a growing acceptance within official donor circles that the debt burden of developing countries was unsustainable and that special actions had to be taken either to forgive debt to free up resources for other areas or to greatly increase aid inflows. By the mid-1990s it was clear that only with debt relief could countries address poverty reduction programs in a sustainable manner, that is, without much greater aid dependence, since higher domestic savings and net exports were not short-term options given the rising poverty levels in Africa. For oil-importing African countries, the terms of trade losses after 1970 cancelled out all the increase in official development assistance (World Bank 2000a). While donor conditionalities remained, they tried to take into account the severe strains that African countries were under.

The enhanced Heavily Indebted Poor Countries (HIPC) Initiative of 1999 (see below) brought about a change in the approach to conditionality. Previously, the basis for IMF and World Bank adjustment programs had been the Policy Framework Paper, which was widely regarded as "made in Washington" and imposed on reluctant governments. Beginning in 2000 the Policy Framework Paper was replaced by the Poverty Reduction Strategy Paper, created by national governments, though still eventually requiring approval by the Bank and the IMF in the context of the provision of concessional assistance by these institutions. The intention was signaled for Africans to be more involved in identifying and prioritizing problems as well as developing homegrown solutions in order to obtain the commitment of implementing agents to reforms.

While there are many positive aspects to the end of the cold war, it has also coincided with donor fatigue at the lack of results in Africa and the need to assist the economic transition from central planning to market economies in the more strategically important countries of Central and Eastern Europe and the former Soviet Union. The share of official development assistance to Sub-Saharan Africa has declined from 35.2 percent in 1989 to 22.5 percent in 1999, and official development assistance per capita has fallen by half, from $45 in 1992 (2002 dollars) to only $21 in 2001–02 (OECD IDS).

Another worrisome trend is protectionism in industrial countries, which prevents African products from competing in Western markets, and subsidies paid to Western agricultural producers, which lead to dumping of low-cost products in African markets. These trade issues in the emerging partnership between Africa and its donors have important implications for how seriously donors take the need for poverty reduction.[1]

The New Pragmatism and the External Focus on Governance, Participation, and Results

A good deal of the blame for Africa's poor development record rests with donor countries. No region in the world is more dependent on aid, and in no other region do donors have as much say over how their aid is used. This has created the problem of donor-driven aid, in which "African governments eager to obtain as much aid as possible . . . have frequently ceded much of the responsibility for identifying, designing, and implementing aid-funded activities to the donors, which have for the most part gladly seized the initiative" (Lancaster 1999, p. 3). The interaction of aid with local institutional development has largely been overlooked. As a result, donors have used aid to displace local institutions—which were very weak anyway, and therefore easy to displace—rather than build them (Easterly 2003). At the same time, some influential research has supported the proposition that aid has been effective in countries with good policies (Burnside and Dollar 2000; World Bank 2000b). Before the end of the cold war, donors were reluctant to stop funding projects and countries in which aid was clearly not effective (Easterly 2003; Lancaster 1999).[2] The basic dilemma was—and remains—that donors either continue to fund failing countries and projects, or apply conditionalities that risk undermining country ownership.

By the end of the twentieth century, donors were exhibiting a new pragmatism based on the realization that throwing money at the problem was not an effective strategy and that official development assistance should increasingly target the deserving poor. Increasingly, donors have called for measurable goals that can be used to determine the effectiveness of assistance. As part of the effort to promote a results-oriented agenda, 191 countries accepted the UN Millennium Development Goals, which set verifiable targets for halving the proportion of people in the world living on less than $1 a day, halving the proportion of people without access to safe drinking water, ensuring universal primary education, reducing the maternal mortality rate by three quarters, reducing the under-five mortality rate by two thirds, and reversing the spread of HIV/AIDS and malaria (White 2002).[3]

In allocating funds there is a movement to take into consideration the success of recipient countries in promoting democracy, human rights, and poverty alleviation policies. In allocating aid, the World Bank and the African Development Bank use similar systems for performance ratings, reflecting economic and social policies and good governance indicators. At the same time, donors are increasingly recognizing the importance of having African development "partners" create their own solutions to economic problems and their own criteria for evaluation.

Initiatives embodying the idea of targeting resources to the deserving poor include HIPC, the African Growth and Opportunity Act, and the U.S. Millennium Challenge Account. HIPC, adopted in 1996, is an IMF and World Bank program to help low-income developing countries with unsustainable debt apply for debt relief; only countries that have undertaken economic reforms are eligible for HIPC relief. The money saved from debt relief is to be targeted to poverty reduction programs. In 1999 HIPC was enhanced to provide deeper and broader debt relief to countries that adopted homegrown poverty reduction strategies, in the expectation that these strategies would be more effectively implemented if countries were accorded more space to design them.

The U.S. government's AGOA operates according to a similar logic, extending preferential access to Sub-Saharan countries to U.S. markets for a limited number of products from 2000 to 2008 (www.agoa.info/). Qualification for AGOA depends on commitment to a set of criteria that includes acceptance of the rule of law, a market-based economy, respect for human rights, and liberal democratic principles. Of course, to benefit from AGOA African countries must have access to the U.S. market (UNECA 2004).

Perhaps the best example of the new results-based aid policies is the U.S. Millennium Challenge Account, announced by President George W. Bush in May 2002. The program promises an extra $5 billion in grants a year by 2006 for countries that can prove they deserve the money based on 16 indicators of good governance, health and education, and sound economic policies. The program is structured as a competition in which countries wishing to apply for additional U.S. assistance are evaluated and compared with one another to determine who receives aid. Seventy-five developing countries participated in the first competition, to gain access to $1 billion. The 16 winners, announced in May 2004, included 8 African countries: Benin, Cape Verde, Ghana, Lesotho, Madagascar, Mali, Mozambique, and Senegal.[4]

The New Partnership for Africa's Development (NEPAD) seeks to create a new basis for Africa's development through a contract between African governments and the people of Africa, recognizing the widespread dissatisfaction within Africa on political governance issues. In addition, it envisages a more balanced partnership between African countries and donors—a relationship in which realistic assessments of needs and performance rather than blind support or conditionalities abound. One of the most innovative aspects of NEPAD is the peer review mechanism, which aims to have African leaders set the governance standards by which they will be judged, as well as undertake the judging. Problems in operationalizing the peer review mechanism get to the heart of the donor-recipient relationship, however. Can African leaders judge themselves and each other objectively, dispassionately, and in a timely fashion to the satisfaction of donors? Relations between Africa and the West take place against a historical background of imperialism, colonialism, and neocolonialism. Since colonial times Western powers have used the euphemism of "partnership" even when the term greatly distorts the true nature of the relationship. Many Africans fear that the old colonial partnership model of inequality has not changed much since independence.

The key question facing current antipoverty initiatives is the degree to which they really represent partnerships among equals—or at the very least partnerships in which the more powerful actors have genuine empathy for Africa and a willingness to take African concerns seriously. Many Africans are looking for Westerners to stop imposing their values and concerns on the continent, while many Westerners are left asking themselves when African countries will be ready to break their solidarity in the face of outside pressure and criticize leaders who are violating agreed upon principles. Both Africans and donors still seem to have important differences over the nature of their new partnership.

Internal Political Cycles and Economic Development

Internal political processes both worked against and contributed to economic development on the continent. In this section, three periods are distinguished: the postindependence period, the "structural adjustment" period of the 1980s, and the round of systemic political changes that started in the early 1990s.

One-party Postindependence Political Systems: 1960–80

At independence, African leaders faced the so-called "politician's dilemma" (Geddes 1994). They had to decide how best to both survive in office and govern efficiently and effectively, nurturing the key institutions needed for sustained economic growth—those that fostered productivity improvements and those that resolved distributional conflicts and ensured a "fair" distribution of resources.[5]

The precedents set during the immediate independence era in Africa set the tone and pace for political and economic developments for the next 25 years. Soon after gaining their sovereignty African leaders turned away en masse—through military coups or peaceful means—from the liberal constitutions inherited from the outgoing colonial regimes, which threatened their tenure, limited their range of action, or both. They instituted one-party states, either de jure or de facto, which guaranteed them security of tenure and provided some of them with the means to intervene in the economy.

Although some leaders acted in good faith, almost all ended up only as survivors: neither the socialists Julius Nyerere of Tanzania and Mathew Kerekeue of Benin nor the consecutive military regimes in Ghana and Nigeria succeeded in bringing about economic development. The political and economic model adopted after independence by African rulers and supported by donor agencies and the World Bank did not produce positive results; the all-encompassing development state failed to improve the lives of ordinary Africans.

The close association between capitalism and liberal constitutions did little to instill the values of political pluralism and private property in newly independent African regimes. Resentful of the colonial racial hierarchies and fearful of continued neocolonial exploitation at the hands of the foreign-owned enterprises dominating the new national economies, many African countries turned to socialism, rapidly expanding the state's role in the economy. Other governments, while not ideologically hostile to capitalism, followed a similar path, establishing single-party regimes and looking to the state to spearhead economic development (Heilman and Lucas 1997). Both socialist and liberal states intervened in the economy to give Africans a greater economic role. In economies in which there was widespread state ownership, Africans were fast-tracked into decisionmaking positions and expected to learn on the job. In countries in which the private sector predominated, credit allocation, employment policy, and negotiation were used to achieve a similar result.

Regardless of ideological persuasion, the postindependence era in Africa failed to produce a state capable of creating an enabling environment for economic development.[6] Not only were states guilty of unproductive interventions in the economy through inappropriate taxation policies, the misallocation of foreign exchange, the undermining of distribution networks, and the redistribution of property; they also retarded economic development through parasitic and corrupt activities that discouraged entrepreneurialism and made business success dependent on political connections (Berman and Leys 1994). Due to its inability to play a nurturing economic role, the African state followed a separate political logic that trumped and undermined economic rationality (Bates 1981).[7]

The implications of the statist development model for poverty reduction were mixed. With the removal of colonial rule and its racial hierarchy, new opportunities were opened up for many Africans, including expanded access to education, health care, and water. But over time the goal of extending cheap or free services to the poor often resulted in a situation in which wealthier urban consumers enjoyed subsidized services to which the poor had no access.

The statist model of economic development adopted in Africa suffered from two key problems. One was that it focused on import-substitution industrialization based on transferring resources from the agricultural sector, where many poor peasants earned their livelihood, to the industrial sector, reducing the resources at the disposal of the rural poor. Another was that African agricultural productivity remained low, incapable of generating the surpluses needed to finance industrialization and an expansion of social services while also allowing rural producers to earn enough to give them an incentive to keep producing for market. Ultimately, the statist development strategy proved to be unsustainable. With the oil price shocks, many African countries could no longer pay for expanded social services, the quality of which declined in the 1970s and 1980s. The oil price shocks also contributed to the debt problem and the rise of structural adjustment in the 1980s, when urban industries were unable to generate foreign currency revenues.[8]

The impact of statist development on pro-poor policies can be seen in the case study on water and sanitation. Attempts by the Ghana Water and Sewerage Company to extend free water to the rural areas by the 1980s could not be maintained by a state enterprise starved of resources. Except in major urban centers, the water and sewerage system fell into disrepair, creating an unintended outcome in which poor people had no water while rich people enjoyed cheap water.[9]

While the state-led model of development was initially able to expand services for the poor, problems led to its decline by the 1970s. With the poor able to require little accountability from the state, programs aimed at providing services to low-income people were frequently transformed into subsidies for better-off urban dwellers. This was possible because avenues of expression and genuine representation were the first casualties of the single-party state. Opposition parties were banned, their leaders were jailed or exiled, legislatures were replaced with rubber-stamp parliaments, and independent judiciaries were subordinated to the party. A similar fate befell autonomous organizations for workers, women, youth, and farmers' cooperatives. This situation of unrestrained power led to, and was in turn reinforced by, a patronage network that in several instances degenerated into extensive rent-seeking networks and prebends. The countries' wealth hemorrhaged into private bank accounts abroad and conspicuous consumption at home. Devoid of any mechanisms for transparency and accountability, authoritarian regimes in Africa trampled on people's rights and aspirations; made decisions that ran their economies into the ground; and failed to correctly assess and adjust to the numerous opportunities, shocks, and bumps in the international environment.

As the ability of the state to provide services and even pay its employees declined, so too did its legitimacy. Poverty reduction was severely impeded in the 1980s as individuals and states turned their attention almost solely to survival. Politically, there was little vision about how to make changes to reverse the decline, and there was no support for major institutional overhauls. Indeed, it was during this period that many crucial state institutions—the judiciary, the parliament, the government administration, the press—collapsed or became compromised. As Levy and Kpundeh (2004, p. 5) say, "With the rise of neopatrimonial rule, the mode of governing bureaucracy shifted from the clarification, monitoring, and enforcement of formal rules to informal rules set without transparency, and sometimes increasingly capriciously, by a country's political leadership." As an important consequence, many of Africa's skilled and trained elite either left the continent, fleeing persecution or seeking more rewarding and secure economic circumstances and becoming the African Diaspora or became marginalized and ineffective. The indigenous business class, small and undeveloped to begin with, became politically dependent and focused on rent-seeking. Africa's capacity to carry out development, which had not been very different from that of other continents at the time of independence, became seriously impaired.

The Politics of Structural Adjustment: 1980–90

The unsustainable political-economic patronage system of the immediate postcolonial era began to collapse by the 1980s—Africa's lost decade—with average per capita GNP falling 0.8 percent a year between 1980 and 1992 (World Bank 1994). Increasing debt, declining outside investment, and deteriorating infrastructure were symptoms of economic decay. African countries experienced frequent power shortages, shortages of essential consumer goods and foodstuffs, and a lack of foreign exchange.

Desperate for funds to keep their economies afloat, as early as 1980 Kenya, Malawi, Mauritius, and Senegal turned to the international financial institutions for structural adjustment loans. By the end of the decade nearly every country in Africa was engaged in structural adjustment programs based on the extension of loans in return for pledges to control budget deficits and the money supply, loosen controls on foreign exchange, remove price controls and subsidies, reduce the size of state bureaucracies, and privatize state enterprises (Clapham 1996).

Although many African leaders initially reacted to structural adjustment by promising to reform and then obfuscating and delaying, some changes were made that had tremendous implications for the African state. Economic decline coupled with loan conditions reduced the resources available to African leaders to pursue the logic of patronage "big man" politics (or even to maintain a state-controlled economy).

As the Uganda case study points out, the leftist-oriented National Resistance Movement (NRM), after taking power in 1986, quickly realized that it did not have the resources to initiate its program of societal revival (chapter 2). Within a year of taking power, the NRM dropped its rigid ideological opposition to structural adjustment and reached an agreement with the IMF that paved the way for a World Bank loan, additional aid, and debt rescheduling. Partly as a result, economic growth reached 7.7 percent in 1988. By 1992 a period of sustained economic growth helped invigorate a reform program that had previously been characterized by pockets of official resistance and inconsistent implementation. As economic growth continued, it strengthened the position of reformers and won converts among the leftists, including President Yoweri Museveni. With internal consensus on the structure of the economy, the NRM government fully committed itself to economic reforms and working with the international financial institutions. A similar process occurred in other African countries, including Ghana and even Tanzania, where the government resisted a structural adjustment deal with the IMF until 1986 and did not fully commit itself to economic reform until President Benjamin Mkapa came to power in 1995.

Following on the heels of structural adjustment were demands for political reforms. A hallmark of the centralized African state created after independence was the concentration of political power in the hands of a leader or a small clique of elites. The lack of term limits and competition for the ultimate position of political authority substantially reduced and in some cases completely removed government accountability to society. Internationally, the cold war alliance system set up a quid pro quo in which African states were free to set up domestic political orders as they saw fit in return for supporting their superpower's geopolitical strategy on the continent (Clapham 1996).

With the collapse of the Soviet Union and communism as a global political force, the West lost its interest in maintaining client states in Africa, opening the door for political change and ushering in the new liberal era of the 1990s. This coincided with the growing internal demand for democracy and an end to corruption and economic mismanagement. While structural adjustment did imply changes in governance, and liberal economic reforms were the beginning of the reassertion of professionalism and the start of efforts to address capacity issues, all too often capacity issues were not addressed and as a result reforms were partial and incomplete. Uganda's experience is again instructive, demonstrating the important contribution made by the renaissance of a strong, highly meritocratic planning and finance ministry to mastermind and implement far-reaching reforms. But it was the end of the cold war that finally allowed outside powers more room to champion the cause of human rights, multiparty politics, a free press, and independent civil society groups.

The combination of economic and political reforms provided donors with the opportunity to form development partnerships with nonstate actors, to hold African states accountable for the use of and management of their domestic economies, and to promote changes that would enhance the ability of emerging civil society groups to hold their governments accountable. If the military coup in Togo in 1962 ushered in the era of political dictatorship in Africa, the National Conference in Benin in 1990 dramatically focused attention on the need to redress a state that had collapsed.

The Emerging Paradigm: Second Political Transition, 1990–2000

Structural adjustment policies were highly controversial, in part because they involved a fundamental reshaping of society. The resulting disruption and change led to new opportunities for some and imposed costs on others. Indeed, a core issue in the debate over structural adjustment was its impact on the poor. Some observers believed it created new opportunities for rural producers of primary products to earn more from sales on the international market and for exporters to expand operations. They justified structural adjustment on the grounds that without basic changes in the national economy sustained economic growth was impossible. They legitimized the painful costs of adjustment using the trickle-down logic that benefits from a growing economy would eventually reach the poor.

Critics, most notably the United Nations Children's Fund (UNICEF), noted that a disproportionate amount of the cost of structural adjustment was being borne by the poor in the form of the removal of state subsidies for agriculture, health, and education. Moreover, privatization, wage freezes, devaluation, and reduction in the public sector had a severe impact on wage earners and the middle class, many of whom were an important resource for extended families because their relative wealth could be tapped to support the education of relatives' children or help cope with a health emergency. Rapley (2002) has suggested that the economic benefits stemming from structural adjustment were arguable and that the costs of such adjustment seemed to fall disproportionately on the poor and middle class, who were typically dependent on the state and state enterprises for their livelihood. Certainly, mistakes were made in the design of adjustment programs. However, Christiansen, Demery, and Paternostro (2003), reviewing available household data, argue that economic policy reforms (improving macroeconomic balances and liberalizing markets) appear conducive to reducing poverty. They also suggest that market connectedness is important to ensure that poor households gain from economic growth; that education and access to land are important to ensure benefit from economic opportunities; and that social risk management strategies are important, given rainfall variation and the high incidence of ill health. It is notable that the countries that sustained growth in the late 1990s—Burkina Faso, Mali, Mozambique, Tanzania, and Uganda—have undergone adjustment programs.

In the wake of structural adjustment, the 1990s marked a second cycle of fundamental political change. Change seemed to lead states along one of two possible paths. One was characterized by an unprecedented acceptance of liberal political and economic reforms. Throughout the continent, constitutional one-party states were replaced by multiparty systems and competitive elections, including elections in Ghana, Malawi, and Zambia in which the ruling parties were thrown out of office. Reinvigorated parliaments challenged the executive, and the judiciary re-emerged from the shadow of the presidency. At the same time, a vibrant electronic and print media as well as a resurgent civil society reshaped the institutional and political and social order of the

African state. While the institutional underpinnings for democracy remain weak in these countries, and the democratic improvements have not yet resulted in better economic outcomes, the potential for pro-poor change has improved. Periodic elections and binding term limits for president; a dynamic system of checks and balances between the executive, judiciary, and legislature; a vibrant, diverse, and free press; and an organized and active civil society will together in the long run limit opportunities for patronage and impunity. They will also establish and strengthen mechanisms for transparency, accountability, and oversight that will hopefully keep pro-poor change at the top of the agenda.

The change to competitive political systems raises at least the theoretical possibility that Africa's rulers can now be held accountable by their citizens, whose votes determine which party will exercise power. Accountability from below is becoming more important as more countries seek to introduce decentralized systems of government with democratic control. There is also greater emphasis on accountability from above, as donor countries and institutions are increasingly looking to allocate assistance to the deserving rather than the needy or needed. Several of the case studies show how the potential for community-driven development is being enhanced by decentralization or challenged by its absence. Countries such as Tanzania and Uganda have been able to make political and economic changes and reverse years of decline. Other African states have not been able to adjust to the new conditions of the post-cold war era, as the state and the patronage system on which it was based was undermined by structural adjustment and increasing conditionality without being replaced by a new national system to make authoritative decisions. In countries such as Liberia, Sierra Leone, and Somalia, state collapse was the path.

Despite the instability of some countries, the trend has been toward a more plural order in Africa, with the military moving out of politics and an independent civil society playing a more central role. The market has slowly replaced the state as the engine of growth. External and internal forces have started forcing politicians to make rational choices and practices by demanding more transparency and providing a brake on government discretion. The extent to which these new trends will lead to real institutional changes remains to be seen, particularly in light of new burdens, most notably the need to slow the HIV/AIDS epidemic and absorb its costs. Reforms continue to suffer from capacity constraints, which tend to be addressed in a piecemeal fashion through training, technical assistance, and right-sizing of organizations rather than through demand-driven reform aimed at restoring a rule-based bureaucracy.

Governance and the Political Economy of the Results Agenda: What Is Changing?

One of the major differences between the postindependence and the liberal era is a broader, albeit fragile, consensus about the central role of markets in driving economic growth and the need for states to play a constructive supporting role in the economy. Politically, there is greater pluralism, with multiparty elections, even for the highest office, increasingly common. The framework for political governance, though still weak in most countries, is improving.

This has created an unprecedented opportunity for strengthening complementary pressures domestically and externally to hold the state accountable and to push political elites to take seriously corruption and the misuse of resources. As the case studies show, competitive elections have forced leaders to recognize voter concerns and explore ways to provide such pro-poor programs as universal primary education and increased access to water as strategies to win votes.

However, political reforms are not leading in a straight line to the institutionalization of impartial professional bureaucracies, democracy, and accountability (Kelsall 2002). Instead, old patronage networks are being restructured to operate in a changed environment, limiting the impact of reforms designed to lead to a more rational use of resources. As a donor official in Tanzania notes, "[The people we see,] the Permanent Secretaries, those who speak the language of 'good governance,' those who talk the talk even if they don't walk the walk, are like a shop window—what is put on public display. But of course the real decisions are made behind the shop window, in the 'smoke-filled rooms' of the CCM [the Revolutionary State Party]" (Kelsall 2002). Still, the CCM needs to obtain a mandate from the people every five years. The return to power of stalwarts of the Kenya African National Union (KANU) under a new party in Kenya's 2003 general election and its difficulties in getting to work, the extensive profiteering from conflicts in Central and West Africa, and widespread corruption throughout the continent suggest that the struggle to reform the state so that it is both willing and able to deliver on pro-poor policies is still a work in progress.

The new environment for poverty reduction at the turn of the century is one of cautious optimism. A new pragmatism has been adopted, and there are incentives and commitment to setting and reaching achievable goals. Outside areas of civil unrest, there is a new emphasis on building institutions that work. Most politicians no longer seek to stay in office at the expense of sustainable rational economic policies. Indeed, they see such policies as a sure way of political survival in the long term.

What Do the African Success Stories Tell Us about the Political Economy of Scaled-up Poverty Reduction?

The previous sections discussed the external and internal forces in the political environment that have combined since independence to support or hinder Africa's attempt to scale up poverty reduction. The case studies in this section show how a conducive political environment can in practical ways translate into effective poverty reduction. Several lessons about the political economy of scale-up can be drawn from these case studies. Although the lessons are African, they are consistent with lessons from other regions as well (World Bank n.d.).

1. *Sound national economic policies that support inclusive, broad-based growth are essential.* Putting these policies in place has proved easier said than done, as Africa has suffered high volatility in economic performance, which has hindered poverty reduction. Countries that have been able to achieve rapid poverty reduction—Chile, China, Costa Rica, India, Indonesia, the Republic of Korea—have done so through sustained per capita economic growth. The range of political systems outside Africa shows that there is no simple correlation between political pluralism and economic performance. What are needed are checks on government power that make governments accountable.

The unique historical circumstances of particular countries determine the political system most likely to succeed in managing the economy in a volatile environment, supporting growth, and making sure that the benefits of growth are distributed to the poor. In the 31 years between 1961 and 2002, China had only 3 years of negative per capita income growth. During the same period Sub-Saharan African countries averaged 18 years of negative per capita income growth. The lesson from the structural adjustment period of the 1980s and 1990s is that, without substantial institutional change, a short period of macroeconomic stabilization followed by donor-led pump-priming does not produce the sustained growth needed for poverty reduction (Rodrik 2003). Sustained growth requires stable and sound economic fundamentals at all levels, including a sound climate for investment and entrepreneurship in all sectors.

The Uganda case study (chapter 2) clearly shows that scaled-up poverty reduction can be achieved when the political system is able to support stable economic policies in a nationally led environment of gradual but continuous reform. By putting the essential building blocks in place early—consistently good macroeconomic management, trade openness, and a focus on getting services to the poor, especially in rural areas—and sticking with the vision as it started to show results, Uganda was able to enjoy one of the longest periods of per capita growth and poverty reduction in the region. Early gains did not collapse because reforms continued throughout the period, supporting structural change in the economy. Consistent donor support has also been important, reducing this potential source of volatility. Uganda was one of the first countries in Africa to develop a national poverty strategy, and it has consistently focused the national policy dialogue as well as the dialogue with donors on implementing this strategy.

Uganda's challenge is to maintain this political and economic momentum while developing a more pluralistic and inclusive political system. With population growth of 3.5 percent a year—one of the highest in Sub-Saharan Africa—Uganda has to maintain a high rate of economic growth and continue to ensure that welfare improvements target the poor to keep the poverty reduction process alive. If it does not, the population will have little stake in supporting the political system. The outcome of ongoing debates in Uganda on the transition to a multiparty democracy with clear pathways for renewing leadership will be crucial if large-scale poverty reduction and welfare improvement are to continue during the next decade.

2. *A competitive economic environment, open to risk taking, innovation, and learning, is essential.* Private sector development as a poverty reduction strategy has long been debated in Africa. Initial skepticism about the private sector, which developed during the colonial period, led African countries to adopt policies and practices that undermine key institutions of private sector growth, such as security of property, sound banking systems, and a competitive environment. Combined with trade restrictions, the result was a decline in Africa's share of world trade and foreign direct investment, resulting in the marginalization of Africa in the global economy.

The development of Kenya's horticultural industry demonstrates the potential of private sector-led development of high-value exports to create income opportunities for farmers and workers (chapter 5). Over a 30-year period horticulture exports have grown to become Kenya's second-largest foreign exchange earner—and they are expected to overtake the current leader, tea, in a few years. Development of the industry was achieved through the transfer of technology, capital, and practices from overseas, adapted by local entrepreneurs. Kenya maintained a policy of secure property rights and encouraged exports through a competitive exchange rate. As a result, entrepreneurs were prepared to take risks and persist in the face of setbacks. Eventually, the government learned to facilitate the growth of the industry through public investment in trade and transport facilitation, in addition to maintaining a stable (albeit corrupt) economic and political environment. Both entrepreneurs and workers have benefited, with employees and self-employed contract farmers earning higher incomes than they could outside the sector, helping to lift their families out of poverty.

When governments have allowed private competition in the domestic market, private investment has helped African countries scale up access to services, providing more flexible and innovative approaches than public sector monopolies. Private mobile phone operators have massively expanded telephone coverage in Mauritius, Tanzania, and elsewhere (chapter 6). The successful reform of the state telephone company resulted in a large increase in the number of fixed-line connections in Tanzania. However, much greater growth occurred in the number of mobile subscribers, which leaped from 1,500 in 1993 to 750,000 a decade later.

3. *More open political processes, which mobilize pro-poor stakeholders, often produce success stories, but leadership is key in translating that mobilization into practice.* An outstanding example is South Africa's drive to extend water supply to 7 million additional rural consumers after 1994 (chapter 10)—a direct result of democracy and the end of apartheid. Leadership from the top has been critical in translating this new political voice into action, especially when the political leadership combines with the technical leadership in the public sector, as in South Africa, where the ambitions of the African National Congress were made possible through dedicated technical leadership at the Department of Water Affairs and Forestry. Another example is the spread of free primary education, a key demand of the poor, which occurred in some East and Southern African countries when politicians began needing votes.

Successful leaders have taken advantage of crises or opportunities for change. In Rwanda the leadership of the Rwandan Patriotic Front

(RPF), under President Paul Kagame, realized the urgency of changing behavior after the genocide (chapter 3). It also recognized the importance of defining and pursuing a vision. For 10 years the RPF leadership has consistently and relentlessly pursued the goal of eliminating ethnic cleavages in Rwanda by building institutions that are ethnically neutral. Similarly, in Tanzania President Nyerere and his successors have provided the visionary leadership for a wide variety of difficult reforms, allowing Tanzania to maintain growth in excess of 6 percent since 1997.

Effective leadership is not a solo act: crucial to leadership is building and empowering a guiding team. A good example of this was the technocratic economic team that President Museveni built in Uganda in the late 1980s and early 1990s, which developed and implemented reform programs with strong political support (chapter 2).

To be effective, leaders must consistently and clearly communicate the need for change to stakeholders, listening to their concerns and bringing them along through clear and inspiring messages. President Museveni's personal communication about the need to change behavior in order to stop the spread of HIV/AIDS was an important element of Uganda's success (chapter 13).

Leaders must also practice what they preach. In Tanzania it was important that President Nyerere himself followed the rules established for ethics and the transition to a multiparty system. Even after retiring, he kept up the pressure for others to follow the rules.

4. *Regional cooperation is important.* Despite political rhetoric, regional integration has made slow progress in Africa as countries have been unable to find the basis for stable regional agreements. The lack of regional integration has meant that Africa, a large and sparsely populated continent, has not been able to achieve economies of scale in areas such as natural resource development and regional infrastructure networks. Africa is subject to significant rainfall variability, which results in droughts and floods requiring regional water management practices and infrastructure. However, river systems are fragmented by national boundaries. Enhanced regional cooperation is a must because investments are often profitable only on a regional basis. International river basins need all stakeholders to agree on investments. Poorly functioning infrastructure and the absence of adequate cross-border trade facilitation and logistics result in a lack of connectivity to markets and services for much of Africa's population, reducing the productivity of capital and labor—and the potential for reducing poverty.

The Senegal River Basin Development Organization (OMVS), a 30-year-old development partnership among three African countries in the Senegal River basin, shows that regional cooperation can achieve scaled-up results and reduce poverty (chapter 4). By jointly owning and managing two dams and the related electricity grid, Mali, Mauritania, and Senegal produce more reliable electricity and water, which results in higher investments and incomes throughout the basin and beyond. The three countries have adopted the benefit-sharing principle by locating investments in a way that maximizes returns and then sharing the benefits equitably. Visionary leadership in all three countries saw the potential long-term gains from the partnership and kept it going through economic and political crises in partner countries. The stability of the partnership spilled over to other areas, preventing regional conflict. The leadership learned from early mistakes and continued to adapt the institutions managed by the OMVS partnership. Guinea, which pulled out of the partnership early on, has now asked to be readmitted.

5. *Empowering the poor through community involvement is key to reducing poverty.* It is now widely recognized that development needs to be based on a broadly owned strategy that empowers the poor. Experience throughout the world, including in Africa, shows that community-driven development projects and processes deliver public investments to poor people faster, cheaper, and better. They do so by building into the project design a strong channel for local communities—the stakeholders—to make their own decisions, within a clear and transparent accountability structure.

All of the case studies involving public investments confirm the potential of this approach to enhance the effectiveness of national and donor public funding. Community empowerment and participation was a key element not only in the two social fund case studies but also in the case studies on rural water and sanitation expansion in Ghana, Lesotho, and South Africa (chapter 10); HIV/AIDS in Uganda (chapter 13); reconciliation in Rwanda (chapter 3); and riverblindness in West Africa, Central Africa, and Eastern Africa (chapter 11). The OMVS responded to problems in managing the ecological environment by increasing community participation and local management of the irrigation infrastructure.

The principle that clients know best—and can, with some technical support, design, operate, and manage their own services when given voice and control—was anathema in Africa until the early 1990s, despite the long existence of capable community structures. In the past, national policymakers and donors have mistrusted communities' ability to diagnose local problems, identify priorities and come up with solutions, and implement projects, including accountability structures. The community-based approach to rural drug delivery to eradicate river-blindness met with initial hesitation from national and international health sector professionals. However, it worked and has been scaled up to cover 20 countries and several other disabling infectious diseases. By trusting communities to actually handle funds themselves, the social funds in Malawi and Zambia (chapter 12) disbursed money more rapidly and more effectively than even the most optimistic predictions of donors had projected.

6. *Institutional change is needed.* The community-driven development approach arose in response to failing central ministries; its success is posing a political challenge to those institutions. While self-standing community-driven development projects are a way of scaling up investments for poor communities, sustainability requires institutional change by the central government.

Governments need to find ways to transform public institutions to increase accountability to the poor by embedding community empowerment in a permanent institutional structure provided by local governments. This implies effective decentralization of administration, resources, and political power, backed by a strong accountability structure. This is now the challenge facing the social funds in Malawi and Zambia. While these projects have demonstrated that even in periods of macroeconomic turmoil and weak governance progress can be achieved in reaching the poor with infrastructure, current weaknesses in the economic policy environment of expenditure management and fiscal and administrative decentralization limit progress.

South Africa and Uganda are two countries that have been able to implement decentralized, community-driven service delivery by using clear and transparent rules of the game and public information to increase the accountability of local leaders. Decentralization in Uganda has increased the percentage of education funds reaching their beneficiaries from 18 percent before decentralization to 80 percent in 2003. The Uganda case study (chapter 2) documents how the central government was able to oversee the use of these funds by giving conditional grants and publicly announcing over the radio the amount that the central government provides to districts. Uganda used a phased approach (another good practice) in which expenditure flexibility was provided gradually as local government planning and implementation capacity grew and institutional structures evolved. In both countries, public information on budget allocations at a very decentralized level is widely available, supporting community monitoring and accountability efforts.

Decentralization is not inherently a better way of allocating funding unless a workable system is put into place to make sure that funds are used properly. This means recognizing that it is often difficult for people at the local level to scrutinize the use of money; to do so, they need to become empowered. Creative strategies must be developed at the local level to ensure local involvement in the use of public resources, and strategies must be creatively pursued to ensure that the central government takes seriously and effectively implements its responsibilities in regard to its oversight functions. The devil is in the details: designing projects carefully, paying attention to implementation, and ensuring local and community level accountability. Decentralization creates the potential for greater accountability, but it can also strengthen patronage networks at the local level.

7. *Pro-poor programs need an effective and transparent state with a stable regulatory environment.* While the case studies provide examples of the private sector innovatively providing more, better, and cheaper services to the poor than the public sector, these same case studies also demonstrate the need for an effective, transparent state.

Microfinance is a good example of this. Owing to its stable macroeconomic environment and tradition of private banking, Kenya has provided a laboratory for microfinance scale-up, providing credit for small business and banking services to the poor. K-Rep Bank successively transformed itself from an aid-funded project to a microfinance NGO and then to a full-service bank specializing in microcredit (chapter 8). In the process, a new business model was developed and the regulatory regime was changed to help other microfinance banks develop. Equity Building Society imported microfinance technology with the support of the United Nations Development Programme, then adapted it to its needs. It pioneered mobile banks and developed new products, including contractual savings, to serve the needs of farmers and low-income clients. The success of these efforts can be attributed to an environment that fostered private sector innovation, rewarding the commitment and drive for results of the leadership, and the relentless focus on low-income clients, which motivated management to stick it out through difficult times.

The expansion of telecommunications through mobile phones also shows that private sector provision of services to the poor has expanded most rapidly in stable regulatory environments that respond proactively to innovation (chapter 6). Community-driven development has also encouraged the growth of the private sector to the benefit of the poor, as communities contracted local private sector contractors who provided more flexibility and better quality than public service providers. In Lesotho private contractors were trained to build latrines, providing an important source of income in rural areas for these contractors, one-quarter of whom are women (chapter 10). The social funds in Malawi and Zambia both used community contracting, which resulted in cheaper and better infrastructure.

8. *Restoring security is a precondition for scaled-up poverty reduction.* During the past two decades violent conflicts have taken an increasing toll on Africa's development prospects, reversing years of economic and social progress in months. In addition to the devastating human toll of conflict, the costs include disruption of public services, infrastructure, public institutions, and social capital. Restoring security and a functioning economy are enormous challenges: about half of all postconflict countries return to war within five years of a peace agreement.

The case studies of Rwanda and Uganda show that restoring security is possible even in poisoned environments and that the benefits to poverty reduction from doing so can be very high. Both countries restored order through an inclusive and pluralistic approach to building institutions. In Rwanda the postgenocide government focused on developing pluralistic institutions and creating a new national identity that transcends ethnicity. Strong efforts were made to demobilize and resettle internally displaced persons. Village and community institutions were used to administer justice and foster truth-telling and reconciliation between perpetrators and their victims, helping restore the rule of law. Solid macroeconomic management and donor support helped normal economic activity resume. Public sector management capacity grew to the point that it can now support a broad-based economic reform and development program. The benefits of the successful postconflict strategy have been steady economic growth and a 10 percentage point reduction in poverty.

In Uganda discipline was restored to the army so that it stopped plundering the countryside, allowing normal economic activity to recommence. A few ministries were built up quickly with capable and trusted staff and given a high degree of authority. Political and fiscal decentralization policies helped foster an inclusive development model, promoting reconciliation and poverty reduction. Nonetheless, low-level conflict has simmered in the north, hindering poverty reduction efforts there.

9. *The classic strategy of innovate, pilot, evaluate, and replicate remains valid in Africa, provided the environment is supportive of innovation.* Many successful scale-ups have involved a visionary change agent who had an idea that produced a quick win, which then fueled more widespread adoption and adaptation, ultimately bringing about systemic change. One example is free primary education in East Africa, which started as a response to political imperatives against the advice and wishes of technocrats and donors (chapter 9). Once the commitment had been made, countries learned from their own and one another's experience. The African Programme for Onchocerciasis Control program to fight river-blindness is a classic scale-up from early pilots in a few West African countries to 20 countries and multiple diseases (chapter 11). The transformation of Ghana's rural water supply program from a centralized supply-driven model to one in which local governments and communities plan, operate, and maintain their own water services was first piloted in several areas (chapter 10). The lessons from these pilots were incorporated in new national programs endorsed by stakeholders. In all cases donor support for the evolution of successful approaches was an important part of the mix, as was a clear monitoring and evaluation process from clients to policymakers. Staff training and capacity building to institutionalize the learning was also key in these scale-ups, as was the institutional transformation of microcredit institutions.

Conclusion

The rhetoric of improvement in the lives of the African people has been on the lips of all Africans in power since independence. The same can be said for donors. Yet until very recently very little if anything concrete had been achieved in turning back the scourge of ignorance, hunger, and disease. Previous sections of this chapter have shown that economic stagnation increases poverty and results from a combination of structural and agency factors in both the internal and external environments. These include authoritarian and undemocratic political systems that stifled dissent and alternative viewpoints, state-led economic systems that ignored market forces and degenerated into fertile grounds for patronage, and narrow protectionist nationalism that reinforced obstructive, exclusionary, artificial social, political, and economic barriers. These factors often resulted in an unstable political kingdom characterized by civil war and social unrest, malfunctioning institutions, and personal rule and dictatorship. The external environment was in some respects also unkind, especially the dynamics of the cold war, unstable terms of trade, and mounting debt. Nor was there an ability to take advantage of windows of opportunity and goodwill.

Even so, the case studies in this volume demonstrate that poverty can be and is being reduced in Africa. The efforts described have been limited in scale, and sustainability remains a challenge. However, they show that committed leadership creating or taking advantage of favorable political conditions to effect change can reduce poverty.

In almost all cases, an open political environment either fueled the pro-poor change or provided the space for change to take place. Recent history suggests that there are sound reasons for this: economic collapse in the 1980s led to economic adjustment and to changes in political systems. In African countries where progress is being made, political and economic change has come through the ballot box. Democracy thus emerges as a key component of enhancing accountability—itself a key ingredient in poverty reduction.[10] After years of authoritarianism without development, both internal and external forces now agree that Africa needs to walk on two legs: democracy and development. For this to happen, peace and social inclusiveness are necessary both nationally and regionally.

With economic growth, greater democracy, and more political openness come risks. First, evidence shows that good macroeconomic indicators take time to translate into jobs, higher incomes, and improved standards of living at the grassroots level. Second, although economic growth is necessary for poverty reduction, it is not sufficient. Several of the countries that have started to experience more sustained growth—such as Mozambique and Tanzania—have also experienced a political backlash from groups who have lost out (managers and employees of state enterprises, civil servants, the urban unemployed) or who perceive that the benefits of growth are accruing excessively to certain groups, such as foreign businesses and certain favored ethnic groups. The state cannot therefore surrender completely to market forces but must design and implement interventions designed to compensate losers and channel the benefits of growth to the poor. To be politically sustainable, those benefits must show up in jobs and better services. This is also a strong message from the East Asian experience (World Bank 2005).

Third, the historical survey in this volume demonstrates that pursuing political survival at any cost leads nowhere. The case studies show that programs can be designed that benefit poor people, but at the end of the day poverty reduction requires sustained, systemic change and reform, as well as good, rational management. Meanwhile, electoral competition of the zero-sum winner-takes-all type strengthens patronage and dependency rather than good governance and endangers economic and social well-being. A balance must be struck, but political leaders must be prepared to take the long view, accept that life can go on without them in power, and tilt toward systemic reforms that ensure peace, unity, accountable governance, and sustained economic development.

The lessons for Africa's development partners are perhaps clearer. Crude conditionality has not worked. Constructive and patient engagement over time with the Museveni government in Uganda, for example, helped win its support for deep economic reforms. Is the same approach valid in the political arena? Countries resist outside interference, either actively and openly by refusing to undertake measures they oppose or passively by appearing to bend and then delaying or slowing implementation. Development partners can help reduce the tradeoffs inherent in the politician's dilemma by judiciously using incentives without appearing to be interfering in countries' internal affairs. Such incentives include not just well-designed aid programs but also open and more favorable trade conditions for Africa as well.

The early twenty-first century may present Africa's best opportunity to scale up poverty reduction. An international consensus now exists that poverty in Africa amid global plenty is intolerable and unjustifiable. There is also agreement that economic growth will be an outcome of open markets, entrepreneurship, trade, and free flow of capital, goods, and services on the one hand and democratic governance on the other. People need food as well as freedom. Economic growth may be increasing in Africa, and poverty numbers may be starting to improve. Democratic governments with pro-poor political visions and determination as well as stronger technocrats are more numerous than they were in the past, and development partners appear more inclined to support them through more aid and perhaps better terms of trade. The African political kingdom can become strong and prosperous at long last.

BIBLIOGRAPHY

AGOA (African Growth and Opportunity Act). 2000. [www.agoa.info/].
BBC (British Broadcasting Corporation). 2004. "BJP Admits 'India Shining' Error." May 28. [http://news.bbc.co.uk/1/hi/world/south_asia/3756387.stm].

Bates, Robert. 1981. *Markets and States in Tropical Africa.* Los Angeles, Calif.: University of California Press.

Bayart, Jean-Francois. 1993. *The State in Africa: The Politics of the Belly.* London: Longman.

Berman, Bruce, and Colin Leys. 1994. "Introduction." In Berman and Leys, eds., *African Capitalists in African Development.* Boulder, Colo.: Lynne Rienner.

Brown, William. 2000. "Restructuring North-South Relations: ACP-EU Development Co-operation in a Liberal International Order." *Review of African Political Economy* 27(85): 367–83.

Burnside, Craig, and David Dollar. 2000. "Aid, Policies, and Growth." *American Economic Review* 90(4): 847–68.

Christiansen, Luc, Lionel Demery, and Stefano Paternostro. 2003. "Macro and Micro Perspectives of Growth and Poverty in Africa." *World Bank Economic Review* 17(3): 317–47.

Clapham, Christopher. 1996. *Africa and the International System.* Cambridge: Cambridge University Press.

East African. 2004. "Why East Africa Was Left out of $1 Billion US Aid Fund." May 31–June 6.

Easterly, William. 2002. "How Did the Heavily Indebted Poor Countries Become Heavily Indebted?" *World Development* 30(10): 1677–96.

———. 2003. "Can Foreign Aid Buy Growth?" *Journal of Economic Perspectives* 17(3): 23–48.

European Union. 2001a. "Generalized System of Preferences: 'EBA'—Everything But Arms." [http://Europa.eu/comm./trade/issues/global/gsp/eba/index_en.htm].

———. 2001b. "Generalized System of Preferences: EU Approves 'Everything But Arms' Trade Access for Least Developed Countries." Press Release. February 26. [http://europa.eu.int/comm./trade/gsp/eba3/htm].

Geddes, Barbara. 1994. *Politician's Dilemma: Building State Capacity in Latin America.* Berkeley, Calif.: University of California Press.

Gibb, Richard. 2000. "Post-Lome: The European Union and the South." *Third World Quarterly* 21(3): 457–481.

Heilman, Bruce. 1998. "Who Are the Indigenous Tanzanians? Competing Conceptions of Tanzanian Citizenship in the Business Community." *Africa Today* 45(3–4): 369–88.

Heilman, Bruce, and John Lucas. 1997. "A Social Movement for African Capitalism? A Comparison of Business Associations in Two African Cities." *African Studies Review* 40(2): 141–71.

Hoekman, Bernard, and Michel Kostecki. 2001. *The Political Economy of the World Trading System.* Oxford: Oxford University Press.

Jackson, Robert, and Carl Rosberg. 1982. *Personal Rule in Black Africa: Prince, Autocrat, Prophet, Tyrant.* Berkeley, Calif.: University of California Press.

Kelsall, Tim. 2002. "Shop Windows and Smoke-Filled Rooms: Governance and the Repoliticisation of Tanzania." *Journal of Modern African Studies* 40(4): 597–619.

Lancaster, Carol. 1999. *Aid to Africa: So Much to Do, So Little Done.* Chicago, Ill.: University of Chicago Press.

Levy, Brian, and Sahr Kpundeh, eds. 2004. *Building State Capacity in Africa: New Approaches, Emerging Lessons.* Washington, D.C.: World Bank.

Lusekelo, Adam. 2004. "Don't the Poor Realize the Economy Is Growing?" *East African*, April 5–11.

Nkrumah, Kwame. 1958. *Towards Colonial Freedom*. London: Panaf Books Limited.

OECD IDS (Organisation for Economic Co-operation and Development International Development Statistics). Online Database. [www.oecd.org/dataecd/50/17/5037721.htm].

Rapley, John. 2002. *Understanding Development*. Boulder, Colo.: Lynne Rienner.

Reno, William. 1998. *Warlord Politics and African States*. Boulder, Colo.: Lynne Rienner.

Rodrik, Dani. 2003. "Growth Strategies." Harvard University, John F. Kennedy School of Government, Cambridge, Mass.

UNDP (United Nations Development Programme). 2003. "UN Millennium Development Goals Brochure." [www.un.org/milleniumgoals/brochure.htm].

UNECA (United Nations Economic Commission for Africa). 2004. *Economic Report on Africa 2004: Unlocking Africa's Trade Potential in the Global Economy, Overview*. Addis Ababa.

USAID (United States Agency for International Development). 2002. "Millennium Challenge Account Update (June 3)." [www.usaid.gov/press/releases/2002/fs_mca.html].

White, Nigel. 2002. *The United Nations System: Toward International Justice*. Boulder, Colo.: Lynne Rienner.

World Bank. 1981. "Accelerated Development in Sub-Saharan Africa—An Agenda for Action." Washington, D.C.

———. 1994. *World Development Report 1994: Infrastructure for Development*. New York: Oxford University Press.

———. 2000a. *Can Africa Claim the 21st Century?* Washington, D.C.

———. 2000b. *Assessing Aid: What Works, What Doesn't, and Why*. New York: Oxford University Press.

———. 2005. *Pro-Poor Growth in the 1990s: Lessons and Insights from 14 Countries*. Washington D.C.

———. n.d. "Conceptual Framework: Scaling Up Poverty Reduction." Washington, D.C. [www.worldbank.org/wbi/reducingpoverty/docs/conceptual.pdf].

2

Sustaining Growth and Achieving Deep Reductions in Poverty
How Uganda Recovered after Conflict

UGANDA MINISTRY OF FINANCE,

PLANNING AND ECONOMIC DEVELOPMENT

Since the National Resistance Movement (NRM) took power in 1986, Uganda has achieved some of the highest growth rates and deepest reductions in poverty in the region. Between 1987 and 2001 GDP grew at an average annual rate of 6 percent (figure 2.1), with inflation averaging about 5 percent a year for much of the period. The stable economy, the increase in foreign capital flows (both official and unofficial), and the strong commitment to poverty reduction allowed Uganda to reduce the proportion of people living in absolute poverty from 55 percent to 35 percent in just seven years (1992–99) and to more than double the number of children attending primary school.

What explains this extraordinary success in a small, land-locked East African country, located in a region mired in

The ministry can be contacted at +256 41 236 205. This case study was produced with the support of Former Minister Gerald Ssendaula and the Permanent Secretary/Secretary of Treasury Chris Kassami. Keith Muhakanizi guided the technical work and Kenneth Mugambe chaired the steering committee for the case study. Warren Nyamugasira, John Okidi, Eric Mukasa, Rosetti Nayenga, Margaret Kakande, Ephraim Kamuntu, and Richard Ssewakiryanga were members of the committee. The committee acknowledges Andrew Mwenda, who wrote the case study as well as conducted the interviews.

| FIGURE 2.1 | **Per capita GDP Growth, 1983–2001** (percent) |

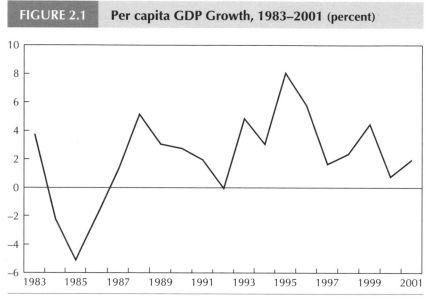

Source: World Bank 2002.

armed conflict and economic stagnation? Strong and single-minded political leadership; capable, committed, and trusted bureaucrats in key ministries; and pragmatic external donors who were prepared to engage with the government at the working level and together achieved a remarkable turnaround in a country that had been ravaged by conflict.

Taking over a Shattered State (1986–87)

When NRM guerrillas seized power in Kampala, Uganda, in 1986 (box 2.1), they took over a shattered state and economy. Between 1971 and 1985 GDP shrank 40 percent, falling 6.2 percent a year between 1973 and 1980 and 2.5 percent a year between 1980 and 1987 (Collier and Reinikka 2001), largely because of the civil war raging in most parts of the country.

State institutions had collapsed. The civil war had killed many government workers and forced many others into exile. Salaries were too meager to encourage hard work. State revenues represented just 5 percent of GDP (Chen, Matovu, and Reinikka 2001), with two-thirds coming from the coffee export tax (de Torrente 2001).

BOX 2.1	Chronology of Reform in Uganda, 1986–2001

January 1986	National Resistance Movement guerrillas, led by Yoweri Museveni, seize power in Kampala.
	Uganda places last in *Institutional Investor*'s ratings of 25 African countries.
May 1987	Mired in economic hardships, the government decides to cooperate with the International Monetary Fund (IMF) and the World Bank and enters loan negotiations.
	The government accepts IMF recommendations and announces measures to tighten budgetary and monetary policies.
	The IMF disburses $73 million to support imports under a Structural Adjustment Facility.
	The World Bank releases $55 million as an Economic Recovery Credit and promises debt rescheduling and additional aid worth $250 million.
	The cabinet decides to embark on a vigorous HIV/AIDS information campaign.
1988–89	The government embarks on a reform process that includes devaluation of the shilling and greater fiscal discipline.
	Foreign assistance, the main source of government revenue, reaches a peak of $786 million (24 percent of GDP).
1990	The government embarks on civil service reform.
1991	The government creates the Uganda Revenue Authority to better manage and increase revenue mobilization.
	The government creates the Uganda Investment Authority to ease investment constraints.
1992	Facing the possibility of losing World Bank/IMF balance of payments support, President Museveni merges the Ministry of Finance with of the Ministry of Planning and Economic Development under strong pro-reform leadership.
	The return of Asian properties confiscated in 1972 begins.
	The Central Bank attempts to ease foreign exchange controls by auctioning foreign currency.

BOX 2.1	Chronology of Reform in Uganda, 1986–2001 (*Cont'd*)
1993	Decentralization begins in 13 pilot districts.
	Coffee prices drop 60 percent.
1994	Interest rates are liberalized. International coffee prices rise. A coffee stabilization tax is imposed to reduce the likely adverse impact of higher transitory incomes.
1996	Presidential elections are held; the provision of universal primary education for all children features prominently.
	The capital account is fully liberalized.
1997	The universal primary education program is started. Primary enrollment more than doubles, from about 2.5 million to about 6 million.
	The Poverty Eradication Action Plan is written.
	The poverty rate declines to 44 percent.
1998	Ninety percent of the total trunk road network in Uganda is rehabilitated.
	Foreign direct investment inflows reach $230 million.
2000	The poverty rate declines to 35 percent.
	First Poverty Eradication Action Plan revision begins.
2001	The second presidential and parliamentary elections are held.
	User fees in the health sector are abolished.

Output declined more than 12 percent a year between 1970 and 1986, and average capacity use was just 5 percent. Nonmonetary output represented more than 40 percent of GDP. Coffee exports, at only 36 percent of their 1970 peak, contributed 92 percent of total foreign exchange earnings; exports of cotton, tea, sugar, copper, tobacco, and tourism were essentially zero (Lateef 1991). Worst of all, Uganda's social and physical infrastructure was in ruins after years of neglect and lack of maintenance.

The NRM government inherited a collapsed state that was under the control of different armed factions. Its first objective was thus to restore peace, law, and order.[1] It succeeded mainly because its armed wing, the National Resistance Army, ended the harassment of civilians by armed forces. This imposition of discipline represented a major achievement, since the tyranny of the country's armed troops (especially their disregard for property rights)[2] and abuses of human rights had stifled commerce and discouraged productive work and investment. However, security remains a lingering concern (box 2.2).

The government's second objective was to rebuild the economy. Initially, it adopted a development strategy that involved barter trade, price and foreign exchange controls, and state ownership of enterprises (Ochieng 1991). The strategy alienated international donors, however, and proved difficult to implement and finance.

Recognizing that the strategy was not viable, Ugandan leaders changed course. "To carry out NRM's programs," the minister of finance at the time recalled, "we needed money. The inputs for the production sector were in short supply and had to be procured from abroad. The NRM government therefore decided in 1987 to cooperate with the IMF and the World Bank in order to attract resources for program implementation" (Kiyonga 1989).

BOX 2.2   Security, a Lingering Concern

The NRM approach to security presumes a convergence of interests with the local populace. At every layer of local government there is a secretary for security. The NRM has trained the civilian population with arms in order to "demystify the gun" and create local self-defense capacity (Museveni 2003).

In the western, central, and some eastern regions, where the population supports the government, political stability has returned. However, the northern region remains mired in armed conflict. The rebels of the Lord's Resistance Army continue to abduct children, destroy infrastructure, and disrupt government programs. As a result, nearly 1.8 million people in the Gulu, Kitgum, and Pader districts live in internally displaced persons camps. An entire region has been rendered unproductive and has to rely on food relief for 90 percent of its nutritional needs (Saleh 2003). Because of the conflict, two-thirds of the region's population lived in poverty in 2002.

Crafting and Implementing a Reform Program (1987–92)

The economic reforms, first implemented in May 1987 as part of the Economic Recovery Programme, cut across sectors (Mpuga 2003). The money supply was sharply reduced and the official exchange rate devalued. Devaluation hurt people on fixed incomes, while tight fiscal and monetary policies forced the government to cut back on programs that had benefited urban constituencies. In response to the cuts, medical workers, students, and lecturers at Makerere University went on strike in 1988 and 1989. However, the NRM, with its support anchored in rural areas, held firm.

As part of its reform effort, the government introduced the "open general licensing system" for private sector imports. It promised to tighten both budgetary and monetary policies in order to control inflation and achieve macroeconomic stability (Sharer, De Zoysa, and McDonald 1995). The IMF responded by disbursing $73 million as import support; the World Bank released $55 million as an Economic Recovery Credit and promised debt rescheduling and additional aid worth $250 million (Sharer, De Zoysa, and McDonald 1995). The economy rebounded, growing 7.7 percent in 1988.

Donor-sponsored policies aimed to disengage the state as a key economic actor in favor of market forces. However, little progress was made on this front between 1987 and 1992 as the NRM dragged its feet on implementing the reforms. The NRM was still a military machine with a narrow and shaky political base, and state control of the economy offered personal and political benefits to those in power who could hark back to the state-led model associated with the 1960s, Uganda's golden period of growth.

Rather than compel Ugandan policymakers to move ahead more rapidly with reform, donors used persuasion and implicit pressure. They remained true to strongly held convictions, especially about budget discipline, but they did not apply punitive penalties when government implementation was inconsistent with their requirements.[3] Their approach increased the clout of the pro-reform group.

Committed Bureaucrats and the President Play Key Roles

Although donors spurred the government to undertake reforms, the main commitment to reform came from the bureaucracy. Initially, the NRM had embraced liberal reforms out of economic desperation.

However, a supportive group in the bureaucracy embraced the reforms and was vital in keeping government on the reform path. Emmanuel Tumusiime-Mutebile and a core of other bureaucrats at the Ministry of Finance, Planning and Economic Development and the Bank of Uganda formed the backbone of the reform movement within the government.

Another force for change was the NRM's populist character. Power was concentrated in the president, enabling clear decisionmaking, especially in the early years. The Presidential Economic Commission, the Army Council, and the Army High Command offered opportunities for policy debates, legitimizing key presidential decisions and avoiding the impression of rule by diktat.

The Economy Begins to Improve

Official inflows to Uganda doubled during the decade that began in 1987–88, reaching about $600 million in 1997–98 (Atingi-Ego and Sebudde 2000). Between 1987 and 1992 foreign assistance averaged $500 million a year, reaching a peak of $786 million in 1988–89, when it represented nearly a quarter of Uganda's GDP (Bank of Uganda 1998).[4] The funds were used to rehabilitate infrastructure, deliver social services, and support the balance of payments—all of which fueled growth.[5] As a result of the resumption in growth and the relatively stable macroeconomic environment, private transfers also rose, from slightly more than $100 million in 1987–88 to more than $500 million in 1997–98.

Agriculture, the largest component of GDP, enjoyed steady gains during this period, growing at an average rate of about 5.8 percent a year between 1987 and 1992. Industry grew at 10 percent a year and construction at 9 percent. Reflecting inconsistency in monetary and fiscal discipline, inflation was erratic, falling from 199 percent in 1987–88 to 2.9 percent in 1989–90 before increasing to 32 percent in 1990–91 and 62.9 percent in 1991–92 (Collier and Dollar 1999).

Despite the precipitous decline in international coffee prices, which fell more than 90 percent between 1987–88 and 1992–93 and cut coffee export values in half, the total value of exports more than tripled, from $180 million in 1990 to $660 million in 1996. Over the same period, imports rose from about $550 million to $730 million. Together with increased domestic industrial production, the rise in imports eliminated scarcities of basic necessities.

Maintenance of security and improvement in the country's economic indicators had extraordinary effects on poverty reduction. In 1992 more than half of Ugandans (about 55 percent) lived below the poverty line. By 1999 the figure had fallen to 35 percent.

The Government Reaps the Benefits of Reform

The benefits of reform increased the political clout of reformists and undermined the left-wingers in the government. Although ideologically a leftist, President Yoweri Museveni and many of his colleagues in the NRM were quick to recognize the benefits of an ideological turnaround on economic growth for stabilizing and consolidating the regime. The leftists were won over by taking advantage of the opportunities offered by the reform process.

Fully Committing to Reform (1992–2002)

Donors responded positively to Uganda's choice of policies, increasing their financial support. That support helped ensure economic recovery, which in turn strengthened political support in Uganda for further reform. As the NRM became stronger politically, the reform process gained momentum. The interplay of these factors produced a dramatic change in 1992, when the government committed itself fully to reform.

The defining moment came when President Museveni merged the Ministry of Finance with the Ministry of Planning and Economic Development in order to integrate the government's budgeting and planning functions within a single institution. The merging of ministries took place at a time when the IMF and the World Bank were withholding balance of payment support because program implementation had gone too far off track. This was the first time the IMF and the Bank had suspended aid since the inception of the Economic Recovery Program in 1987. The suspension caused macroeconomic indicators to decline, making clear the costs of abandoning reform.

Although President Museveni had been convinced as early as 1989 about the efficacy of the liberal economic model,[6] it took the suspension of balance of payments support and declining macroeconomic indicators for him to take action. An important lesson is that politicians may procrastinate on key issues out of political expedience, even when they support reform.

Putting a Strong Team in Place

President Museveni appointed Emmanuel Tumusiime-Mutebile, the leading supporter of liberal reform within the bureaucracy, permanent secretary in the Ministry of Finance, Planning and Economic Development and secretary to the Treasury. To establish institutional coherence and efficiency, Tumusiime-Mutebile ensured that the ministry recruited staff on the basis of professional merit, not political or other considerations. By increasing staff remuneration, initially supplementing wages with donor funds (Foster and Mijumbi 2002), he built a solid team with a strong esprit de corps. He was also receptive to foreign technical support to supplement internal capacity.

Staff continuity in key positions has been maintained at the ministry, and a culture of hard work, high achievement, and commitment to common goals has been established. The excellent staff have ensured the efficiency and relative autonomy of the ministry—important factors for policy reform, implementation, and the formulation of poverty policy.

Improving the Investment Climate

The government recognized that sustained growth and poverty reduction required a strong private investment response.[7] It thus set investment promotion as a top priority. Uganda had a long way to go in improving its investment climate: in 1986 *Institutional Investor* rated it last out of 25 African countries.

Repatriating wealth from overseas. By 1992 two-thirds of Uganda's private wealth was held abroad (Collier and Reinikka 2001). Repatriating this wealth would be an important source of investment and growth, as well as a signal to foreigners to invest in Uganda.

The government agreed that the return of properties once owned by Asians and confiscated by Idi Amin in 1972 would help Uganda regain a positive image as an investment destination. This was a difficult political decision for the government, but after considerable foot-dragging, repossession began in early 1992. By October 1993, 3,327 applications had been received and 2,647 properties had been returned to their previous owners (Mugisa 1993). The returning Asians invested in renovating their assets and setting up new businesses in large towns and cities, providing employment to people in urban areas.

Remittances from Ugandans living abroad increased from $400 million in 1998 to $650 million in 2002, becoming the largest source of foreign exchange inflows (Uganda Ministry of Finance, Planning and Economic Development 2003a). These funds spurred the construction industry and brought a welfare dividend, as many households receive remittances from rich relatives (Harris 2003). By 1997, 17 percent of private wealth held abroad had been repatriated (Collier and Reinikka 2001).

Although there is no direct evidence on the contribution to poverty reduction, a plausible argument can be made that the repatriation of wealth increased employment, raising incomes and consumption in urban areas. The reduction in urban poverty from 28 percent in 1992 to 17 percent in 1997 and 10 percent in 2000 may well have resulted partly from this private investment response.

Promoting investment. With substantial donor support, in 1991 the government created the Uganda Investment Authority as the institutional hub of investment promotion and facilitation. It also simplified licensing procedures for new businesses. These measures were buttressed by a strong political commitment to economic liberalization and macroeconomic stability. These actions restored investor confidence in Uganda, as the improvement in the *Institutional Investor* confidence rating from 5.2 in 1986 to 22.9 in 2000 indicates. To further improve the investment climate and ease supply-side constraints, the government initiated programs aimed at enhancing the environment for private sector growth. These programs—the Medium-Term Competitiveness Strategy, the Program for the Modernization of Agriculture, and the Strategic Exports Program—also aimed to increase growth and bring about the structural transformation of the economy that is necessary to raise living standards significantly.

As confidence in Uganda improved, investment increased, rising from 8 percent of GDP in 1998 to 21 percent in 2003 (Kassami 2003). The $230 million in foreign direct investment in 1998 was concentrated in export-oriented agribusiness (flowers, vanilla, fish processing) and services (media, mobile telephones, supermarkets, restaurants), mainly in urban areas (Uganda Ministry of Finance, Planning and Economic Development 1999).

Stimulating private sector growth. Foreign aid has played a key role in Uganda's reform and growth process, but the bulk of the country's recovery has come from a close partnership between the government and the private sector. The stimuli created by an enabling macroeconomic environment have promoted wider private activity in both small and large enterprises.

Government recognition of impediments to private enterprise led to the design and implementation of the Medium-Term Competitiveness Strategy for the Private Sector and the Strategic Exports and Investment Plan. Implementation of these initiatives has been sluggish, however, and the share of private investment in the economy has not grown as rapidly as expected.

Improving the Trade Regime

To improve the trade regime, the government removed import bans, abolished licensing requirements, reduced tariffs, removed export taxes, and in 1993 floated the shilling. The pegged exchange rate had offered many opportunities to those in positions of influence to obtain foreign exchange cheaply at the official rate and sell it dearly on the black market. Opposition to floating the currency came from many sources, but the government moved ahead with the reform.[8] By removing import bans, reducing import tariffs, and liberalizing import trade in the context of a liberalized foreign exchange market, the government reduced scarcities of basic consumer goods and created a handsome welfare dividend.[9]

The government also opened doors for private participation in the trade sector. During the 1994–95 coffee boom, farmers received 43 percent of the international market price for their coffee—nearly twice the 23 percent they received in 1991. The increase improved farmer incomes and rural consumption (Uganda Ministry of Finance, Planning and Economic Development 2003a) and pushed GDP growth to 11 percent in 1995–96 (Uganda Ministry of Finance, Planning and Economic Development 1997, 1998). By 1999–2000 farmers were receiving 80 percent of the world price (Uganda Ministry of Finance, Planning and Economic Development 1999, 2000a). Coffee in Uganda is grown mainly by a large number of family-based small producers, many of whom were presumably below the poverty line in 1992 (there are no official statistics on poverty before 1992). High coffee prices in 1994–96 dramatically reduced poverty in the cash-crop sector.

With the help of foreign direct investment, liberalization also encouraged export diversification. Tea estates were rehabilitated, and export earnings from flowers, vegetables, fish, hides, skins, tobacco, and tourism increased. Nontraditional export earnings rose from

$39.4 million in 1993 to $253.2 million in 2000 and $437.6 million in 2003 (Uganda Ministry of Finance, Planning and Economic Development 2003a). Coffee's contribution to foreign exchange earnings declined from 92 percent in 1986 (Museveni 2001) to 20 percent in 2003 (Uganda Ministry of Finance, Planning and Economic Development 2003a). Despite the greatly reduced dominance of coffee, however, Uganda's exports have remained primarily agricultural, with little value added, leaving the country highly vulnerable to external shocks.

Reforming the Civil Service

In 1990 the government set out to reform the civil service, with the aim of eliminating bloat and creating a lean and efficient bureaucracy. The plan was to reduce the number of staff from 320,000 in 1990 to 80,000 in 1995. Generous compensation packages were provided, and the wages of those who remained improved. Thirty-eight ministries were collapsed into 22 by 1992 and 17 by 1998.

However, reform ran into serious opposition from politicians and bureaucrats who were not committed to the reform, with many believing that it had been imposed by donors.[10] By mid-1995, 153,000 employees remained on the payroll—still well short of the planned 80,000 (Uganda Ministry of Public Service 1999).

The government wanted results, but it was difficult to reform and reorient the entire civil service quickly. To move ahead, it created semi-autonomous bodies, including the Uganda Investment Authority, the National Environment Authority, the Civil Aviation Authority, and the Uganda Revenue Authority. Staff at these agencies were offered better terms and conditions of service in exchange for implementing key policy reforms. The results were positive: the Uganda Revenue Authority, for example, increased domestic revenue mobilization significantly.

What initially was a temporary response to short-run bureaucratic weakness turned into a long-term strategy for institutional development. Abandoning its original strategy of transforming the entire civil service, the government sought to create islands of efficiency. Today the country has more than 70 semiautonomous agencies, most of them created with donor support (Kassami 2002). Donors, particularly the IMF and the World Bank, cultivated a bureaucratic elite committed to reform. They helped create specially funded units within key ministries, established a research center and a master's degree program at Makerere University, and trained government workers. Technical assistance from the World Bank and other donors strengthened capacity and expertise in the institutions handling economic reform (World Bank 1998).

Creation of islands of excellence has facilitated the implementation of reform, but it has had negative effects on the civil service. Differences now exist between public servants undertaking similar tasks, which undermines motivation and incentives in the public sector (Kassami 2002). The lesson is that successful institutional reform requires transforming the entire civil service, not just parts of it.

The Results of Reform

Partly because of the high cost of public administration, the fiscal deficit grew from 5 percent of GDP in 1995 to 13 percent in 2003 (Uganda Ministry of Finance, Planning and Economic Development 2003a). Growth and poverty reduction since 1992 have been sustained by consistent fiscal policy and by macroeconomic stability. However, because of large foreign aid inflows and the high cost of public administration, the central bank raised interest rates on treasury bills to sterilize the money supply. That increased the cost of borrowing by the private sector, impeding realization of the objective of rapid, broad-based, and sustainable private-sector-led growth (figure 2.2).[11]

| FIGURE 2.2 | Growth in GDP, Agriculture, Industry, and Services in Uganda, 1991/2–2001/2 |

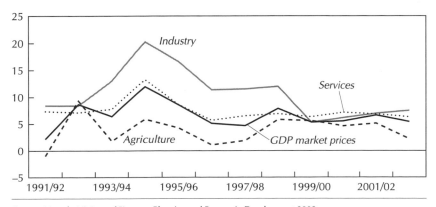

Source: Uganda Ministry of Finance, Planning and Economic Development 2003a.

Focusing Reform on Poverty Reduction (1992–2003)

Uganda's early economic reforms did not specifically address poverty. They were aimed at stabilizing the macroeconomic environment and promoting growth, in the hope that economic changes alone would improve the lives of poor people.

By 1992 the government and donors realized that adjustment was hurting some social groups, causing disenchantment and possibly threatening the reform process. Initial actions that addressed the adverse implications of the reforms included the Program for the Alleviation of the Social Costs of Adjustments (PAPSCA), which provides services in areas where people affected by the reforms live, and targeted credit programs, such as the Rural Farmers Credit Programme and seed capital programs, which help skilled groups and individuals who lack the capital to initiate investment projects.

The political campaigns for the Constituent Assembly elections of April 1994 and the presidential and parliamentary elections of May and June 1996 prompted a sharper focus on poverty. Government leaders, in contact with wide parts of rural Uganda as they canvassed for votes, realized that growth had not trickled down to the very poor in the countryside. NRM leaders returned from campaign visits to the countryside with a new awareness of the extent of poverty.

In September 1995 President Museveni brought members of Parliament, donors, and government ministers to the Luwero district so that donors and politicians could see firsthand the state of roads, schools, and dispensaries and the extent of poverty in the countryside. "We all felt threatened," Keith Muhakanizi, director of economic affairs in the Ministry of Finance, Planning and Economic Development, says of this trip, "because the president was attacking the very foundation on which our leadership in economic reform was based."[12]

Indeed, equitable economic growth would demand that, for the majority of the population to benefit from growth, they would need to participate in the processes that bring about such growth. That is, they would need jobs and a share of the benefit from public services.

The 1997/98–2000/01 Poverty Eradication Action Plan

The politicians' concerns convinced them to make the fight against poverty the government's top priority. Between 1997–98 and 2000–01 Uganda nearly doubled the proportion of its spending on poverty reduction, from 17 to 32 percent. Much of the increase came from earmarking Heavily Indebted Poor Country (HIPC) Debt Initiative savings and donor commitments for use in the fight against poverty.

The blueprint for reducing poverty in Uganda is the Poverty Eradication Action Plan, adopted in 1997. The plan is based on achieving rapid and sustainable economic growth, which is necessary for private sector growth and poverty reduction. It has become the blueprint for poverty reduction strategies and public expenditure programs in Uganda and a model for other countries in the region and beyond.

The Poverty Eradication Action Plan is Uganda's national development framework and medium-term planning tool. It is also its Poverty Reduction Strategy, guiding the formulation of government policy and the implementation of programs through sectorwide approaches through a decentralized system of governance. The main strength of the Poverty Eradication Action Plan derives from powerful implementation mechanisms tied into the national budget process. The main technical tool is the Medium-Term Expenditure Framework, which guarantees an increase in pro-poor allocations of public expenditure over three-year periods and creates a mechanism to assess whether funds are being used for pro-poor purposes. The budget process has been opened up, with budget documents such as the Background to the Budget summaries and the Poverty Monitoring Reports now made public. The Medium-Term Expenditure Framework is supported by sector strategies and spending plans, which indicate how resources will be used for poverty reduction, and sector working groups, which include government, civil society, and donors. These working groups help build consensus among key political actors.

The 2001–03 Poverty Eradication Action Plan

The revised Poverty Eradication Action Plan has four pillars:

- Creating an enabling environment for rapid and sustained economic growth and structural transformation.
- Maintaining good governance and security.
- Increasing the ability of the poor to raise their incomes.
- Increasing the quality of life of the poor by investing in primary education, clean water, health care, and sanitation.

Creating an enabling environment for growth is critical to poverty reduction. Indeed, the most significant reductions in poverty in Uganda—

between 1992 and 1997—occurred mainly because of growth, not redistribution. Central to growth are markets for cash crops overseas and food crops in the region driven by urbanization at home. One challenge for Uganda is to increase domestic savings to finance investment. The most effective instrument here is developing a mortgage market to encourage savings. A second challenge is to promote exports of higher value-added products by developing more agro-processing industries.

The revised Poverty Eradication Action Plan aims to reduce the poverty rate to 10 percent by 2017—a goal that will be very difficult to achieve. Even if growth were to reach the target of 7 percent a year, it would have to be very pro-poor to meet the target for poverty reduction (Kassami 2003). Achieving the target would require doubling exports from 12 to 24 percent of GDP and increasing investment from 21 to 26 percent of GDP, industry from 19 to 35 percent of GDP, and savings from 6 to 23 percent of GDP (Kassami 2003).

To enable itself to meet the Poverty Eradication Action Plan goals, the government has contained public spending, adopting a cash budgeting system and categorizing spending into priority and non-priority areas. Priority areas included rural feeder roads, primary education, primary health care, rural water, agricultural research, and extension. Spending in these areas was protected from cuts whenever there were shortfalls in revenue (Uganda Ministry of Finance, Planning and Economic Development 2003a).

In addition, in 1998 the government established the Poverty Action Fund to protect poverty spending from in-year budgetary cuts. The fund channels resources from debt relief to priority areas for poverty reduction, as determined by the Poverty Eradication Action Plan and the more detailed sector plans and budget consultations. It also receives additional budget support from bilateral donors. Resources are disbursed to ministries and districts to fund pro-poor priorities; they cannot be reallocated to other activities. The main beneficiaries are primary health care, primary education, and water and sanitation. New items can be included in the Poverty Action Fund if they can be shown to affect the delivery of services for the poor. The Poverty Action Fund now includes all major poverty-sensitive expenditures identified in the Poverty Eradication Action Plan, with its expenditures fully integrated in the budget.

The share of budget expenditures funded by the Poverty Action Fund rose from 17.5 percent in 1997–98 to 37 percent in 2001–02. Civil society is helping the government and donors monitor the fund on a quarterly basis, assessing pro-poor delivery against budget allocation. Although the fund undermines flexibility in the budget process by earmarking some areas of expenditure, some technocrats in the government feel that it is a useful tool for protecting pro-poor funding from other expenditures, such as defense.

Uganda's reforms have had an extraordinary effect, reducing the poverty rate from 56 percent in 1992 to 44 percent in 1997 and 35 percent in 2000 (figure 2.3). (The rate rose to 38 percent in 2003, partly as a result of adverse weather conditions, large declines in international commodity prices, and increased inequality in the distribution of income.[13]) What specific actions did Uganda take to achieve these results?

Rehabilitating and Maintaining Roads

Between 1987 and 1998, 90 percent of the trunk road network in Uganda was rehabilitated and 65 percent of the feeder road network restored (Museveni 2001). Feeder roads continue to present the greatest barrier to investment and growth, however (Uganda Ministry of Finance, Planning and Development 2003b), because their poor

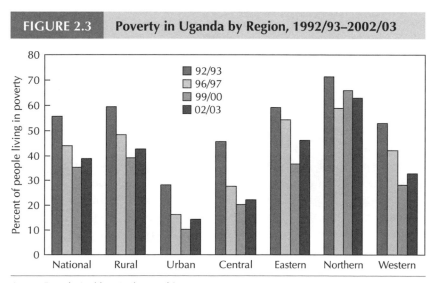

FIGURE 2.3 **Poverty in Uganda by Region, 1992/93–2002/03**

Source: Data obtained from Appleton and Ssewanyana 2003.

condition makes them impassable during rainy seasons, making it difficult for farmers to reach markets (Museveni 2001).

In 1996 the government launched a 10-year road development program focused on rehabilitating national roads. With World Bank assistance, it expanded the plan in 2002 to include feeder roads. Construction of main and feeder roads, coupled with the construction and rehabilitation of schools and health centers, has been a major source of jobs and income for the rural poor.

Empowering Communities

Empowering local communities in the management of their own affairs was a key part of the government's agenda. As guerrillas the NRM had established peoples' committees to involve the population in the management of their security and local affairs. On coming to power in 1986, the NRM made these peoples' committees the basis of local administration. President Museveni appointed a renowned political science professor, Mahmood Mamdani, to chair a commission of inquiry into local government. The Mamdani Commission recommended devolving more power and responsibilities to local governments and retaining the district as the unit of local administration.

Decentralizing Spending

Decentralization was introduced gradually, first in the form of political decentralization (1986), then in the form of administrative decentralization (1993), and finally in the form of fiscal decentralization (1995). The Local Government Act of 1997 gave local authorities responsibility for delivering almost all services within their districts. Budgetary transfers to districts increased from 11 percent of the national budget in 1995–96 to 20 percent in 2000–01 (Foster and Mijumbi 2002) and 34 percent in 2002–03.[14]

The Ministry of Education initially objected to decentralized budgeting, fearing that districts lacked the institutional capacity to manage the budgetary responsibilities. The Ministry of Health, which had a national plan to build dispensaries and hospitals and to recruit staff using a national projects approach, also objected. To overcome their concerns, the Ministry of Finance presented a study that showed that for every shilling spent on universal primary education before decentralization, only 18 percent reached the intended beneficiaries, while under decentralization the figure rose to 38 percent.[15] Expenditure tracking studies undertaken in 1996 showed similar results: a large proportion of funds intended for schools and health facilities actually went toward administrative costs at higher levels of government (Foster and Mijumbi 2002). The challenge for the government was to increase spending on priority areas under the Poverty Eradication Action Plan through the districts while ensuring that the funds disbursed reached the intended beneficiaries.

The government introduced conditional grants with clearly defined purposes, and compelled local governments to develop work plans and comply with reporting requirements. The conditional grant system has made it possible for the Ministry of Finance, Planning and Economic Development to impose national expenditure priorities through sector expenditure allocations to local governments. By 2001 conditional grants made up 80 percent of local government financial resources.

To ensure public participation in the budgetary process, the disbursement of central government funds to districts is published in the newspaper and announced on the radio. Explanations of how the funds will be used must be posted on notice boards at local government headquarters. Beneficiary institutions, including schools, health facilities, and water and sanitation works, must post similar information when they receive local government funds.

Decentralization has dramatically increased the effectiveness of spending: today 80 percent of funds released in Uganda reportedly reach the intended beneficiaries.[16] Decentralization has also increased employment opportunities at the district level and increased local power.

Investing in Education

One of the greatest successes in the Ugandan reform experience has been in education. The priority placed on the sector suggests that Ugandans have become more confident about the future and are beginning to think and invest long term.

The results of reform have been astonishing. In just six years (1996–2002), primary school enrollment doubled. Furthermore, the increase has been pro-poor: children from the lowest income bracket are now just as likely as those from well-off families to be enrolled in school (Foster and Mijumbi 2002).

The commitment to universal primary education was born in the 1996 presidential elections, which pushed Uganda's leaders to address the concerns of the poor. President Museveni's challenger, Paul Ssemogerere, promised primary education for all, while Museveni promised primary education for four children per family.

Donors provided early support to the education sector, financing the construction of classrooms and the recruitment and training of teachers. The education program and the World Bank Poverty Reduction Support Credit established targets to be achieved by May 2003. Those targets included reducing the student-teacher ratio from 63 to 48, the student-classroom ratio from 121 to 92, and the student-textbook ratio from 6 to 3 (Foster and Mijumbi 2002). Under the Schools' Facility Grant to districts, more classrooms have been built, more teachers recruited, and more books purchased. As a result, by June 2003 the targets were almost achieved, with 54 students per teacher and 94 students per classroom (Uganda Ministry of Finance, Planning and Economic Development 2003a). The average distance from school also declined, falling from 1.8 kilometers in 1992 to 1.4 kilometers in 1999, and the proportion of classrooms in good condition increased from 10 percent to 25 percent over the same period (Foster and Mijumbi 2002).

These achievements have come mainly from two sources: higher government spending on education, particularly primary education, and greater transparency and accountability for funds spent. Public expenditure tracking studies show that the proportion of funds remitted by the central government reaching the schools rose from 20 percent in 1995 to 80 percent in 2001 (Reinikka and Svensson 2003). The usefulness of public expenditure tracking as a means of promoting accountability for public funds has been extended to other sectors, including health and water, and it is being used as a model by other countries as well.

The sudden increase in primary school enrollment has been accompanied by a decline in the quality of education, however. Parents cite lack of supervision of teachers, lack of textbooks, large class sizes, inadequate numbers of classrooms, automatic promotion of students to higher grades, and late arrivals of funds as causes of poor quality education (Uganda Ministry of Finance, Planning and Economic Development 2002b).

Secondary education in Uganda has also expanded, with private provision as the engine. In 2003, 655,908 students were enrolled in secondary school (317,763 in government schools and 338,145 in private schools). That figure represents a 79 percent increase over 1997, when 366,022 students were attending secondary school (255,335 in government schools and 110,687 in private schools). Total secondary school enrollment is expected to more than double in 2004 to reach 1.4 million (*The Monitor*, August 6, 2003).

University enrollment has also increased, from 4,828 in 1986 to more than 52,000 in 2002. Private sponsorship, which did not exist in 1992, covered 77 percent of students in 2002.[17]

Improving Health—and Dealing with HIV/AIDS

Uganda had one of the best public health care systems in Africa in the 1960s, with the largest and best-equipped referral hospital in the region, well-functioning hospitals in almost every district, and well-equipped dispensaries at the county and subcounty levels. By 1986 the system was functioning poorly, the result of neglect and mismanagement in the 1970s and early 1980s. Staff at health centers were rarely present and diverted most drugs and other supplies to private clinics. According to household surveys, less than a third of people requiring health care used government health facilities, which they avoided because of frequent lack of drugs, poor facilities, the absence of qualified health workers, and long waiting times (Ablo and Reinikka 1998; Deininger and Mpuga 2004a).

To improve the performance of the health system, the government adopted several reforms, including decentralization. Under the new arrangements the district health system delivers a package of health services to the population, while the Ministry of Health is responsible for policy formulation, standards and guidelines, overall supervision, and monitoring (Uganda Ministry of Health 2000a and 2000b). At the same time, efforts were made to restore the functional capacity of the health sector, reactivate disease control programs, and reorient services to preventive and primary care rather than curative interventions.

The results have been impressive. The infant mortality rate fell from 122 per 1,000 in 1986 to 98 in 1988 and 81 in 1995, rising to 88 in 2001.[18] Under-five mortality dropped from 203 per 1,000 live births in 1986 to 143 in 2000—a significant decline, although the figure remains high. Over the same period the maternal mortality rate fell from 900 to 506 deaths per 100,000 women giving birth (Uganda Ministry of Finance, Planning and Economic Development 2003c), and the doctor to patient ratio rose from 1 per 23,000 people to 1 per 18,000. The abolition of fees reduced the number of days lost due to sickness (Deininger and Mpuga 2004a). Improvements in safe water have been even more remarkable, with the proportion of the rural population with access to safe water—a major contributor to health—rising from just 10 percent in 1987 to 60 percent in 2000 and 75 percent in 2002 (Uganda Ministry of Finance, Planning and Economic Development 2003c).

Uganda took steps early on to fight HIV/AIDS, which had a devastating effect on the Ugandan army in the 1980s. In 1986 the Ministry of Health established the AIDS Control Program. In 1987 the cabinet urged government officials to use every public speaking opportunity to bring up the virtues of abstinence, safer sex, and faithfulness to one partner. President Museveni felt that these initiatives were not sufficient, however, and in 1990 established the Uganda AIDS Commission in the President's Office to coordinate the fight against AIDS. The government also created the Joint Clinical Research Center within the army to spearhead research on finding a cure for HIV/AIDS. Recognizing that the military lacked the facilities and personnel needed to manage the research, the government later created a partnership between the center and the Ministry of Health.

The heart of Uganda's efforts is its nationwide prevention program, known as A, B, C (Abstinence, Be faithful, use a Condom). As part of the campaign, condoms were distributed in schools, advertised in the media, and sold widely in shops. An extensive public education and sensitization campaign used print media, electronic media, and billboards to address the problem of HIV/AIDS. By breaking the taboo about talking openly about sex, the campaign opened the door for parents and teachers to talk to children about safer sex, abstinence, and faithfulness.

The results of these efforts have been remarkable, with the HIV prevalence rate dropping from 30 percent in 1986 to 6 percent in 2002. The program worked because the government addressed HIV/AIDS openly, forged a range of partnerships with all of Uganda's main faith communities, and approached HIV/AIDS as a development rather than a health issue.

Lessons and Remaining Challenges

Before the government came to power and established peace, GDP in Uganda had plummeted, state institutions were in disarray, and the country's infrastructure was weak and deteriorating. By establishing peace, the government has allowed the millions of Kenyans who were forced to engage in subsistence agriculture to move back into market-based activities. It has halted the flight of capital and spurred new investment by private firms. It has also invested in poverty reduction—with outstanding results.

How did the government effect these changes? What lessons can be learned from its experience?

- *Strong leadership is critical, especially early on.* Attempts to reform generate struggles among vested interests and parties with different ideological orientations. To overcome such logjams, the initial stages of reform may require a clear and uncontested center of power. A lead agency—in Uganda's case, the Ministry of Finance, Planning and Economic Development—is important for driving the process. As the reform process progresses, decisionmaking should become less personal and more institutional.

- *Competent and committed bureaucrats are essential to implementing policy reforms.* Insiders must be committed to the reform process; without internal bureaucratic support, no amount of political commitment or donor pressure can bring about the desired results. Cultivating bureaucratic allies is thus the first step in successful institutional reform. Institutional reform must target the entire bureaucracy, not create pockets of competence.

- *Strong macroeconomic performance requires macroeconomic stability and fiscal discipline.* A stable currency is healthy for both firms and households, because it allows for transforming temporary income windfalls into productive investments. However, success requires policy consistency, because slippages can undermine achievements, as in 1984 (Edmonds 1989) and 1991 (Collier and Dollar 1999). Since 1998 Uganda has had a rising fiscal deficit, generated mainly by high public expenditure. This should be curbed so that the gains of earlier years are not lost.

- *Structural reforms that remove price-distorting policies and promote private involvement in the economy and openness to trade reduce poverty.* In a predominantly agricultural society such as Uganda's, access to markets for agricultural produce generates income and reduces poverty. Poor farmers reap the benefits of agricultural markets best when foreign exchange transactions and the marketing of agricultural products are liberalized, because liberalization allows competition to drive up farm-gate prices so that farmers receive a larger share of the world price (or domestic urban price) for their produce. Necessary reforms include liberalizing the foreign exchange market, removing import restrictions, eliminating direct and implicit export taxes, abolishing the monopoly of government marketing boards in the purchase and export of cash and food crops, and diversifying exports.

■ *A good working relationship between the government and donors is vital for policy formulation and implementation.* This demands that all stakeholders see reform as a shared effort to which everyone contributes.

■ *Foreign aid is critical for economic growth and poverty reduction.* The donor-funded Poverty Action Fund is the most important source of funds for districts in Uganda. Three-quarters of these funds are spent in the districts, where they provide poorer communities with social services.

■ *Decentralizing public spending helps reduce poverty.* Public spending increases the incomes of the rural poor more when local governments control their own budgets. Building schools and dispensaries and repairing and maintaining roads creates nonagricultural employment. These jobs have been a major source of increased income and consumption for rural Ugandans. In addition, the share of funds that actually reaches beneficiaries is much higher when spending is decentralized.

■ *Technical assistance alone is not adequate for reducing poverty.* Trying to replicate Uganda's program without strong political commitment to poverty reduction at the top and a core of competent and powerful government officials to turn that commitment into reality will not yield the desired results.

Economic growth in Uganda was robust over the past decade and a half, but recent years have witnessed a marked slowdown. For the first time since 1987–88, economic growth fell below 5 percent in 2002–03. The deterioration in growth was attributed mainly to the impact of prolonged dry weather on agricultural output, lower growth in food crops, and higher fuel prices.

Income poverty has also increased. Inequality has risen; health and fertility outcomes have been stagnant; insecurity continues to afflict many Ugandans, including the 1.6 million displaced persons; and the fiscal outlook is much more constrained than in the recent past.

To address these problems, policymakers need to confront four key challenges:

■ *Restoring security, dealing with the consequences of conflict, and improving regional equity.* The government needs to end armed conflict in all parts of the country in order to enable internally displaced persons to return home or find new livelihoods. Only when security is restored can the government begin to repair the war damage to the economies of the North and Northeast.

■ *Restoring sustainable growth in the incomes of the poor.* Per capita consumption needs to rise significantly and increases in inequality must be halted or reversed.

■ *Promoting human development.* Uganda has greatly improved access to primary education, but quality and drop-out remain concerns. The prevalence of HIV/AIDS, which had fallen dramatically, has recently leveled off, and recent progress in reducing child and infant mortality and adult fertility has been very disappointing. Family planning services are inadequate, and more needs to be done to make Ugandans aware of their responsibility to support their children.

■ *Using public resources transparently and efficiently to eradicate poverty.* The major expansion of resources in the late 1990s and early 2000s is unlikely to continue, so the focus has to be on improving the efficiency of resource use. The government needs to reduce corruption and increase accountability in the use of resources. It needs to educate the public about procedures for reporting corruption, since the lack of such knowledge increases households' risk of being subjected to bribery and significantly reduces the quality of public service delivery (Deininger and Mpuga 2004b). The government also needs to improve the allocation of public resources by giving high priority to actions identified in the Poverty Eradication Action Plan and reducing the proliferation of uncoordinated initiatives.

BIBLIOGRAPHY

Ablo, E., and Ritva Reinikka. 1998. *Do Budgets Really Matter? Evidence from Public Spending on Education and Health in Uganda.* World Bank Research Paper 1926. Washington, D.C.

Amsden, Alice. 1989. *Asia's Next Giant: South Korea and Late Industrialization.* New York: Oxford University Press.

Appleton, Simon, and Sarah Ssewanyana. 2003. "Poverty Estimates from the Uganda National Policy Research Centre, Uganda."

Atingi-Ego, M., and R. K. Sebudde. 2000. "Uganda's Equilibrium Real Exchange Rate and Its Implications for Nontraditional Export Performance." Bank of Uganda Staff Paper 2(1). Kampala.

Bank of Uganda. 1998. "Balance of Payment Statement." Analytical presentation.

Chen, Duanjie, John Matovu, and Ritva Reinikka. 2001. "A Quest for Revenue and Tax Incidence." In Paul Collier and Ritva Reinikka, eds., *Uganda's Recovery: The Role of Farms, Firms and Government*. World Bank Regional and Sectoral Studies. Washington, D.C.

Collier, Paul, and David Dollar. 1999. *Aid Allocation and Poverty Reduction*. Washington, D.C.: World Bank.

Collier, Paul, and Ritva Reinikka, eds. 2001. *Uganda's Recovery: The Role of Farms, Firms and Government*. World Bank Regional and Sectoral Studies. Washington, D.C.

Deininger, K., and P. Mpuga. 2004a. "Economic and Welfare Impact of the Abolition of Health User Fees: Evidence from Uganda." Working Paper 3276. World Bank, Washington, D.C.

———. 2004b. "Does Greater Accountability Improve the Quality of Delivery of Public Services? Evidence from Uganda." Working Paper 3277. World Bank, Washington, D.C.

de Torrente, Nicolas. 2001. "Post Conflict Reconstruction and International Community in Uganda, 1986–2000: An African Success Story?" Doctoral thesis. London School of Economics and Political Science, London.

Dollar, David. 1998. *Assessing Aid: What Works, What Doesn't and Why*. World Bank Policy Research Report. Washington, D.C.: Oxford University Press.

Edmonds, Keith. 1989. "Crisis Management: Lessons for Africa from Obote's Second Coming." In Holger Hansen and Michael Twaddle, eds., *Uganda Now: Between Decay and Development*. London: James Currey.

Firimoni, Banugire. 1989. "Uneven and Unbalanced Development: Development Strategies and Conflict." In Kumar Rupesinghe, ed., *Conflict Resolution in Uganda*. Athens, Ohio: Ohio University Press.

Foster, Mick, and Peter Mijumbi. 2002. "How, When and Why Does Poverty Get Budget Priority: Poverty Reduction Strategy and Public Expenditure in Uganda." ODI Working Paper 163. Overseas Development Institute, London.

Harris, John. 2003. "Reconstruction and Poverty Alleviation in Uganda: 1987–2001." World Bank, Washington, D.C.

Hansen, Holger, and Michael Twaddle, eds. 1989. *Uganda Now: Between Decay and Development*. London: James Currey.

———. 1991. *Changing Uganda: The Dilemmas of Structural Adjustments and Revolutionary Change*. London and Kampala: James Currey and Fountain Publishers.

Henstridge, Mark, and Louis Kasekende. 2001. "Exchange Reforms, Stabilization and Fiscal Management." In Paul Collier and Ritva Reinikka, eds., *Uganda's Recovery: The Role of Farms, Firms and Government*. World Bank Regional and Sectoral Studies. Washington, D.C.

IDRC (International Development and Research Council). 1986. *Economic Development and Long-Term Development in Uganda*. Toronto, Canada.

IMF (International Monetary Fund) and IDA (International Development Association). 2002. *Uganda: Updated Debt Sustainability Analysis and Assessment of Public External Debt Management Capacity*. Washington, D.C.

Investment Authority. 1999. "Analysis of Investment Performance 1991–98." Media and Management Information Services Division. Kampala.

Johnson, Chalmers. 1982. *MITI and the Japanese Miracle: The Growth of Industrial Policy, 1925–75*. Palo Alto, Calif.: Stanford University Press.

Kassami, Chris. 2002. "Budgetary Aspects of Public Administration." Paper presented at a Public Expenditure Review meeting, May 21, Kampala.

———. 2003. *PEAP: Lessons from the Past and Challenges for the Future*. PEAP Revision, July 16, Kampala.

Kiyonga, Cryspus. 1989. *The State of the Economy as Inherited by the NRM Government in 1986: The Economic Challenges and Policy Direction Taken*. Speech given at the Government Seminar on the Economy, December 12–16, Kampala.

Kreimer, Alcira, Paul Collier, Colin S. Scott, and Margaret Arnold. 2000. *Uganda— Post Conflict Reconstruction*. Country Case Study Series. Washington, D.C.: World Bank.

Lateef, Sarwar K. 1991. "Structural Adjustment in Uganda, the Initial Experience." In Holger Hansen and Michael Twaddle, eds., *Changing Uganda*. London: James Currey.

Mamdani, Mahmood. 1989. *A Critical Analysis of the IMF Program in Uganda*. Presentation at a public lecture, Makerere University, March 10.

Mpuga, P. 2003. "Demand for Rural Financial Services in Uganda." Unpublished doctoral dissertation, Johannes Kepler University, Linz, Austria.

Mugisa, Anne. 1993. "DAPCB Gets New Team." *New Vision*. November 27.

Museveni, Yoweri. 2001. *Consolidating the Achievements of the Movement*. Election Manifesto. Kampala.

———. 2003. "Arrow Boys Are UPDF Reserves." *The Monitor*, September 8.

Mutebi, Frederick Golooba. 1998. "Decentralization and Development Administration in Uganda; Limits to Popular Participation." Doctoral thesis, London School of Economics, London.

Ochieng, E. 1991. "Economic Adjustment Programs in Uganda 1985–89." In Holger Hansen and Michael Twaddle, eds., *Changing Uganda*. London: James Currey.

Reinikka, Ritva, and Jakob Svensson. 2001. "Confronting Competition: Investment, Profit and Risk." In Paul Collier and Ritva Reinikka, eds., *Uganda's Recovery: The Role of Farms, Firms and Government*. World Bank Regional and Sectoral Studies. Washington, D.C.

———. 2003. "The Power of Information: Evidence from a Newspaper Campaign to Reduce Capture." World Bank Discussion Paper. Washington, D.C.

Reno, William. 2002. "Uganda's Politics of War and Debt Relief." *Review of International Political Economy* 9(3): 415–35.

Rowden, Rick, and Warren Nyamugasira. 2002. "Poverty Reduction Strategies and Coherence of Loan Conditions, Do the New World Bank and IMF Loans Support Countries' Poverty Reduction Goals? The Case of Uganda." ActionAid, Kampala.

Saleh, Salim. 2003. "Proposal to End the War." Security and Production Programme, A proposal by the Presidential Advisor on Military and Political Affairs in the North. Kampala.

Sharer, R., H. De Zoysa, and C. McDonald. 1995. *Uganda: Adjustment with Growth*. Occasional Paper 121. International Monetary Fund, Washington, D.C.

The Monitor, August 6, 2003. Kampala.

Transparency International. 2001. *Global Corruption Report: 2001*. Berlin.

———. 2002. *Global Corruption Report 2002*. Uganda Demographic and Health Survey, 2000–2001. Berlin.

UIA (Uganda Investment Authority). 1999. "Analysis of Investment Performance 1991–98." Media and Management Information Services Division, UIA, Kampala.

Uganda Ministry of Agriculture, Animal Industry and Fisheries and Ministry of Finance, Planning and Economic Development. 2000. *Plan for the Modernization of Agriculture: Eradicating Poverty in Uganda*. Kampala.

Uganda Ministry of Finance, Planning and Economic Development. 1997. "Background to the Budget 1997." Kampala.

———. 1998. "Background to the Budget 1998." Kampala.

———. 1999. "Background to the Budget 1999." Kampala.

———. 2000a. "Background to the Budget 2000." Kampala.

———. 2000b. *Medium Term Competitive Strategy for the Private Sector*. Kampala.

———. 2000c. *Learning from the Poor: Voices of the Poor*. Uganda Participatory Poverty Assessment National Report. Kampala.

———. 2001. *Poverty Eradication Action Plan: 2001–2003 (Vol. 1)*. Kampala.

———. 2002a. *Deepening the Understanding of Poverty*. Uganda Participatory Poverty Assessment Process, Second National Report. Kampala.

———. 2002b. "Second Participatory Assessment Report." Participatory Poverty Assessment Process. Kampala

———. 2003a. "Background to the Budget 2003." Kampala.

———. 2003b. "Strategies to Promote Economic Growth." Progress report. Report presented at the fourth Consultative Group Meeting, May 14–16, Kampala.

———. 2003c. "Uganda's Progress in Attaining PEAP Target in the Context of the Millennium Development Goals." Paper presented at the Donor Consultative Group Meeting, May 14–16, Kampala.

Uganda Ministry of Health. 2000a. *Health Sector Strategic Plan, 2000/01–2004/05*. Kampala.

———. 2000b. *Statistical Abstract, 2000*. Kampala.

———. 2002. "Uganda Demographic and Health Survey, 2000–2001." Kampala.

Uganda Ministry of Public Service. 1999. *Public Service Reform Program (PS: 2002) Report of the Year 1998*. Administrative Reform Secretariat. Kampala.

Wade, Robert. 1990. *Governing the Market, Economic Theory and the Role of Government in East Asian Industrialization*. Princeton, N.J.: Princeton University Press.

World Bank. 1992. *Project Completion Report, First Economic Recovery Credit*. Washington, D.C.

———. 1993. *Uganda: Growing Out of Poverty*. Washington, D.C.

———. 1996. *The Challenge of Growth and Poverty Reduction*. Washington, D.C.

———. 1998. *The World Bank Experience with Post Conflict Reconstruction, Volume VI: Uganda Case Study*. Washington, D.C.

———. 2000. *Uganda, Post Conflict Reconstruction, Country Case Study Series*. Washington, D.C.

———. 2002. *World Development Indicators 2002*. Washington, D.C.

Zake, Justin. 2002. *Tax Compliance and Operations of URA*. Uganda Revenue Authority, Kampala.

————. 2002. *Tax Obligations, Domestic Revenue Mobilisation and Options for Widening the Tax Base.* Uganda Revenue Authority, Kampala.

Interviews

Abdi Alam, Chairman of Uganda Manufacturers' Association, Kampala, July 15, 2003.

Robert Blake, former World Bank Country Resident Representative in Uganda, 2004.

Walter Mahler, International Monetary Fund, on Monitor FM, June 12, 2002.

Lars Christian Moller, formerly with Poverty Monitoring and Analysis Unit, Ministry of Finance, Planning and Economic Development, on Monitor FM, October 13, 2001.

Interviews picked from Monitor FM archives

Keith Muhakanizi, Director of Economic Affairs in the Ministry of Finance, Planning and Economic Development, Kampala, October 15–16, 2003.

Brig. Jim Muhwezi, Minister of Health, former Minister of State for Primary Education, Kampala, July 2003.

President Yoweri Museveni, State House Nakasero, December 31, 1999.

Edward Rugumayo, Minister of Tourism, Trade and Industry, and his Permanent Secretary, Sam Nahamya, Cancun, Mexico, September 14, 2003.

Col. Kahinda Otafiire, Minister for Lands, Water and Environment, Kampala, June 13, 2003.

Maj. Rubaramira Ruranga, National Coordinator of the National Guidance and Empowerment Network of People Living with HIV/AIDS, also chair to the 11th International Conference of People Living with HIV/AIDS, October 19, 2003.

Bidandi Ssali, former Minister of Local Government, October 15, 2003.

Emmanuel Tumusiime-Mutebile, Governor of the Central Bank, June 16, 2002.

Nimrod Waniala, Executive Director of Private Sector Foundation Uganda, Cancun, Mexico, September 13, 2003.

James Wapakhabulo, Second Deputy Prime Minister and Minister of Foreign Affairs, and Tom Butiime, Minister of State for Regional Cooperation, regarding bureaucratic performance in the Ministry of Foreign Affairs, Kampala.

PART Two

Improving the
Investment Climate

3

Ensuring Security and Justice
Routes to Reconciliation in Rwanda

BOB BURGOYNE AND
MATTHEW MAGUIRE

In the decade since it experienced one of the worst genocides in history, Rwanda has transformed itself from a fragile, fragmented state with a shattered economy and a population at constant risk from attacks by insurgents to a secure country that has experienced sustained economic growth for 10 years. This remarkable transformation was achieved through exceptional efforts at reconciliation, an emphasis on the unity of the state, and the (re)creation of a strong sense of Rwandan identity that transcends ethnicity.

Several lessons can be learned from the extraordinary progress Rwanda has made since the genocide. Other states emerging from conflict can learn much from the way Rwanda entrenched security and created an environment conducive to progress and development.

Bob Burgoyne is private enterprise development consultant at the U.K. Department for International Development, Rwanda; he can be contacted at +250 87 74 98 66. Matthew Maguire is with the U.K. Department for International Development, Rwanda; he can be contacted at m-maguire@dfid.gov.uk. The interviews were conducted by Shyaka Kanuma, who wrote the preliminary draft of the case.

The 1994 Genocide

It is often argued that people living in exile develop a strong sense of national identity. For the Rwandans exiled from their country following the massacres of 1959, this feeling manifested itself in the 1987 formation of the Rwandan Patriotic Front, which, according to one of its founders, was driven by a need to reclaim and rebuild the country (box 3.1).

During the early 1990s the Rwandan Patriotic Front launched a series of incursions into Rwanda, but in 1993 it signed a peace agreement with the Mouvement Révolutionnaire National pour le Développement (MRND) in Arusha, Tanzania. However, the agreement, known as the Arusha Accords, acted as little more than a smokescreen for the benefit of the international community: hardliners in the MRND stalled implementation of the accords while planning the atrocity that followed.

The origins of the Rwandan genocide have been the subject of much examination, discussion, and debate, but the horrifying process itself has been well documented. For months leading up to April 1994, extremist elements in the MRND government, known as the *Akazu*, had been planning to kill a large number of Tutsis, whom they referred to as cockroaches. The Hutu population was subjected to a barrage of

---

BOX 3.1	**A Brief History of Rwanda**

Unlike many African countries, Rwanda has been a recognizably distinct "state" for centuries. Originally inhabited predominantly by the Twa ethnic group, by the mid-Eighteenth century the country was predominantly ethnic Hutu but ruled by a Tutsi *mwami,* or king. Before the ascension of Kigeri IV in the mid-nineteenth century, the country had been characterized by clan hierarchies rather than ethnicity. It was Kigeri who molded Rwanda into a Tutsi-dominated structure to consolidate his power.

Rwanda became a German protectorate in the 1890s and then came under Belgian control after World War I. The Belgians did not significantly adjust the social structures of the country, but they did entrench ethnic identities by introducing an ethnic identity card system.

In 1959 tensions between the Tutsis and the Hutus forced some 100,000 Tutsis to flee the country. Since Belgium granted Rwanda independence in 1962, Rwanda has experienced periodic outbreaks of violence, which culminated in the events of 1994.

anti-Tutsi propaganda and told to fear for their lives. Radio and other media were used to incite violence. To prepare for the massacre, the *Akazu* purchased machetes and grenades and drew on Rwanda's well-developed administrative structure and its population's traditions of obedience. Extremists maneuvered into key positions, and a militia, the *Interahamwe*, was trained by the *Akazu*. Numerous terrorist atrocities such as bombings and assassinations were carried out. The government blamed the Rwandan Patriotic Front, but today most commentators suspect that the *Akazu* were using "action as propaganda" to instill fear and whip up further hatred of the Tutsis.

Rwandan President Juvénal Habyarimana, a Hutu, was killed on April 6, 1994, when his plane was shot down on the way back from Dar es Salaam, where African heads of state had insisted on implementation of the Arusha Accords to end the conflict. This event appeared to trigger the genocide in which more than 800,000 Tutsis and moderate Hutus were killed. About 2 million Rwandans fled to neighboring countries. Another million became internally displaced. The massacre was halted with the military victory of the Rwandan Patriotic Front in July 1994 (box 3.2).

While fleeing the country, former members of the Forces Armées Rwandaise looted Rwanda, adopting a scorched-earth policy in their retreat. The *Interahamwe* militia destroyed all the fixed installations they could and drove most available vehicles across the border to the Democratic Republic of Congo. In the towns, fleeing forces often cut off water and electricity.

The interim government that had planned the genocide took all of the central bank's foreign currency reserves with it when it fled Kigali. Nothing was left in the public coffers.

Following the military victory the Rwandan Patriotic Front formed a government of national unity on July 19, 1994. Rwanda's first postwar prime minister, Faustin Twagiramungu, outlined an eight-point program to steer Rwanda toward stability. In some ways, this government was a return to the one envisaged in the Arusha Accords: it was created along power-sharing lines, with only the MRND and other extremist groups excluded from power.

The government was led by the Rwandan Patriotic Front, which brought skills and international experience developed in exile. However, the government faced many challenges, and the price of failure would have been high—the likely recurrence of civil conflict. The first priority during the early years was therefore security, a policy that

BOX 3.2	**Chronology of Events in Rwanda Before and After the 1994 Genocide**

April 6, 1994	President Juvénal Habyarimana's plane is shot down.
April 7, 1994	The genocide of more than 800,000 Tutsis and moderate Hutus begins.
July 19, 1994	The Rwandan Patriotic Front takes power. A government of national unity is sworn in. The government launches an eight-point development plan.
November 8, 1994	Security Council Resolution 955 establishes the International Criminal Tribunal for Rwanda.
1996	About 1.3 million refugees are repatriated to Rwanda.
	Rwanda routs extremist elements in refugee camps in the Democratic Republic of Congo.
1997	The Demobilisation and Reintegration Commission is set up.
	At the instigation of the Office of the President, village meetings are held throughout the country.
1998	Rwanda's development plan, Vision 2020, is launched.
1999	The National Unity and Reconciliation Commission begins broad-based consultations.
March 1999	First local elections held for committees at the local administration levels of the cellule and the sector.
2000	National police force is disbanded, and local police forces are set up.
2001	A revised *Gacaca* system is instituted for trying people suspected of having participated in the genocide.
March 6, 2001	First local elections held in communes. Decentralization goes into effect.
July 27, 2001	The Law Reform Commission is set up.
June 2002	The government releases its Poverty Reduction Strategy Paper.
Late 2002	Rwanda Defense Forces pull out of the Democratic Republic of Congo.
April 2003	The Sun City Peace agreement is signed in the Democratic Republic of Congo.
June 4, 2003	The Constitution is signed after lengthy consultations.
2004	The Law Reform Commission package of proposals is put before Parliament.

directly addressed the needs of the poor, who prioritize security above justice (Republic of Rwanda 2001b). But security could not be achieved by military means alone. In a country where a large share of the population had directly participated in a genocide, reconciliation was essential to prevent further outbreaks of violence.

As well as reconciling Rwandan civilians, the new government faced the demobilization of thousands of soldiers and accommodation of millions of returning refugees, some of whom had been in exile since the 1960s. In short, the challenges were immense and the response had to be extraordinary.

The government's ultimate goal was to achieve stability, unity, and reconciliation by creating a Rwandan identity that is unrelated to ethnicity. According to Protais Musoni, the minister of state in the local government ministry, "The new ideology of the oneness and unity of all Rwandans was something different from the winner-takes-all scenarios of the past. Sectarian politics have no place in the new Rwanda and are best confined to history."

Achieving and Embedding Security

For some time after the expulsion of Forces Armées Rwandaise in July 1994, the northwest—Rwanda's breadbasket—suffered from insurgent-led insecurity. At the same time, about 1 million people were displaced within Rwanda's borders, and close to 2 million more had fled—to Tanzania, Burundi, and eastern Democratic Republic of Congo (then Zaire). The challenge facing the Rwandan Patriotic Front was to repatriate this displaced population while defending the people of Western Rwanda against the Forces Armées Rwandaise troops that had fled to the Democratic Republic of Congo.

Responding to Attacks by the Forces Armées Rwandaise

The massive movement and external settlement of refugees hid the reconstituting of the civil and military structures of the Habyarimana administration from many outside observers. Militias from the Forces Armées Rwandaise established themselves in refugee camps in eastern Democratic Republic of Congo, across from northwest Rwanda. Described by one officer of the Rwandan Patriotic Army as "a transplanted refugee administration," the camps were used to regroup, recruit, train, rearm, and then attack. All of this took place under the eyes of the international humanitarian community, which was ill-equipped to differentiate between genuine refugees and perpetrators of genocide (de Waal 1997).

Mid-1994 saw several incursions in the northwest. The incursions continued regularly for two years, creating a climate of fear and insecurity. The situation improved markedly after a concerted response to a series of attacks in early 1996. Brigadier Kayumba Nyamwasa, the former chief of the defense staff, outlined the Rwandan position. "Despite efforts to bring this problem to the attention of everyone, regionally and internationally, no one has contained the militias in the camps," he asserted. "Rwanda cannot afford to sit and look on as this security threat builds and explodes on us once again." Forces of the Rwandan Patriotic Front entered the Democratic Republic of Congo and, in alliance with Zairean rebel groups, broke up the camps that sheltered those who had carried out the genocide.

Repatriating Refugees

Even as it was continuing to deal with the external threat from former Forces Armées Rwandaise troops, the government focused on the return of refugees. It was at pains to stress that all would be welcomed back, regardless of "ethnic" origin.

Rwanda is the most densely populated country in Africa, with an average of 410 people per square kilometer. With the huge numbers of returning refugees, the potential for violent conflict over property was high. Between November 1996 and January 1997, about 1.1 million people returned to their homes, the largest and swiftest repatriation in the history of the office of the United Nations High Commissioner for Refugees. Many of those who flooded back to the country in the mid-1990s were the survivors of the pogroms of the late 1950s, 1960s, and 1970s—"old case refugees." Rather than the usual procedure of keeping returnees in camps, the government insisted on their immediate return to permanent settlements.

The Arusha Accords stipulated that all Rwandans had a right to land and that those in exile had a right to return, but it did not give refugees the right to reclaim land they had lost through ethnically motivated attacks. Instead, it was agreed that the government would help returning refugees find alternative land. Vacant government land, including parts of the Gishwati Forest and Akagera National Park, was identified for settlement.

Rather than settle in these areas, however, many "old case refugees" returned to the land that they once owned, which was empty. Later, "new case refugees" (survivors of the genocide) found "their" land occupied by the original owners. Facing these complex and potentially conflictual situations, the government either persuaded competing claimants to share the land (with the support of local NGOs) or settled people in villages on vacant government land—a policy known as *imigugdugu* (villagization). By the end of 2000 more than 100,000 homes for returned refugees and other displaced or vulnerable households had been constructed, at an estimated cost of $183 million. Conflicts remain, however, and these short-term measures are now being supplanted by a new land policy.

Reintegrating Former Combatants

The government also recognized the need to demobilize and reintegrate former troops of the Forces Armées Rwandaise and the Rwandan Patriotic Army into civilian life. In 1997 a demobilization program was set up to run through June 2005. The program successfully demobilized and began reintegrating 18,692 soldiers between 1997 and 2001.

Beginning in 2001, under the framework of the World Bank's Multi-Country Demobilisation and Reintegration Plan, the demobilization plan was stepped up. Ex-combatants attend demobilization and reintegration camps, where they are given advice on how to use their reintegration packages and how to access grants and loans to establish cooperatives and small businesses. They are also sensitized to the need for national reconciliation and taught about civilian life in modern Rwanda. Ex-combatants are provided with medical screening, including voluntary HIV testing and counseling, and they are given "basic needs" kits and follow-up advice and support to facilitate their reintegration. Of the estimated 40,000 former members of the Forces Armées Rwandaise who returned to Rwanda in 1996 after the dissolution of the refugee camps in the Democratic Republic of Congo, the government has reportedly reintegrated some 15,000 into society, in accordance with the Arusha Accords (box 3.3).

Responding to Attacks in the Northwest

Despite this success, the northwest continued to suffer incursions throughout 1997 and 1998, as the Democratic Republic of Congo

BOX 3.3	Putting Down Arms: Returning to Civilian Life in Rwanda

"Life as a civilian cannot be compared to that in the army. The life we are living is definitely a lot better than before," says Hassan Kayumba, a former member of the Rwandan Patriotic Front. Today Kayumba is the leader of the Ubumwe (Unity) Collective set up by demobilized former combatants in 2001, with assistance and initial funding from the Demobilization Commission. The collective, which includes four former Forces Armées Rwandaise soldiers and four civilians, performs carpentry work and owns several small shops. It earns about 100,000 Rwanda francs ($178) a month.

Source: IRIN 2004.

began to provide military assistance to armed groups from the former Rwandan Army. The rural poor of the northwest suffered disproportionately from these incursions, intended to destabilize the Rwandan administration. Unable to exploit the potential of the land, Rwanda's breadbasket could not provide food to the country, resulting in sporadic food insecurity.

In August 1998 the Rwandan Patriotic Front and Ugandan forces again entered the Democratic Republic of Congo. The security situation improved along the border, but a complex multiparty war in the Democratic Republic of Congo was ignited, and sporadic insurgencies continued in northwest Rwanda. (A ceasefire, the Lusaka Agreement, was signed in July 1999 but was not implemented immediately. The conflict was finally halted only following concerted international pressure in mid-2003, with the signing of the Sun City Agreement and installation of a transitional national government in the Democratic Republic of Congo, although doubts about its durability remain.)

Working Toward Unity and Reconciliation

While the Rwandan Patriotic Army tried to secure the country's borders, the government engaged in vigorous domestic efforts to entrench the peace. As part of its commitment to unity and reconciliation, the government was assiduous in consulting broad sections of the population in developing public policy through, for example, village meetings, begun at the behest of the president in 1997. These meetings have had an impact on a number of government policies, and in 1999 gave rise to the implementation of a key component of the Arusha Accords, the creation of a National Unity and Reconciliation Commission.

The mandate of the National Unity and Reconciliation Commission was to organize open discussions across the country so that all Rwandans could air their views on the causes of past divisions and provide new ideas for national reconciliation. Government ministers were required to visit communities around the country to explain and discuss government policies and national unity. Ministers also visited refugee camps outside Rwanda to explain the government's policies and encourage refugees to return home. In March 1999 Rwanda consultations began at the grassroots level, with special efforts to reach marginalized groups, including women and the Batwa ethnic group. Within a year consultations had been held in 154 of Rwanda's 180 *communes.*

Promoting Decentralization and Democratization

The village meetings also provided the impetus for the government's decentralization and democratization program. The government's aim is to build democracy from the bottom up by empowering local communities to engage with local government and by improving basic services. It believes that democracy built in this way, with its emphasis on social participation and inclusion, will act as a counterbalance to political divisionism and extremism. Elections of officials to committees at the *cellule* (the smallest administrative unit) level were held in March 1999, followed by a more formal decentralization law in late 2000. Fiscal decentralization occurred in 2001, when local councils were given revenue-raising powers.

The thing that marks out Rwanda is that it has been so single-minded about reconciliation. I don't think I have come across a country that is so single-minded about it. Look at Gacaca (the process of truth-telling and reconciliation between perpetrators and victims), for example. To implement the policy must have taken a lot of courage, keeping in mind the kind of wounds it would open and the fury it could cause between Tutsis and Hutus. That they have gone ahead with programs like these is testimony of how courageous the Rwandans are.

—Baroness Lynda Chalker,
former British minister for overseas development

Some observers argue that the political system in Rwanda has been influenced by Ugandan President Yoweri Museveni's ideology of a "single-party democracy," and that for this reason the government moved slowly in opening up political debate. The Arusha Accords envisaged a transition to an elected government in 22 months, but in 1999 the government extended the transitional arrangements another four years. It felt that, given the fragility of the country and Rwanda's devastating experience with the power of hate radio, greater reconciliation and security needed to be achieved before political openness could be increased.

Establishing the International Criminal Tribunal for Rwanda

In 1994 the legal system in Rwanda was stripped bare. The Supreme Court had been disbanded in 1978 and the judiciary placed under the direct control of the executive—there was thus no recent tradition of an independent and impartial justice system to build on. To make good on the social contract and to achieve reconciliation and security, the government needed to show genocide survivors that justice would be done.

The international community attempted to help bring justice to Rwanda by establishing the International Criminal Tribunal for Rwanda (ICTR), set up by Security Council Resolution 955 on November 8, 1994, with the purpose of contributing to the process of national reconciliation and maintaining international peace and security in the region. The aim of the ICTR was to prosecute people responsible for genocide and other serious violations of international humanitarian law committed in Rwanda between January 1, 1994, and December 31,

---

I would say that everybody has worked well in contributing to making a difference from the 1994 situation. In the current situation there is stability, there is progress and reconciliation, we have been involved with decentralization where provinces, districts are taking a lot of activities in their hands, the responsibilities are being handed over to the population. It is very difficult to imagine you could overcome this very complex situation in such a short time.

—President Paul Kagame,
June 2003, BBC

1994. From the start, however, there were several concerns about the appropriateness of the tribunal—a mechanism of international law used to address the reconciliation needs of a deeply traumatized country. Rwanda had a seat on the UN Security Council in 1994 and was the only country to vote against the establishment of the court.

The ICTR had indicted more than 70 genocide suspects, more than 60 of whom were arrested. Thirteen trials were completed, resulting in 12 convictions and 1 acquittal; 8 trials, involving 20 defendants, are currently in progress. Those convicted include Jean Kambanda, the prime minister of Rwanda during the genocide and the first head of government ever to be convicted on genocide charges. Fourteen ministers of the previous government are in custody awaiting trial.

While useful precedents in international criminal law have undoubtedly emerged from the ICTR, most Rwandans perceive that the court has been unable to deliver justice for the survivors of the genocide. The court's slow arrests and prosecutions and its high operating costs (the ICTR has spent $537 million since 1996) are causes of skepticism, frustration, and even indifference for many survivors. This undermining of the tribunal's standing in the eyes of the ordinary Rwandan citizen makes it difficult for it to make a strong contribution to national reconciliation. The government has to look to other options.

Using Gacaca to Try Genocide Suspects

Influenced by Western norms of justice, the government initially rejected the South African Truth and Reconciliation Commission model, believing that only when the guilty had been punished would it be possible for Rwandans to create a joint future together. With some donor support, Rwanda set about rebuilding the justice sector. More than 100 projects have been established, including projects to train lawyers, judges, investigators, and police officers and to conduct exercises on administrative procedures and court reform. Despite these efforts, however, by early 2000 only about 3,000 suspects had been processed through the conventional court system, and it was clear that the justice system could not work any faster to clear the backlog of cases. Of the more than 100,000 prisoners in Rwanda in 2003, 85 percent were awaiting trial for genocide-related crimes. By one estimate, moving at the pace of conventional courts, it would take 150 years to try all of these genocide suspects.

As early as 1998 the government began to consider how a traditional, community-based means of conflict resolution—*Gacaca*—could be transformed into the principal mechanism for trying those accused of participation in the genocide. The new *Gacaca* system was created by the government in 2001. It is made up of about 11,000 jurisdictions, each with 19 elected judges known for their integrity in their communities. For many generations Rwanda has been a hierarchical society with an efficient local administrative apparatus. This apparatus was capitalized on when open-air elections were held and more than 254,000 *Gacaca* judges elected in October 2001. These judges received training in 2002 before the courts began to function.

The genocide law passed by the government in 1996 divides suspects into four categories:

- Planners, organizers, and leaders of the genocide; people who acted in a position of authority; well-known murderers; and people who committed rape and sexual torture.
- People guilty of voluntary homicide, people who participated—or were complicit—in voluntary homicide or acts against people that resulted in death, people who inflicted wounds with intent to kill or committed other serious violent acts that did not result in death.
- People who committed violent acts without intent to kill.
- People who committed crimes against property.

Suspects in the first category are judged by the regular courts; all other cases are tried by *Gacaca*.

Former Rwandan ambassador to the United States Richard Sezibera explains,

> *"Traditionally,* Gacaca *would be a method of arbitration between families, a situation in which wise men would sit together. It would only deal with minor infractions, or minor disputes. . . . When we revived* Gacaca, *we wanted to tap into the tradition of arbitration that it embodied, but to use it to deal with the genocide. But note that we do call what we're setting up 'Gacaca courts,' not just plain 'Gacaca'. . . . We've looked at other arbitration systems, in the United States and elsewhere. But no one has ever tried to use such a system to deal with a genocide. Mainly, we're trying to merge our traditions with current international law"* (quoted in Cobban 2002).

The main aims of *Gacaca* are to speed up trials, reduce prison populations, and reconcile victims and perpetrators through truth-telling. Critics have noted that using *Gacaca* to try crimes is inconsistent with international norms and principles of due process, since defendants are under to pressure to incriminate themselves and there is no legal representation, legally reasoned verdict, or separation between prosecutor and judge. Defenders of the use of *Gacaca* note that these elements of due process were not designed to try crimes arising from circumstances in which as many as 1 million people died nor were they designed to make a significant, identifiable contribution to national reconciliation.

Initially disparaged by commentators used to Western norms of justice, *Gacaca* is now regarded as a bold, innovative socio-judicial experiment that is reducing the cost of upkeep of prisons; speeding the processing of genocide suspects, thereby ending the feeling among victims that there is a culture of impunity; and helping reintegrate people who committed genocidal acts into society through community service sentences. Such sentences can be passed for category 2 suspects who confess or category 3 or 4 suspects who are convicted. Services consist of unpaid work within the community for a fixed period of time in a specialized institution.

The Reform Agenda: Rwanda's Eight-point Plan

From the beginning, Rwanda's new government recognized that economic growth and an environment characterized by the rule of law are important guarantors of continuing security. In July 1994 Faustin Twagiramungu, Rwanda's first postwar prime minister, outlined an eight-point plan for development. In addition to reconciliation and the restoration of peace, the plan includes development of the economy and consolidation of democracy as key goals for the new administration.

By 1998 the government had formalized these goals in its flagship development document, Vision 2020, which sets out the steps to be taken for Rwanda to become a middle-income country. Building on the more secure environment achieved in Rwanda by mid-1998 and running parallel to the efforts at reconciliation, the government's program of reform has ensured economic growth and confirmed its determination to rebuild the country to benefit all Rwandans. The program is continually evolving as the government collaborates with external partners and consults with civil society through village meetings.

Achieving Macroeconomic Stability and Spurring Growth

The government has tried to maintain the macroeconomic stability needed for sustained growth. In March 1995 it liberalized the exchange regime. In 1997 a revised central bank statute was adopted that gives the Banque National de Rwanda independence with respect to monetary policy. Current account restrictions have been abolished. Domestic price controls have been eliminated for the majority of commodities, and laws are being modified to reflect the policy of price liberalization. Budget allocations for social sectors have increased since 1998 (and are protected from cuts), and spending on defense has fallen, dropping from $31.2 million in 1999 to $14.9 million in 2003. Economic governance has been improved through the creation of a number of parastatal institutions, described below.

Liberalizing and Promoting Trade

Rwanda has made significant progress in liberalizing trade, with the maximum tariff rate reduced from 100 percent before 1995 to 25 percent in early 1999. State marketing boards for coffee and tea have been put on a commercialized footing, and the tariff on coffee was eliminated in early 1999. The government has engaged consultants to help develop primary product sectors by differentiating products and encouraging Rwandan industries to move up the value chain. Rwanda joined the World Trade Organization in 1996 and the Common Market for Eastern and Southern Africa (COMESA) in 2003. Rwanda's external partners have recognized these efforts at creating a free trade environment. As a result of the changes, for example, Rwanda qualifies for tariff-free exports of certain products to the United States under the African Growth and Opportunity Act (AGOA).

Creating Semi-autonomous Parastatals

The government recognized the need to establish relatively autonomous agencies in certain key economic areas and to staff these agencies with highly qualified personnel. Although they report to the Ministry of Finance, Rwanda's parastatals are semiautonomous institutions with outcome-based strategic plans. By offering enhanced pay scales, they have been able to attract and retain skilled staff.

The National Tender Board, created in 1997, promotes transparency, economy, and equity in the public procurement process. The Rwanda

Revenue Authority (RRA), also established in 1997, is an independent body devoted to tax reform. In addition to introducing the value-added tax in 2001 and reforming income and property tax regimes, it has engaged in a vigorous public information campaign to encourage Rwandans to meet their tax obligations. The result has been a high level of compliance with the tax regime—about 90 percent, according to the RRA—by larger businesses in Rwanda.

In 1998 the government created the Rwandan Investment Promotion Authority (RIPA), a body tailored to facilitate inward investment. RIPA guides international businesspeople through the process of registering and running a business in Rwanda and informs them of the tax concessions available to those willing to make a serious commitment to investing in the country. Some bankers have noted that it is currently very difficult to obtain a court order to sell property held as security and that bribery on the part of debtors can delay this process. These problems are being addressed through comprehensive law reforms.

In 1999 the government established the Auditor General's Office. This body examines the budgets and expenditures of government departments and reports its findings to Parliament. An ombudsman was recently created with responsibility for eliminating and preventing corruption and injustice in both the public and private sectors and providing a mechanism for receiving complaints on the implementation of judicial decisions.

Establishing the Rule of Law

Although the *Gacaca* are beginning to lighten the burden on the formal justice system, the courts remain overwhelmed by cases relating to the genocide. In addition, in rural areas, where 90 percent of Rwandans live, people have little access to formal justice, and there is a lack of legal literacy and awareness of rights, as well as a very limited supply of paralegal and legal services offering free advice to litigants. Rwanda has only about 100 lawyers, most of them practicing in Kigali.

International and local NGOs have proved to be useful partners in helping address these capacity issues in the judicial sector. The Danish Centre for Human Rights has helped create a corps of judicial defenders—numbering 115 as of 2003—located in each of Rwanda's provinces. Their principal task is to provide assistance during genocide cases, but they also offer advice in other cases. A few NGOs and the National University in Butare also provide legal and paralegal advice. The NGOs Haguruka and AVEGA offer advice to women at the local level. The government is also making efforts to improve civic education (through the Ministry of Education) and human rights education (through the National Human Rights Commission).

Rwanda has acknowledged problems of corruption in the judicial sector. For example, in order to be exempted from paying court fees, poor citizens must reportedly obtain a certificate of impoverishment from their local administration—a process that, ironically, can involve paying a bribe. There are also problems of corruption among magistrates: defendants sometimes pay to have cases against them delayed significantly.

Reform of the judiciary is now a priority for the country and has been championed by the president. The government created an independent Law Reform Commission in 2001 that has developed comprehensive reforms that are currently before Parliament. These reforms include the expedition of cases in lower courts; the development of pretrial mediation; the establishment of an independent, better-paid judiciary; and the development of a code of ethics. To improve the business environment, the government is in the process of establishing a "fast-track" court for the processing of commercial cases.

Adopting a New Constitution That Promotes Unity

The Constitution has been developed with input from the Rwandan people themselves. The long consultative process, begun by the government in 1995 through village meetings, culminated on June 4, 2003, with the adoption of a new constitution. Rather than simply condemning the past, it seeks to learn lessons from the experience. The first two sections of the preamble commit the state to fighting the ideology of genocide and eradicating divisions, ethnic or otherwise. The constitution recognizes these aspects as prerequisites for economic development and social progress. It also recognizes the "privilege of having one country, a common language, a common culture, and shared history," confirming that the people of Rwanda are determined to build on the historical unity that once existed.

The constitution emphasizes the importance of national unity. Article 50 refers to activities that promote "national culture." Article 54 prohibits political organizations based on race, ethnic group, or tribe. These aspects derive from the government's commitment to eliminating discrimination on the basis of ethnicity. The constitution also mandates that women should hold 30 percent of posts in decisionmaking organs, a mandate that will help Rwanda meet the third Millennium Development Goal. Currently, 49 percent of parliamentarians in the National Assembly are women—the highest percentage of any country in the world.

Ensuring Citizens' Rights

The constitution contains an extensive exposition of the rights of every Rwandan citizen. While the detailed legislation and implementation of some rights are still being worked out in some cases, the fact that rights to equality, liberty, and life are enshrined in the constitution represents an important pledge to the people of Rwanda. The right to property—now widely recognized as an essential component of a pro-poor developmental agenda—is guaranteed in the constitution.

Opening Up the Political Process

Rwanda held its first national elections on September 30, 2003. Although criticized by some observers, they marked an important step on the road toward a fully democratic state. In keeping with Rwanda's continuing focus on consultation and unity, the country's model of democracy will continue to differ somewhat from the traditional Western parliamentary model, however. Political parties are organized in a "consultative forum" in order to facilitate the exchange of ideas and consolidate national unity. Citizens will participate in political processes not only by voting but also through continuing consultation and input into government policy. The constitution confirms this, identifying "the constant quest for solutions through dialogue and consensus" as a fundamental principle. The judiciary (in particular the Supreme Court) is accorded a significant function in reviewing or amending laws and therefore constitutes an important check on the power of the executive.

What Has Rwanda Achieved in Terms of Development?

What have been the results of Rwanda's efforts at reconciliation and reform? Significant progress has been made since 1994—in economic performance, poverty reduction, and human development.[1]

Economic Performance

Postconflict countries grow rapidly, because their starting point is often very low (box 3.4). Even within this context, however, Rwanda's achievements have been significant. Through sound macroeconomic management, Rwanda's economy rebounded by 70 percent between 1994 and 1997, and it grew by an average of 7.7 percent a year between 1998 and 2002; inflation was reduced from 64 percent in 1994 to 3 percent in 2000–02 (figure 3.1). The Ministry of Finance and Economic Planning estimates that given rapid population growth, real GDP growth of at least 7 to 8 percent will be needed over the next 15 years to ensure continued poverty reduction.

The fiscal deficit, excluding donor grants, declined from 13.8 percent of GDP in 1995 to 9.5 percent in 2001, while the current account deficit declined from 19.1 percent of GDP to 16.4 percent over the same period. Rwanda is highly indebted, with an external debt of about $1.5 billion. It is looking to meet enhanced Heavily Indebted Poor Countries (HIPC) Initiative targets that will allow it to access $810 million of relief over the coming years.

Economic growth has been broad based, although improvements in living standards have been primarily urban. Agriculture and construction have been the main sources of growth since 1998, stimulated by the return of refugees and internally displaced persons. Other key subsectors, such as utilities, manufacturing, and tourism, are still below the levels of the early 1990s.

BOX 3.4	How the Genocide Affected Rwanda's Economy and Demographics

Statistics on Rwanda in 1994 are sparse, but an estimated 78 percent of the population was living below the poverty line when the Rwandan Patriotic Front took power (Republic of Rwanda 2002). After the genocide real GDP fell 50 percent, and the rate of inflation rose to 64 percent—up from 12.4 percent in 1993. Government revenue declined to 5.8 percent of GDP in 1995, and Rwanda became largely dependent on foreign assistance.

The genocide also dramatically changed Rwanda's demographics. The population became predominantly female (54 percent) and young, with large numbers of widows, orphans, and children. More than 3 million Rwandans became refugees or internally displaced persons.

| FIGURE 3.1 | Real GDP and GDP Growth in Rwanda, 1982–2002 |

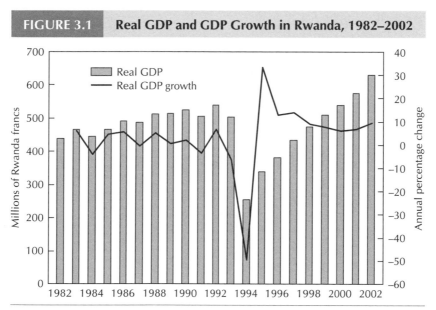

Source: Cropper 2003.

Human Development

It is extremely difficult to determine whether a particular episode of growth benefits the poor disproportionately (Ravallion 2001). Although figures are sparse, those that are available show that improvement and significant progress is being made in meeting the Millennium Development Goals. Rwanda's infant mortality rate fell from 210 per 1,000 live births in 1995 to 95 in 2003, and the incidence of poverty fell from about 70 percent in 1994 to 60 percent in 2002 (United Kingdom, Department for International Development 2004).

In the health sector the immunization rate for childhood diseases for 2002 was 80 percent, which compares favorably with the Sub-Saharan average of only 58 percent of one-year-olds immunized against measles. HIV/AIDS remains a key challenge, which the government and partners are addressing. HIV/AIDS education efforts have boosted awareness of the disease to 70 percent of the population.

Education indicators are now stronger than they were before 1994. In 2002 the net primary school enrollment rate was 75 percent, up from 65 percent in 1990.

What Accounts for this Progress?

Direct causal links cannot be drawn between the improving security environment and reforms on the one hand and economic growth and reduction in poverty on the other—but the correlation is suggestive. A secure environment is itself a critical component of a poverty reduction agenda. Businesses cannot function in a climate of insecurity, and the poor, who cannot afford private protection, will always suffer disproportionately. In addition to the secure environment, the government's commitment to sound economic management, trade promotion, and institutional reform has enabled the country to bounce back rapidly over the past 10 years. Challenges remain in the areas of land policy and justice, but they are being addressed following broad countrywide consultations, consultations that in their openness characterize the formulation of public policy in Rwanda.

The role of the government. The broad consultation process used by the government in developing its policies has meant that they are widely accepted—as suggested by the relatively high percentage of taxes paid. Although the consensual nature of Rwandan democracy has meant that development of policies is sometimes rather slow, it also means that when agreement is reached policies can be implemented rapidly. In addition, on issues on which urgent leadership is needed, the presidency has shown itself willing to act with focus and determination. The president has also shown a personal commitment to the eradication of corruption. Providing civil servants with short-term contracts, coupled with the cultural expectation that a job in government is not necessarily a "job for life," has meant that when corruption is detected it is addressed.

The strong growth exhibited by the Rwandan economy must also be partly attributed to the government's single-mindedness and determination. Perhaps building on its military origins, the government has exhibited discipline and resolve to realize its agenda for change. While listening to input from other sources, the government has not let itself be distracted. Tough choices have been translated into necessary reforms.

The role of donors. Rwanda's budget has been supplemented by international aid flows, with nearly $2.2 billion disbursed by bilateral and multilateral donors between 1995 and 1999. These external inflows have financed Rwanda's large current account deficit. The provision of resources has allowed donors to have an influence on government policies such as the creation of parastatal institutions,

which donors supported. The government has quickly embraced policies that it recognizes as beneficial to its overarching goals of developing the country.

Conclusions and Lessons

The Rwandan experience holds some key lessons for other postconflict
societies. The enormous scale of the problems overcome by the government should provide hope that similar achievements can be made
elsewhere.

Early on the government recognized that security and reconciliation, as well as being ends in themselves, were essential to economic
and social recovery and progress. Conversely, in conjunction with
political efforts, sustained economic growth has made a relapse into
conflict less likely.

Rwanda's recent history demonstrates the dangers of ethnic frag-
mentation and extremism but also the progress that can be made in
creating a national identity that transcends ethnicity. The forging of
such an identity is a political project to which the government has
devoted immense effort.

Rwanda had to deal with the largest exodus and return of refugees
in recent memory. In addition to this logistical challenge, it had to
prevent conflict between "old case" and "new case" returnees. A key
lesson is that, with logistical assistance from international agencies
and the presence of grassroots NGOs to help with mediation, large
movements and reintegration of people can be managed successfully.

The *Gacaca* experience has shown that, for extraordinary challenges,
bold, unconventional responses are sometimes necessary. In the context of countrywide trauma, the need for "restorative" justice was acute,
and the ideals of due process and formal trials proved to be far too
time consuming to address these needs. The government has shown
that, with determination and a willingness to involve the people, such
experiments can be made to work.

Rwanda has also shown that a relatively closed political system is
able to involve its citizens in political processes through "bottom up"
democratization, similar to that seen in China. Rwanda has used the
more than 11,000 administrative areas in the country to rapidly reach
and consult with a broad sector of the population.

Many challenges remain, and the results of the most recent reforms
are still pending. However, Rwanda's remarkable progress toward

reconciliation and poverty reduction shows what a determined, focused, and receptive government can achieve.

BIBLIOGRAPHY

Adelman, H., and A. Suhrke. 1999. *The Path of a Genocide: The Rwanda Crisis from Uganda to Zaire.* New Brunswick, N.J.: Transaction Publishers.

Arendt, H. 1973. *The Origins of Totalitarianism.* Eugene, Ore.: Harvest Books.

Bledsoe, D. 2003. "Rwanda Land Policy and Land Law Assessment." Rural Development Institute, Seattle, Wash.

Cobban, H. 2002. "The Legacies of Collective Violence." *Boston Review* 27(2).

Cropper, B. 2003. "The Economic Effects of Genocide on Rwanda: Post-Conflict Reconstruction and Aid Allocation in Light of New Research on the Economic Effects of Civil War." M.A. dissertation. University of Nottingham, School of Economics, United Kingdom.

De Soto, H. 2003. *The Mystery of Capital: Why Capitalism Succeeds in the West and Fails Elsewhere.* New York: Basic Books.

de Waal, A. 1997. *Famine Crimes: Politics and the Disaster Relief Industry in Africa.* Bloomington, Ind.: Indiana University Press.

Ernst & Young. 2003. "Doing Business in Rwanda." New York.

Galtung, J. 1969. "Violence, Peace and Peace Research." *Journal of Peace Research* 6(3): 167–91.

Harrell, P. E. 2003. *Rwanda's Gamble: Gacaca and a New Model of Transitional Justice.* Lincoln, Neb.: Writers Press Club.

International Crisis Group. 1999. *Five Years after the Genocide in Rwanda: Justice in Question.* Brussels.

IRIN (United Nations Integrated Regional Information Networks). 2004. "Rwanda: The State of Demobilisation, Reintegration of Excombatants." United Nations Office for the Coordination of Humanitarian Affairs, New York.

Jackson, R. 1990. *Quasi-States: Sovereignty, International Relations and the Third World.* Cambridge: Cambridge University Press.

Khan, M. H. 2002. "State Failure in Developing Countries and Strategies of Institutional Reform." Paper presented at the Annual Bank Conference on Development Economics, June 24–26, Oslo, Norway.

Khan, M. H., and K. S. Jomo, eds. 2000. *Rents, Rent-Seeking and Economic Development: Theory and Evidence in Asia.* Cambridge: Cambridge University Press.

Liversage, H. 2003. "Overview of Rwanda's Land Policy and Land Law and Key Challenges for Implementation." U.K. Department for International Development and Government of Rwanda, Ministry of Lands, Resettlement and Environment, Kigali.

Multi-Donor Demobilisation and Reintegration Programme. 2004. "Country Profile: Democratic Republic of Congo." Washington, D.C.

———. 2004. "Country Profile: Rwanda." Washington, D.C.

Obidegwu, C. 2003. "Rwanda: The Search for Post-Conflict Socio-Economic Change, 1995–2001." Africa Region Working Paper 59. World Bank, Washington, D.C.

Olson, M. 2000. *Power and Prosperity: Outgrowing Communist and Capitalist Dictatorships.* New York: Basic Books.

Penal Reform International. 2003. "Research Project on *Gacaca* Courts." London. [www.penalreform.org/english/frset_theme_en.htm].

Piron, L. H. 2003. "Justice Reforms in Rwanda: Recommendations to Government and Donors." Overseas Development Institute, London.

Prunier, G. 1995. *The Rwanda Crisis: History of a Genocide.* New York: Columbia University Press.

Ravallion, M. 2001. "Growth, Inequality and Poverty: New Evidence on an Old Debate." *World Development* 29(11): 1787–1966.

Republic of Rwanda, Ministry of Finance. 2000. "La Vision du Rwanda à l'Horizon 2020." Kigali.

———. 2001a. "Rwanda en chiffres 2001." Kigali.

———. 2001b. "Report on Poverty Profile Survey in Rwanda." National Poverty Reduction Programme, Kigali.

———. 2002. "Poverty Reduction Strategy Paper." Kigali.

———. 2003. "Vision 2020." Kigali.

Republic of Rwanda, Ministry of Internal Security. 2004a. "Rwanda National Police Strategic Plan—2004–2008." Kigali.

———. 2004. "Sector Policy." Kigali.

Republic of Rwanda, Ministry of Lands, Environment, Forestry, Water and Natural Resources. 2004. "Draft National Land Policy." Kigali.

Smyth, F. 1994. "The Horror." *The New Republic* 210(25): 19–21.

The New Times. "FRW 4.2bn Lost in Shady Govt Deals." March 8–9.

———. 2004. "Massive Corruption Reported in MVK." March 8–9.

———. 2004. "No Political Influence in Bank Loans–Kanimba." January 8–11.

———. 2004. "Police to Dismiss 150." March 1–3.

United Kingdom, Department for International Development. 2003. "A Scoping Study of Transitional Justice and Poverty Reduction." London.

———. 2004. "Rwanda Country Assistance Plan" London.

USAID (United States Agency for International Development). 2002. "Assessment of the Judicial Sector in Rwanda." Washington, D.C.

Uvin, P. 2000. "The Introduction of a Modernized Gacaca for Judging Suspects of Participation in the Genocide of 1994 in Rwanda." Discussion paper prepared for the Belgian Secretary of State for Development Cooperation. Brussels.

World Bank. 2003. "Rwanda Data Profile." *World Development Indicators Database.* Washington, D.C.

4

Fueling Cooperation
A Regional Approach to Reducing Poverty in the Senegal River Basin

UNDALA ALAM AND OUSMANE DIONE

In a series of conventions and other agreements beginning in 1963, the four coastal countries in the Senegal River Basin—Guinea, Mali, Mauritania, and Senegal—agreed to cooperate in developing and managing the river and its resources. Motivating them was a belief in pan-African unity and the realization that they could all get more from the Senegal River—and at a lower cost—by cooperating in its development than by proceeding unilaterally. Their experience shows that regional cooperation rather than unilateral development of a shared resource can help tackle poverty.

History of Cooperation in the Senegal Basin

In 1963 the Bamako Convention, signed by Guinea, Mali, Mauritania, and Senegal, recognized the Senegal River's

Undala Alam can be contacted at ualam@worldbank.org, and Ousmane Dione at odione@worldbank.org. The case study was a joint effort made with critical inputs from Mohamed Salem Ould Merzoug, High Commissioner of the Senegal River Basin Development Organization; Khalil Gueye and his team at Generation Television Senegal; and Robert Liebenthal and Louise Fox. The authors thank them for their efforts.

international status and created the Interstate Committee (CIE) to manage the river. Colonial conferences on the status of Africa's rivers had not recognized the Senegal River as an international river, as it belonged to a single colonial power. After independence landlocked Mali sought to have the Senegal River's international status recognized in order to ensure navigation rights. Freedom of navigation on the Senegal River derives from the principle of reciprocity, not universal access.

Driven by a strong will to cooperate, the countries signed the Labé Convention, creating the Organization for the Coastal States of the Senegal River (OERS) on March 24, 1968, with the mandate to develop the basin by facilitating closer coordination beyond the water and agricultural sectors. In a wide-ranging development plan the countries pledged to cooperate in other areas through OERS; harmonize civil legislation; improve education, industrial growth, transport, and telecommunications; and facilitate trade and labor movements across borders. In conformity with the Organization for African Unity Charter, the countries adopted a resolution calling for unprecedented levels of cooperation and integration. The aim was, as President Modibo Keita of Mali put it, for all citizens to "regard themselves as citizens of the Senegal River states rather than Guineans, Malians, Mauritanians, or Senegalese."

On March 11, 1972, Mali, Mauritania, and Senegal signed the Nouakchott Convention, reconfirming the river's international status and establishing the Senegal River Development Organization (OMVS) and dissolving the OERS. Although Guinea was not a party to the convention, it did not oppose it (box 4.1).

The resulting forum, often referred to as the "OMVS space" (*l'espace OMVS*), has three organs: the executive organ, which includes the Heads of State Summit and the Council of Ministers; the technical organ, including the High Commission, based in Dakar; and the consultative organ, made up of the Permanent Water Commission and the Regional Steering Committee, which advise the High Commission. Learning from the OERS experience, OMVS incorporated changes. First, OMVS was given a narrower mandate, focusing on developing the basin's water resources and related economic activities. Second, a stronger decisionmaking process was established. Links to the executive organ were strengthened, so that if, in exceptional circumstances, a unanimous decision could not be reached, the heads of state could intervene to move matters forward.

BOX 4.1	Chronology of Cooperation in the Senegal River Basin

1963 Guinea, Mali, Mauritania, and Senegal establish the Interstate Committee and declare the Senegal River an international river.

1968 The four basin countries form the Organization for the Coastal States of the Senegal River (OERS) and define a basinwide development program.

1972 Mali, Mauritania, and Senegal create the Senegal River Development Organization (OMVS) to implement the development program outlined by the OERS.

1978 Mali, Mauritania, and Senegal sign a convention establishing the legal status of common works.

1982 Mali, Mauritania, and Senegal sign a convention on financing the common works.

1984 Twelve donors support building the Manantali and Diama Dams.

1986 The Diama Dam becomes operational.

1990 The Manantali Dam becomes operational.

1992 The OMVS-Guinea protocol is signed.

1997 The Regional Hydropower Project begins.

2000 The Diama Dam Management Company (SOGED) and the Manantali Dam Management Company (SOGEM), the dams' management agencies, are established.

2002 Electricity generated at Manantali is transmitted to Bamako, Dakar, and Nouakchott. Mali, Mauritania, and Senegal sign and ratify the Water Charter.

2003 Guinea participates in the OMVS Heads of State Summit in Nouakchott.

2004 The first interministerial meeting between Guinea and the OMVS member states is held in Nouakchott.

   The first technical meeting on establishing an inclusive framework for the basin's joint management is held in Conakry.

Focusing on Benefits, Not Allocations

The Senegal River Basin countries' decision to cooperate marked a significant shift in how international river basins are developed. By choosing to develop the Senegal River jointly, Mali, Mauritania, and Senegal focused on generating the services they needed—and then sharing them equitably. Referred to as the "principle of benefit sharing," this approach is unique in that it focuses on benefits rather than allocations. The international donor community is beginning to embrace this approach. By working as partners rather than competitors, the countries face their common challenges of reducing poverty and sustaining economic growth together.

The strong political commitment to joint management and common works has reinforced intrabasin relationships and built trust that the benefits will be shared equitably and that the country hosting the common works will respect their joint ownership. Assane Diouf, the Director of Energy Transportation at the Senegal National Electric Company (SENELEC), explains why the Senegal Basin countries chose to forgo unilateral planning: "After independence, African countries were confronted with budgetary constraints. To facilitate the search for funds, the only way was for the riparian countries to manage the Senegal River jointly." This spirit remains uncommon, obstructed in many cases by a lack of trust, which can take time to build and be politically very difficult. Lack of trust often prompts countries to choose unilateral options, despite the higher returns on investments in cooperative development and the greater impact on poverty.

Providing Infrastructure for Basic Needs

The OMVS countries created two types of shared infrastructure. Physical infrastructure includes water management works, telecommunication networks, and transportation links. Institutional infrastructure includes the OMVS and related agencies, which seek to harmonize national planning and legal frameworks to promote trade and labor flows. Both are needed for the basin's development. As Madia Fall, technical advisor in Senegal's Ministry of Agriculture and Water, explains, "The dams have favored the development of potable water, electricity, and telecommunications—not only in the valley but also for other crucial geographical areas not in the basin, such as Bamako, Dakar, and Nouakchott."

Increasing the Power Supply

Owned jointly by the OMVS countries, the Manantali Dam and its network of 1,300 kilometers of transmission lines came on line in 2002. Mali's national grid was connected in January, Senegal's in July, and Mauritania's in November. Since May 2003 the station has been working at full capacity, generating 200 megawatts (MW).

Manantali Dam was built on the Bafing River, entirely within Mali. It has a storage capacity of 11.3 cubic kilometers and an annual generating capacity of 800 gigawatt-hours (GWh). It regulates the flow at 300 cubic meters per second. Electricity generation in the region is still not sufficient, but since 2002 it has become more reliable and is slowly transforming the lives of people in Mali, Mauritania, and Senegal (box 4.2).

The Diama Dam, located 23 kilometers from the Senegal River's mouth, was built to block intrusion into the river by the Atlantic Ocean, to facilitate perennial irrigation, and to improve the water supply of Dakar and Nouakchott by filling Lac de Guiers in Senegal and Lac R'Kiz in Mauritania. Used jointly with the Manantali Dam, the Diama Dam has ensured a water supply for Dakar and reduced irrigation costs (figure 4.1).

In 1997 the OMVS countries initiated the Regional Hydropower Project at Manantali. The project installed electricity-generating turbines with a capacity of 200 MW and laid transmission lines to Bamako, Dakar, and Nouakchott. It also established the institutions to operate the generating system. Two operating agencies, the Manantali Dam Management Company (SOGEM) and the Diama Dam Management Company (SOGED), were commissioned in 2000. In addition, an independent entity from the private sector was appointed to operate the Manantali Dam under SOGEM's supervision. Mirroring OMVS's Permanent Water Commission, which advises on water allocation, the Permanent Technical Committee on Interconnection was created, along with a Management Committee for Interconnection, to define the program of production, supply, and regulation of electricity production.

The Regional Hydropower Project provided an opportunity for the countries to introduce efficiencies that would benefit more than the energy sector. For example, the transmission lines that connect Manantali to the three national grids use dual-purpose fiber optic technology, which can be used for telecommunications. As a result of this technology Senegal has one of Africa's most modern telephone

BOX 4.2	A Tale of Two Countries: How Cooperation Has Affected People's Lives in Senegal and Guinea

In a suburb of Dakar, Demba Ndiaye and his friends and siblings started a cooperative in 2001. The 10 young men and women were faced with university strikes and other difficulties that threatened their studies. Rather than lose time, they decided to open a cybercafe to provide them with income and make the Internet more accessible to other young people. They bought three computers and established a connection with SONATEL, Senegal's main telecommunications provider. Today the cooperative has two cybercafes, with average daily revenues of $82 from 12 computers.

The cooperative survived during a period of frequent electrical outages. Not owning its own electrical generators, it was completely dependent on SENELEC. As Demba explains, "When there was no electricity, nothing worked. We would stop working during those hours and on occasions lost a whole day's business." Before the electricity supply stabilized, the business's average daily turnover was $16—a fifth of what it is today.

Electrical outages were not the only obstacles. Frequent breakdowns in equipment also hampered business. Lack of security, another consequence of the outages, forced the cybercafes to close at 8 p.m. Outages still occur today, but they are less frequent and shorter than before. As Assane Diouf, the director of energy transportation at SENELEC, notes, "Since the end of outages, when Manantali came on line, we have noticed less frustration among households and more constant activity at small and medium industries."

The situation is far different in Guinea. Mamadou Diallo, the owner of a cybercafe in the central part of the country, is angry about electricity outages, which cost him a third of his revenues. Mamadou uses 10 liters of fuel a day to generate his own electricity during outages. The fuel costs him $0.67 a liter if it is available from legitimate suppliers. If it is not, he is forced to buy it on the black market at $2 a liter. Mamadou's fuel bill alone ranges from $6.70 to $20.00 for every day of outage. The drop in revenues has forced him to cut his staff from four employees to two. Because of the problems, Mamadou is considering closing his business and emigrating to Europe or the United States.

For other enterprises in Guinea the story is much the same. Unreliable electricity is threatening the incomes of butchers and women selling fish or fruit juices, who are losing their inventory because they cannot keep their products cool. In hospitals, medical centers, and pharmacies, vaccines and medicines, already in scarce supply, cannot be stored properly. Guinea's difficulties are linked to its lack of infrastructure and the lost opportunity to be part of the transformation occurring down the Senegal River in Mali, Mauritania, and Senegal.

FIGURE 4.1   The Senegal River Basin

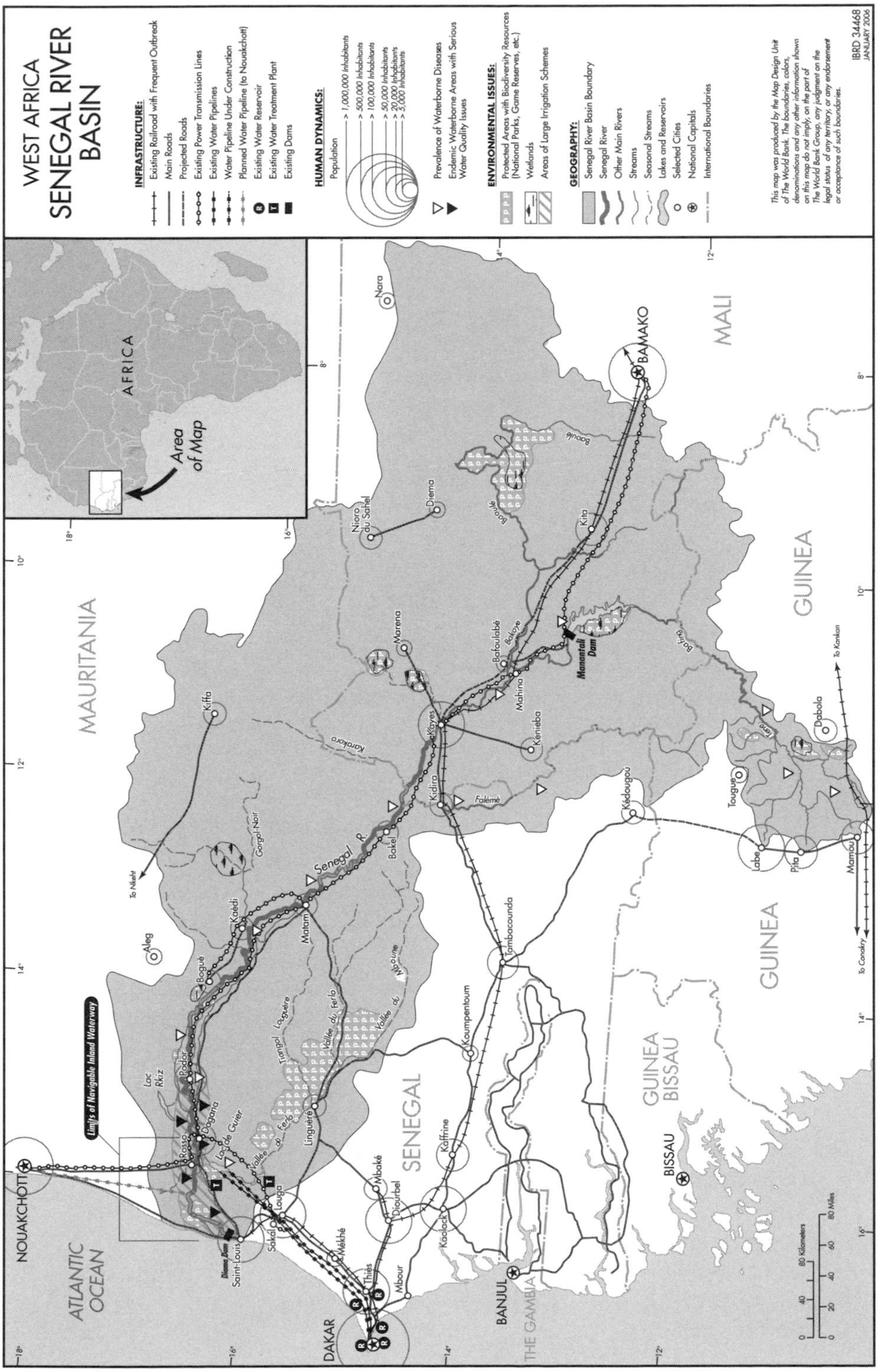

Source: World Bank.

networks—80 percent of it already digital—with links to international networks in Europe and Asia. Its lower rates give it a comparative advantage in developing telecommunication services such as call centers.

In 1999, before the dam came on line, Mali's installed electrical power was 123 MW, of which 100 MW was on an interconnected transmission network already at the saturation point. Due to the lack of capacity, Mali Energy (EDM) was forced to cut off approximately 46.5 GWh, at an estimated loss of $38.3 million, disrupting economic activities and triggering social turmoil.

In 2002 Manantali's commission reduced the cost of electricity to $0.15–0.17 per kilowatt-hour in the basin and minimized outages in all three countries. It has also reduced Mali's imports of fuel to generate electricity. (As a non–oil producer, Mali is highly dependent on imports.) The positive impact of Manantali is evidenced by the closure of the Balingue, Dar Salam, and Kita central fuel depots.

SOGEM sells electricity to EDM at $0.05 a kilowatt-hour, a price EDM raises to $0.13 a kilowatt-hour at resale. Access to electricity remains difficult in Mali because of the country's size, high tariffs, and low population density outside the Bamako area. Even so, the number of subscribers increased from 66,175 in 1995 to 101,800 in 2003, and total consumption rose from 245 GWh to 384 GWh.

Improving the Supply of Water

As a result of the dams Senegal's rural population is enjoying improved water supply, although many people still rely on untreated water drawn directly from the river. In the Dagana municipality the population is benefiting from water stations and distribution networks financed mainly by expanding agribusinesses, such as the Senegal River Development Agency (SAED). The dams will provide 62 villages on the valley's left bank with potable water. Work is also under way to increase Nouakchott's daily water supply of 50,000 cubic meters to 170,000 cubic meters by 2020 by using water from the Senegal River through the Aftout-es-Saheli.

The Diama Dam straddles the river between Mauritania and Senegal, 27 kilometers from its mouth. It stops the ocean's intrusion upriver during the dry season, increases irrigation, and improves the filling of Lakes Guiers and R'Kiz, as well as other depressions such as the Aftout-es-Saheli. It also supplies potable water. Embankments along the river were built to create a freshwater lake, managed at 1.75 meters above sea level, which allows farmers upstream to pump water for rice cultivation at a lower cost. Together the dams aim to increase the irrigated area from less than 50,000 hectares to 375,000 hectares in Mauritania and Senegal and to provide Mali with access to the Atlantic Ocean.

Dakar's metropolitan area experienced recurrent and seasonal water shortages (estimated at 65,000 cubic meters a day during the dry season) due to the pressures of growing demand (expected to triple over the next 30 years) and the need to close contaminated boreholes. Dakar's heavy reliance on the nearby Littoral Nord fossil aquifers was unsustainable (recharge rates were low), overexploitation was already leading to saltwater intrusion, and an additional 35,000 cubic meters a day could be drawn from the aquifers only through 2005. To tackle the problem, groundwater extraction needed to be reduced to 3,300 cubic meters a day by 2005. Doing so meant providing an alternative water source from Lake Guiers, about 240 kilometers away, which relies on water levels in the Senegal River regulated by the Diama Dam (box 4.3). A water treatment plant at Ngnith currently provides 40,000 cubic meters of treated water a day to Dakar and its surrounding area. A second plant is being constructed on the lake, which will provide an additional 65,000 cubic meters a day, allowing the aquifers to be sustained.

Financing Infrastructure Jointly

The most valuable outcome of cooperation is the strong intrabasin relationships that have been formed, which have facilitated economic growth through joint development of infrastructure. For example, in addition to the common interest in establishing and maintaining a reliable energy supply, Mali wanted navigation to the sea and Mauritania and Senegal wanted to expand irrigation in the valley. Rather than pursue these goals unilaterally, the OMVS countries chose to share the burden of large loans to fund their development plans, so that each economy would not need to carry the full weight of the investments.

The countries could have followed the common international practice of preserving sovereignty and minimizing commitments to other countries by opting to share the benefits based on a minimum common denominator or by "splitting the difference." Instead, the Senegal Basin countries opted to act as a single community and to maximize

| BOX 4.3 | Changing People's Lives by Providing Clean Water |

The Senegal National Water Company (SONEES) has changed the lives of hundreds of thousands of people by installing fountains in Dakar and other urban areas. Upon request, local communities and individuals can be connected without having to pay the $10 connection fee or the $23 water meter fee. Alioune Mboup, a resident of Thiaroye, near Dakar, explains, "My wives no longer need to go to the communal fountain, which was a source of a lot of conflict. My water bill is around $25 every two months, but we can wash better and whenever we want. As a father, it makes me proud to see my family well."

Improvements have occurred in the area around Lake Guiers, too. According to Sogui Ba, a Ngnith resident, "Before running water arrived in the house, everyone went to the lake for all domestic needs. It has been a long time since I have gone to the lake. Now only children go there to play. Our water invoice is around $33, which we find very expensive given that Lake Guiers is so close to us. People have said to us that if they lived so close to the river, they wouldn't have connected to SONEES. But we will never give up the running water, even if it costs a lot, because we know what the costs would be to use the lake's water. There was a local belief that the lake's water didn't contain any microbes if it was collected early in the morning or after leaving it in the sun. This belief disappeared with the arrival of running water. Today we wash ourselves when we want. The women do not have the drudgery of collecting water. And the children are always clean."

Maimouna Diop is a housewife living in St. Louis. "I live with my husband, four children, and son-in-law. The connection with the SONEES changed our lives, because before that there wasn't a fountain nearby. Each day I would walk with my daughter several blocks to draw water to drink. For the dishes and laundry we used the well by the side of the house. If I had had my own tap when I was younger, I wouldn't have aged so quickly and would have better health. I am a woman who likes cleanliness," she says. "My greatest satisfaction is to see my children clean."

their common interest. Their decisions were based on consensus and the principles of solidarity and equity. Solidarity means joint fiscal responsibility for shared infrastructure, even if the immediate outcomes do not benefit a particular country. Equity means that each country's share of the benefits is congruent with its needs.

To obtain financing for the Diama and Manantali Dams, the countries needed to define common ownership and the related principle of financial solidarity. The countries agreed to guarantee and repay construction loans according to a formula that apportioned repayment based on benefits received. Doing so allowed donors to conclude agreements directly with each country for its share of the total loan repayment.

The loans to construct the Diama and Manantali Dams were guaranteed equally by Mali, Mauritania, and Senegal, but loan repayment is proportional to the benefits each country derives from the dams. Under the current benefit-sharing formula, 42.1 percent of the benefits accrue to Senegal, 35.3 percent to Mali, and 22.6 percent to Mauritania. To revise the formula, a country applies in writing to the OMVS Council of Ministers.

This approach ensured an equitable allocation of water to different sectors, including irrigation and joint exploitation of the basin's hydroelectric potential. Mali receives 52 percent (104 MW) of the electricity generated at Manantali, Mauritania 15 percent (30 MW), and Senegal 33 percent (66 MW). Expansion of irrigation was also divided equitably, with the irrigated area increasing from 20,000 hectares in 1980 to 120,000 hectares after the dams began operating, with most of the increase in the valley between Mauritania and Senegal. Agricultural intensification also helped smooth the unequal balance of payments among the OMVS members. As Assane Diouf, notes, "[The dam] is a project that is not easy to manage because all the decisions have to be made unanimously. But it has lasted for 25 years."

Avoiding Armed Conflict

Joint ownership of infrastructure has meant that the basin countries have a common interest in safeguarding the works and the benefits that flow from them. As Babacar Ndao, Director of OMVS's national cell (*cellule*) in Senegal states, "OMVS is really an integrating factor for the three countries."

The Manantali and Diama Dams and the relationships established through the OMVS helped pull Mauritania and Senegal back from armed conflict. Ethnic violence triggered by a simmering dispute over animal grazing rights erupted in the valley in mid-April 1989. At least 50,000 people fled their homes as tensions escalated. The Organization of African Unity attempted to mediate the conflict in 1990 but was unsuccessful.

Remarkably, in July 1991 Mauritania and Senegal worked out an agreement themselves, based on recognition of their shared interests in the jointly owned dams. Even though diplomatic ties had been ruptured, the two countries managed to continue to collaborate through OMVS. The lessons the two countries had learned from their OERS experience and the fact that OMVS continued to operate during the conflict gradually eased tensions between them, initiating a process of normalization, with refugees returning to the valley and diplomatic ties resuming in May 1992.

Managing Extreme Hydrological Events

Using their common physical and institutional infrastructure, which includes the shared collection of hydrological data, Mali, Mauritania, and Senegal work together to manage extreme events such as floods and droughts. Hydrological data are transmitted simultaneously by satellite to OMVS headquarters in Dakar, to SOGEM at Manantali Dam, to SOGED at Diama Dam, and to the national water companies in Bamako, Dakar, and Nouakchott. Each receiving station has the same modeling software to determine the necessary action in the event of unusual water flows. A coordinated response is critical to minimizing loss of life and socioeconomic damage.

In 2003 the Senegal Basin experienced floods of a severity not seen in a century. Damage to the basin's economy and the impact on poverty was reduced by OMVS, coordinating the countries' technical efforts, and by using the local radio network to keep communities along the river informed. The handling of the situation contrasts sharply with that in Mozambique in 2000, where real GDP declined 23 percent after massive flooding. Much of the damage in Mozambique could have been avoided by better cooperation among the riparian countries.

Stimulating Economic Activity

Evidence is growing that reliable supplies of water and electricity encourage income-generating activities, making investments less risky in the OMVS economies (see boxes 4.2 and 4.4). As SENELEC's Assane Diouf notes, "Electricity is not a tangible product, it is a service made available to consumers. Permanent availability stimulates economic activities that generate income and reduce poverty among our people."

BOX 4.4	Keeping Fish Cold in Senegal

At Dakar's central fish market, the price of ice is usually $31 a ton. But when an electrical outage leads to a shortage, the price can rise to $33–$37, increasing the price of fish. Seydou Diaw, a fish wholesaler in Dakar, notes, "If electricity continues to be regular—and above all if the costs are reduced and we are assisted with transport—we could deliver fresh fish every day to the smallest village in Senegal."

Reliable electricity and water have encouraged various kinds of entrepreneurial activities:

■ Video halls for viewing large events, such as football matches, have opened in Mauritania. The average entrance fee is $0.08 a person.

■ Using water that travels 200 kilometers from Lake Guiers to Dakar's peri-urban area of Sebikotane, farmers in an area of low employment are using modern farming techniques to grow higher value off-season crops (green beans, melon, asparagus, cherry tomatoes), mainly for export to the European Union.

■ Irrigation has allowed year-round cultivation and yields that are almost 50 times those of rain-fed agriculture.

■ In Mauritania an intensive shrimp fishery that employed local fishers was set up in 1997.

■ Rice cultivation in the valley has driven the creation of small industrial units, with microenterprises providing key inputs such as tractors and pumps.

In investor surveys, Senegal's low-cost and reliable electric power is consistently singled out as a reason for locating factories in Senegal and for expanding capacity.

Tackling the Environmental and Social Challenges

Regulation of the Senegal River has created some problems. The Diama Dam changed the ecology and livelihoods along the lower Senegal River in Mauritania and Senegal. The Manantali Dam affected traditional river recessional agriculture in Mali.

Getting Rid of Aquatic Weeds

The delta's water salinity used to fluctuate daily with the tides and seasonally with rainfall. Local communities had adapted their livelihoods to the dynamic and diverse ecosystem. Before the river was regulated, the ecosystem ensured that no single species of aquatic plant could dominate. The Diama Dam produced a uniform freshwater environment in which one species, *typha australis*, could thrive. The resulting proliferation of the aquatic weed increased the incidence of bilharzia and malaria.

Water hyacinth (*salvinia molesta*), another species of weed that bloomed in the uniform environment, was successfully controlled by introducing the weevil (*cyrtobagous salviniae*) into the Senegal delta in May 2000. It proved a very effective biological control: by April 2002 water hyacinth was no longer a problem.

Biological control does not exist for *typha australis*. The weed can be eliminated only by removing it mechanically, which is expensive and slow, or by altering the river's saline balance by allowing salt water to enter through the Diama Dam, a step that could hurt the valley's agribusinesses and reduce the area's income.

A Mauritanian company, Enterprise des Routes et du Bâtiments, won a bid issued by the Senegalese government to clear stretches of the delta in Senegal. Funded entirely by the government, the $6.6 million program started in December 2003 and is due to last a year. Using an amphibious mower, the project has already cleared 160,000 square meters of the invasive weeds. The plan is to clear 1.3 million square meters. Productive uses for *typha australis*, as fodder and fuel, are also being researched.

Restoring Lost Livelihoods and the Ecosystem

Work is under way along the river's length to restore livelihoods lost by the drought and the alteration of the river's flow. To restore the valley's ecological diversity and rural livelihoods, Mauritania and Senegal together established Djoudj National Park (in 1971) and Diawling National Park (in 1991) on their sides of the river. Each park covers about 16,000 hectares.

The decline of the ecosystem forced men to leave the area in search of work, leaving behind women, children, and the elderly as permanent residents. To reverse the trend, Diawling National Park aimed to integrate conservation with development. A multidisciplinary team of experts worked closely with local communities, integrating indispensable knowledge of the former ecosystem's functioning into the park's management plan. The team recognized that the pre–Diama Dam flood cycle would need to be restored for local people to resume their traditional activities or develop new ones, such as ecotourism and market gardening. This activity would need to be supported by transport facilities, such as access roads, embankments to facilitate the economic revival, and adequate supplies of drinking water.

Market gardening proved successful in providing an alternative income source. Women organized themselves into cooperative groups, each contributing about $2 to a joint fund. The fund provided start-up materials such as fencing, agricultural equipment, and seeds to each cooperative, depending on its needs. A local advisor provided technical advice for six months to see the cooperatives through the first season, after which the women managed their activities independently. The area around Birette became a major exporter of vegetables to Nouakchott and now employs agricultural workers, who receive half of the profits.

To support local fisheries, two sluice gates were added. The Berbar gate allows fish migration to and from the spawning grounds in the Diawling-Tichilitt basin; the Lekser sluice gate allows shrimp to migrate. The fishers received help to purchase fishing equipment. Focusing on the hydraulic infrastructures where fish concentrated, fishers harvested 15,000 kilograms in 1996, which sold at $0.30–$0.40 per kilogram. Higher water levels and more exchanges with the Diawling Basin increased the catches to 400 kilograms a day in 1997.

The ecosystem's regeneration also stimulated wildlife. In 1993 a waterfowl census noted 2,000 waterbirds in the park. By 1995 the figure had risen to nearly 50,000. Subsequent studies have shown a clear relation between maximum flood levels and the number of birds.

Upstream of Diawling and Djoudj National Parks efforts are being made to mitigate the environmental impact of the Manantali Dam. Under the Regional Hydropower Project, a program was designed to mitigate the environmental impacts of the infrastructure, ensure stakeholder participation in determining the transmission lines' routes through local and national coordination committees, and guarantee the annual artificial flood from Manantali under the Water Charter.

Encouraging Stakeholder Participation

To encourage public engagement in decisionmaking, the OMVS is reaching out to stakeholders, providing for representation on the Permanent Water Commission, OMVS's consultative arm. Local coordination committees were established in Mali, Mauritania, and Senegal to allow communities to take part in decisions about the transmission line routes from the Manantali Dam. The Global Environment Facility (GEF) Senegal Basin Project is doubling the number of such committees in all basin countries, including Guinea. Building on existing institutional structures and experiences in the Senegal Basin under GEF's Small Grants Program, the project will facilitate microfinance opportunities by working with local communities at key sites across the basin. Guinea, Mali, Mauritania, and Senegal will each identify and prepare national priority action plans to guide improving livelihoods and managing the basin's resources.

Working directly with local communities helped resolve conflicts between water users in Diawling National Park (box 4.5). From the outset in 1991, respected village elders were recruited as "guards" to assist with surveillance, and the park's head of surveillance was a respected local *cherif*. Stakeholder meetings were held, but the composition of the meetings and their procedures were left to the village chiefs.

BOX 4.5	**Resolving Conflicts among Water Users in Diawling National Park**

Women's cooperatives in Diawling National Park depend on *sporobolus robustus,* a grass they use to make mats, their main source of income. For the *sporobolus robustus* grasses to achieve optimal lengths, rain needs to fall before the water body is flooded. But fishers in the park did not want to wait for rain. They wanted to flood an area within the park early, because the tilapia were ready to spawn; waiting for the rains would shorten the tilapia's growing season and reduce the fishers' income.

The two groups reached a compromise in which a thin layer of water was released to cover crucial parts of the floodplain in July; it was followed by flooding later. The women harvested grass stems that were more than 2.5 meters high, improving the quality of their mats. Selling at $50, each mat represented two weeks' labor for five women. The fishers harvested sizable catches.

Increasing Investment and Social Inclusion

The Senegal Basin countries' innovative cooperation has created an enabling climate for investments and social inclusion, opening the door to both large and small private sector enterprises. Several factors were key in creating an enabling environment for investment:

- *Commitment and political economy for change.* In their policies and declarations, the countries have repeatedly shown their commitment to change. The Nouakchott Declaration, issued by the heads of state in May 2003, calls for closer cooperation between Guinea and the OMVS countries. The Cross-Border Initiatives Program was signed by Guinea, Mali, and Senegal in 2001. National policies encourage private sector involvement through deregulation, and privatization is under way in the basin's energy sector. Regional integration is being tackled step by step. (For example, goods landing at the Dakar port en route to Mali can now land tax free.)

- *Institutional innovation.* The OMVS countries created institutions under which member countries give up some sovereignty for the basin's greater good. The countries jointly own the infrastructure. In raising funds the OMVS can commit member countries to terms it negotiates with the international financial community. The decisionmaking process is based on equality, but the benefits and burdens of development are shared equitably based on solidarity.

- *Learning and experimentation.* Since 1962 there have been three different basin organizations, their mandates evolving with experience. The CIE focused on the technical aspects of river basin development. The OERS promoted total integration based on the countries' political aspirations. Recognizing the limitations of both, the countries established the OMVS, politically less ambitious than the OERS but with a broader mandate than the CIE. The OMVS countries understood that to optimize their shared development in the basin, an inclusive decisionmaking framework would have to include Guinea—and all stakeholders. Recognizing that public participation in decisionmaking is essential, the OMVS included representatives from civil society organizations. Realizing the need for closer environmental monitoring of the basin, it has created an environmental observatory.

■ *External catalysts.* The countries took advantage of the political opportunities in the postindependence drive for pan-African unity by creating basinwide institutions to jointly develop the Senegal Basin. The severe droughts of the 1970s also served as a catalyst, spurring the OMVS countries to jointly build infrastructure to safeguard their economies. The 2003 floods prompted the OMVS system to coordinate its activities with local communities along the river. Conflict in neighboring countries encouraged the basin countries to establish greater cooperation with each other.

What about Guinea?

Guinea has not benefited from the improved water and electricity supply or the institutional changes within the OMVS space (see box 4.2). Shortages of electricity and water are common, seriously handicapping economic activity and making life hard for households. As a result, the Guinean government is seeking to establish stronger links with its neighbors in the Senegal Basin.

The weak investment climate in Guinea has hampered growth. With more than 30 percent of the world's known bauxite reserves, Guinea has been the second largest producer after Australia since 1971. But foreign investment is low due to uncertainties about the fiscal and policy regime for major investments. In the 1990s the water and electricity sectors were opened to private investment, but the Guinean government nationalized them in 2001. According to Mohamed Said Fofana, director of the National Directorate of Trade and Competition, "Guinea had broken up the state monopolies in all sectors and liberalized the energy sector. However, it was necessary to rescind this decision for the energy sector because it is very strategic and the government was not satisfied with the sector's liberalization." Guinea Electric (EDG) was created after the dissolution of the private companies. Although EDG follows commercial rules, it is a public sector entity. The government intends to involve the private sector once again, using the build-operate-transfer approach.

Guinea, despite its location in an area where average rainfall is 4 meters a year and 14 international rivers originate, is again experiencing water and electricity shortages. According to Sidy Diallo, a spokesman for EDG, the shortages are due to weak rainfall in 2002. Before 1997 Guinea had outages that paralyzed economic activity. Production capacity increased following construction of the Garafiri generating station (which cost more than $200 million, or nearly a third of the country's annual budget) and the Tombo III thermal stations, which add 44 MW of power.

Neither station is functioning at full capacity, however, and they are unable to meet Guinea's demand of 138 MW a day. In January 2004, after several months of electricity shortages, with EDG struggling to supply 26 MW, the government had to spend 5 million Guinean francs ($2,494) a day on fuel to ensure the regular supply of electricity in the country's large urban centers. The expenditures had repercussions for the balance of payments and government budget. The government has called on the private sector to assist in dealing with the shortage. The Guinean company Futurelec will invest $8.9 million in the energy sector to buy a new thermal generating station and to repair the Tombo station.

Guinea is looking to strengthen its ties within the Senegal Basin and beyond. Its participation in basinwide decisionmaking will create more cost-effective opportunities to augment existing energy supplies, which could boost the basin's development. Participation would complement the forthcoming West African Power Pool, which is to work on priority issues such as connecting the Mali and Côte d'Ivoire grids. Because Manantali's production will be saturated by 2005–06, studies are exploring other ways to tap the Senegal River's hydropower potential. Creating dams at Félou and Gouina could potentially add 100 MW of power at each site.

Against the broader background of the New Partnership for Africa's Development (NEPAD), the four Senegal Basin countries are looking to strengthen their integration through partnerships with each other, with the international community, and with the private sector. Recognizing that a basinwide institution is needed to tap the basin's full development potential, they are already moving toward an inclusive framework for decisionmaking on water management.

The four basin countries have already collaborated in preparing the GEF project on the Senegal River Basin. Significantly, the OMVS was designated as the recipient and executor of the GEF grant, on behalf of the member countries and Guinea. As an indication of its political commitment to cooperate, Guinea was invited to attend the OMVS Heads of State meeting in Nouakchott in May 2003, which Guinean Prime Minister Lamine Sidime attended on behalf of President Lansana Conté. A joint declaration was issued articulating the desire to establish an inclusive framework for managing the Senegal River Basin. Outside OMVS, Guinea, Mali, and Senegal drew up the Cross-Border Initiatives Program in November 2001 to improve trade among the countries by harmonizing customs, facilitating the flow of traffic and people, and joining forces in the fight against HIV/AIDS.

Lessons from the Senegal Basin Initiatives

Cooperative development of the Senegal River has benefited the economies of Mali, Mauritania, and Senegal by increasing the reliability of electricity and water. Widespread perceptions of improved services are driving further cooperation within OMVS—and beyond, to Guinea. Although the process is far from over, lessons can be drawn from the Senegal Basin's experience in collectively addressing poverty:

- *Grasp opportunities through cooperation.* The success of Mali, Mauritania, and Senegal in collectively raising external investment for their joint infrastructure shows that more can be done with less if parties cooperate rather than act unilaterally. Even natural disasters such as the severe droughts of the 1970s can bring opportunities for change by focusing attention on key issues. Mali, Mauritania, and Senegal combined national efforts to address the crises with regional ones, facilitating joint operations. Together with the oil crisis of the early 1970s, the droughts made the countries recognize that they had to jointly develop their shared water resources to mitigate the effects of external shocks on their economies.
- *Engage top political leaders.* From the outset, the basin countries' political leaders committed to jointly developing their shared water resources. The political commitment manifested itself in meetings of heads of state, innovative legal conventions, and joint development and ownership of infrastructure. Political will is fundamental to engendering trust between basin countries and with key partners in the international community.
- *Develop a shared vision for development.* Regional approaches can optimize development of a basin's resources by providing the basin countries with new opportunities and by addressing national limitations and priorities. From the outset, development of the Senegal Basin was based on a plan that reflected country priorities that could be met only through a regional approach.

- *Engage all stakeholders.* To tap regional opportunities, stakeholders at all levels—from governments to communities—need to participate in identifying and developing opportunities and sharing benefits. All four basin countries have maintained a dialogue since OMVS's creation, leading to the current discussions on establishing an inclusive framework for managing the basin's resources. Stakeholder participation in the basin's water resource management has been encouraged by the establishment and expansion of OMVS's Permanent Water Commission.
- *Examine the impacts of infrastructure at the local, national, and regional levels.* As the Senegal Basin countries are discovering in Djoudj and Diawling National Parks, income-generation activities and other outcomes can come from sectors not usually included in impact assessments, such as the environment, fisheries, and recessional agriculture.
- *Bind cooperation with legal instruments.* Successful cooperative processes are underpinned by mutual trust and political commitment, but legal instruments capture the agreements and bind future cooperation. Building on the region's tradition of cooperation, the basin countries signed conventions that were remarkable expressions of international cooperation based on equity, solidarity, and equality. The legal instruments remain open to Guinea's joining.
- *Promote private sector involvement.* Private sector involvement can boost the flow of funds needed to access opportunities and help transfer knowledge to the public sector. Providing an enabling environment for the private sector requires options that target the full range of private sector actors, from market women to large companies. The Senegal River Basin countries understood that having more reliable supplies of water and electricity reduces the risk on investments by small entrepreneurs in the basin. They also understood that national and regional policies are necessary to get private companies involved in key sectors. It is critical to maintain a consistent policy for private sector involvement.

5

Exporting Out of Africa
The Kenya Horticulture Success Story

PHIL ENGLISH, STEVE JAFFEE,
AND JULIUS OKELLO

With more than 70 percent of the poor in developing countries living in rural areas, agricultural growth must play a significant role in poverty reduction. Local markets can provide some opportunities, but in many cases urban markets are too small or too poor to generate significant new demand, or their principal demands cannot be efficiently met by local producers. Especially in small, low-income countries, export growth will be essential to take advantage of external markets in industrialized countries and in fast-growing middle-income countries. But traditional commodities offer few prospects for significant growth in volume, and prices are expected to continue to decline.

Prospects are much more positive for horticultural products (vegetables, fruits, and cut flowers), for which demand has grown rapidly since the mid-1990s. Exports of these products now represent the single largest category in agricultural trade, accounting for more than 20 percent of

Phil English can be contacted at penglish@worldbank.org, Steve Jaffee at sjaffee@worldbank.org, and Julius Okello at okellojj@hotmail.com. The authors wish to give special thanks to Hasit (Tiku) Shah, Director of Sunripe, for providing regular advice along the way, as well as for presenting this case study at the Shanghai Conference on Scaling Up for Poverty Reduction.

117

world agricultural exports—a larger share than that of all traditional tropical commodity exports combined.

Developing countries have been expanding their share of this growing market. Sub-Saharan Africa's horticulture exports now exceed $2 billion (4 percent of world exports), and there is plenty of room for more expansion. Not surprisingly, the horticultural sector has attracted the attention of policymakers, the donor community, and the private sector in low-income countries that remain heavily dependent on traditional exports.

The business of horticultural exports can be complex, with the sophistication required to compete at the high-value end of the market rivaling that of many manufactured products. Changing consumer demands, rising standards, and just-in-time delivery necessitate careful supply chain management and close cooperation with the overseas client.

Because foreign individuals and companies have often played a large role in the sector, some observers question the impact that the industry is having on poverty reduction. But the experience in Kenya shows what can be achieved. Horticultural products account for two-thirds of all growth in agricultural exports and have surpassed coffee to become the second-largest merchandise export (after tea). Kenya is the second-largest horticultural exporter in Sub-Saharan Africa (after South Africa), the second-largest developing-country exporter of flowers in the world (after Colombia), and the second-largest developing country supplier of vegetables to the European Union (after Morocco). About 135,000 people are now employed in the sector, in farming, processing, and packaging. Most of them are poor Kenyans whose lives have been changed by the industry.

What were the key factors behind this success? What has been the impact on ordinary Kenyans?

The horticulture industry can be defined in several different ways. The broadest definition, used here, includes three segments: processed fruits and vegetables, fresh fruits and vegetables, and cut flowers. Some farmers may grow vegetables for immediate export as fresh produce, while others sell them to local processors, who then export the processed product. The same entrepreneur may sell both fresh and processed fruit. The same exporter may deal in both fresh vegetables and cut flowers, and vary the mix over time as market conditions evolve. Processed fruit and vegetables are usually treated as manufactured products, but their complexity and value added can actually be lower than for some flowers and prepackaged fresh produce.

A Long and Winding Road

The Kenyan horticulture story began more than 60 years ago.[1] During World War II the colonial administration launched an experiment with irrigated smallholder vegetable production to provide dehydrated vegetables for the Kenyan army and Allied troops. Shortly thereafter a canned pineapple export project was begun, first relying on European settler farmers, but eventually including many African smallholders. Some fresh vegetables were also exported to Djibouti, Somalia, Yemen, and the United Kingdom. A few carnations and orchids were exported before independence in 1963.

The 10-year period following independence witnessed a gradual expansion in all three segments of the industry. A British company initiated a new vegetable dehydration project for export, modeled largely on its wartime precursor. The pineapple cannery brought in Del Monte to manage the operation in order to exploit its international marketing expertise. A Swiss company developed a passion fruit juice export business, and a Danish firm (Dansk Chrysanthemum and Kultur) made a multimillion-dollar investment in chrysanthemums. By 1973 there were 36 registered exporters of fresh fruits and vegetables, drawn from domestic wholesalers and retailers and medium-size farmers. An important component was the sale of "Asian vegetables" (okra, capsicums, dudhi, zucchini, brinjals, and karella) to the rapidly growing South Asian immigrant community of London, where Kenyan Asians put family connections to good use.

Growth over the next 30 years can be roughly divided into three periods. The export horticulture sector took off between 1974 and 1980, beginning with the expansion of canned pineapple (box 5.1), which accounted for roughly half of all horticulture exports by 1977. This was accompanied by a steady but less dramatic increase in fresh fruits and vegetables, notably French beans, which became the industry leader in this sector. In contrast, cut flowers stagnated.

The 1980s saw a slowdown in growth (figure 5.1). New sources of supply were entering the market, and competition was driving down prices for some products. Rising transport costs in 1979 after the second oil price shock placed Kenya at a major cost disadvantage with

BOX 5.1	**Multinational Company Shows the Way: Del Monte and Canned Pineapples**

In 1948 a British company established Kenya Canners to process and can pineapples for export. Initially based on supplies from European settler farms, it expanded to include African smallholders, who helped keep the project alive after the exodus of Europeans following independence. In 1965 the company decided to expand and to bring in California Packing Corporation (Del Monte) in order to benefit from its management and marketing expertise. Three years later Del Monte acquired a majority interest in the company. The agreement between Del Monte and the Kenyan government included both an expansion of the smallholder program and the lease of 5,000 acres for a nucleus estate. At the time, farmers were finding coffee and tea more attractive, and Kenya Canners faced major supply problems. They thus proposed expanding their estate by 18,000 acres and phasing out their purchases from smallholders. The government agreed, over the objections of some small farmers and their parliamentarians. It also gave the company a 10-year monopoly on local pineapple processing, along with reductions in rail, wharfage, and handling charges.

The deal looked too good to some critics, but the company continued to lose money, with annual sales remaining in the range of 10,000 metric tons. Finally, in 1975, business took off. By 1977 Del Monte was exporting 45,000 metric tons a year, at a value of $25 million. Further expansion raised sales to 61,000 metric tons in 1989 ($36 million.) and 91,000 metric tons in 1996 ($69 million), supplemented by sales of pineapple juice of about $10 million.

Although new problems emerged in the late 1990s, the success of this one company has made canned pineapple the largest single manufactured export from Kenya and placed the country among the top five exporters of pineapple in the world. Kenya Canners employs 6,000 workers, two-thirds of them on the plantation, the remainder in the factory. While the failure of the original smallholder scheme may have been unfortunate, adherence to this approach might well have jeopardized the entire project.

Del Monte has continued to maintain a prominent presence in Kenya's horticulture as an exporter of canned pineapples. The company is currently working to correct its poor public image, an image that is tied to allegedly poor working conditions and the company's withdrawal from spot market purchases and the outgrower scheme, both of which benefited small farmers. At the same time Del Monte is redefining its trade policy following its recent merger with Cirio to form Cirio-Del Monte. Cirio-Del Monte has increased sales of its products in the domestic markets, a market dominated until recently by South Africa's Ceres juices. All the major local supermarkets are now packed with many varieties of Del Monte fresh, natural juices.

Source: Jaffee 1994, 1995.

FIGURE 5.1	Exports of Major Horticultural Products Rise Rapidly in the 1990s (US$ millions)

Source: Jaffee 2003 and authors' estimates.

respect to North Africa, which effectively replaced Kenya as a supplier of sweet peppers and zucchini. Fresh vegetables continued to expand in volume, but growth was lower in value terms. In processed horticulture there was some growth in the pineapple business, and a significant canned bean project was started by Njoro Canners. Cut flowers, notably roses, provided more dynamism, with sales rising from $8 million in 1980 to $38 million by the end of the decade.

In the past 10 years, fresh fruits and vegetables and cut flowers have enjoyed impressive growth, which appears to have accelerated since 1995 (figure 5.1). The value of fresh fruits and vegetables rose from $29 million in 1991 to an estimated $164 million in 2002, while cut flowers expanded from $39 million to $175 million. Total horticulture exports were estimated to exceed $350 million in 2003, representing 35 percent of all Kenyan agricultural exports.[2] This exceeds the value of coffee exports and is approaching the value of tea exports ($450 million in 2001).[3] Horticulture export prices are also more stable than those for coffee or tea.

The growth of horticulture exports needs to be placed in the broader context of Kenyan economic policy and performance. In the first 10 years after independence sound economic management and political stability made Kenya a relatively attractive place for investors. While officially adopting the path of "African socialism," Kenya in fact pursued a mixed economy approach and adopted an openness to foreign investment that was more liberal than many other African countries. It also paid considerable attention to the agricultural sector, giving priority to smallholders.[4] Many large European farms were broken up and redistributed when their owners departed, but others remained intact and were taken over by Kenyans. In general, agricultural policy was fairly pragmatic in this respect. Macroeconomic policy was characterized by fiscal responsibility and prudent monetary policy. For these and other reasons, Kenya enjoyed strong economic growth, averaging 5.5 percent a year, between 1963 and 1978 (O'Brien and Ryan 2001). These conditions helped the horticulture business establish a foothold.

Economic and political circumstances deteriorated by the late 1970s. Two oil price shocks created balance of payments problems while raising the cost of international trade. Coffee and tea booms ended abruptly, and the East African Community was terminated in 1977. The political leadership of the aging Kenyatta led to policy drift. The expulsion of Asians from Uganda increased hostility toward Asians in Kenya, tensions that were exacerbated in 1982 after a failed coup attempt. The country was sending a different signal to investors at home and abroad.

In 1980 an extended period of structural adjustment began that ebbed and flowed over the next 20 years. The economy slowed under the initial belt-tightening measures, recovered somewhat, and then sank into recession in 1992–93. Inflation hit 55 percent. Donor balance of payments support was suspended from 1991 to 1993 because of the slow pace of reform, new political problems, and concerns over corruption. A fresh round of reforms was introduced, but by 1997 the situation was again deteriorating. The International Monetary Fund suspended its support, and the World Bank stopped lending. Civil unrest grew, putting Kenya's long record of political stability in serious jeopardy.

Against this backdrop, the surge in horticultural exports is particularly impressive. Despite the overall decline in the export/GDP ratio since independence, performance of the horticulture sector has been strong.[5]

The Many Paths to Poverty Reduction

Export horticulture represents an opportunity for reducing poverty by generating income by smallholders, rural laborers on larger farms, and unskilled or semiskilled workers in processing factories. Reliable employment figures are not available, partly because it is difficult to separate the export segment from the much larger, domestically oriented business, but the rough orders of magnitude for total horticulture employment can be estimated (table 5.1). Each smallholder farm employs more than one person from the household on a part-time basis, as well as some laborers. Assuming that the average Kenyan farmer or laborer supports at least three other people, the industry affects roughly half a million Kenyans.[6]

Horticultural production is significantly more profitable for a smallholder than the traditional maize-bean intercropping system that is most common among subsistence farmers. The gross margin (value of output minus all input costs) per hectare per season of maize and beans is about Ksh 13,000. As a typical farmer would produce two such crops a year, with somewhat lower yields during the second short rainy season, total earnings would be on the order of Ksh 20,000–25,000. In contrast, the gross margin for French beans is about Ksh 50,000–75,000 per harvest per hectare.[7] Given the labor-intensive nature of French beans, small farmers normally dedicate no more than 0.5 hectares to them, but it is possible to produce three crops a year under rain-fed conditions (and more with irrigation). Thus small farmers likely earn Ksh 75,000–120,000 a year on a half-hectare plot, roughly four times the return from the maize-bean combination.[8] A farmer would normally engage in both cropping systems, with horticulture providing an important source of cash

TABLE 5.1	Employment in the Horticulture Export Industry, 2003
Category	People employed
Smallholders (fruits and vegetables)	35,000–40,000
Processing industry workers (fruits and vegetables)	5,000–10,000
Packhouse and farm laborers (fruits and vegetables)	40,000–50,000
Cut flower industry	40,000–50,000
Total	120,000–150,000

Source: Authors' estimates based on company interviews.

income and maize and beans satisfying much of the household's food needs.

More commercial horticulture cultivation is very labor intensive and hence provides employment for many farm workers. A medium-scale farm of about 10 hectares can employ 38 to 50 women a day to weed, pick, and grade and about 17 men to spray and irrigate the fields, transport produce from the farm to the grading shed or cooler, and load it into vehicles for delivery to exporters' factories or collection centers. Most of these workers are paid a wage that is greater than the government-mandated minimum agricultural wage. Because competing employment opportunities often do not exist in rural areas, such wages may be well above the level of earnings in the alternative income sources. Indeed, because farm laborers typically own little or no land of their own, they tend to be poorer than smallholders, especially those engaged in fruit and vegetable production. Consequently, their employment in the horticulture industry has a more direct impact on poverty reduction.[9]

A recent carefully conducted survey provides detailed information on the incomes of a sample of workers in the horticultural sector and comparative data for a control group of people not involved (McCulloch and Ota 2002). Information was collected from packhouse workers and nonpackhouse workers living in the same residential areas of Nairobi, workers on farms owned by exporters, workers on large commercial farms, smallholders engaged in horticulture, and nonhorticulture smallholders farming in the same region (table 5.2).

These figures indicate that horticulture smallholders are much better off than nonhorticulture smallholders, with a mean income that is four times as large. Even workers on exporter-owned farms and independent commercial farms do significantly better than nonhorticulture smallholders. Poverty rates are much lower among workers employed in the horticulture sector, with almost three-quarters of horticulture-growing smallholders above the poverty line.

The situation in urban areas is a little more complicated. Average income for the control group is somewhat higher than for the packhouse workers, but the figure reflects the relatively high incomes of a small minority. The median packhouse employee fares significantly better than the median control group worker, and levels of poverty are much higher among nonpackhouse workers.[10] At the same time, packhouse workers worked longer hours, at least during the peak season, and they enjoyed fewer fringe benefits than nonpackhouse workers.

| TABLE 5.2 | Income and Poverty Levels for Horticulture and Nonhorticulture Households, 2001 | | | | | |

| | Packhouse worker | Nonpack-house worker | Exporter-owned farm worker | Large farm worker | Smallholders | |
					Horti-culture	Nonhorti-culture
Household income						
Mean (Ksh)	55,490	59,294	29,886	18,767	55,528	12,902
Median (Ksh)	46,853	28,747	21,330	17,144	32,431	5,658
Share below poverty line						
Food poverty (%)	15.0	31.7	30.8	40.0	25.0	73.2
Total poverty (%)	42.5	63.4	41.0	55.0	27.8	80.3

Source: McCulloch and Ota 2002.

Several major exporters have initiated changes that allow women to return to work after maternity leave, limit the number of hours worked per day to 10, and offer overtime pay (box 5.2).[11] Through the Fresh Produce Exporters Association of Kenya, the industry has adopted a voluntary labor code that exceeds Kenyan government norms and may well establish a new standard in the developing world. Observance of the code will be monitored by independent auditors.

To be confident that it is really the horticulture industry that is making a difference, the analysis needs to take other factors into account that may result in higher incomes. These may include the education level and gender of the household head, the size of the household, and the ownership of land and livestock. Taking these factors into account, horticulture employment does indeed make a significant difference to household well-being. The incomes of households of nonpackhouse workers were slightly more than half those of otherwise identical households of packhouse workers. Rural horticulture smallholders were somewhat worse off than urban packhouse workers but not significantly so.

The relative standing of other rural households was consistent with that shown in table 5.2: workers on exporter-owned farms were the next best off, followed by workers on large farms, with nonhorticulture smallholders at the bottom. While these workers did own some land, they had less than the nonhorticulture smallholders (much less in the case of workers on large farms). Across urban and rural sectors,

BOX 5.2	Agnes Aronya, Packhouse Employee

Agnes Aronya, a married woman with three children, completed form four in 1994. For two years she was a casual employee at the village market, working as a cleaner with a daily wage of Ksh 130. In 1996 she left this job because of low pay, joining Company A, where she worked in the prepared/prepack packhouse section as a casual worker with a daily wage of Ksh 220. Her capacity to learn and willingness to work long and flexible hours resulted in a change in her status to three-month renewable contracts with a monthly salary of Ksh 6,000. However, a downturn in the export market forced the company to return her to daily employment status and eventually lay her off. She was unemployed for two weeks before being hired by Company B in 2001 as a casual worker with a daily wage of Ksh 180.

"I was desperate for a job," she recalls. "I had children who needed to be fed. I kept turning up at the gates of exporters for two weeks without being taken. Then one day I tried Company B. They wanted people with some experience. When I mentioned working at Company A, they took me. The salary was lower, but I wanted a job." It took her six months to match her last wage at Company A. She now earns Ksh 240 a day and with overtime pay she can earn Ksh 120 in just two hours.

Agnes appreciates Company B, even though she does not have a monthly contract. "I feel that this company cares about my family. When I get a call that my child is sick, they let me go and attend to him, and they pay me that day's wages no matter what time I leave. Elsewhere, I would either be denied permission to leave or lose the hours I am out. In addition, when I took [unpaid] maternity leave, they kept my job and took me back when I was ready. Besides, there is free transport to and from work and free lunch. And when I am sick, I get treated at the dispensary for free. These benefits mean more than higher pay to me."

Agnes manages to balance her long hours and her family responsibilities with the help of her husband, who helps with the children. "I am the one who seeks overtime. Company B has a good overtime package and so I go for it whenever I can." She has been able to save some money, which she and her husband combined with his savings and used to buy a plot in her husband's home town. Now she is saving some money to use in developing the plot.

smallholders not involved in horticulture had incomes that were just one-fifth those of urban packhouse workers.[12]

This analysis provides strong support for the conclusion that urban employees draw substantial benefits from involvement in the horticulture sector (see box 5.3) and that rural laborers are also better off

BOX 5.3	David Tinega, Packhouse Manager

David Tinega (not his real name) graduated in 1992 with a B.Sc. in horticulture from the Jomo Kenyatta University of Agriculture and Technology. For lack of alternatives, he started his career as an untrained teacher, but the low pay left him unsatisfied with his job. He got his first job in the horticultural industry with Company D, working in the quality control department, at a monthly salary of Ksh 2,500. At the end of the probation period, his salary rose to Ksh 5,000.

After the company collapsed at the end of 1995, David took a job with Company C, as an acting quality control manager, at a monthly salary of Ksh 8,500. He was later redeployed to raw material procurement, where he earned Ksh 22,000 a month. During this period he received regular training and acquired significant skills in the physical assessment of product quality. However, his work required him to put in long hours of work, which his parents and fiancée disliked.

David recalls, "During the 1995–98 period, there was an acute shortage of technical people in the horticultural industry. At the same time, most exporters were seeking local skills to replace expatriates. The exporters were therefore luring skilled technical people from each other by offering attractive packages."

With the benefits of his training at Company C, David was approached by Company B in 1997. The company offered him a job as raw material manager, with a monthly salary of Ksh 35,000, in addition to direct contact with clients, shorter working hours, and paid vacations. At the end of 2000 he was promoted to packhouse manager, with a monthly salary of Ksh 70,000.

David attributes his rapid rise in the industry to the years he worked as quality control manager, which, he says, "were very instrumental in developing my career because I got to understand the product. I am able to determine what products should be taken in and what the packers can get out of it, in addition to how long I can hold the product [shelf life]. I have been lucky to work under people who would go out of their way to train you for the next stage of your career and then inform you when you are ready for it."

Asked how working in the industry has affected his life, he replied, "I would not have achieved what I have now, much less have the aspirations I have now, had I not changed fields. Working in the industry has enabled me to save and to set up a stationery supply business for my wife, who was unable to get a job after graduating. I have also been able to buy a car, educate my brother up to college level, and support my parents. There is no way I would have been able to achieve all this if I worked for the government, where the pay is Ksh 16,000 a month. I am now hoping to build a house in Nairobi."

as a result. Because the comparison between smallholders inside and outside the sector is not complete, however, the difference in household incomes between these two groups is probably exaggerated. The analysis does not account for the fact that horticulture smallholders are much more likely to have irrigated land and that their land holdings are significantly larger. These farmers would probably have been better off even if they had not been involved in horticulture, although horticulture provided them with an opportunity to exploit their assets that they might not otherwise have had. Some of these farmers remain below the poverty line, but they are not the poorest farmers. The laborers hired to work on horticulture farms are undoubtedly drawn from the poorest farmers (the average landholding of workers on large commercial farms is less than 0.5 hectares).

Women are actively involved in two segments of the horticultural industry. An estimated 70 to 80 percent of packhouse workers, or "table operatives," are women, who wash, chop, and pack produce. Many of these women are the heads of their households. The survey of Kenyan workers found that 62 percent of all packhouse workers came from households headed by women, while all nonpackhouse urban households were headed by men. This makes the relatively good income performance of the packhouse households all the more impressive.

Women also tend to play a leading role in vegetable production on smallholder farms, by one estimate accounting for two-thirds of the hours worked over the course of a season (box 5.4) (Dolan 2001). Vegetables have traditionally been considered a woman's crop, since they were grown for home consumption and sale on the local market, while men focused on cash crops. In some cases of contract farming, exporters have signed contracts with—and therefore paid—the male head of the household, because he is the owner of the land. Women have often had trouble getting what they consider to be their fair share of the revenues generated.

The attractiveness of export horticulture has also led some husbands to put pressure on their wives to allocate more of their labor and land to this end. Women typically have customary rights over a small garden area used for food production; the arrival of export horticulture has sometimes encouraged men to retract the traditional right of women to decide how to use this land. Export horticulture has thus created pressures within the household and may have reduced the independence of many women, at least in the short run. But it also appears to be spurring women to find ways to resist the inequity of

BOX 5.4	**Jane Mutuli Munyoki, Smallholder Farmer**

Jane Mutuli Munyoki is a 34-year-old single mother of two who started growing French beans in 1992. She recalls that it was an "amazing business" then. Unlike coffee, which was the major crop in her area and which she grew up weeding and picking every year, French beans had very quick and handsome returns. Jane was among the first farmers to start growing beans in a wave that saw hundreds of small farmers in her village join the fresh vegetable export industry. At the time she had no children, so her income was mainly for personal needs.

In 1995 Jane married and stopped growing French beans. The marriage did not work out, and she returned to her parents' home in 2000 with two young children. She recalls how difficult it was providing for her children and herself. Her parents, who had been coffee farmers for many years, were having difficulty feeding their now larger family because coffee prices had plummeted. Worse still, the French bean exporter that used to buy beans in the area had pulled out after farmers demanded compensation for the requirement that they comply with good agricultural practice standards. "I was desperate. I did not know what to do. I considered taking up a job as a house helper, but the pay was so low," Jane recalls.

Then in 2002 a broker came to the area and asked farmers to start producing beans and snow peas for him. The response was poor. Farmers did not take him seriously and were afraid that the exporter would pull out. "In despair, I decided to take the plunge," says Jane. That year she planted three-tenths of an acre of French beans, selling about 150 kilos. "The pay was low—sometimes as low as Ksh 25 per kilo—but I was able to get enough money from it to meet my basic financial needs," recalls Jane. After deducting purchased input costs, she retained some Ksh 2,500. "Though little, the money made a whole lot of difference. I was able to buy my son new clothes for the first time after separating from my husband."

Jane intends to continue growing fresh export vegetables. She has diversified into growing snow peas as well but laments that she has to work long hours, doing most of the farm operations herself, especially bucket-irrigating the crops, because she cannot afford to hire labor. She does hire two women, at Ksh 100 a day each, to help pick and grade the beans, creating employment in a small way.

gender relations. How this plays out is not clear. These problems are less likely to emerge when women are paid directly by exporters, a practice that should perhaps be encouraged. They may disappear completely in the many households headed by women that result from male migration to the cities.

The impact of horticulture is also beginning to affect consumers' diet and health. There has been a slow but gradual increase in the sale of fruits and vegetables through local supermarkets. Some export companies have embarked on a strategy to develop domestic outlets for their surplus produce by educating domestic consumers on how to use vegetables, such as French beans, that were traditionally grown only for export. As these export vegetables are now subject to strict pesticide application regimes, they may well be safer and healthier than the traditional vegetables consumed domestically. The consumption of fruit salads has increased tremendously in recent years, sold mainly at lunch time in small roadside shops in urban centers.

Sunripe: From Family Farm to Global Player

The Shah family entered horticultural farming in 1962–03, growing Asian vegetables (cucumbers and capsicums) and green beans, which were shipped to France and the United Kingdom. In 1969 the Shah family and some partners founded Sunripe Ltd. to market the family's vegetables. The move to integrate forward into marketing was motivated partially by the good prices being obtained in Europe. While Sunripe has also exported fruit (pineapples and avocados), the mainstay of its business has been vegetables.

For Sunripe the 1970s was a period for defining its export business. The company tried many new ideas, including shipping fruit to Europe and strengthening its European trade in general. During this period it resolved to move out of other export crops, such as cotton and sisal, in order to concentrate on high-value horticultural crops. In the early 1980s the company introduced cherry tomatoes; in 1988 it was among the first to add value by producing prepacked produce (washed, chopped, packed, and bar-coded) for the European retail market. This move to higher-value products was a response to stiff competition from West African and North African countries, which have lower freight charges because they can ship their fresh vegetables to Europe by sea.

In the 1990s Sunripe made bold moves, building three packhouses and diversifying production into Arusha, Tanzania (box 5.5). The company is now planning to start an outgrower scheme in Uganda as well. One of the Shah brothers, the head of marketing, spends every other month in Europe collecting market information and intelligence, which the company uses to develop new strategies and product lines.

BOX 5.5	Tiku Shah, Sunripe Director

Tiku Shah is a Kenyan of Asian origin. Born and raised in Kenya, he went to the United States to get an engineering degree and a master's degree in applied mathematics and finance, returning to Kenya in 1987.

Unable to find a job for four months, Tiku decided to join Sunripe, a family business, as an information technology specialist. He started by setting up a telex machine and computerizing the business, quickly moving up the ladder to his current position as director. Today he manages the company, along with his two brothers, and has just been named chairman of the Fresh Produce Exporters Association of Kenya (FPEAK).

The path to leadership of Sunripe Ltd. has not been an easy one. "My parents used to warn me that doing business in such a dynamic industry as horticulture requires a lot of effort and selflessness. And they were right. I have to put in 16 to 18 hours a day of work. They, however, laid down the foundation we are building on. I don't mind it, you are young only once," he says.

Tiku is known in the industry for his aggressiveness, which serves him well in this fast-paced sector. When the industry altered its focus from supplying fresh bulk produce to prepackaged goods, his company did the same. Sunripe recently forged a partnership with a horticultural firm in Arusha, Tanzania, to take advantage of ecological and climatic differences. "The diversification of our production base helps us meet our orders throughout the year, because when it is dry in Kenya, it could be raining in Arusha. We can't afford to lose our share of the market by being unable to source enough produce to meet our orders." Because the future growth potential of vegetables now seems limited, Sunripe is planning to diversify further by expanding into cut flowers.

Tiku appreciates working in this dynamic industry. He particularly enjoys the exposure that working in Sunripe and FPEAK has accorded him. "I meet all sorts of people in my jobs, from the little farmer in Timau, to the high and mighty, such as European business executives and government officials. Frankly, I would not be what I am now if I were working for the government as an electrical engineer."

These strategies have enabled Sunripe to stay ahead of the competition and to supply more than 17 countries, from Singapore to Canada, with French beans, avocados, and a variety of other vegetables, including green peas, runner beans, baby corn, snow peas, broccoli, and several Asian vegetables. Growth in sales has averaged about 20 percent a year over the past 15 years, increasing from about $1 million in 1988 to $13 million in 2003. The company now employs 1,200 full-time and 1,000 part-time workers. In addition to its large farm suppliers, it buys from 1,000 smallholders, predominantly through contract farming arrangements. Many contracts are with female farmers.

The past emphasis, by Sunripe and other export companies, on French beans and Asian vegetables reflected the lack of government involvement. The absence of public investments prevented Kenya from developing its own sea-freight capacity for pineapples and other less perishable fruits until the late 1980s, by which time other suppliers were well established. Belated investments in research and development, limited arrangements for the propagation of planting materials, and official barriers on the importation of varieties favored by foreign consumers greatly constrained the development of competitive exports for many commodities, including most fruits. These weaknesses in official services proved less important for French beans and Asian vegetables, since their cultivation was similar to more traditional crops and the older varieties grown in Kenya continued to be accepted by European customers.

A telling exception was avocados, where the initial stimulus for smallholder production came from a seedling propagation program at the National Horticultural Research Station in the late 1970s and early 1980s. Farmers in nearby areas received free seedlings and informal technical advice—despite the government's stated policy that support should go only to medium-size farmers planting at least five hectares. Once production began, however, the government's Horticultural Crops Development Authority collected and marketed the crop, since there was inadequate demand from private exporters. By 2002 avocados were the second-largest category of fruit and vegetable export (after French beans), accounting for 50 percent of all fresh fruit exports by value. An estimated 10,000 smallholders dominated production of this crop, as larger commercial farmers found it too hard to make a profit.

More recently, partnerships have developed between individual exporters and European trading partners for research and development (Dolan and Humphrey 2000). These partnerships have led to the introduction of some new types of vegetables, such as runner beans, baby corn, mangetout, broccoli, and green peas, which have accounted for most of the growth in terms of both volume and value. These new crops have tended to be grown under large-scale production, since most require a higher level of sophistication.

The sector generally benefited from the decision by the government to leave marketing in the hands of the private sector, in sharp contrast to most other cash crops in Kenya in the 1970s and 1980s. The number of licensed exporters increased from 36 in 1973 to more than 100 in the mid-1980s, generating intense competition for supply. Exporters sought out new regions to expand and diversify their sources, provided free technical advice, and sometimes competed directly for the output of established vegetable farmers by paying higher prices. While this occasionally undermined the contractual arrangements that farmers had agreed to, it stimulated entry by smallholders.

The government intervened indirectly in marketing in an effort to promote new Kenyan African exporters, in a reaction to the domination of the sector by Kenyan Asians and demands by the well-connected who saw the money that could be made.[13] Kenyan Africans were given preference at government-sponsored trade fairs and training programs, as well as periodic preferential access to air-freight facilities at Kenya Airways. Most of these exporters eventually failed, due to the lack of relevant experience and their efforts to conduct this business as a part-time, small-scale operation. Ironically, the government did not intervene in the same way in the cut flowers and processed fruit and vegetable sectors, where non-Kenyans dominated the export business.

Smallholder farmers have traditionally played a major role in the production of fresh fruits and vegetables (box 5.6). Some 14,500 smallholders are estimated to have been involved in the sector in the mid-1980s, accounting for roughly 50 percent of export production (Jaffee 1995). More recent official figures are not available, but with the growth of the industry this number has probably risen close to 20,000. Company interviews in late 2002 suggest that smallholders account for 27 percent of fresh vegetable exports and 85 percent of fresh fruit exports, for a combined average of 47 percent.[14] The number of smallholders in export-oriented vegetable production has probably fallen slightly over the past 10 years, but there has been a significant increase in the number involved in avocados.[15]

The landscape for smallholder participation is changing, however, and at least for export vegetables, the role of smallholders seems destined to decline. Some of the new crops, such as runner beans, which require artificial lighting, are unsuitable for small farmers. Several major supermarket chains in the United Kingdom have made large investments to carry a broad range of "exotic" fruits and vegetables

BOX 5.6	Ben Mwangi, Farm Owner, Contract Grower

Ben Mwangi is a 63-year-old retired shipping and freight worker. Upon retirement, he started growing cabbages for the domestic market. He quickly realized that growing cabbages did not pay, as he had to compete with farmers who illegally raised their crops in the government forest, where land was "free." He then started growing pyrethrum, which was profitable but which he abandoned because of late payments that made it difficult to pay his workers.

Ben approached Sunripe and offered to grow peas and broccoli for them. He feels very happy growing horticultural export crops. Comparing his current situation with his former one as a freight worker, Ben notes, "Unless you are super-skilled, company employment pays you just what is enough to live each day. My biggest joy is that I now work for myself and my kids. In addition I get enough return to employ people."

Ben currently employs 35 women and 12 men as daily workers on his two-acre horticultural plot, as well as 7 men and 1 woman who work for him on a permanent basis. During harvesting, he employs up to 50 women a day. Those who come from the neighborhood do not have alternative employment sources. Unlike Ben, who sunk a borehole, they cannot engage in horticultural production, since they have no source of water to irrigate their crops. "I feel good that I am able to help people get some income by employing them on my farm. The lives of the people who work here are totally different. They have invested their incomes in educating their kids and a number are building stone houses. A number of them send remittances back home, especially those from Western Kenya, who are far from home."

Being a new entrant in the industry, Ben has had to make many investments to meet European Union grades and standards and become EUREPGAP compliant, meeting the standards of Good Agricultural Practices set forth by the Euro-Retailer Produce Working Group, an international organization promoting safe and sustainable agricultural practices. But he does not mind. "Making these investments will always help me find a buyer, even if Sunripe were to leave," he says. "And compliance with EU requirements could pave the way to exporting directly in the future."

and prepared food products and to establish their brand name as a signal of high quality, thereby justifying a higher price. While this has created important new opportunities for Kenyan exporters, it has also placed a premium on a steady, reliable supply, since the chains typically have fixed weekly requirements. The contract farming arrangement has proven insufficiently reliable for many vegetable exporters, given the potential for farmers to break their contracts in order to obtain a higher price from competing buyers.

Also important is the growing consumer concern about food safety certification and compliance with environmental and ethical standards. Some export companies have organized their smallholder farmers into small groups, with an agronomist assigned to each group to oversee compliance with market requirements. But farmers who fail to meet certain criteria are being dropped, and some exporters have concluded that traceability can be ensured only by establishing their own farms. Meeting these requirements presents a real challenge to smallholders, and many observers worry that more and more small farmers will find themselves out of business.

At the same time, the rising standards in parts of the European market have provided the industry as a whole with an important opportunity to assert its superiority over new low-cost competitors. By investing in highly sophisticated, climate-controlled packhouses with specialized personnel and tight management of the entire supply chain, the top Kenyan companies have established a reputation for meeting some of the highest standards in the global export vegetable industry. This reputation has enabled them to charge higher prices and increase sales, leaving others to grapple with the falling profitability of traditional bulk produce, where price-based competition remains dominant. Thus while fresh vegetable exports have increased only 75 percent in volume terms over the past 10 years, they have grown 400 percent in value (figure 5.2).

FIGURE 5.2	**Fresh Vegetable Exports from Kenya, 1991–2002**

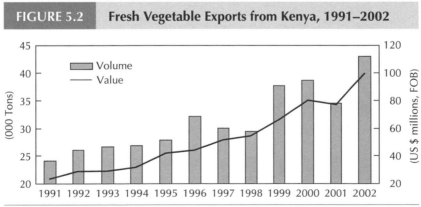

Source: Jaffee 2003.

Learning the Tricks of the Trade: Njoro Canners and Smallholders

Contract farming has been one of the principal mechanisms for involving small farmers in export crops in Africa.[16] The Kenya Tea Development Authority scheme is one of the most famous, but a similar approach has also been instrumental in the success of cotton production in francophone West Africa and in other agricultural sectors elsewhere in Africa. Contract farming has invariably been based in the public sector or heavily dependent on public resources, and contract buyers have usually enjoyed exclusive rights to purchase the crop in question.

Njoro Canners is the largest private sector contract farming operation in Kenya, producing a high-quality product for a competitive international market with no state support or monopsony powers. As developing country agricultural strategies move toward greater emphasis on the private sector, it is reassuring to know that at least some elements of contract farming are transferable to private operations. It is also important to understand its limitations.

Kenya's reputation as a source of high-quality fresh green beans prompted the largest French vegetable processing firm, Saupiquet, to try importing canned beans from the country, specializing in the demanding "extra-fine" category. For four years, from 1977 to 1981, it collaborated with a leading Kenyan fresh vegetable exporter, Corner Shop, to no avail. Corner Shop established a large estate, but found it too difficult to manage the large number of workers required for this labor-intensive product. Next Saupiquet tried working with large-scale farmers, but its staff had trouble covering the large geographic area involved and farmers found the financial returns too low. The company then turned to smallholders, only to be confronted by a range of technical and organizational problems. By 1981 the project had ground to a halt.

Unwilling to give up, Saupiquet sent to Kenya the manager of a Moroccan project in which the company played a more direct role, to explore the possibility of establishing a similar venture. The only interested party was Njoro Canners, a small, unused cannery owned by a Kenyan Asian businessman. Saupiquet offered to manage the project and guarantee the sale of all its output for five years if the local partner would finance expansion of the factory as well as a scheme to procure the raw material.

Drawing on its experience in Morocco as well as the lessons learned from Corner Shop, Saupiquet put in place a smallholder contract farming arrangement. Inputs were supplied on credit, with the cost to be deducted at the time of delivery of the harvest. The initial focus was on the Vihiga area in Western Kenya, which had also been involved in the Corner Shop experiments. The area was deemed suitable because of its large population (and hence readily available labor), suitable agro-climatic conditions, and remoteness from major towns (which would lower the risks of crop leakage into alternative markets).

The first year was full of problems. The crop was hit by disease and pests for which the extension staff was not prepared, farmers took on more seed than they could handle, inputs were sold on the local market rather than used for production, farmers misunderstood their contracts, yields were low, and everyone lost money. Nonetheless, during the second year, 1983, the number of farmers doubled, from 1,500 to 3,000. Many changes were introduced, including a limit on the amount of seed provided to any one farmer, an amount that corresponded to a plot of a mere 170 square meters. Problems remained, but yields improved and the factory began to operate at close to capacity.

Encouraged by this outcome, the company expanded the factory and increased the number of participating farmers to 10,300. By 1988 some 21,000 farmers were involved in the project, receiving about $400,000 a year in cash payments (Njoro Canners' total revenues were about $3 million). Another 500 local people were employed in the field and collection system.

The success of the joint venture generated new problems, however. Local politicians and administrators became jealous of the apparent success and started demanding "donations" from the company. When they were unsuccessful in doing so, they stirred up discontent among participating farmers. Accusations of exploitation began to surface. To stifle these challenges (and reduce agro-climatic risk), Njoro Canners developed similar schemes in other regions and let it be known that it would pull out of areas where its efforts were not appreciated. True to its word, when political interference emerged in one of its schemes (in Kisii), the company shut down its operations.

Staff at all levels within the company also sought to increase their share of the profits. Some collection center clerks colluded with farmers, issuing receipts for beans not actually delivered and sharing the proceeds with farmers willing to play. Discrepancies of up to 10 percent were recorded in 1984.

These problems were brought under control by a strong performance-based incentive system for all staff. The system emphasized the interdependence of employees at different stages of the operation and promoted a significant degree of self-policing. However, in 1989 several senior staff members began demanding "commissions" from local transporters and suppliers of other goods and services in return for winning tenders. In addition, local (junior) staff complained that senior managers were appropriating their salaries while threatening to fire anyone who dared blow the whistle. In the political context of Kenya at the time, such behavior was perhaps not surprising. Fortunately, Njoro Canners was able and willing to fire the offenders.

The 1990s ushered in new challenges, as Saupiquet was acquired by its biggest competitor in France, Bonduelle. The acquisition forced the company to change its modus operandi, as Bonduelle was not interested in managing Njoro Canners. It proceeded to remove the French managers from Njoro Canners, replacing them with advisors and eventually volunteers. In addition, Bonduelle chose to buy only premium- quality product, due to the development of new hybrid cultivars that facilitated low-cost production of other varieties within Europe. Njoro Canners was forced to reduce its production and to more carefully screen out product that failed to meet the extra-fine quality demanded by Bonduelle, while seeking other buyers for lower-grade product.

Bonduelle also began encouraging other firms inside and outside Kenya to begin production of a similar product in order to reduce its dependence on Njoro Canners. From a peak of 24,000 in 1989, Njoro Canners cut back the number of farmers to 15,000–18,000 over the next five years. Production fell before recovering in 1995. Njoro Canners also diversified into the canning, freezing, and dehydration of vegetables and the production of tomato paste, building three additional factories, all focused on the export market and all relying on small farmers as the primary source of supply.

The increasingly competitive nature of the canned green bean market forced the company to cut the number of participating farmers and to lower the price paid for beans. Disputes arose between Njoro Canners and the farmers over prices. The company also encountered problems with bean rust disease toward the end of the 1990s, exacerbated by the cheating of staffers employed to spray the beans.[17] Meanwhile, farmers, who were struggling to meet the quality standards required by Njoro Canners, demanded an increase in pay. The company considered the behavior of the sprayers and the farmers improper and shut its operations in Western Kenya (Vihiga), relocating near Nakuru. Eventually, it lost its contract with Bonduelle and now markets its produce through another local processor and directly to the local market. Today only a few hundred farmers are engaged in green bean production for Njoro Canners.

The Njoro Canners green bean project in Western Kenya represented a major infusion of money into a hitherto isolated local economy with little access to cash income. It enabled women, who formed the majority of the farmers, to earn supplemental income, which went toward paying school fees, purchasing basic household items, and making home improvements. The company had significant backward linkage effects. It stimulated the development of local goods and services that the company needed to operate, including transport, packaging materials, and a local seed company. Small towns in the area experienced a mini-boom in new shops and services.

One of the particularly interesting features of the project was the decision to limit the amount of beans produced by any one farmer to a relatively modest amount. Initially adopted as a way to control seed wastage, reduce company risk, and standardize the input package, the decision had several beneficial results for farmers. It meant that more—and smaller—farmers could participate and that they did not become overly dependent on the success of the venture. The French bean system became integrated into their normal lives, avoiding some of the negative social consequences observed in other contract farming projects, notably those involving sugar or resettlement schemes.

From Bust to Boom: Letting a Thousand Flowers Bloom

What started as a humble cottage industry underwent a significant transformation in 1969 when the Danish company, Dansk Chrysanthemum and Kultur (DCK), made a large-scale investment on a 6,000-hectare estate in Eastern Province. The Kenyan government supported the project by providing land (under a low-cost, long-term lease), exclusive growing and trading rights for eight years on several types of flowers, unlimited work permits for expatriate workers, and a 25-year guarantee not to change laws on foreign investor taxation and profit repatriation. The Danish government provided a grant equal to one-third of the total investment costs. DCK expanded its operations in the 1970s, acquiring two additional estates, a large-scale farm in Naivasha for producing carnations and a smaller one in Updown, near Nairobi, to be used as a nursery. The original estate did not work out, and in 1976 the main Danish shareholder suddenly pulled out, throwing the company into a financial crisis.

The DCK farms then passed into Kenyan hands. Leading government officials became major shareholders in the Updown farm, and a political decision was made to restructure the farm into a small-holder outgrower scheme to expand Kenyan participation in a rapidly growing industry controlled largely by European expatriates. Unfortunately, Updown collapsed in 1978, shortly after its takeover by the Agricultural Development Corporation, a government-owned company that had dismissed all the expatriate personnel. Most of the farmers who had acquired floriculture skills under the scheme continued growing flowers for commercial purposes, including one group of 300 smallholders who formed a flower trading cooperative. Many used the marketing services provided by former expatriate employees of DCK who had set up their own small companies.

Brooke Bond, which ran many of the tea estates in Kenya, invested some of its profits in the Naivasha operation and chose to retain some of the DCK expatriates. The farm, renamed Sulmac, soon enjoyed considerable success. Some 120 hectares were planted with 50 different varieties of carnations, making it the largest operation of its kind in the world, and by 1979 it accounted for 90 percent of Kenya's flower exports. Sulmac further diversified its flower mix to include roses, and it remains one of the major players in Kenya's flower industry today.

Several other major investments occurred in the 1980s, tied to international sponsors. One such investment was by a U.S. firm, Yoder Bros., whose operation was managed by a former DCK manager. Another, more substantial investment, Oserian Development Company, was made by a Dutch family in Kenya. Located next to Sulmac at Naivasha, Oserian ran Kenya's largest vegetable growing operation in the 1970s, producing for both export and local processing companies. Dissatisfied with the profitability of vegetables, the company decided to diversify into cut flowers, using its existing irrigation and cold storage facilities and, once again, former DCK employees. Despite major logistical and marketing problems at the start of its flower operations, Oserian determined that its viability in the flower trade depended on reaching a critical threshold of production that would allow it to charter its own air-freight planes. To gain greater control over the marketing side, the company integrated forward into the Dutch market, establishing a subsidiary company called East African Flowers.

A few other relatively large cut flower investments involving joint ventures with Dutch companies were also established in Naivasha. There were several dozen new small-scale investments in the mid-1980s, including spin-offs by managers and staff from Sulmac and Oserian. Other spin-offs were by some of the larger fruit and vegetable production/export companies and by prominent public officials. Spin-offs founded by prominent officials typically take the form of joint ventures or use technical assistance from expatriate flower specialists from Israel and the Netherlands.

The 1990s witnessed a surge in the production of cut flowers, with area doubling and the value of cut flower exports increasing threefold. Investment promotion efforts contributed to the strengthening of the technical support network for the flower industry. Improvements in infrastructure, including the new airport at Eldoret, helped stimulate the westward expansion of the industry. But much of these gains can be attributed to reduced government intervention: liberalization of Kenya's foreign exchange control regime; streamlining of importation procedures (equipment, planting material, and other inputs); and withdrawal from the air-freight market.

The government's attempt to control air-freight rates, ostensibly to improve the horticulture industry's competitiveness, constrained air-freight supply, stifling the industry. Tight restrictions on foreign exchange transactions and official concerns about the non-repatriation of foreign exchange earnings by some horticultural exporters led to a situation in which flower exporters were required to specify a fixed FOB price for their sales.

Since the market was dominated by commission-based or auction transactions, many of the export transactions involved fictional pricing. The larger firms managed to retain sufficient foreign exchange abroad to purchase the necessary imported inputs, but small firms suffered. Smaller players were also adversely affected by constrained access to the newest planting materials, because the government refused to sign the International Convention for the Protection of New Plant Varieties (UPOV). Larger companies were less affected, as they conducted a more diverse array of financial transactions abroad, which enabled them to surreptitiously pay plant breeder royalties.

At the same time, the private sector was innovating in various ways. In marketing, for example, direct Dutch auctions had been the main outlets for Kenyan flowers. When rising imports began to hurt local profits in the mid-1990s, Dutch growers lobbied to secure a strict import policy, including quotas and a total ban on imports of certain flower varieties during the summer. To circumvent these trade restrictions, Oserian, through its subsidiary company, East African Flowers, initiated an alternative auction, the Tele Flower Auction. Buyers purchased flowers remotely, through computers at their offices, rather than at auctions. The distribution system eliminated much of the product handling and hence reduced the risk of physical damage to the product. Delivery was faster (within half an hour), and prices were lower. The Tele Flower Auction now handles 20 to 30 percent of Kenyan flower imports into the Netherlands, as well as imports from the other major exporting countries.

The industry is now undergoing significant changes. Oserian is the industry leader, and production for export is concentrated in about two dozen large-scale farms, which account for 75 percent of the industry. These larger growers are supplemented by some 4,000–5000 small-scale growers (growers who own no more than one hectare of land), who currently account for 10 to 15 percent of production.

These small-scale farmers face an uncertain future because of declining demand for lower-quality flowers and increasing production and marketing costs. These problems are exacerbated by their lack of access to adequate credit and inputs, as well as logistical constraints associated with transport, haulage, air-freight, and cold storage facilities. Changing to a new regime of farm chemicals, meeting the UPOV royalty requirements, and making the investments needed to comply with the Kenya Flower Council and other European codes of practice entail significant costs. Complying with these standards represents a real challenge for small-scale farmers, leading some experts to predict a major shake-up of the Kenyan cut flower industry.

Meanwhile, nongovernmental organizations have been putting pressure on the industry to take bolder steps to preserve the environment. The flower industry has been blamed for the ecological problems facing Lake Naivasha: ground water pollution, emigration of the flamingoes, a drop in the water level, and a decline in fish populations. A few flower farms have taken steps to address some of these concerns by building water treatment and water harvesting facilities in order to meet the Good Agricultural Practices standard, as well as the

Sanitary and Phytosanitary code of practice. A related issue is that of competition between flower farms and households for water in and around urban centers (such as Ngong in Nairobi). There is a growing demand for subjecting such farms to higher water charges, even though doing so would reduce profit margins, which have already declined due to high input costs.

Lessons

Each national experience is to some extent unique, defined by initial conditions and circumstances at different points in time. Kenya has benefited from various special factors—the early experience with Asian vegetables for the domestic Asian community and their subsequent marketing links with overseas Asians, a climate particularly conducive to flower cultivation, and the booming tourism industry, which created both a local market for quality horticultural produce and significant air-freight space for shipments to Europe. Nonetheless, certain lessons can be drawn from this experience that may prove relevant for other countries embarking on an export diversification path in this or a similar sector.

External Catalysts Are Critical

Foreign investors and partners played a critical role in launching and expanding the horticulture industry in Kenya. Dutch companies started flower export businesses, and Dutch and Israeli advisors have been important sources of technical support. In the fresh fruit and vegetable trade, the industry leader (Homegrown) was created by a British entrepreneur who broke into the British supermarket sector. These supermarkets have opened up important new opportunities, which account for most of the growth in this subsector. Donors, in contrast, played a relatively minor role.

Domestic players who were regarded as "external" by many Kenyans were equally critical to the industry's success. Asian Kenyans' connections with overseas relatives and friends provided reliable marketing support, which was particularly useful in the early phases, when Kenya was an unknown player. Asian Kenyans accounted for an estimated 64 percent of Kenya's fresh fruit and vegetable exports in 1991. European Kenyans were responsible for another 17 percent, as well as 25 percent of cut flower exports (Jaffee 1995).

Experimenting, Learning, and Adapting to
Changing Circumstances Are Critical

The industry's development now spans more than 50 years, during which time countless problems have been surmounted. None of the big initial investors had an easy time in the early stages. DCK collapsed after six years, the Del Monte project lost money for many years, and the first year of the Njoro Canners French bean experiment was a disaster. Major changes in strategy have been required. Del Monte dropped its smallholder scheme in favor of running its own estate. Oserian diversified from vegetables into flowers and then developed its own alternative marketing arrangement in the Netherlands. Exporters had to drop out of zucchini, sweet peppers, and other "off-season," temperate vegetables when competition from North Africa became too stiff.

The success of the industry is in large measure a testimony to the capacity of the private sector to adapt to changing circumstances, including the failure of old actors and the rise of new ones. This is perhaps best underlined by the remarkable growth of the late 1990s, when economic mismanagement by the state and political turmoil were undermining investor confidence and the capacity to conduct business.

A Coherent and Constructive Approach from
the Public Sector Would Have Helped

The performance of the Kenyan government in promoting the horticulture sector has been mixed. Research and extension were minimal; lack of cold storage facilities discouraged the development of perishable fruits, such as strawberries; and the failure to invest in sea-freight capacity blocked the growth in bulkier fresh fruit, such as pineapples. Meanwhile, the government imposed many trade restrictions typical of the 1970s and 1980s. Import duties of 25 percent or more on many inputs raised the costs of production, and compensatory schemes to reimburse these expenses functioned with long delays if at all. Failure to sign the UPOV barred access to the newest flower planting materials. Foreign exchange controls, pre-shipment inspections, and corruption also raised the cost of doing business.

The biggest problem may have been the program of Kenyanization, notably in the fresh fruit and vegetable segment, which was dominated by Kenyan Asians. African exporters were favored, and Asian-owned firms were often obliged to take on African partners—usually prominent government officials. Such harassment, combined with the expulsion of Asians in neighboring Uganda, undoubtedly discouraged many Kenyan Asians from making long-term investments.

In contrast, the government got many of the biggest issues broadly right. It has been more supportive of the private sector and foreign investment than most other African regimes. Its commitment to a realistic exchange rate was critical in protecting the industry's competitiveness, as was its liberal approach to foreign work permits for expatriates. Its direct assistance to the Del Monte and DCK projects may well have been key to the initiation of the canned pineapple and flower industries. The National Horticultural Research Station played an important, if somewhat inadvertent, part in starting avocado cultivation. The Horticultural Crop Development Authority had the good sense to resist active involvement in marketing at a time when state trading was the norm in Kenyan export agriculture. The government's concern for smallholder development probably helped promote smallholders' participation in the industry.

Broadly speaking, the government's approach to the export horticulture sector has improved over time, to the point where it is now serving as a fairly effective facilitator when needed. The Kenya Plant Health Inspectorate Service, formed in 1997, is working with the private sector to implement plant variety protection laws and help meet international standards by inspecting exported produce in a timely fashion. The horticulture sector would have blossomed sooner had the public sector adopted a more coherent and constructive approach.

Contract Farming Is Vital, But Employment of Laborers May Be More Important for Poverty Reduction

The Njoro Canners French bean project proved that contract farming could be successfully transferred to the private sector. However, farmers contracting with one firm and then selling to a different firm offering a higher price has been a common problem. Ways need to be found to strengthen the contractual arrangement, especially with the growing importance of reliable supply volumes and traceability of inputs and agricultural practices.[18] Contracts that complement rather than monopolize farmers' lives create a healthier relationship, with less potential for negative impact on food security. Where women are the principal growers, dealing directly with them will likely reduce the potential for tensions within the household and make for more sustainable contracts.

While it is probably desirable for reasons of political economy to ensure some participation by smallholders, it is not clear that their involvement is more pro-poor than the involvement of larger farms. Given the need for irrigation, hired labor during peak periods, and increasing quality standards, the poorest smallholders are unlikely to meet the requirements of contract farming schemes, but they may be able to work part-time on larger farms. Such farms, regulated with appropriate labor laws, may actually reach poorer rural workers more effectively. Entrepreneurs should probably be allowed to experiment with various sources of supply in order to determine which works best given the crop and circumstances involved. Meanwhile, the government can facilitate the continued participation of smallholders in various ways, including disseminating good practices in contracting, raising awareness about export standards, certifying compliance, and supporting producers' associations.

BIBLIOGRAPHY

Collinson, Chris. 2001. *The Business Costs of Ethical Supply Chain Management: Kenyan Flower Industry Case Study.* National Resources Institute Report 2607. Chatham, U.K.

Dolan, Catherine S. 2001. "The 'Good Wife': Struggles over Resources in the Kenyan Horticultural Sector." *Journal of Development Studies* 37(3): 39–70.

Dolan, Catherine, and John Humphrey. 2000. "Governance and Trade in Fresh Vegetables: The Impact of UK Supermarkets on the African Horticulture Industry." *Journal of Development Studies* 37(2): 147–76.

FAOSTAT (Food and Agriculture Organization Statistical Databases). [http://apps.fao.org/default.jsp].

Gabre-Madhin, Eleni, and Nicholas Minot. 2003. "Promoting Africa's Horticultural Exports: Successes and Challenges." World Bank, Washington, D.C.

Humphrey, John, Neil McCulloch, and Masako Ota. 2004. "The Impact of the European Market Changes on Employment in the Kenyan Horticulture Sector." *Journal of International Development* 16(1): 63–80.

Jaffee, Steven. 1994. "Contract Farming in the Shadow of Competitive Markets: The Experience of Kenyan Horticulture." In P. Little and M. Watts, eds., *Living Under Contract: Contract Farming and Agrarian Transformation in Sub-Saharan Africa.* Washington, D.C.: World Bank.

———. 1995. "The Many Faces of Success: The Development of Kenyan Horticultural Exports." In Steven Jaffee and John Morton, eds., *Marketing Africa's High-Value Foods.* Washington, D.C.: World Bank.

————. 2003. "From Challenge to Opportunity: The Transformation of the Kenyan Fresh Vegetable Trade in the Context of Emerging Food Safety and Other Standards." Agriculture and Rural Development Discussion Paper 1. Washington, D.C.: World Bank.

Jaffee, Steven, and Gilbert Bintein. 1996. "French Bean Connections: Sustaining Success in a Kenyan Contract Farming Venture." *African Rural and Urban Studies* 3(3).

McCulloch, Neil, and Masako Ota. 2002. "Export Horticulture and Poverty in Kenya." Institute of Development Studies Working Paper 174. Sussex, U.K.

O'Brien, F. S., and Terry C. I. Ryan. 2001. "Kenya." In S. Devarajan, David Dollar, and T. Holmgren, eds., *Aid and Reform in Africa*. Washington, D.C.: World Bank.

Swamy, Gurushri. 1994. "Kenya: Patchy, Intermittent Commitment." In Ishrat Husain and Rashid Faruqee, eds., *Adjustment in Africa: Lessons from Country Case Studies*. Washington, D.C.: World Bank.

Thoen, Ronaldt, Steven Jaffee, Catherine Dolan, and Lucy Waithaka. 1999. "Equatorial Rose: The Kenyan—European Cut Flower Supply Chain." In R. Kopiki, ed., *Supply Chain Development in Emerging Markets: Case Studies of Supportive Public Policy*. Boston: MIT Press.

6

Leapfrogging into the Information Economy
Harnessing Information and Communications Technologies in Botswana, Mauritania, and Tanzania

JOSEPH O. OKPAKU, SR.

In perhaps one of the most dramatic developments since the Industrial Revolution, information and communications technologies (ICTs) have fundamentally changed the lives of people and national economies all over the world. In Africa these technologies offer an important means of delivering much-needed services more efficiently, allowing the continent to reap more value from limited resources. ICT can help build sustainable economies, scale up efforts to reduce poverty, and increase the ability of individuals and institutions to promote their own development through vastly increased access to information.

Joseph O. Okpaku, Sr. can be contacted at Okpaku@aol.com. The author thanks Paul Noumba Um, Mavis Ampah, and Louise Fox, all of the World Bank, for their guidance of this study and engaging dialogue in reviewing drafts of the report. Gratitude is also due to Yves Vivier, Country Manager, and Hawa Cisse Wague, Economist, of the World Bank Office in Mauritania. For generously granting access and interviews, the author gratefully acknowledges individuals and government officials in Botswana, Tanzania, and Mauritania, particularly the Honorable Fatimetou Mint Mohamed-Saleck, Secretary of State for New Technologies, Mauritania; Adolar Mapunda, former Director General of the Tanzania Telecommunications Corporation, Tanzania; and Cecilia Mamelodi, Manager for Corporate Affairs, Botswana Telecommunications Corporation.

Africa was late in entering the ICT arena, and many African countries are handicapped by inadequate infrastructure and access. Nevertheless, many countries—including Botswana, Mauritania, and Tanzania, which together represent a microcosm of Africa as a whole—have embarked on embracing ICT as one of the engines to drive their development, especially to combat poverty.

Although the reform process began fairly recently (in 1999 for Mauritania, in 2003 for Tanzania, and not yet in Botswana), the framework was laid down through telecommunications reform, as the antecedent of ICT reform. With World Bank assistance in formulating, implementing, and building capacity for policy reform, Mauritania has dramatically expanded the sector by liberalizing and partially privatizing its incumbent public telephone and telegraph. In the process, Mauritania has also attracted foreign direct investment for ICT at a time when the global trend would predict otherwise. Tanzania has built on a long-term strategic effort at developing the sector, which has resulted in the proliferation of access across the country, including through several thousand public access points, as well as in rural access. For its part, Botswana aims to use ICT to build a new sector, that of becoming a regional hub in financial services.

Sector reform has greatly accelerated the development of ICT in the study countries and advanced the use of ICT for development. Liberalization has brought about competition, which in turn has greatly increased access, especially in mobile telephony. Privatization has introduced the dynamics of commercial enterprise with its expected attendant increase in efficiency. The establishment of formal policy, legal, and regulatory frameworks through regulatory authorities has brought much-needed structure to the sector, with much clearer rules, processes, and regulations and the corresponding increase in transparency. Challenges remain, including high costs, the threat of technological obsolescence, and the need to provide human resource capacity building to support the sector. The promise and achievements already made, however, outstrip the threats.

Adoption of Information and Communications Technologies in Africa

Although still modest by comparison with Western economies, an explosion in the development of ICT infrastructure has occurred in Africa over the past decade. The number of fixed telephone lines rose from 12.5 million in 1995 to more than 21 million in 2001 (Jensen 2003) and 25 million in 2003 (ITU 2004). In addition, the quality of the infrastructure improved tremendously, with many networks switching from purely analog technology to a hybrid of analog and digital systems and a few countries having fully digital networks.

The change in mobile telephone service has been even more dramatic. In 1995 very few African countries had mobile telephone services. Today every country on the continent has at least one mobile operator, and by 2001 the number of mobile subscribers had overtaken the number of fixed-line subscribers. Sub-Saharan Africa had an estimated 18 million mobile telephone subscribers in September 2003, while the continent as a whole had an estimated 51 million subscribers by the end of the year (World Bank 2004b; ITU 2004).

This quantum leap in voice telecommunications infrastructure and services has been matched by a parallel development in Internet use. In 1995 only a handful of African countries had Internet service. By the end of 2003 there were about 4.5 million Internet subscribers and some 52,000 Internet hosts in Sub-Saharan Africa (excluding South Africa), and 12.4 million subscribers and 350,000 Internet hosts in Africa as a whole. Today Internet service is available in every country in Africa, especially in cities and towns, and a large number of Africans, mostly students and young adults, have free email addresses. As of the end of 2003 there were an estimated 4.2 million personal computers in Sub-Saharan Africa (excluding South Africa) and an estimated 10.4 million personal computers in all of Africa (box 6.1) (ITU 2004).

Despite this rapid growth, ownership of telephone and personal computers remains limited. This has been partly mitigated by the explosion in public access facilities such as telecenters, Internet kiosks, and cybercafes, which have mushroomed across the conti-

---

BOX 6.1	**How Plugged in Is Africa?**

As of the end of 2003, Africa's 750–800 million people owned about 94 million radio sets, 50 million television sets, 25 million fixed telephone lines, and 10 million personal computers. The continent had 25 million fixed telephone lines, 51 million mobile subscribers, and just over 12 million Internet subscribers, nearly 200,000 cable television subscribers, and 8 million users of home-based satellite antennas.

Source: ITU 2004.

nent. Mauritania alone has about 3,500 public kiosks, and Tanzania has more than 1,000 cybercafes.

The new technology is being used in innovative ways. Wireless technologies are being used to improve "last-mile access," the stretch between the nearest switch and the subscriber's terminal equipment, in countries with inadequate copper wire or optical fiber cable networks. Global positioning technology is being used to communicate with nomads in the deserts of Mauritania (box 6.2).

Advances in technology have increased access, but they have not reduced prices: Africans continue to pay more than $1,000 per access line, regardless of the technology used. These high prices are preventing African countries from taking full advantage of ICT.

The explosion in ICT infrastructure and services in Africa over the past decade reflects several factors:

- The global reach of mass media, which has created local demand for world knowledge and information.
- The increase in public awareness, including greater knowledge of the right to information.
- The focus on self-actualization, as the internecine conflicts once endemic in Africa are increasingly giving way to development priorities.
- The expansion of the African diaspora (and the desire for families to stay in touch).
- The increasing maturity of the knowledge-based economy and its consequences for economic and social empowerment.
- The shrinking job market, which has compelled young people to become entrepreneurs and exposed them to the promise of ICT.

BOX 6.2	**Using Mobile Phones to Communicate with Nomads in the Sahara Desert**

Global positioning technology is allowing people who live in towns and cities in Mauritania to communicate with nomads living in the Sahara Desert, using satellite phone service provided by Mauritel and Mattel, in collaboration with the satellite operators Inmarsat and Thuraya. The same technology could be used to provide online services—tracking, education, and emergency services—to the one-third of Mauritania's people who are nomads.

The impact of these developments in ICT in Africa, in terms of both ICT development (increased infrastructure and access) and ICT for development (adoption of ICT applications), has been to advance the process of development itself, in terms of ICT for development. The result of this duality of sector transformation has been itself dually vast. On the one hand, it has facilitated the delivery of services such as education, health, better governance (on the part of both the leadership and the governed), enterprise and business development, as well as their overall contribution to socioeconomic well-being (especially poverty reduction), political stability, and self-actualization. On the other hand, the transformation has increased demand for more and better services, faithful to the adage that once people have tasted honey, they crave more. This, in turn, has been good for governments, as it has provided a flexible and potentially inexpensive means of establishing an interactive dialogue with the people, the basis of democratic governance.

Reform of the Telecommunications Sector in Botswana, Mauritania, and Tanzania

The development of ICT policy in the three countries is fairly recent and still in its nascent stage for different reasons in each country. Botswana does not have a national ICT policy; in November 2003 it awarded a contract to a Canadian consulting firm to draft a policy. The draft will be reviewed through a series of dialogues with various stakeholders in the country. The National Information and Communications Technologies Policy for Tanzania was published only in March 2003. The Act of Parliament establishing the Tanzania Communications Regulatory Authority (TCRA), which is responsible for implementing and administering the policy, was promulgated on May 23, 2003. The TCRA has since taken over from the Tanzania Communications Commission. Mauritania published its National Strategy for the Development of New Technologies (2002–06) in November 2001, and the Plan of Action six months later. Reform of the ICT sector was preceded by reform of the narrower telecommunications sector through telecommunications policies (as distinct from broader ICT policies).

As a result of the serious commitment of the governments to ICT development in these countries and the growing awareness of the benefits of ICT (and demand for them) by the public, the sector has seen substantial growth in all three countries. For example, the number of telephone subscribers in all three countries has skyrocketed in the past six years, with most of the growth coming from mobile lines. The increase in teledensity (the percentage of subscribers in the population) has been unprecedented. Between 1998 and 2003 teledensity rose from 7.5 to 34.0 in Botswana, from 0.6 to 12.1 in Mauritania, and from 0.5 to 3.0 in Tanzania (table 6.1 and figure 6.1).

These figures are impressive, but small increases in the number of subscribers can have very dramatic effects on teledensity in very small countries. A more useful way of comparing the growth of telecommunications technology may therefore be to look at the rate of growth of teledensity across the three countries (figure 6.2).

Botswana

The reform process in Botswana began in earnest in 1996, following promulgation of the Telecommunications Policy in 1995 and the enabling Telecommunications Act of 1996, which established the Botswana Telecommunications Authority. The Broadcasting Act of 1998 came into law in 1999. A National Information and Communications Technologies Policy was contracted out in November 2003.

Liberalization of the telecommunications sector, which began with the issuance of two mobile telecommunications licenses in 1997, significantly changed the landscape in the sector. As a result of the introduction of competition into the mobile telephony sector, the number of mobile subscribers rose from about 15,000 in 1998 to 435,000 by the end of November 2003. For a population of only 1.7 million people, this represents a mobile teledensity of 25.6 percent.

The much slower increase in the fixed-line network, from 102,000 to 142,000 over the same period, partly reflects the effect of growth in mobile telephony on fixed-line subscriptions. Although fixed-line teledensity hovers around 8 percent, the subscriber base actually declined 3.7 percent between March 2002 and March 2003 (Botswana Telecommunications Authority 2004).

Mauritania

Telecommunications sector reform in Mauritania began in 1998, when the government, with World Bank assistance, set out to restructure the sector in order to transform it into a key instrument for addressing

TABLE 6.1	Telecommunications Access in Botswana, Mauritania, and Tanzania, 1998–2003						
Item	1998	1999	2000	2001	2002	2003
Botswana						
Number of fixed-line subscribers	102,016	123,819	135,900	142,600	142,362	142,400
Number of mobile subscribers	15,190	92,000	200,000	316,000	435,000	435,000
Total number of subscribers	117,206	215,819	335,900	458,600	577,362	577,400
Total teledensity (percent of population)	7.5	13.4	20.4	27.3	35.67	34.0
Rate of growth in teledensity (percent)		78.67	52.54	33.46	23.06	1.16
Mauritania						
Number of fixed-line subscribers	15,000	16,525	18,969	24,856	31,529	31,500
Number of mobile subscribers	0	0	15,300	110,463	247,238	300,000
Total number of subscribers	15,000	16,525	34,269	135,319	278,767	331,500
Total teledensity (percent of population)	0.6	0.7	1.3	3.7	10.4	12.1

(continued)

TABLE 6.1	Telecommunications Access in Botswana, Mauritania, and Tanzania, 1998–2003 *(Cont'd)*					
Item	1998	1999	2000	2001	2002	2003
Rate of growth in teledensity (percent)		40.3	111.7	179.1	177.8	16.0
Tanzania						
Number of fixed-line subscribers	121,769	149,611	173,591	148,464	161,590	149,100
Number of mobile subscribers	17,940	50,950	180,200	426,964	780,000	891,000
Total number of subscribers	139,709	200,561	353,791	575,428	941,590	1,040,100
Total teledensity (percent of population)	0.5	0.6	1.1	1.7	2.7	3.0
Rate of growth in teledensity (percent)		40	71.4	63.9	58.7	8.1

Source: From official data.

| FIGURE 6.1 | Teledensity in Botswana, Mauritania, and Tanzania, 1998–2003 (Percentage of Population Subscribing to Fixed-line or Mobile Phone Service) |

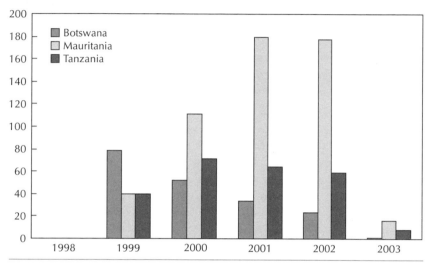

Source: From official data.

| FIGURE 6.2 | Annual Change in Teledensity in Botswana, Mauritania, and Tanzania, 1998–2003 (Percentage Change over Previous Year) |

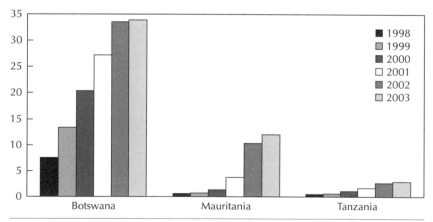

Source: From official data.

development priorities. A new law in May 1999 established a regulatory authority for the sector.

The government took a two-pronged approach to transforming telecommunications services, namely through liberalization of the sector to encourage competition and privatizing the state-owned telephone company (Nair and Tintchev 2001). Despite initial hiccups attributable to legacy anxieties about the potential challenge of sector expansion to national security, the government's determination to succeed, combined with the benefits of best practices elsewhere and alongside the concerted efforts by the World Bank to help guide the preparatory process in order to minimize the threat of Mauritania's low investment appeal and the pervasive global crisis in telecommunications investment, produced dramatic results.

From the introduction of telecommunications services in Mauritania in 1974 until the introduction of reform in 1999, the country had developed only 16,525 fixed lines. With measured steps, the government first broke the Office of Posts and Telecommunications into a telecommunications company (Mauritel) and a postal service company (Mauripost). In June 2000 it then liberalized the sector by issuing a mobile license to Mattel, a consortium made up of Tunisia Telecom and local partners.

Liberalization preceded privatization of Mauritel, which took place half a year later, when Maroc Telecom bought a 46 percent stake for $48 million. At the end of 2001 a cabinet-level office headed by the Secretary of State for New Technologies was established within the Office of the Prime Minister. The same year the office published its strategic five-year plan, the National Strategy for the Development of New Technologies, 2002–06 (NERA 2003; Wilhelm and Mueller 2003). It released a Plan of Action in May 2002.

Increases in ICT in Mauritania have been dramatic. The number of mobile subscribers jumped from zero in 1999 to 300,000 at the end of 2003.[1] The number of fixed-line subscriptions nearly doubled, rising from 16,525 to 31,500, but the increase does not reflect reform, as competition does not exist in the fixed-line sector.

Tanzania

Tanzania published its National Information and Communications Technologies Policy in March 2003. Two months later Parliament established the Tanzania Communications Regulatory Authority, which is responsible for implementing and administering the policy. The new agency is both more powerful and more independent than its predecessor.

The number of fixed lines in Tanzania experienced marginal growth since the reform process began, increasing from 125,703 in 1993 to 149,100 in 2003. However, the number of mobile subscribers leaped from 1,500 in 1993 to 891,000 in 2003. Overall teledensity rose from 0.32 to 3.0. In 1993 there was a single Internet service provider and just 10 Internet subscribers; by 2003 there were 23 Internet service providers (with all but 2 or 3 fully functioning) and some 14,000 subscribers. Over the same period, Internet bandwidth rose from 64 to 44,000 kbits, the number of television broadcast licenses issued jumped from 1 to 24, and the number of radio broadcast licenses rose from 2 to 18.[2]

Efforts have been made to establish telecenters in district capitals (Nielinger 2003c). However, as a primarily rural country (70 percent of the population lives in rural areas, and 80 percent of the workforce works in agriculture), it is the deployment of ICT in rural areas that is of primary importance to Tanzania (Intelecon 2002). The National Telecom Policy of 1997 made provisions for a Rural Telecommunications Fund. The National Information and Communications Technology Policy of 2003 calls for the operationalization of the fund. It also calls for universal access to telecommunications, for "special incentives for investors to deliver broadband connectivity to hitherto disenfranchised and isolated populations in the country," and for the building of "awareness that investment in and through ICT in remote areas is a potent means of reducing the cost of rural-urban transactions" (Tanzania Ministry of Communications and Transport 2003).

How Has ICT Improved People's Lives?

Reforms, although still in their early stages in Botswana, Mauritania, and Tanzania, are already yielding dividends—for individuals, for the private sector, and for government:

- Access to communications facilities has improved, making communicating and accessing information much easier for many people.
- Increased access to the Internet has allowed more and more people to communicate electronically and to take advantage of the

educational, informational, and entertainment content of the Internet.

■ The private sector has benefited from improved communication with buyers and suppliers; expanded market access, including access to global markets; higher productivity and profitability (in both agriculture and urban trade); and greater access to information—about markets, competitors, and best practices—from around the world.

■ A new economic sector has emerged, spawning entrepreneurship and job creation at Internet service providers, telecenters, kiosks, and cybercafes (box 6.3).

■ Financial and administrative efficiency have increased.

■ The ability to serve remote populations through online applications—such as distance education, e-health, e-commerce, and e-government—has increased.

BOX 6.3	**Selling ICT Products and Services in Botswana, Mauritania, and Tanzania**

At the shopping mall next to the Cresta Hotel in Gaborone, Botswana, young boys and girls sit at card tables holding mobile handsets. For a pre-paid fee customers can use the phones to make or receive telephone calls. The tariff is $.32 a minute for a call to a fixed line or a number on the Mascom mobile operator network and $.64 a minute for a call to an Orange (formerly Vista) mobile line. Calls outside Botswana but within Africa cost $1.28 a minute, while overseas calls cost $2.56 a minute. Customers expecting calls can give callers the number of the service operator at whose stand they plan to await the call. Each of the 10 phones at the station reportedly brings in $75 a day in revenues.

In the capital city of Nouakchott, Mauritania, a two-block portion of the main street looks like a street bazaar at its busiest. A stretch of shops sells mobile handsets and telecommunications accessories. The street is also home to several large Internet cafes, some of them with more than 50 personal computers. One cafe, located across the street from a secondary school, gets its heaviest traffic when school is out, when boys and girls from the school pour in to use the Internet.

Joseph Ng'ombe is a supervisor at the MEaLZ Internet Cafe in Dar es Salaam. "If not for this Internet cafe," he says, "I would not be employed. People come here searching for information and goods to buy, even cars to buy from Japan."

- Where governments have created Web sites (as they have in Tanzania and to some extent Mauritania), access to public information has increased.
- The greater efficiency, cost effectiveness, and transparency that ICT makes possible have enabled governments to deliver more and better services.
- Increased knowledge and information obtained through the Internet have improved the quality of public dialogue, which creates an enabling environment for national integration and the establishment and entrenchment of peace and tolerance.
- The increased demand for ICT services as their value has become broadcast is resulting in the emergence of small and medium-size ICT enterprises, such as telecenters, kiosks, and cybercafes, which create much-needed employment for young people.
- The growing adoption of ICT in business and government, spreading increasingly from the national level to the state, provincial, and local government levels, creates a demand for staff with ICT skills. An increasing number of young men and women seek daytime or evening extramural courses to acquire ICT skills to meet these demands.

In all three countries reform has increased competition and expanded access under the guidance of credible regulatory authorities. Competition has promoted the creation of appropriate institutional frameworks for regulation in the utilities sector, benefiting other sectors as well. In Mauritania reform has also improved the investment environment, as reflected in the investment of $28 million in 2000 for a mobile license and $48 million for partial privatization of the incumbent operator, Mauritel (Nair and Tintchev 2001).

Building an Information-based Economy: Key Components of Success

Several factors are critical to building an information-based economy—and to putting ICT to work to reduce poverty. Commitment to developing ICT must be strong. Champions of reform must be willing to spearhead, implement, and support reform. Institutional changes must be made, and partnerships must be forged—among development agencies, donors, nongovernmental organizations, and returning nationals with skills in ICT and entrepreneurship.

Commitment and Ownership

Development partners have played a critical role in promoting the need for sector reform and facilitating a paradigm shift in the way policymakers view ICT. Such paradigm shifts would be short-lived and unsustainable, however, without indigenous commitment. Recognition of the need for reform and the commitment to undertake it must come from within the countries themselves, and the promise of reform must be consistent with a country's strategic vision. The countries and the people must take ownership of the reform process in order to derive maximum value from the effort and make it sustainable for the long term.

African policymakers are committed to increasing access to and use of ICT for a variety of reasons. In recent years African leaders have tried to build their countries' economies and stem the tide of poverty. As the source of economic strength has shifted from material resources to knowledge and intellectual capacity, they have come to realize the importance of acquiring, creating, and mobilizing their countries' own knowledge and expertise as critical tools to drive a new development thrust, especially in scaling up poverty reduction efforts. Several factors have played critical roles in pushing African leaders to move ahead more quickly to increase access to ICT:

- More than ever, Africa's leaders at the beginning of the new millennium share a common desire to turn over a new leaf. As part of this effort, they want to join forces to develop ICT capacity across the continent.
- Policymakers recognize the potential of ICT to overcome the limitations of distance, terrain, and limited human and financial resources to deliver such services as health, education, and recently banking through Internet-based online applications.
- Policymakers recognize the empowering impact of global Internet access, especially for young people, and its ability to enable citizens to discover and share information that can improve their lives in a variety of ways.
- Governments are more aware of the compelling need to deliver good, accountable, responsible, and responsive governance to the people. They also recognize the ability of the people to gauge the performance of their governments as well as to express their dissatisfaction through access to information tools.

■ Policymakers understand that, especially where financial resources are very limited, good governance and economic development require greater efficiency. ICT has the potential to improve governance, allowing governments to get more bang for their development buck.

■ The rapid transformation of the world into an information- and knowledge-based environment makes the benefits of ICT tangible and palpable.

■ The success stories from Asia, especially China, India, and Malaysia, have proved very compelling.

Champions of Reform: Committed Leaders, Dedicated Bureaucrats, Able Regulators—and an Informed and Eager Public

By themselves, motivation, appropriate policies, and privatization of the sector are insufficient to have an impact on development. A champion of reform is needed, someone from the public or private sector who is powerful enough to promote major changes and has sufficient authority and control over financial resources to direct them in support of needed change.

As champions cannot make things happen by themselves, loyal, enlightened, and committed deputies are needed, especially at the ministerial and principal secretary level, and dedicated bureaucrats committed to change are needed throughout the civil service. In addition, a knowledgeable, enlightened, fair, and transparent regulatory authority is needed to lead the development of the ICT sector by encouraging and interacting flexibly with the private sector and creating an environment in which competition is open and fair. Most important of all is an informed public that is enthusiastic about the empowering potential of ICT and willing and able to experiment with new technologies without worrying about jeopardizing enduring value in tradition.

In Botswana the main driver of transformation has been Cuthbert M. Lekaukau, executive chairman of the Botswana Regulatory Authority. Mr. Lekaukau has been active in all of the relevant forums with potential impact on ICT in Africa, including the International Telecommunication Union (ITU) and the Telecommunications Regulatory Authority of Southern Africa (TRASA), the regional grouping of telecommunications authorities in the 16 member states of the Southern African Development Community. He is backed by a team of young, smart men and women who have solid backgrounds in the field and are actively engaged in the regional, continental, and global exchange of ideas in the sector.

In Mauritania the key driving force has been President Maaouya Ould Sid Ahmed Taya. According to Fatimetou Mint Mohamed-Saleck, the secretary of state for new technologies, "The president believes in new technologies as a solution for development, for crossing barriers to development, for creating a short-cut to development." The president's commitment is matched by that of the secretary of state. The director for new technologies for information and communications, B. A. Houssey-nou Hamady, and the president of the Mauritania Regulatory Authority, Moustapha Ould Cheikh Mouhamedou, play important roles in imple-menting reforms. The Ministry of New Technologies has accomplished a lot since it was created by presidential decree in 2000, crafting an ICT strategy and a plan of action and implementing changes to the sector.

In Tanzania championship of ICT comes from the University of Dar es Salaam, which is also taking the lead in expanding access to distance education. This is a direct result of the country's modern political his-tory and the legacy of founding head of state and pre-eminent visionary President Julius Nyerere, whose philosophy and commitment centered on education, knowledge, and information. At independence young politicians, academics and intellectuals, the media, and budding entre-preneurs in most African countries belonged to the same social group. Except during a rebellion by the armed forces, which was quickly put down, Tanzania has never experienced a separation between the intel-lectual class and the political leadership. Academics and intellectuals have continued to play an important role in Tanzania's development process. Together with the stability that Tanzania has enjoyed since independence, their participation has enabled Tanzania to rely heavily on internal expertise to craft its development strategies.

Tanzania's ICT policy was drafted by a broad-based task force chaired by Matthew Luhanga, vice chancellor of the University of Dar es Salaam, following an extended process of dialogue with all stakehold-ers, including a special session with Parliament. The fact that the min-ister of transport and communications is an ICT specialist and former professor at the University of Dar es Salaam, and that many university graduates serve in Parliament, has helped spur ICT development in Tanzania. More people with academic training in ICT are probably working in the policy, regulatory, and operational sectors of the eco-nomy in Tanzania than in most countries in the world. This cadre of well-trained people has enabled Tanzania to develop and implement a sound ICT strategy.

Leaders in all three countries understand the scope and long-term nature of developing ICT as a tool for reducing poverty. As Dr. Maua Daftari, the deputy minister of transport and communications of Tanzania, noted, "We in Tanzania are trying, but we have a long way to go. We have to provide connectivity for our rural populations."

Institutional Innovation

The most important institutional innovation governments can adopt is establishment of an e-government platform, which serves not only to enhance administration and the delivery of public services but also as an example to nongovernmental institutions of the value of ICT. Tanzania has an ambitious and comprehensive e-government platform. Mauritania recently awarded a contract for the design of an e-government platform. In contrast, Botswana appears reluctant to create a robust e-government platform, limiting its ICT involvement to interconnecting government ministries (COMNET-IT and UNESCO 2002).

A good indicator of the importance government places on the use of ICT for improved delivery of administrative and public services is the location of the office responsible for ICT. In Mauritania the Ministry of New Technologies is placed within the Office of the Prime Minister. In Tanzania it is located in the Presidency.

Working with Partners

Donors and development partners are playing a key role in all three countries, supporting the development of policy, strategies, and rules for implementing sector reform, such as licensing and privatization tender rules and procedures; helping implement policy; and developing legal and regulatory frameworks and instruments to manage the sector. Many of these interventions have failed to promote indigenous enterprises or to draw on local players to create the ICT sector. The absence of African experts as consultants in strategic situations that require the long-term commitment that only comes with ownership and responsibility is a flaw that development partners need to address.

Even with donor assistance, government cannot do everything. Public-private partnerships are needed, as well as partnerships between government and civil society. In Tanzania NGOs are playing a major role in the development and deployment of ICT for development (Nielinger 2003a).

In all three countries foreign nationals living abroad have helped drive the sector. As a result of the cooling off of the high-tech industry in the United States and Europe, many ICT–savvy Africans have returned home and become key players in the ICT sector, especially in Tanzania.

Can ICT Reduce Poverty?

The relationship between ICT and poverty reduction is complex. ICT is not likely to have an effect on the poorest of the poor in the short term, as it affects economies in a structural and systemic way. By simplifying the way things can be done—and often making possible things that might otherwise have been impossible or unprofitable—ICT acts as a driver of economic change. Only in the wake of this transformation does employment—and the education and skills training it demands—begin to respond. Investment in ICT for poverty reduction must therefore be crafted as a long-term strategy in order not to create false hopes of early returns.

Thus, the promise of ICT for reducing poverty should be viewed as a multistep process. Early on ICT can increase the government's ability to deliver basic social services and create two-way communications between leadership and the people. ICT can make government more responsive and more transparent—and therefore more likely to address poverty reduction.

Later ICT can improve education, enabling "the poor to understand their own circumstances" (Pigato 2001, p. x) and improve health outcomes (through telemedicine, for example). In this trajectory the long-term strategic impact on poverty reduction becomes self-evident and self-propelling.

In addition to these indirect effects, ICT also has a direct impact on development and poverty reduction by creating jobs (Pigato 2001). The bustling activity on the main street of Nouakchott, Mauritania (see box 6.3) has an effect on poverty reduction in urban areas. The challenge will be using ICT to reduce poverty in rural areas, where few people would be able to afford even inexpensive ICT services.

Lessons and Recommendations

Two primary lessons emerge from the brief experience with reform in Botswana, Mauritania, and Tanzania:

■ *Sector reform greatly accelerated the development of ICT and advanced the use of ICT for development.* Liberalization brought competition, which has greatly increased access, especially in mobile telephony. Privatization introduced the dynamics of commercial enterprise, with its emphasis on efficiency. The establishment of formal policy, legal, and regulatory frameworks through regulatory authorities has brought much-needed structure to the sector, with much clearer rules, processes, and regulations and a corresponding increase in transparency.

■ *ICT is a potent tool for development—and one that is within the reach of all African countries.* To take full advantage of its promise, policymakers need to develop a strategic vision that recognizes the importance of knowledge and information, and affordable public access to both, as key elements of national development. It also requires a recognition that public access to shared knowledge is not a threat to government but rather a facilitator of open and meaningful dialogue between leaders and the people they govern, to the benefit of all concerned. Political leaders need to have the courage to make the bold decisions required to adopt ICT—especially when doing so threatens established power and authority systems and interests. And they need to lead by example, by developing e-government.

Several recommendations also emerge from experience with ICT development in Botswana, Mauritania, and Tanzania and elsewhere in Africa:

■ ICT development should be planned, not ad hoc, based on strategies that reflect local conditions and resource availability.

■ ICT should be widely adopted, so that economies of scale can be enjoyed and a paradigm shift in the way of doing business produced. Governments can do much to spur this process by increasing e-government capacity at the national, state, provincial, and local government levels.

■ Resources should be allocated to areas in which ICT will have the most immediate impact, especially on income and job creation (and therefore poverty reduction) in order to build the momentum necessary to sustain the process until longer-term impacts can be felt. In the meantime, ICT should be used to increase productivity and efficiency in the productive sectors of the economy.

- ICT is an expensive undertaking that does not pay off in the short term. Expectations must therefore be long term in order to avoid disillusionment and retrenchment before the benefits of the technology are realized.
- ICT cannot simply be thrust on a country with the expectation that people will adopt it. Adopting new technology requires a new mindset, which may require public education. One approach would be to include ICT education as part of the basic school curriculum.
- ICT is prone to rapid change—and to rapid obsolescence. African countries should avoid adopting obsolete technology, which industrial countries often dump on them.
- Pilot-testing projects is a good way of avoiding large investments in ICT projects that may not prove cost effective. Pilot projects must perfect each step of the transformation in order to prevent costly mistakes.
- ICT is not sustainable if it is not approached as an industry. Efforts should be made to increase ICT capacity in local content development, software development, technology and applications adaptation, and outsourcing in order to entrench ICT as a productive sector of the economy. Acquiring ICT capacity without developing the collateral scientific and technological expertise or creating production facilities greatly limits the benefits of ICT. Some form of industrialization, possibly undertaken as a collaborative effort by several African countries, is necessary.
- Governments in the region need to support research and development in ICT.

Future Challenges and Opportunities

Each of the three countries studied has its own vision for its future and the future of its people. Each is taking different steps to achieve its vision.

Botswana, one of the richest economies in Africa, is trying to diversify its economic base away from a heavy reliance on mining and agriculture. It hopes to develop into a Hong Kong–style regional center for financial services and outsourcing—sectors that require world-class

ICT infrastructure and human resource capacity. Botswana is seeking to build a science and technology sector to support this strategy.

Mauritania discovered offshore oil reserves in 2001 and is expecting the oil industry to come onstream in 2005. The discovery of oil has the potential to help Mauritania overcome poverty, but policymakers are well aware of the trauma that oil discovery has caused other African countries. To avoid the same fate, Mauritania will need to establish new institutional arrangements. ICT can help. The oil industry depends heavily on global information and communications infrastructure and systems—and trained people to service them. Mauritanian officials are eager to implement a program for rapid human resource capacity building in all aspects of ICT support services.

Tanzania is facing new challenges with the impending end of the exclusivity period for its incumbent fixed-network operator, and needs to develop innovative strategies to develop its information and communications infrastructure to meet the needs of all Tanzanians, especially its very large rural population. The country's strategy is to focus on building expert capacity at all levels and using this capacity to chart a new course for the country. The academic expertise at the University of Dar es Salaam, as well as key experts in the public and private sectors, are helping to develop a new strategy to build on the successes of earlier reforms in the telecommunications sector.

Annex A. Statistics on the Environment for Information and Communications Technologies in Botswana, Mauritania, and Tanzania

Botswana

TABLE 6.2	Information and Communications Technology Statistics for Botswana as of November 30, 2003	
Name of operator	Network type	Number of subscribers
Botswana Telecommunications Corporation	Fixed line	134,493
Mascom Wireless	Mobile network	310,160
Orange Botswana	Mobile network	173,251

Source: From official data.

TABLE 6.3	Subscriber Base and Teledensity in Botswana as of November 30, 2003	
Network type	Total subscriber base	Teledensity
Fixed line	134,493	8 percent
Mobile network	483,411	29 percent

Source: From official data.

TABLE 6.4	Other Licensed Operators in Botswana as of November 30, 2003
Type of operator	Number of licensed operators
Internet service providers	13
Private data networks	8
Data network service providers	9
Number of Internet subscribers	40,000–60,000 (estimate)

Source: From official data.

Mauritania

TABLE 6.5	Information and Communications Technology Statistics for Mauritania as of End of December 2002	
Name of operator	Network type	Number of subscribers
Mauritania Telecom (Mauritel)	Fixed line	30,456
Mattel	Mobile	—

Source: From official data.

Mauritania also has two GMPCS satellite operations designed to service the thin and highly dispersed nomadic desert populations. These consist of partnerships between the two standard operators, Mauritel and Mattel, and satellite operators Inmarsat and Thuraya.

TABLE 6.6	Subscriber Base in Mauritania as of End of December 2002
Network type	**Total subscriber base**
Fixed line	30,456
Mobile	243,650
GMPCS	145

Source: From official data.

Mauritania also has 65 cybercafes and 3,419 public phone kiosks.

Tanzania

TABLE 6.7	Information and Communications Technology Statistics for Tanzania, 2003 (2003 figures)
Name of operator	**Network type**
Tanzania Telecommunications Company, Ltd. (TTCL)	Fixed line
Celtel (subsidiary of TTCL)	Mobile
Mobitel	Mobile
Vodacom	Mobile
Zantel (Zanzibar Telecom)	Mobile

Source: From official data.

TABLE 6.8	Subscriber Base in Tanzania, 2003	
Network type	**Total subscriber base**	**Teledensity**
Fixed line	234,640	–
Mobile	750,000	–
Overall teledensity	–	1.22

Source: From official data.

TABLE 6.9	Other Licensed Operators in Tanzania, 2003
Type of operator	**Number of licensed operators**
Internet service providers	23
Data network service providers	16

Source: From official data.

TABLE 6.10	Other ICT Services in Tanzania, 2003
Service	**Number**
Internet subscribers	14,000
Cybercafes	1,000
Television licenses	24
Radio broadcast licenses	18

Source: From official data.

BIBLIOGRAPHY

Botswana. 1996. "Telecommunications Act." Gaborone.
Botswana Telecommunications Authority. 1999. "Botswana Telecommunications Regulations." Gaborone.
———. 2003. *Annual Report 2001/2002.* Gaborone.
———. 2004. *Annual Report 2002/2003.* Gaborone.
Botswana Ministry of Works, Transport and Communications. 1995. "Telecommunications Policy for Botswana." Gaborone.
Chowdhury, Shyamal K., and Susanne Wolf. 2003. "Use of ICTs and the Economic Performance of SMEs in East Africa." Discussion Paper 2003/06. Helsinki: United Nations University and World Institute for Development Economics Research.
COMNET-IT (Commonwealth Network of Information Technology for Development) and UNESCO (United Nations Educational, Scientific and Cultural Organization). 2002. "Country Profiles." [www.comnet.mt/unesco/Country%20Profiles%20Project/Profiles.htm].
Dasgupta, Susmita, Somik Lall, and David Wheeler. 2001. "Policy Reform, Economic Growth and the Digital Divide: An Econometric Analysis." Policy Research Working Paper 2567. World Bank, Washington, D.C.
Dutta, Soumitra, and Mazen E. Coury. 2003. "ICT Challenges for the Arab World." In Soumitra Dutta, Bruno Lanvin, and Fiona Paua, eds., *The Global Informa-*

tion Technology Report 2002–2003: Readiness for the Networked World. New York: Oxford University Press.

Fink, Carsten, Aaditya Mattoo, and Randeep Rathindran. 2002. "An Assessment of Telecommunications Reform in Developing Countries." Policy Working Paper 2909. World Bank, Washington, D.C.

Government Gazette. 1998. "Botswana: Broadcasting Act." Supplement A. August 13.

Hanna, Nagy K. 2003. "Why National Strategies Are Needed for ICT-Enabled Development." ISG Staff Working Paper 3. World Bank, Information Solutions Group, Washington, D.C.

Hesselmark, Olof. 2003. "ICT in Five African Countries." Stockholm: Swedish International Development Cooperation Agency.

Intelecon Research and Consultancy Limited. 2002. "Tanzania: Rural ICT Market Opportunity Report." African Connection Centre for Strategic Planning, Johannesburg, South Africa.

ITU (International Telecommunication Union). 2001. "Effective Regulation Case Study: Botswana 2001." Geneva.

———. 2004. *African Telecommunication Indicators 2004*. Geneva.

Jensen, Michael. 2003. "The Current Status of Information and Communications Technologies in Africa." In Joseph O. Okpaku, ed., *Information and Communications Technologies and African Development: Assessment of Progress and Challenges Ahead*. New York: UN ICT Task Force.

Mauritania. 2001. "Stratégie National de Développement des Technologies Nouvelles 2002–2006." Nouakchott.

———. 2002. "Stratégie National et Plan Directeur pour le Développement des Technologies (2002–2006)." Nouakchott.

Nair, Govindan G., and Svetoslav Tintchev. 2001. "Liberalizing Telecommunications in Mauritania." Findings Infobriefs 71. World Bank, Washington, D.C.

NERA (National Economic Research Association). 2003. "Evaluating the Effectiveness of Telecommunications Regulators in Sub-Saharan Africa: The Case Study of Mauritania." Report for the World Bank. London.

Nielinger, Olaf. 2003a. "Fact Sheet: ICT-Utilisation by Non-Governmental Organisations (NGOs) in Tanzania." Institute of African Affairs, Hamburg, Germany.

———. 2003b. "Fact Sheet: ICT-Utilisation of Small and Medium Enterprises (SMEs) in Tanzania." Institute of African Affairs, Hamburg, Germany.

———. 2003c. "Rural ICT Utilisation in Tanzania: Empirical Findings from Kasulu, Magu, and Sengerfema." Institute of African Studies, Hamburg, Germany.

OECD–DAC (Organisation for Economic Co-operation and Development–Development Assistance Committee). 2003. "Information and Communications Technology (ICT) in Poverty Reduction Strategy Papers (PRSPs) as of January 2003." OECD Global Forum on Knowledge Economy, March 4–5, Paris.

Okpaku Sr., Joseph O. 2000. "Developing Knowledge Societies: Challenges and Opportunities." ASEAN Preparatory Conference for Global Knowledge, Conference II, January 26–27, Kuala Lumpur.

———. 2001. "E-Culture, Human Culture and In-Between: Meeting the Challenges of the 21st Century Digital World." International Telecommunication Union Conference on Creating New Leaders for e-Culture, August 20, Coventry, U.K.

————. 2002. "The Role of Information and Communications Technologies in the African Development Agenda." Keynote Address to the CAFRAD/UNDESA/NEPAD Regional Workshop on Building e-Governance Capacity in African Countries, October 28, Johannesburg.

————. 2003. "Information and Communications Technologies as Tools for African Self-Development." In *Information and Communications Technologies and African Development: Assessment of Progress and Challenges Ahead.* New York: United Nations ICT Task Force.

————. 2003. "SMART e-GOVERNMENT—Adopting Information and Communications Technologies to Enhance Strategic Development without Undermining Fundamental Human Priorities." Keynote address to the e-Government Africa 2003 Conference, September 15, Johannesburg.

————. 2004. "Information and Communications Technologies and HIV/AIDS." In Scholastica Kimaryo, Joseph O. Okpaku Sr., Anne Githuku-Shongwe, and Joseph Feeney, eds., *Turning a Crisis into an Opportunity: Strategies for Scaling Up the National Response to the HIV/AIDS Pandemic in Lesotho.* New Rochelle, N.Y.: Third Press Publishers.

Pigato, Miria. 2001. "Information and Communication Technology, Poverty and Development in Sub-Saharan Africa and South Asia." Africa Region Working Paper Series 20. World Bank, Washington, D.C.

Sawe, David. 2003. "African Government without Borders: Integration & Process Change for Customer-Centric Services." Microsoft Government Leaders' Forum, September 16, Rome.

Tanzania Ministry of Communications and Transport. 2003. "National Information and Communications Technologies Policy." Dar es Salaam.

Terrab, M. 2002. "Telecom Reform: The Moroccan Case. Knowledge for Development—MENA." World Bank, Global Information and Communication Technologies Department, Washington, D.C.

University of Dar es Salaam. 1995. "Information Technology Masterplan for the Development of Administrative Information Systems and Data Communication Infrastructure." Dar es Salaam.

Wilhelm, Vera, and Susanne Mueller. 2003. "The Ingredients of Capacity Enhancement: Three Case Studies in Telecommunications." WBI Working Paper. World Bank Institute, Washington, D.C.

World Bank. 2004a. "Scaling Up Poverty Reduction: Conceptual Framework." World Bank, Washington, D.C.

————. 2004b. *World Bank Group Experience in Telecommunications Sector Reform: A Decade's Achievements and Efforts Made.* Washington, D.C.

————. 2004c. *World Development Indicators 2004.* Washington, D.C.: World Bank.

World Markets Research Centre. February 2003a. "Telecoms Country Report: Botswana." London.

————. February 2003b. "Telecoms Country Report: Tanzania." London.

PART Three

Delivering Services
to Poor People

7

Equity Building Society
Scaling Up Microfinance in Kenya

TAMARA COOK

Equity Building Society (Equity) is a homegrown success story that has only recently attracted international attention. Equity's beginning 20 years ago was inspired by an entrepreneurial vision of the potential demand for financial services by Kenya's underserved, low-income population. Despite high hopes for serving this market, Equity's first 10 years were characterized by a difficult environment, fierce competition, and a lack of institutional knowledge of how to operate a profitable financial institution. On the verge of collapse in 1993, Equity brought in outside experts

Tamara Cook can be contacted at tcook@worldbank.org. This case study was originally published as "Equity Building Society: A Domestic Financial Institution Scales Up Microfinance," in CGAP (Consultative Group to Assist the Poor) and World Bank Financial Sector Network, *Scaling Up Poverty Reduction: Case Studies in Microfinance,* Washington, D.C., 2004. Changes to the original text are made with the permission of CGAP and the author. The author gratefully acknowledges the Equity Building Society management and staff, and in particular James Mwangi, for access to information, input, and review of the case study, and for building Equity into the institution described in this case study. Martin Holtmann, Anne Folan, and Kristin Hunter, all of CGAP, provided significant comments. In addition, MicroSave provided permission to use information from *Understanding the Rebirth of Equity Building Society in Kenya* cited in the bibliography.

and committed to radical steps to turn the institution around. This commitment led to improved financial performance and increased outreach.

Between 1993 and March 2004 the number of Equity depositors grew from 12,000 to more than 297,000, representing more than 13 percent of all bank accounts in Kenya (figure 7.1). This growth can be attributed to committed staff and leaders, high-quality customer service, effective marketing, low barriers to access (especially compared with traditional commercial banks), appropriate product design, an acceptable enabling environment, and, recently, external support from donors.

Equity's History—From Failure to Success

Equity opened its doors in 1984 with the goal of bringing financial services to ordinary Kenyans, especially those who had no access to the formal banking sector. The founders, who hailed from senior positions in government and business, shaped the institution based on their in-depth understanding of the sociopolitical circumstances, their commitment to the government's rural development policy, and their ability to turn a commercial profit in Kenya.

| FIGURE 7.1 | Number of Deposit Accounts, 1994–2004 (thousands) |

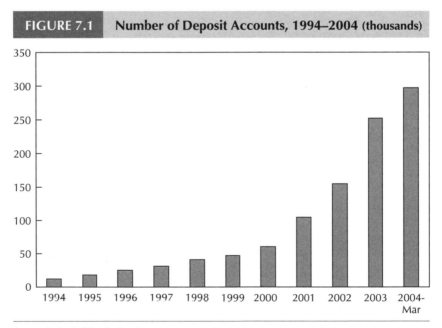

Source: Equity Building Society data.

Taking advantage of new rules allowing Kenyans to open formal, licensed financial institutions, they registered Equity as a building society—an affordable option in terms of license fees and capitalization. The building society legislation influenced Equity's decision to offer savings services and mortgage loans.

Equity realized, however, that it was servicing a microfinance market for low minimum balance deposits and loans that were rarely used for housing. According to one of Equity's founders, J. K. Mwangi, "With very small deposits from short-term depositors, we have never been into serious mortgage finance. . . . We have been 'infringing' on the Societies Act since our inception by lending very small amounts for different purposes and continuing to lobby [the Central Bank of Kenya] about this."

In its early years Equity faced fierce competition from a multitude of locally owned financial institutions that were set up during this time. In contrast to other financial institutions, Equity resisted the temptation to attract deposits from government agencies and state-owned companies. Instead, it mobilized individual clients by one-on-one marketing, entrenching a culture of service excellence from the start. For its first decade of operations, Equity struggled to maintain clients and cover costs, while other small institutions closed and confidence in the sector eroded.

Despite Equity's dedicated efforts in a difficult environment, in 1993 the Central Bank of Kenya reported that the institution was technically insolvent, that board supervision was poor, and that management was inadequate. Nonperforming loans represented 54 percent of Equity's portfolio, and accumulated losses totaled Ksh 33 million ($570,000), against a paid-up capital of Ksh 3 million ($52,000). Deposits were being used to meet operating expenses. Equity's liquidity ratio stood at 5.8 percent, far below the required 20 percent. Despite these problems, the Central Bank of Kenya did not request the closure of Equity, which, for the sake of existing clients committed to the institution, was given a chance to turn itself around.

Realizing the need for a radically new and professional approach to retail banking, Equity's board recruited two experts, a promising banker (who later became the finance director) and an experienced trainer. The goal was to help staff meet the challenges of the new environment, expand marketing, and generally enhance Equity's efforts. The original culture of good customer service and teamwork was revived, and the number of depositors grew.

Efforts to turn Equity around were assisted by a new political atmosphere taking hold in the early 1990s. The country was moving away from a one-party political system, and more freedom was evident. The government allowed employees to bank at financial institutions not under government control, a change in policy that allowed Equity to attract new depositors. Equity also succeeded in mobilizing deposits from churches. Many foreign banks converted from retail to corporate banks during this period, leaving a vacuum in the retail sector. At the same time, banks were closing their rural branches and rationalizing urban branches, generating a flood of new deposits for Equity.

Equity also formalized its commitment to smaller clients in a new mission statement that recognized how financial services contribute to the welfare of clients as well as the national economy. Deposit mobilization increased 40 to 60 percent a year, and profits grew. In August 2003 a marketing and public relations campaign celebrating Equity's 20th anniversary of "providing financial solutions to Kenyans" yielded spectacular increases in the number of new savings accounts.

During its first 15 years, Equity relied entirely on its own resources. It did not solicit assistance from international partners, and none was offered. This began to change in 1999, when Equity undertook two small projects with EU-Micro-Enterprise Support Program and UN Development Programme (UNDP)-MicroStart. Deeper partnerships were developed with Swisscontact and MicroSave-Africa. Both relationships have concentrated on providing local and regional technical expertise and on jointly developing new products and services. MicroSave-Africa in particular helped Equity focus on services and product design based on client demand. This led Equity to redesign its products to reflect a tighter focus on clients. The marketing department was restructured and eventually devoted much more time to market research.

The Financial Deepening Challenge Fund of the U.K. Department for International Development (DFID) supported the launch of Equity's mobile banking program. DFID currently provides technical assistance for specific targets. The UNDP-MicroStart program played a role in upgrading and computerizing the management information system, which has had a tremendous impact on Equity's turnover and portfolio growth. In 2003 Africap, a regional microfinance investment fund of international financial institutions, chose Equity for its first African investment—$1.54 million, accompanied by technical assistance valued at $244,000.

Equity's turnaround is reflected in the improved ratings by the Central Bank of Kenya. After 1993 the overall rating rose to marginal, then to fair, and finally, in 2002, to satisfactory. Equity's board and management were deemed competent to govern and manage a financial institution. Capital adequacy and asset quality were rated satisfactory. Management, earnings, and liquidity were rated as strong. One representative of the Central Bank of Kenya Inspection Team had the following to say about Equity, "EBS [Equity] is a good idea, well executed and giving very good results. We at the Central Bank of Kenya commend the board, management, and staff of EBS for touching many Kenyans positively and not in an exploitative manner. We feel extremely fine that EBS is managed professionally and is giving service appropriately."

In its 2003 report the Central Bank of Kenya rated Equity's overall financial condition as satisfactory. Capital adequacy, earnings, and liquidity were all rated as strong. Asset quality dropped to marginal (19.2 percent portfolio at risk), however, and management was rated as satisfactory. The senior management team takes the report very seriously and is revamping its credit operations and methodologies to improve credit risk management and administration. Improvements to the management information system, which the report found deficient, are also already under way.

Equity's profile from March 2004 shows an institution that is consistently profitable and fully computerized. Equity maintains 15 branches and 25 mobile units. It has 384 staff members, 8 directors, 2,470 shareholders, 297,000 depositors of Ksh 3.8 billion ($50 million), and a loan portfolio of Ksh 2.1 billion ($28 million).

The Challenges of Scaling Up

The dramatic turnaround and scaling up of Equity was not easy or quick. Once Equity regained its footing, it strove to serve a large number of its target clients—economically active low- and medium-income clients. The key challenges facing the institution were enhancing management capacity and internal systems, recruiting and professionalizing staff, improving and expanding branches, bolstering perceptions among current and potential clients, and monitoring the competition.

The management team during the turnaround needed to be reinforced by a second rung of high-quality managers to ensure that proper systems were put in place and properly administered. Before the turnaround all functions of Equity had been handled by senior management, an approach that would not be sustainable if the institution were to grow. The board recognized that managers needed to be recruited from outside the institution in order to bring in the expertise needed in areas such as financial management, marketing, human resource management, and internal controls and auditing. Equity succeeded in recruiting managers from other high-performing businesses in Kenya. It created new departments for these managers to head and delegated substantial responsibilities to them.

The newly created Human Resources Department played an essential role in professionalizing Equity's staff by providing substantial training, recruiting more qualified applicants, and creating intensive orientation programs. Given the huge increase in staff—from 35 in 1993 to 384 in 2004—the essential role of the Human Resources Department must not be underestimated. In addition to recruitment and training, this department also handles staff welfare, including benefits, internal disputes, promotions, and performance incentives.

To leverage the increased staff capacity, Equity needed to enhance its branch infrastructure. Following the turnaround in 1993, Equity acquired new branch offices for almost all of its up-country branches in order to expand client services and professionalize the image of its branches. It also opened new branches in Nairobi and the Central Province. By 2003 Equity had branches in four provinces and plans to open additional branches. These refurbished and new branches have attracted attention and been pivotal in recruiting new clients.

Building on the new look of the branches, Equity's marketing team has implemented an aggressive strategy for establishing Equity as a recognized brand name and preferred financial service provider in Kenya. Prior to this effort, Equity was traditionally associated with a particular tribe and regional area. Because of its classification as a building society, most potential clients did not understand the breadth of financial services it provided. The marketing team conducted market research to develop appropriate products for clients and to determine the most effective way to market the institution and its services.

The new marketing effort has given Equity a competitive edge in attracting new clients, some of them drawn from competitors. Equity has anticipated client needs by improving its services—extending its hours beyond those of traditional banks, for example. According to one branch worker, "Customers love our long opening hours. It became nonsense to tell a woman from Gikomba who came in with a million shillings after 3 o'clock to go back and come again the following day."

Impact Analysis—Success by Several Measures

Financial services help poor and low-income households increase their incomes and build the assets that allow them to mitigate risk; plan for the future; increase food consumption; and invest in education, health, housing, water, and sanitation. Equity decided to focus on poor and low-income clients to help them improve their lives. Although it reaches a wide range of clients, the majority of its clients are smallholder farmers, low-end salaried workers, and micro and small businesses (figure 7.2).

Although average account size is not a perfect indicator of poverty level, it suggests the level of income and accumulated wealth of Equity's clients. As of December 2003, 73 percent of Equity's savings accounts held less than $70 (Equity allows clients to open accounts without a minimum deposit; the figure does not include the 50,000 new accounts to which no deposits had yet been made). Although most of Equity's savings accounts have very low balances, 63 percent of Equity's total deposit

FIGURE 7.2   Distribution of Clients

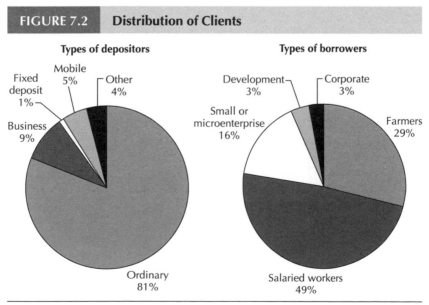

Source: Equity Building Society data.

volume is made up of corporate savings accounts and fixed deposits of more than $1,000 (figure 7.3). Given the volume of clients with small accounts, Equity staff members spend most of their time handling small depositors. Equity is nevertheless able to attract relatively large deposits, which provide stability and often supply longer-term funding.

On the credit side, about 80 percent of outstanding loans have outstanding balances of less than $400, although they account for only about 18 percent of the total outstanding loan balance (figure 7.4). On average, small-scale farmers take out the smallest loans ($132), which are usually evaluated on the basis of projected remittances from the Kenya Tea Development Authority or other farm produce marketing agencies. Farm input loans are also provided for dairy, coffee, and other crops on a smaller scale. Salary-based loans, including education and medical loans, have slightly higher average outstanding balances ($201). Loan repayments are deducted automatically from salaries that are directly deposited into clients' savings accounts at Equity.

Equity's Corporate Branch in Nairobi caters to a higher-end market, in which business loans average $9,500. In contrast, other branches cater to smaller businesses, with an average loan of $922. Equity's business loans have been based on revenues demonstrated by turnover

| FIGURE 7.3 | Distribution of Deposit Size by Number of Depositors and Deposit Balance |

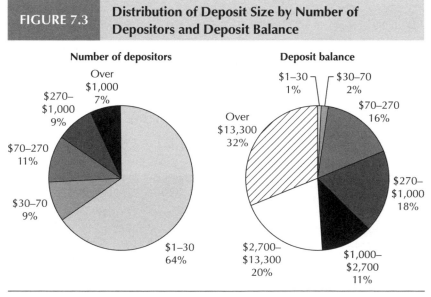

Note: Overdrafts and new accounts with 0 balances have been excluded.
Source: Equity Building Society data.

| FIGURE 7.4 | Average Loan Size by Borrower Category (US$) |

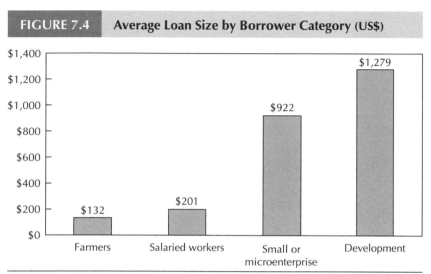

Notes: Corporate loans for medium-size businesses average $9,500.
Development loans are for longer-term construction and land development
provided to all three categories of clients.
Source: Equity Building Society data.

in savings accounts and secured with collateral such as land and vehicles. A new microcredit product targeting even smaller entrepreneurs is slated for pilot testing in 2004. It will require reorientation of credit methodology (including more flexible security requirements with a strict emphasis on the analysis of regular cash flows) and substantial training for credit officers.

In mid-2003 the United Nations Capital Development Fund (UNCDF), in conjunction with Equity's market research team, conducted a qualitative impact assessment of Equity, using tools developed by MicroSave-Africa. The assessment examined the nature, scope, and depth of client impact at the individual, household, and enterprise levels. Twenty-three focus group discussions were conducted at eight rural and urban branches. The findings provided insight into how clients use Equity's services to manage risk and meet household and business cash flow demands. Equity's clients reported using savings and loans to invest in business activities (inventory, salaries); save for the future (education, medical costs); manage household cash flow needs (rent); invest in assets (land, housing, appliances); and cope with crises or special life events (illness, marriages, funerals). Clients reported growth in their incomes and assets over the past 10 years—growth in which Equity appears to have played an important role (box 7.1).

BOX 7.1   The Path to Independence: A Client's Story

Stella Maina (not her real name) opened a savings account with Equity in 1992. She was primarily a housewife and received little money from her husband for subsistence. But she believed that women could control their finances and followed the Swahili adage "haba na haba hujaza kibaba" (little by little, the coins fill up a large bowl).

Stella dreamed of lining up at the credit counter like other clients, but she knew that she had no source of income to repay a loan. During this time, women in Kenya were given more opportunities to contribute to society, including the business sector. With support from her husband, Stella opened a small kiosk in front of their house. The location enabled her to care for the house and the children while running a small business. She was then able to approach Equity for a loan.

The memory of that first loan of Ksh 20,000 ($250) brings a smile to her face. She was able to stock the small neighborhood shop with sugar and flour and all the little things that bring in clients. By 1996 the shop had grown, and she was ready to move to a nearby center in a busy area. Equity supported her expansion with a Ksh 50,000 ($650) loan.

In 1997 Stella seized a golden opportunity to buy out a mini-market to expand her business once again. The loan from Equity was accompanied by business advice from Equity staff that helped her use the loan wisely. Throughout this time, she continued to save and was able to access her next loan at a lower rate because it was secured by a fixed deposit.

In 1999 Stella's business was not performing well, and she was having difficulty repaying her loan. Although Equity took steps to repossess her security, it was willing to listen to her situation and work out a new repayment plan. The plan enabled Stella to focus on the growth and profitability of her business—and ultimately to clear the loan. In 2003 she decided to upgrade the mini-market into a supermarket. Perhaps someday, with the help of Equity, she thinks she might even be able to grow as big as Uchumi, one of the largest local supermarket chains in Kenya.

Equity's support has had an important impact on Stella's business and family. It has allowed her to cover educational and medical expenses, and it has made her more independent, because she understands how to manage her finances and never needs to ask her husband for money. As Stella puts it, "Even others and I have shown that housewives can be good money managers. For the small, Equity is our kind of bank!"

Equity's commitment to increasing educational opportunities and addressing health care needs for Kenyans permeates the institution. Rates on education and medical loans are reduced if the funds are paid directly to the educational institution or medical provider. Equity encourages saving for education through its Super Junior account for children, which includes free banker's checks for school fees for Super Junior account holders. It also offers favorable pricing for others on the issuance of banker's checks required for the payment of school fees. The Jijenge savings account, a monthly contractual savings product, helps clients develop the discipline to save regularly, and it allows clients to borrow against their savings at favorable rates.

Equity's impact can also be viewed in terms of its financial return. By the beginning of 1994, Equity had accumulated losses of Ksh 33 million ($570,000)—a figure that exceeded the Ksh 31 million it held in deposits. After the dramatic shift in its operations in 1994, Equity reported its first profitable year; by 1997 Equity had accumulated profits of Ksh 6 million ($100,000), which grew to Ksh 393 million ($5.2 million) by the end of 2003 (figure 7.5).

In the 1980s and 1990s, Equity's growth was financed entirely by mobilized (domestic) savings and the personal investment of the founders and shareholders. To survive, they had to use their resources

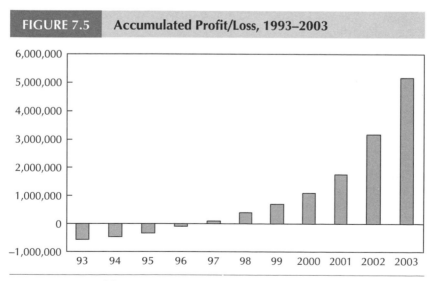

| FIGURE 7.5 | Accumulated Profit/Loss, 1993–2003 |

Note: Currency is Kenya shillings.
Source: Equity Building Society data.

efficiently, especially to dig themselves out from the crisis in 1993. The recent technical assistance and financial investments in Equity are beginning to reap results, but it is too early to measure their full impact.

Driving Factors Behind Equity's Success

Equity's success can be attributed to the dedication of its management and staff, as well as to its ability to innovate and maintain an extremely high level of client focus. Equity's success attracted limited external support in 1999 and more substantial support after 2002, but support followed and reinforced, rather than created, "homegrown" success.

Commitment and Political Economy for Change

Internal and external commitment to change pushed Equity in the right direction. Internally, Equity's management and board governed the institution effectively during a period of generally weak governance in Kenya. The decision to concentrate on the lower end of the market shielded the organization from political influence. In addition, Equity's leadership focused operations in a single region (the Central region) to provide the best services to the target market. This focus helped develop institutional capacities without overstretching management, operations, and internal controls. Equity's recent growth is built on the foundation of high-quality services and strong institutional capacities.

Equity's founding and turnaround benefited from external reforms catalyzed by key decisionmakers who shared Equity's vision. Equity was established under new rules in the 1980s to create locally owned formal financial institutions with the hope that such institutions would serve populations neglected by the commercial banks. In the early 1990s, when Equity was finding its footing again, multiparty democracy and financial and market liberalization helped it attract new clients such as government employees who were (finally) allowed to deposit their salaries directly at financial institutions that were not controlled by the government. Influenced by World Bank and International Monetary Fund financial sector reform requirements and lobbying by building societies (especially Equity), Parliament revised the Building Societies Act to widen the scope of activities they could participate in to include almost all of those permitted under the Banking Act. Finally, regulators sympathetic to Equity's mission granted it one last chance to shape up after the Central Bank of Kenya rated Equity technically insolvent in 1993.

Institutional Innovation

Equity's most important institutional innovation may be the way in which it motivates and sensitizes its staff to embody the company pledge, which commits staff to "take pride in the noble responsibility of offering financial services and solutions, to empower our clients to face the future with dignity and realize our full potential." Equity has a tradition of recruiting young people who are well educated but have little or no experience. Its emphasis is on instilling its corporate culture of customer service. This strategy has worked exceptionally well, as illustrated in the work ethic and culture of Equity's staff. Staff members are encouraged to see their work as a calling, not just a job. This view unites staff around Equity's vision and has the added benefit of inducing them to work long hours to achieve this vision when needed. According to staff, "Equity has been built through our sacrifice."

Equity is committed to bringing financial services to rural clients, who make up 63 percent of its clients but only 28 percent of total deposit volume, given the relatively lower average savings account size of rural clients (figure 7.6). Building on its branches in small towns, in

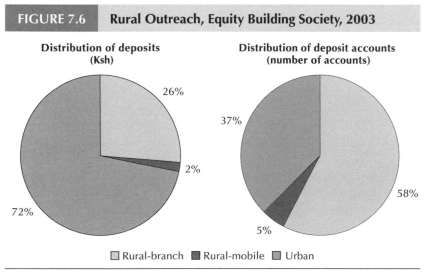

| FIGURE 7.6 | **Rural Outreach, Equity Building Society, 2003** |

Source: Equity Building Society data.

2002 Equity launched mobile banking (with support from DFID) to deliver services deeper into rural areas. The mobile units are designed as stand-alone mini-branches, wholly contained in a fortified sport utility vehicle with satellite connection to the branch, solar power, and a fold-down teller window. The mobile mini-branch drives up near factories when wages are paid, for example, serving clients directly from the vehicle. More often, the vehicles are used to transport two or three staff along with two armed security officers over rough rural roads to rented offices in which Equity opens temporary mobile branches at least one day a week. These minimally equipped rented locations generally have a counter for staff and an area for clients to wait for service. The mobile branch downloads information for clients from the branch onto a laptop (it also brings a hard copy of the data in case there is an electricity shortage or satellite connection with the branch is lost). All transactions by the mobile office are uploaded at the branch before running the close-of-day report.

The mobile branches are a cost-effective way to increase access to rural clients without the significant investment needed to open a full-scale branch. As of December 2003 Equity had 25 mobile units serving 12,161 clients (5 percent of all clients) with an average deposit size of about $100 (a significantly lower average than for other savings products). The mobile units earn a profit, in part by charging a small fee to clients, which is less than the cost of transportation to the nearest branch.

Innovations in information technology can dramatically affect an institution's ability to serve its clients well. For more than 16 years, Equity survived despite the growing difficulties of a manual information system—problems that were amplified at every level of growth. Both clients and staff felt the strain of the manual system as the volume of Equity's business expanded over the years. With support from UNDP-MicroStart, in June 2000 Equity launched its computerized management information system, completing the installation in a record four months. Computerization increased Equity's efficiency in collecting and reporting data and improved its service delivery to clients. The new system allowed Equity to reduce its client turnaround time at the counter from 30–40 minutes to about 5 minutes.

The new computerized system has been a major factor in Equity's growth, demonstrating the importance of technology to banking in general and to high-volume, low-value microfinance in particular. Currently, Equity is investing in a wide area network to connect all of its branches on a real-time basis, in data warehousing to facilitate better reporting and to prepare for potential credit scoring, and in upgrades to its information system to increase functionality and reliability.

Learning and Experimentation

Since its inception Equity has been relentless in focusing on clients. Recently, Equity has marketed itself as "the listening, caring financial partner" in an aggressive marketing campaign that includes radio, newspaper, and television spots. In addition, it continues to rely on the important role of informal marketing by key members of society. Far from just a marketing tool, Equity's slogan represents how it runs its business. In the words of one client, "Equity ni mama ya kila mtu (equity is mother of all). Equity has a very unique way of serving clients; they listen, whether you have money or not. They serve all categories of people."

Learning and experimentation play key roles in Equity's ability to attract and retain clients. Equity uses various mechanisms to solicit client suggestions about current products, needs for new services, and perceptions about Equity. Focus group discussions have helped Equity improve service, and they have demonstrated Equity's "caring" to clients in a tangible way. MicroSave trained Equity's bright and energetic marketing team on designing and conducting these discussions for maximum impact. After new products are launched, MicroSave uses "mystery shoppers" to determine how well staff know and deliver the products. Equity managers have an open-door policy at the branches and head office, and they welcome hearing about clients' experiences with Equity. The owner of a cybercafe cited this open-door policy as one of the reasons she chose to bank with Equity.

Equity's approach to learning from clients contributed to the successful launch of the Jijenge savings account, a contractual savings product intended to help clients "realize their dreams." The account was designed to meet the needs of lower-end clients seeking discipline to save for needs such as school fees, weddings, and household items. Jijenge clients can access low-cost loans of up to 90 percent of their accumulated savings account for urgent needs. The product was designed using client input, pilot tested, refined through discussions between the head office and branch management, and successfully rolled out with support from the marketing team.

External Catalysts

Since 1999 Equity has selectively accessed external resources that propel it toward its mission. Key medium- to long-term donors and investors formed a steering committee to coordinate support and guidance for Equity. This harmonized approach has encouraged complementary inputs by donors and investors and reduced Equity's transactions costs in managing relationships with external supporters. Equity has received technical support and funding from Africap, DFID, the European Union, MicroSave, SwissContact, and UNDP-MicroStart.

Lessons

Equity's more than 20 years of ups and downs offer lessons for institutions, donors, and governments committed to scaling up financial services to the poor.

Lessons for Financial Institutions

- Understanding poor and low-income clients is essential for identifying niche markets, designing appropriate products and services, and developing and maintaining client loyalty.
- Appropriate technology, particularly computerized information systems, can increase efficiency and outreach (by facilitating mobile banking in rural areas, for example).
- Investing in staff training and developing meaningful incentives help staff internalize and be motivated by the vision of the institution, which leads to tangible results.
- Visionary leaders and top management, while vital to the success of an institution, must be supported by strong and technically competent middle management.

Lessons for Donors and Service Providers

- A consortium approach to funding, a medium- to long-term commitment, and an emphasis on results work best.

■ Targeted and timely technical assistance that is consistent with the institution's own vision and objectives can help an institution manage growth. For optimal impact, donors should focus on strategic support.

■ Domestic financial institutions, including nonbank institutions, exhibit great potential as mechanisms for massive outreach. Donors should explore relationships with local partners who have demonstrated the capacity to grow through visionary leadership, existing infrastructure and client base, and brand recognition in local markets.

Lessons for Governments and Policymakers

■ Government can create enabling environments for the creation, proper regulation, and expansion of indigenous financial institutions with the potential for scaling up.

■ Nonbank financial institutions can play an important role in providing services to clients who are not served by banks, if the government gives them the mandate to do so.

Equity's Future: Managing the Sustainability of Scaling Up

At the end of Equity's first decade of operations, it was a defunct building society. During its second decade, Equity emerged as an organization with great potential. As it enters its third decade, Equity needs to transform itself into a high-performance institution. The main challenges will be managing growth, transforming the institutional culture of what was a family-like business, and balancing the enormous success in mobilizing deposits by expanding and improving the quality of lending operations.

Continued growth and expansion will require significant enhancement of Equity's organizational architecture, especially at the governance level (advancing the executive oversight function of the board of directors, for example). Planned changes in lending practices, including greater emphasis on recovery and portfolio quality, will need to be rolled out. Internal controls need to be strengthened, an effective asset liability management system developed, and the staffing and middle management capacity built up. Equity has demonstrated that it is capable of managing these challenges and should continue to scale up its success in the years to come.

BIBLIOGRAPHY

Coetzee, Gerhard, Kamau Kabbucho, and Andrew Mnjama. 2002. *Understanding the Rebirth of Equity Building Society in Kenya.* Nairobi: MicroSave-Africa.

Craig, Kim, and Ruth Goodwin-Groen. 2003. "Donors as Silent Partners in MFI Product Development: MicroSave-Africa and the Equity Building Society in Kenya." CGAP Case Studies in Donor Good Practices 8. World Bank, Consultative Group to Assist the Poor, Washington, D.C.

Equity Building Society. Various dates. *Annual Report and Accounts* for 1999, 2000, 2001, 2002, and 2003 (draft). Nairobi.

———. Various dates. Internal documents. Nairobi.

Negre, Alice, and Josephat Mboya. 2001. "PlaNet Rating: Equity Building Society, Nairobi, Kenya." PlaNet Rating, Paris.

United Nations Development Programme. 2003. *Client Impact Assessment Report.* New York.

Wright, Graham A. N., and James Mwangi. Forthcoming. *Equity Building: Society's Market-Led Approach to Microfinance.* Nairobi: MicroSave.

8

From Donor-sponsored Microfinance Project to Commercial Bank
Increasing the Outreach of the Kenya Rural Enterprise Programme

JOHN NYERERE AND SHARON MAVIALA

Transforming microfinance institutions organized or run by nongovernmental organizations into licensed and regulated commercial institutions is essential for meeting the immense unmet demand from the poor for access to financial services. Such transformation also offers the potential for increasing outreach by commercial sources of funding. K-Rep is the only NGO microfinance institution in Africa that has gone through this process. Its success offers a model for other African microfinance institutions and regulators.

NGOs began providing microfinance services to low-income communities in the 1970s. Among the pioneering institutions were ACCION in Brazil, established in 1973, and Grameen Bank in Bangladesh, established in 1976. By the mid-1970s a few banks in Indonesia had demonstrated that microfinance could be commercially

The authors are deeply grateful to Kimanthi Mutua, managing director of K-Rep Bank Ltd.; Aleke Dondo, managing director of K-Rep Development Agency; John Kashangaki, managing director of K-Rep Advisory Services (Africa) Ltd.; William Steel, senior adviser to the World Bank; and John Kamau, J. M. Mungai, Salome Njeri, and Margaret Wangechi, K-Rep Bank customers, who cheerfully volunteered their time to reveal how K-Rep has transformed their lives.

successful. PRODEM of Bolivia pioneered the transformation of an NGO microfinance institution into a commercial bank.

In Africa many credit unions, rural banks, and NGO projects launched microcredit programs in the 1980s—with varying degrees of success. These programs were generally small and not financially self-sustainable. More recently, the microfinance industry has been growing very rapidly in many African countries, particularly where financial system development has been slowed by war, poor economic performance, or government control.

In Uganda, where the cooperative and rural financial sector had collapsed, commercial banks such as Centenary Bank are providing financial services to more than 45,000 active borrowers and 390,000 savers in both urban and rural areas. In Ethiopia one microfinance institution has a customer base of 214,000 and the "big four" microfinance institutions have a combined portfolio of more than $80 million. In South Africa consumer finance has proliferated since the late 1990s, particularly for poor blacks who previously had no access to credit, with one institution now listed on the Johannesburg Stock Exchange. In Ghana several small rural banks are beginning to take an interest in microfinance. With assistance from K-Rep's consulting arm and support from a number of international development agencies and the government of Ghana, their portfolios are beginning to expand rapidly. In Tanzania there is keen interest in microfinance from a wide range of institutions, which the government is spearheading by developing a suitable policy framework for the growth and development of the sector.

K-Rep and a few other institutions pioneered the concept of microfinance in Kenya, adapting methodologies used elsewhere to suit the African context. As a result of the initial success of these efforts, the concept spread to other institutions, such as the Kenya Women Finance Trust, NCCK-MESP, CAREWEDCO, and Faulu, which together with K-Rep Bank Ltd. now provide microfinance services to more than 200,000 customers across the country.

From USAID Project to NGO: K-Rep's First Decade

In 1984 World Education, Inc., a U.S.-based NGO, launched K-Rep as a five-year project funded by the U.S. Agency for International Development (USAID). Its mission was to provide grants, training, and technical assistance to address the financial, management, and technical needs of NGOs involved in developing small and micro-enterprises. A 1986 USAID evaluation concluded that the project had limited development impact, was not cost effective, and should be terminated at the end of the five years. The report prompted K-Rep founders to question the sustainability of the project. It also raised issues about relying on a single donor for funding and on subgrantees for results.

This crisis—in which the decision to terminate or continue operations depended on one donor—planted the seed for creating a sustainable institution that would focus on long-term strategies to alleviate poverty by delivering microcredit and other financial services. K-Rep's board and management responded to the evaluation with a series of changes that transformed K-Rep from a project to an institution with many of the characteristics it has today. In 1987 the project was registered as WEREP Ltd., a Kenyan-owned company. Right away it began addressing some of the concerns prompted by the audit review. It started seeking other donors to broaden its funding base, and it changed its strategy from being solely a service provider to other NGOs to also developing its own loan portfolio.

Offering Microcredit Products to Customers

After exchange visits with microfinance institutions in Bangladesh and Latin America, K-Rep introduced a group-based lending approach among its partner NGOs and launched its own lending program in September 1990. The program, known as *juhudi*, was modeled after the Grameen Bank's group-based lending method and modified to the Kenyan environment. *Juhudi* loans are co-guaranteed by peer groups of five to seven members (called *watanos*) within larger groups of five to six *watanos* (known as a *kiwas*). Before receiving loans, the groups receive two months of initial training on group dynamics and the importance of savings.[1]

Responding to demand and in an effort to increase outreach, in 1991 K-Rep targeted the indigenous rotating savings and credit schemes, located primarily in rural areas, by lending to groups of borrowers known as *chikolo*. Lending to *chikolo* was initially a cost-effective way of increasing outreach, since a single check was issued to each group, which was then responsible for allocating the loan funds among its members. Between 1994 and 1995, however, repayment rates fell to 90 percent due to a lack of cohesiveness within the larger *chikolo*. As a result, K-Rep changed many features of the scheme and began disbursing loans to individual members within the group. It also encouraged the formation of smaller groups and weekly repayment, in line with the *juhudi* lending approach. These changes were very successful in improving the standards of living of the poor and helping them cope with the financial vulnerability that comes with poverty (box 8.1).

Becoming an NGO

In December 1991 WEREP Ltd. changed its name to the Kenya Rural Enterprise Programme (K-Rep) Ltd. It received its NGO certificate of registration in 1993, in compliance with the NGO Coordination Act of 1990. In 1996 it changed its name to K-Rep Holdings Ltd. In 2000 it became K-Rep Group Ltd.

During the 1990s K-Rep expanded rapidly and began extending larger loans. Delinquency and desertion rates rose, with many customers hesitating to co-guarantee the larger loans. Growth was so rapid that credit officers were unable to effectively manage their portfolios and provide the necessary customer follow-up.

In 1994 changes were made to turn the situation around. K-Rep stopped all wholesale lending to NGOs due to their increasing arrears.

BOX 8.1   Helping the Poor through Credit

John Kamau works as a tailor at the Kenyatta Market. A married man with two children, he has been a K-Rep customer for more than 10 years. "The economy has been bad, affecting our customers and our incomes," he says. "It could have been extremely difficult—or even worse—if I had not been able to access loans to grow my business or even maintain it in these hard economic times."

Margaret Wangehi started her embroidery business in 1990, before she got married. She now has two children. "When I started, I was making $250 a month and it was not sufficient to meet my needs. Today we are able to make more than $1,875, and we can meet our needs and invest. I now have four machines. I employ three ladies and pay them well. The loans have enabled me to expand and start other business, such as importing clothes from Uganda. They have also helped me raise poultry for eggs and broilers. The desire to get a loan makes you think about how to generate income in order to pay it back."

It began to focus on lending directly to low-income communities, merging the administration of the *juhudi* and *chikolo* lending methodologies. It also began to address concerns about its long-term financial sustainability, its growth, its continued dependence on donors, and the appropriateness of the NGO institutional form. Based on what it learned about global trends in microfinance (including the transformation of PRODEM into Banco Sol in Bolivia), K-Rep's board commissioned a feasibility study that led to the articulation of K-Rep's second transformation strategy.

In preparation for this change, K-Rep organized itself into two divisions, the Financial Services Division and the Nonfinancial Services Division. The Financial Services Division administered the microfinance activities. The Nonfinancial Services Division performed research and evaluation of K-Rep's programs and those of the NGOs it supported. In partnership with the government and other institutions, it also conducted studies on the informal sector of the economy. The studies, disseminated through seminars and publications, covered a broad range of issues of interest to K-Rep and similar institutions. The research also helped K-Rep develop new products, understand customers, and improve its methodologies. The Nonfinancial Services Division eventually engaged in activities that were not only strategic but also profitable, and it helped build K-Rep's capacity to enhance outreach of microfinance through consulting services.

Transformation from a project to an NGO with two divisions increased both the number of customers and the institution's ability to reach the poorest of the poor. In just seven years the number of customers increased more than tenfold, and the outstanding loan portfolio and the volume of total assets rose more than sixfold (table 8.1).

K-Rep's outstanding loan portfolio in 1991 stood at $0.6 million. It peaked at $4.6 million in 1995 before K-Rep decided to scale back lending. The decision to cut lending reflected K-Rep's fear that continued rapid growth would conceal the deteriorating quality of the loan portfolio and the difficulty the institution was having raising funds for lending. To consolidate its lending activities in preparation for the transformation to a commercial lending institution, K-Rep wrote off some old NGO loans and implemented a back to basics program in 1996.

Under the back to basics program, K-Rep retrained all of its credit officers, reiterating the institution's philosophy and the fundamentals

TABLE 8.1	Outreach and Performance, 1991–98			
Year	Active loan customers	Outstanding loan portfolio ($)	Average loan size ($)	Total assets ($ millions)
1991	1,253	580,607	463	0.9
1992	2,852	982,991	344	1.2
1993	4,331	1,087,100	251	2.1
1994	5,149	3,514,797	682	5.0
1995	11,137	4,601,441	413	5.0
1996	12,885	4,534,323	351	5.0
1997	10,958	3,622,043	330	5.8
1998	13,150	3,816,639	290	6.3

of microfinance and reemphasizing its commitment to the micro-enterprise sector. Service delivery changes were also introduced to help customers gradually learn the habit of making weekly deposits, and collateral requirements were revised.[2] The outstanding loan portfolio fell to $3.6 million in 1997, then increased gradually to just under $4 million in 1998. By late 1998 total member savings had risen to more than $1.37 million and delinquency rates had fallen drastically, with arrears more than one day past due down from 20.9 percent in 1997 to 9.7 percent. The number of active borrowers rose from 11,137 in 1995 to 13,150 in 1998, while 4,149 members held savings but had no loans. It became clear that increasing savings was both desirable as a service to customers and necessary to finance further scaling up and ensure K-Rep's long-term self-sufficiency.

From NGO to Commercial Bank: K-Rep's Second Decade

K-Rep's vision of transformation to a regulated financial institution began in 1994, when it prepared a concept paper on possible transformation. A 1995 feasibility study funded by the Ford Foundation showed that the idea was indeed viable.

The decision to become a commercial bank was based on several factors that limited K-Rep's potential. First, the NGO structure prevented K-Rep from attracting funds from investors and inhibited the potential benefits of private ownership. Accessing additional sources of capital, particularly from customer savings (by mobilizing deposits), would permit sustained scaling up of credit to the target population.[3] Second, cross-subsidization of nonfinancial services from lending operations was impeding the scaling up of lending activities. In addition, the energy and focus required to oversee the microlending program was overshadowing the potential for new product development and expansion of nonfinancial activities. Third, the savings of K-Rep's customers were deposited in commercial banks, but neither K-Rep nor its customers could access loans from the banks. Transformation to regulated financial institution status was expected to allow K-Rep to redress the inequity of customer savings being lent to wealthier customers of formal banks. Fourth, transformation was believed to help ensure the institutional permanence of K-Rep's microcredit program by improving governance and increasing profitability, giving customers, the government, and partners confidence in the viability and sustainability of microfinance as a long-term solution to tackling poverty.

Initially, some board members had reservations about K-Rep's transformation to a commercial bank.[4] They feared loss of control to new investors with different views, ideas, and missions. Once these reservations were overcome, a nine-person advisory team that included K-Rep's chairman, managing director, and a third board member was formed to manage the transformation process. Their responsibilities included preparing a business plan, presenting the plan to potential investors and the Central Bank of Kenya, educating Central Bank officials on microfinance as a commercial proposition, and negotiating the licensing requirements for the proposed K-Rep Bank.

Creating a New Organizational Structure

The transformation of K-Rep into a commercial bank required major organizational, financial, and operational changes. Three new legal entities were created: K-Rep Group Ltd., a holding company with the largest equity holding in K-Rep Bank; K-Rep Bank Ltd.; and K-Rep Advisory Services (Africa) Ltd. (KAS) (figure 8.1).[5] K-Rep the NGO was renamed the K-Rep Development Agency (KDA).

The K-Rep Group transferred the financial assets, liabilities, and activities of the Financial Services Division to K-Rep Bank. The assets, liabilities, and activities of the Nonfinancial Services Division remained with KDA, which was then split into two divisions, the Microfinance

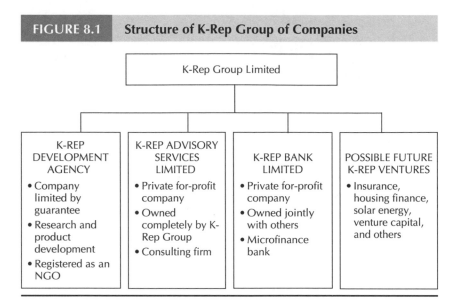

FIGURE 8.1   **Structure of K-Rep Group of Companies**

Research and Innovations Division and the Microfinance Capacity Building Division. In 2001 the assets, liabilities, and activities of the Microfinance Capacity Building Division were assigned to K-Rep Advisory Services, which was incorporated to provide fee-based microfinance consulting services.

The new structure was intended to preserve K-Rep's original vision of providing both financial and nonfinancial services to the poor. Each institution provides different services within the microfinance and microenterprise sector. The institutions within the K-Rep Group are separate legal identities, each with its own board of directors, mission, vision, core values, and organizational culture.

K-Rep Group Ltd. K-Rep Group Ltd. is the holding company of the K-Rep group of companies. It has the largest equity participation in K-Rep Bank (28.8 percent) and wholly owns both subsidiaries in the group (KDA and KAS). The board of directors of the K-Rep Group includes all the directors who were present at the transformation of K-Rep from an NGO to a commercial bank plus one additional director, the managing director of KAS. This board continues to be the mission bearer for the K-Rep Group, ensuring that all of the entities remain united in one overarching mission, "to empower low-income people, promote their participation in the development process, and enhance their quality of life."

K-Rep Development Agency. KDA focuses on product research and innovation, as well as the dissemination of results to the microfinance industry. Its strategy is to identify, test, and develop new microfinance products for the poor that enable them to organize their financial lives and to facilitate partnerships with institutions that can deliver these products and services to poor customers.

KDA has developed a variety of innovative products, including financial service associations (autonomous, user-owned and -managed, self-financed savings and credit schemes); health care financing and insurance for the poor; microloans for smallholder dairy farms; low-cost housing finance; and rural savings mobilization in which rural communities pool savings to access higher returns (by purchasing Treasury bills, for example). KDA shares its findings with all interested parties and helps implement new product lines within development organizations other than K-Rep. Donors continue to support KDA with the understanding that its services are valuable resources for microenterprise development in Africa.

K-Rep Advisory Services (Africa) Ltd. Incorporated in January 2001, KAS is a profit center with its own board of directors and capital structure. As the advisory and consulting arm of the K-Rep Group, KAS provides a wide range of fee-based services, including institutional capacity building and training; project management; and business, financial, and strategic planning for microfinance institutions. It also manages an exposure program that hosts visitors from all over the world. The program gives visitors insight into the activities of the K-Rep Group and other leading microfinance institutions in Kenya. KAS continues to provide management and technical support to the NGOs that K-Rep originally served.

K-Rep Bank Ltd. K-Rep Bank began operations as a full-fledged commercial bank on December 23, 1999. It is the only commercial bank in Kenya licensed and regulated by the Central Bank that caters to low-income communities. It is also the first microfinance NGO in Africa to transform itself into a regulated banking institution. The Bank is headed by Kimanthi Mutua, a founder of K-Rep, who has turned management of the sister institutions over to others in order to devote all of his time to the new bank.

Dealing with Internal and External Obstacles to Transformation

K-Rep's transformation took four years. It forced K-Rep's board to make difficult decisions and to be persistent in looking for investment partners who could help overcome the Central Bank's concerns with the proposal. The board also dealt with a variety of other internal and external issues.

Internal issues. The board had several concerns about commercializing the institution. First and foremost, it feared mission drift—the risk that commercial banking considerations would drive K-Rep Bank to serve higher income customers at the expense of scaling up the mission of serving low-income and poor people. K-Rep needed to resolve the apparent contradiction between financial and social objectives, and it needed to locate partners who shared the original vision and objectives. Becoming a commercial bank also meant that K-Rep would have to submit to the rigors of supervision and prudential guidelines of a regulatory authority with a different tradition and culture.

Before deciding to transform itself into a commercial bank, K-Rep considered other options, including becoming a finance company (a nonbank financial institution) or a cooperative or building society. Workshops were held to solicit the views of external stakeholders, including customers, the government, the Central Bank, and other microfinance stakeholders. At the same time, internal operations were assessed to determine if systems were well grounded and supported by adequate staff capacity and strong leadership capable of operating as a commercial financial institution.

The finance company format initially appeared to offer the best fit, with a lower capital and liquidity requirement than a bank. This option was rejected by the Central Bank, however, which was pursuing a universal banking policy (banking that includes investment services as well as savings and loan services). The cooperative society presented a good option for including customers in the ownership structure, but it had a weak regulatory framework.

External issues. Skeptics and doubters were many, the fiercest being the Central Bank of Kenya, which regulates Kenya's financial industry. Bank officials questioned the viability of microfinance, given its unconventional lending practices and the fact that it had hitherto been a donor-funded activity. They also questioned whether an NGO could own a bank, given that an NGO has no real owners. The Central Bank worried that there would be no one to hold responsible if things went wrong and that allowing this to happen would set a bad precedent. Their concerns were heightened by the fact that five Kenyan banks had recently been placed under Central Bank management due to lack of liquidity and the National Bank of Kenya (the fourth-largest bank in Kenya) had nearly collapsed. The Central Bank therefore decided not to license any new banks, and K-Rep's application was placed on hold.

The Central Bank's reluctance to approve the commercialization of K-Rep was eventually overcome following a lengthy lobbying process. Donors helped central bankers become familiar with microfinance regulation in other countries. With international financial institutions as investors in K-Rep Bank and the requirement that K-Rep provide minimum capital of $6.3 million, the Central Bank agreed to allow the proposal to go forward.[6]

K-Rep had sufficient loans, cash, and other assets to meet the minimum paid-up capital requirement, but it needed at least three other investors to comply with a 25 percent ownership limit per single investor. K-Rep restricted its subscription to $1.82 million in equity and invested $2.06 million in income notes (a convertible debt redeemable after five years); another $4.48 million was offered to other investors. The search for local investors was not successful, as the few that were identified sought returns of more than 20 percent. Donor agencies supported a search for foreign investors, which finally bore fruit.

To resolve both mission drift and investment issues, the board developed criteria for potential investors that would enable K-Rep Bank to achieve its scaling-up objectives and remain true to its mission by fostering a creative tension between financial and social goals. It sought institutional investors who would provide a common ownership profile, avoid pressure for profit maximization, and provide for a managed exit when K-Rep Bank went public. Priority would be given to institutions with social objectives that were similar to K-Rep's. It sought international development finance institutions that would provide access to sizable investments; help influence regulators; and increase public confidence, recognition, and credibility. In addition, it sought investors who understood the microfinance industry and who would counterbalance more commercially oriented investors while facilitating appropriate governance and direction.

To accommodate the interests of founders and staff members, an employee stock ownership program was established as a means of rewarding performance and ensuring support from all K-Rep Group staff members.

The Advisory Team met with nine potential investors for many months. Eventually, it reached agreement with six investors who combined financial expertise with the commitment to K-Rep Bank's social mission (table 8.2).

Meeting the Challenges of Transformation

Despite extensive staff training and systems development and simulation before transformation, a variety of problems was encountered once K-Rep became a commercial bank. The new regulatory requirements and the culture clash between "old" and "new" staff reduced morale. Data migration did not proceed smoothly, and tensions between different groups of shareholders adversely affected governance. The commitment of management and staff to resolving these challenges of transformation was severely tested over a transition period that stretched through the first year of K-Rep Bank's operations.

Complying with Regulatory Requirements

As an NGO, K-Rep Bank had faced no stringent external regulator. Having to meet Central Bank regulatory requirements was a new experience for the institution.

The first inspection visit by the Central Bank, six months after commencement, rated the bank as strong, largely because of its strong capital base. It expressed concern, however, about high operating costs, the slow growth of deposits, low earnings, and difficulties migrating data. Surprisingly, the Central Bank took issue with the fact that K-Rep Group held more than the maximum 25 percent of total shares, even though the 28.8 percent shareholding had been negotiated with the licensing department of the Central Bank. The Central Bank also questioned the legitimacy of K-Rep's field offices, which were not licensed as bank branches and did not meet the minimum requirements in security and infrastructure.

Central Bank inspectors advised K-Rep Bank to book large loans and attract large deposits to increase earnings and reduce costs—advice that contradicted the Bank's fundamental objectives. This demonstrated to K-Rep Bank that more work needed to be done before the Central Bank fully understood microfinance. Management worked to resolve the other issues by formally applying for a waiver of the 25 percent ownership limit, redefining field offices as "marketing offices" rather than formal branches and securing approval for them, lobbying for a Microfinance Regulation Bill (approved by the cabinet

TABLE 8.2	Breakdown of Shareholding in K-Rep Bank, December 1999		
Investor	**Type of institution**	**Initial investment ($ millions)**	**Shareholding (%)**
K-Rep Group	The holding company of a private development group, promoter and founder of the bank	1.82	28.8
Shorebank Incorporated	A U.S.-based private development bank that provides commercial and development loans to small and microenterprises; offers a unique combination of commercial banking expertise and commitment to poverty alleviation through microlending.	0.85	13.4
International Finance Cooperation (IFC)	A public financial institution that is an independent member of the World Bank Group with projects in more than 160 countries. IFC brought financial expertise and political clout that have been critical elements in persuading the Central Bank to approve the bank license.	1.06	16.7
The African Development Bank (AfDB)	A multilateral development agency for Africa, AfDB provides access to funding sources and potential linkages to other countries and programs in the region. It also offers extensive expertise in organizing and governing institutions in Africa.	0.96	15.1

(continued)

TABLE 8.2	Breakdown of Shareholding in K-Rep Bank, December 1999 (*Cont'd*)

Investor	Type of institution	Initial investment ($ millions)	Shareholding (%)
KWA Multipurpose Cooperative Society (ESOP)	A cooperative society, KWA facilitates the ownership of the bank by K-Rep employees and board members and acts as a motivator of employee performance and commitment to the organization in the future.	0.63	10.0
Triodos Doen	A Dutch private bank, Triodos brings microfinance expertise and long-term investment commitment and banking expertise to K-Rep.	0.70	11.0
Netherlands Development Finance Company	A Dutch development bank targeting the expansion of private enterprise in emerging markets; brings funding and expertise in managing banks.	0.32	5.0
Total equity investment		6.33	100.0
K-Rep Group Income Notes		2.06	
Total startup capital		8.39	

in 2004), and encouraging the Central Bank to establish a microfinance unit within its supervision department (set up in early 2004).

Migrating Data and Harmonizing Operations

Despite substantial training and systems simulation, staff members were overwhelmed with new products (such as deposits) and procedures, and the accuracy and timeliness of data were adversely affected by the centralization of the system. The new savings products doubled transaction volumes. K-Rep Bank was initially licensed to operate only one branch. K-Rep's head office therefore assumed the accounting and recordkeeping functions that had previously been spread out over more than 17 field offices. The distance of many field offices from the head office presented a serious challenge, however: transactions had to be booked at the head office and accounts closed daily, but data transfer from the field offices took several days to reach the head office.

So that these urgent problems would not continue to divert management's attention away from business development, management decided to hire consultants to address the problem, train staff, and restructure the process of data migration. While this action resolved the problems within six months, it also increased the cost of operations. The reduction in profitability below the projections in the business plan and past performance became a cause of concern to the Central Bank and to K-Rep Bank's board.

Strengthening Governance

The new regulatory environment was more stringent about governance. Board members represented diverse shareholder interests. Representatives of international financial institutions changed frequently, had limited understanding of microfinance, and mistook the transformation difficulties to mean that microfinance was not profitable. They supported the Central Bank's recommendations for nonmicrofinance products to improve profitability. Some board members became involved in details of management rather than formulating policy, assisting management, and directing the institution.

The resulting tensions led to mistrust between management and the board, diversion of energies from productive activities, and loss of confidence. Following consultations with investors, the situation was resolved by replacing some of the people who had represented investors on the board. The board brought in a mix of professionals who represented broad interests, understood microfinance, and shared common objectives. It also addressed tensions at the board level by ensuring that other directors were trained and exposed to the dynamics of microfinance.

Independent board directors who did not represent institutional investors were invited to join the board to provide a broader perspective and different experience. Initially, the KWA (the investment vehicle through which staff members in the K-Rep Group of Companies own an equity stake in K-Rep Bank) did not have a board representative. KWA shares were originally designated as nonvoting shares, to prevent possible board intrusion by staff. The category was changed to ordinary shares in 2003, and one of the "independent" directors was allowed to represent KWA when it established a trust to manage the employee stock ownership program.

Combining Corporate Cultures and Maintaining Staff Morale

Difficult decisions had to be made in determining which board and staff members would move to the new K-Rep Bank and which would remain with the NGO (KDA). Staff who were not asked to join the bank felt insecure, as they were not convinced that KDA would survive. Some of those who did move to the Bank were not convinced of the viability or necessity of transformation—especially after the difficulties encountered in the first few months. At the board level only two directors moved to the K-Rep Bank board. The others felt left out of an institution they had helped to establish.

During the first three months of bank operations, productivity decreased. To handle regulatory and banking operations requirements, K-Rep Bank hired traditional bankers to run functions (front and back office operations, clearing functions, compliance, treasury management) that required competencies that existing staff lacked. To attract the new staff, the bank had to pay salaries that were higher than those they paid existing staff. The new staff came in with a new culture, and it tended to look down on the old microfinance staff. For their part, the old staff disdained the new staff and their lack of microfinance knowledge.

Two different and seemingly diametrically opposed working cultures emerged. The commercial bankers were less sympathetic to microfinance customers. They focused more on conventional banking practice and adherence to strict procedural rules and regulations. In contrast, the original staff were more sympathetic to their poor customers and embraced microfinance best practices. The resulting culture conflicts and personality clashes slowed operations and polarized K-Rep Bank. The tension, however, presented an excellent opportunity for creating a new culture that embraced the best of both sets of values.

K-Rep Bank held meetings to bring staff together to discuss the issues affecting them. Professional bankers were taken into the field to learn about microfinance; former NGO staff members were sent to banks as tellers and clerks to give them a feel for traditional banking. Training activities were carried out across cadres rather than across disciplines, which would have increased the gap between the professional bankers and the former NGO staff. Some of the old staff who could not take up the new challenges were transferred to KDA; other staff members, old and new, who could not adjust were let go. It took time before the two groups worked harmoniously.

To overcome feelings of having being left out, staff and board members who did not move to the bank were given a sense of ownership in it through equity participation through the employee stock option program. The new organizational structure also provided an opportunity to give new responsibilities to board members who did not move to the K-Rep Bank board. Coupled with a biannual get-together of all staff and board members of the K-Rep Group, these measures helped maintain K-Rep as one family with a single development vision that is being pursued through different objectives and corporate entities.

Avoiding Mission Drift

To demonstrate its commitment to serving the poor, K-Rep Bank located its headquarters in Kawangware, one of the largest slums in Nairobi. It also undertook corporate social responsibility activities, such as supporting school activities, local theaters, and women's groups located near customers' homes.

K-Rep Bank encountered many challenges with respect to mission drift, despite having prepared for the problem. After the first inspection visit, regulators and some board members urged the bank to move into more profitable lending activities. Some of the new staff from the banking sector tried hard to instil conventional lending practices that would exclude poor customers. Had the board and top management not included key proponents, it would have found it difficult to overcome these challenges. In the event, K-Rep Bank managed to maintain its mission.

The nature of K-Rep Bank's product did not change after transformation, although new loan and savings products were introduced. The Bank continues to target poor and low-income people. Both before and after transformation, the average loan size was less than $500 (exceptions were 1994 and 2001). The average size of a first loan is $263; the average deposit size is $247.

How Did Transformation Affect Scaling Up, Services, and Customers?

K-Rep quickly achieved its primary objective in scaling up, tripling its outreach in its first four years as a commercial bank (table 8.3).

Impact on Scaling Up

Despite teething problems in the first two years, K-Rep increased the number of loan customers considerably. Growth skyrocketed in 2002, when the number of loan customers rose more than 70 percent, and it continued in 2003. The loan portfolio quadrupled, rising from $4.7 million in 2000 to $20.4 million in 2003. Although some of this increase came from nonpoor customers, the number of poor customers was three times as high in 2003 as it was before transformation. The ability to accept savings brought in new customers, many of them poor.

This phenomenal growth in outreach is due in part to increased marketing activities by K-Rep Bank. The much publicized opening of

| TABLE 8.3 | Client Outreach Before and After Transformation, 1991–2003 |

Year	Active customers With loans	Active customers With savings	Loan portfolio ($ thousands)	Average loan size ($)	Deposits ($ thousands)	Average deposit size ($)	Total assets ($ millions)
Before transformation (NGO)							
1991	1,253	0	581	463	0	0	0.9
1992	2,852	0	983	345	0	0	1.2
1993	4,331	0	1,087	251	0	0	2.1
1994	5,149	0	3,515	683	0	0	5.0
1995	11,137	0	4,601	413	0	0	5.0
1996	12,885	0	4,534	352	0	0	5.0
1997	10,958	0	3,622	331	0	0	5.8
1998	13,150	0	3,817	290	0	0	6.3
1999	13,636	0	3,228	237	0	0	6.3
After transformation (commercial bank)							
2000	17,139	19,863	4,718	275	3,512	177	12.64
2001	22,659	28,584	9,458	417	5,377	188	15.42
2002	38,739	46,969	14,535	375	10,779	230	22.00
2003	45,379	62,643	20,389	449	15,481	247	28.58

its Mombasa branch two years after K-Rep Bank's launch demonstrated viability and strength. Today customers can access K-Rep's services through 27 field marketing offices located in market centers and small towns across the country.

The K-Rep Group's outreach has also been enhanced through the development focus of KDA, particularly through its support in developing and disseminating the financial service association model. By late 2003, KDA had established 67 financial service associations, half in arid areas. The institutions had some 48,000 shareholders, most of whom use the association to save and withdraw when needed, and an outstanding loan portfolio of $0.5 million. Other projects supported by KDA—in HIV/AIDS, agriculture, health care, and low-cost housing—reach another 9,000 poor people, largely in rural areas.

Impact on Products and Services

Transformation led to several new banking products, including individual loans, wholesale loans, bank overdrafts, consumer loans, and health loans. The new products have permitted the bank to accommodate more group-based customers, as well as new customers, including small and medium-size enterprises, which were targeted as a source of new deposits. Deposit instruments include passbook savings, which are attractive to the poor, and time deposits, used to mobilize savings from small and medium-size enterprises, among others. The success of these products and management's commitment to work through the teething problems have enabled K-Rep Bank to move from the 27th to the 5th largest bank in Kenya in just three years.[7]

Loan products. K-Rep Bank continues to offer group-based lending to individual members for a maximum of 24 months, charging an interest rate that is higher than that on standard commercial bank loans. Repayment frequency may be daily, weekly, or monthly. An important principle of this method is the graduated loan size: subsequent loans are larger and for longer periods, based on a customer's ability to repay.

Before transformation K-Rep offered only group-based loans (the *juhudi* and *chikolo* products had been merged). The group loan product did not change as a result of transformation, but the proportion of group-based loans was reduced to diversify risks. Although the share of group-based lending in the portfolio decreased from 81 percent to 49 percent, volume grew—from $3.7 million in 2000 to $10.1 million in 2003 (table 8.4).

TABLE 8.4	Breakdown of K-Rep Bank's Loan Portfolio in December 1999–2002			
	1999	2000	2001	2002
Group-based loans (US$ mil)	3,743	5,769	8,443	10,197
% of Total	81	63	45	49
Wholesale loans (US$ mil)	–	2,861	3,609	6,604
% of Total	0	31	19	32
Individual & other loans (US$ mil)	863	574	6,863	4,088
% of Total	19	6	36	20
Total portfolio (US$ mil)	4,606	9,204	18,915	20,890

As a commercial bank K-Rep has been able to expand its credit products to cater to both conventional customers and customers from its core market who have outgrown the group-based method. Individual loans are issued to customers within the group structure but are not co-guaranteed by group members. K-Rep Bank also offers individual loans to customers who have grown their businesses, have substantial savings, and have at least three years of successful repayment experience with K-Rep Bank. Previously, such customers would have had to seek loans from commercial financial institutions, with little chance of success.

K-Rep Bank also now offers traditional collateral-based individual lending to new customers and a credit product, known as *Kati-Kati*, for individual entrepreneurs with high-potential businesses and credit needs that exceed $1,250. Overdraft facilities are available for current account holders—a standard banking product positioned competitively with other commercial banks and aimed at attracting small business accounts as a source of funds.

After transformation the outstanding loan portfolio grew nearly 200 percent, from $4.6 million in 1999 to $9.2 million in 2000, $18.9 million in 2001, and $20.9 million in 2002. The primary focus remains on the poor: 80 percent of the loan portfolio continues to represent loans advanced to microenterprises through the group-based loan products.

Savings products. One key objective of transformation was to mobilize a larger volume of deposits. A study of customers and noncustomers within the target population was conducted in 1996 to determine the level of interest in opening savings accounts. It revealed that the majority of respondents (92 percent of entrepreneurs and 86 percent of nonentrepreneurs) were willing to open a savings account. Their interests, in order of importance, were access to credit, low minimum balance, proximity, good customer relations, fast service, and competitive interest rates.

Before its transformation K-Rep could use only compulsory savings as security for its loans. K-Rep Bank now offers five main kinds of savings products: group savings accounts,[8] standard savings accounts (for voluntary savings), children's accounts,[9] current/checking accounts, and term/fixed-deposit accounts.

During the first year after transformation, K-Rep Bank attracted $3.5 million in deposits, most from group savings held at other banks. By the end of 2003 deposits had grown substantially, to $15.5 million, mobilized from a wide spectrum of customers. Despite this growth K-Rep Bank has a funding gap, which it covers with lines of credit. The vast majority (96 percent) of K-Rep Bank's depositors are microsavers whose savings balances average less than $247. Savings by this group account for 38 percent of total deposits. Depositors with balances of more than $13,000 contributed 39 percent of deposits as of the end of 2003 (table 8.5).

Other services. Transformation has enabled K-Rep Bank to offer services other than credit and saving services, including traditional banking services such as current accounts. In January 2000 K-Rep Bank had no current accounts; by the end of the year it had mobilized more than $590,000. Check transactions are now commonplace, offering

TABLE 8.5	Average Deposit Sizes for K-Rep Bank Customers as of December 2003			
Deposit size ($)	Customers	Share of total (%)	Amount ($ thousands)	Share of total (%)
Less than 650	60,267	96	5,861	38
650–1,300	1,605	3	1,480	10
1,300–6,500	634	1	1,601	10
6,500–13,000	58	0	508	3
Above 13,000	79	0	6,054	39
Total	**62,643**	**100**	**15,504**	**100**

convenience and integrating the poor into the monetary transaction world.

Together with KAS, K-Rep Bank is developing additional structured financing services. One initiative helps customers start a community telephone business. KAS works in partnership with a community phone distribution company in structuring the financing, training the business owners, and marketing the product; K-Rep Bank provides loans of $1,000–$1,400, repayable in six months. As of March 2004, six months after the initiative began in earnest, 421 mobile phone sets had been sold, with K-Rep Bank customers forming the vast majority of owners.

Interest rates. Because its funds came from grants during the 1990s K-Rep Bank was able to offer its group-based loans at an average annual interest rate of 33 percent—comparable to commercial bank lending rates, despite the relatively high operational costs of microfinance. Despite the higher cost of commercially sourced funds after transformation, K-Rep Bank was able to reduce interest rates to 31 percent in 2001 and to 30 percent in 2002. These rates were higher than commercial bank rates, which averaged 14.5 percent in 2004.

Before transformation K-Rep did not offer wholesale or term loans because its mandate as an NGO did not extend to doing so. As a commercial bank it has been able to offer these products. The average interest rate fell from 25 percent in 2000 to 14 percent in 2003—from slightly above to comparable to commercial bank rates.[10] The cost of finance to customers has thus been declining (at least in nominal terms) as access to credit has expanded.

Impact on Customers

K-Rep Bank has maintained its focus on providing financial services to poor customers, especially women, who would not normally be able to access commercial sources of finance (box 8.2). Although nonpoor customers were added in order to facilitate scaling up, the overwhelming majority of K-Rep's customers are still using the group-based products designed for low-income customers. In 2002, 11,000 first-time borrowers participated in *juhudi* and *chikolo* groups. More than 52 percent of customers surveyed in 2003 were women, and 12 percent were categorized as very poor. More than 70 percent of the 48,000 shareholders in financial service associations are considered poor, and 49 percent are women.

| BOX 8.2 | **How Did K-Rep's Transformation Affect Poor People in Kenya?** |

Becoming a bank has helped K-Rep change the lives of Kenyans like Margaret Wangechi and J. M. Mungai. "After K-Rep became a bank, it is not like before," says Margaret. "Things have become easier. Products are many, interest rates have gone down, and paying back loans has been easier than before. The savings product enables us to keep money for a rainy day. K-Rep does not require large deposit for opening accounts. It is a bank for the small people and responds to their needs."

J. M. Mungai, an entrepreneur, agrees. "I cannot shift to another bank, because the services I receive from K-Rep are good. My questions are responded to, there are no threats when you have delays in repayment, no harassments, and we operate according to our mutual agreement. We also keep savings for emergency loans to help the group member so that we sort each other out in case of unforeseen circumstances."

What Accounts for K-Rep's Success?

K-Rep's experience in searching for a model of sustainability while maintaining a consistent focus on the poor provides some lessons on the factors that lead to successful scaling up and implementation of institutional change. Each transformation stage—from project to NGO and then from NGO to a corporate enterprise—presented challenges of implementation. Institutional commitment, a political economy for change, innovation, and adaptation, a learning culture, and external catalysts helped the institution adapt successfully.

Commitment and a Political Economy for Change

Transformation threatened the ability of K-Rep to remain focused on poverty by forcing it to deal with external investors and the Central Bank and to hire staff who came from a purely commercial banking culture. A key success factor was management's readiness to recognize problems and treat them as challenges to be overcome and its commitment to the institution's original mission of serving the poor. This is reflected in the back to basics program of staff training and the fact that women represent more than 60 percent of K-Rep Bank's current borrowers.

External factors helped create a political economy for change. The government's growing focus on developing a strategy for poverty reduction helped increase officials' receptivity to microfinance. International partners played a catalytic role through donor-supported activities such as sponsored trips to successful microfinance institutions in South America and Asia and through the willingness of international financial institutions and investors to provide capital and help persuade the Central Bank of the viability of K-Rep as a commercial institution. Public and private institutions worked together to hold seminars to develop guidelines that would make it easier for other microfinance institutions to join the financial sector.

K-Rep's commitment to reducing poverty is demonstrated by the decision to appoint a seasoned leader from within (rather than an outside banking professional) to launch and manage K-Rep Bank. Under his leadership K-Rep Bank developed new products to attract deposits from new types of customers, such as small and medium-size enterprises, while innovating to better serve poor customers. More important, he and other key board members convinced doubters that microfinance methodologies could be modified to work in a viable commercial business.

The K-Rep Group has also demonstrated its commitment to reducing poverty through the collaborative efforts of its subsidiaries. They have developed and introduced new financial products for the poor and shared K-Rep's experience in alleviating poverty with institutions in Kenya and abroad.

K-Rep's group-based model proved an important success factor by making beneficiaries active participants in the loan methodology and rewarding their successful application of a hitherto unmarketable asset: their social capital. In the initial stages, even customers were apprehensive, as it was inconceivable that loans could be accessed without collateral or any form of tangible commitment. As time went by and the group methodology was strengthened with the participation of communities, visible improvements in living standards and microenterprises raised credibility among the poor. The success of K-Rep Bank remains based on a participatory process involving both staff and customers.

The regulatory environment was a significant barrier to transformation. The board chairman and the managing director identified and targeted the governor of the Central Bank as a key person critical to the success of transformation. They built a solid working relationship, confidence, and trust with the governor, and they educated Central Bank officers on microfinance.

Management continued these efforts after transformation to a bank, helping regulators better understand the mechanics of microfinance. They successfully responded to issues raised by regulators without requiring special exemptions, thereby instilling credibility in microfinance. As a result of their efforts, the Central Bank established a microfinance unit and legislation was drafted that will make it easier for NGO microfinance institutions to become commercial institutions and for the Central Bank to regulate the industry. Other microfinance institutions are developing institutional frameworks for self-regulation that will help them prevent disreputable players from bringing the industry into disrepute.

Institutional Innovation

K-Rep's innovativeness created an environment that has helped other microfinance institutions and encouraged other stakeholders to support the industry. From the beginning K-Rep established a tradition of experimenting with credit methodologies to adapt international best practices to the Kenyan context. Institutions such as the Equity Building Society (with more than Ksh 2.5 billion in deposits) and the Cooperative Bank of Kenya, Ltd. (with more than Ksh 20 billion in deposits) have joined the industry with a commercial orientation toward microfinance.

Whereas the first institutional transformation, from project to NGO, involved internalizing and taking direct control of services in a single institutional transformation, the second transformation required externalizing different functions into separate but interrelated organizations. The holding company organizational design provided for legal ownership and created structures that are distinct but depend on each other in pursuit of common objectives. Creating three separate institutions was an innovative approach to resolving potentially divergent objectives by allowing each institution to specialize while working toward the overall group mission of serving the poor.

Governance of the new organizational structure was complicated by having to bring in external investors to meet regulatory requirements. An important success factor was the establishment by the board and management of guidelines that enabled suitable partners to be selected. Even this proved insufficient, and additional efforts were needed to ensure that the individuals representing these partners on the board had the right skills and understanding to help the new institution fulfil its dual mission of achieving financial sustainability and reaching the poor.

Institutional change such as the one that K-Rep went through can be devastating to staff morale. K-Rep introduced innovations to deal with two human resource problems: allocation of staff between the "new" bank and the "old" NGO, and the clash of culture between existing staff and new staff brought in to help address Central Bank compliance issues. Inclusion of K-Rep pioneers and staff in ownership of the new venture through an employee stock ownership program helped reinforce their commitment. Management's humility and readiness to take corrective action were critical with respect to new staff. They recognized the need to recruit seasoned bankers in order to quickly meet Central Bank requirements. To prevent the inevitable clash of cultures between the two groups from impeding the institution's effectiveness, they provided special training to familiarize "new" staff with microfinance methodologies and K-Rep's mission and "old" staff with commercial banking techniques. The result is a blended workforce that enables K-Rep Bank to serve low-income communities in a profitable, commercial way.

Learning and Experimentation

K-Rep is a learning organization. Very quickly learning that its initial integrated model of packaging nonfinancial services with finance might not attain the objectives of outreach and sustainability, it shifted to a minimalist model focusing on developing financial products appropriate for its target population of the poor. It then experimented with new products, such as the *juhudi* credit scheme (an adaptation of Grameen Bank methodology).

A study of K-Rep's initial phase as a service wholesaler indicates that the objectives of the microfinance institutions it assisted were not consistent with its objectives of outreach and sustainability. In response, it began providing financial services directly to the poor.

In response to waning donor interest and funding, K-Rep embarked on a second transformation. It had learned from experience that microfinance was not only viable but also sustainable if the right models were implemented. Seeking to combine the drive for profit as a commercial bank with its mission to serve the poor is its latest venture in learning and experimentation.

Learning was institutionalized by the creation of a research and development department that tests products and adapts them to customer requirements. The department laid the foundation for the eventual emergence of KDA, whose mandate continues to be experimentation, leaving K-Rep Bank free to focus on earning profits while the other subsidiaries undertake the risks of experimentation and pass on the benefits. This model has facilitated outreach in terms of learning: the advisory and consulting services provided by KAS have enabled the K-Rep Group to extend its experience to more than 15 countries in Africa.

Conclusions and Key Lessons

Institutional transformation for scaling up is a difficult undertaking that requires focused leadership and commitment from donors, government, and other stakeholders. K-Rep's experience demonstrates that it is possible to pursue a profit objective and achieve social objectives by carefully structuring the organization to create the tensions and cross-fertilization necessary for adaptation and innovation in ever-changing circumstances.

To succeed in proactively overcoming obstacles in the external environment—and eventually changing it—institutions need to marshal a broad coalition of partners that can facilitate the process of change. Important external catalysts in K-Rep's success included microfinance institutions in other countries, which demonstrated the feasibility of the model and of transformation into a commercial enterprise; donors, who helped educate regulators; and investment partners, who provided credibility and lobbied for change.

A key lesson is the need for institutions to remain dynamic and relevant to the environment in which they operate. K-Rep was initially one entity, but when the time was right the board made the somewhat painful decision to spin off the Financial Services Division into what is now K-Rep Bank. Later it decided to spin off the Microfinance Capacity Building Division into what is now K-Rep Advisory Services. This flexibility demonstrates that K-Rep's leadership is bold and dynamic enough to let go of projects incubated by KDA. KDA is currently piloting several projects, including financial services associations. KAS is incubating a community phone project. K-Rep's structure is designed in such a way that when the board feels that the time is right, it could institutionalize these projects, spinning them off to become K-Rep entities in their own right.

The creation of K-Rep Bank, according to Kimanthi Mutua, one of the leaders of K-Rep's transformations, was not an end but a means of fulfilling an ongoing mission. His comment represents a suitable mantra for leaders engaged in the institutional development process. K-Rep is in the process of a major consolidation. That process will likely be followed by further transformations to take advantage of the skills and potential of the three institutions in the group and to harmonize their mission and objectives in order to maximize benefits. Scaling up and transformation are part of a continuous evolutionary process.

The leadership of institutions seeking to replicate this kind of scaling up and transformation needs to understand and foresee the implications of doing so, particularly with respect to the structures needed to maintain the institution's core mission and objectives. In Kenya the Cooperative Bank is successfully scaling up its microfinance activities as a result of increased awareness and a regulatory climate that is now more conducive to microfinance. K-Rep benefited from establishing a research and development department that would keep it informed of trends in the industry and experiment. The importance of testing new methodologies locally and adapting them to suit local circumstances requires the creation of an organization that is capable of learning both internally and externally.

Government support is critical in establishing a regulatory climate that will allow sustainable microfinance institutions to service poor customers. Donors should be understanding, flexible, and accommodative of the unique situations institutions operate in. They should provide opportunities that seek to empower leadership, forging linkages to international networks to expose managers to best practices and nurture leadership capabilities. In the initial stages, to build the confidence of other partners, donors could assume the risks of investments for social reasons. For their part, leaders must continuously transform institutions and develop their human resource capacities in response to customer demands and the changing environment.

Annex. K-Rep Bank Performance Indicators

TABLE 8.6	Comparative Financial Results

Microfinance institution: K-Rep Bank
Peer Group: Africa, large microfinance institutions
Year of data: Dec. 31, 2003, 2002
Currency: U.S. dollars (Exchange rate: 76.15)

	K-Rep Bank 12/31/2003	K-Rep Bank 12/31/2002	Average for Africa large microfinance institutions 12/31/2002	Average for all microfinance institutions 12/31/2002
Institutional characteristics				
Age (years)	12	11	9	8
Offices	28	27	27	19
Total assets ($ millions)	28.6	22.0	29.0	7.9
Employees	264	195	278	120
Financing structure				
Capital / assets ratio (%)	32.1	36.5	25 0	42.7
Debt / equity ratio (%)	2.1	1.7	4.5	1.9
Deposits to loans (%)	40.4	37.5	95.1	15.3
Deposits to total assets (%)	28.8	24.8	45.2	12.3
Gross loan portfolio/ total assets (%)	71.3	66.1	59.6	70.9
Commercial funding liabilities ratio (%)	110.2	63.3	114.8	70.9
Outreach indicators				
Women borrowers (%)	52 .0	52.0	48.2	62.9
Average outstanding loan size ($)	449	373	423	532
Active borrowers	45,379	38,739	30,341	15,553
Voluntary savers	17,269	8,230	82,052	3,345
Total savers	62,648	46,969	112,393	18,898
Total savings/deposits ($ millions)	15.5	10.8		
Voluntary savings ($ millions)	8.2	5.4	11.8	1.2
Average savings balance per saver ($)	131	721	131	269
Average deposit per saver ($)	247	230		

(continued)

TABLE 8.6	Comparative Financial Results (*Cont'd*)			
	K-Rep Bank 12/31/2003	**K-Rep Bank 12/31/2002**	**Average for Africa large microfinance institutions 12/31/2002**	**Average for all microfinance institutions 12/31/2002**
Gross loan portfolio ($ millions)	20.4	14.5	15.3	5.3
Macroeconomic indicators				
Deposit rate (%)	3.4	5.5	1.7	4.7
Inflation rate (%)	2.7	2.0	4.6	7.4
Overall financial performance				
Adjusted return to assets (%)	2.3	2.5	3.7	0.1
Adjusted return to equity (%)	6.9	6.1	14.1	2.3
Operational self-sufficiency (%)	132.0	133.0	148.0	115.0
Financial self-sufficiency (%)	126.0	127.0	133.0	104.0
Operating income				
Adjusted profit margin (%)	16.9	21.5	21.5	0.3
Adjusted financial revenue ratio (%)	20.2	20.2	18.6	27.1
Nominal yield on gross portfolio (%)	28.9	31.2	31.9	39.8
Real yield on gross portfolio (%)	25.6	28.7	29.8	33.6
Adjusted total expense ratio (%)	15.3	15.8	14.4	27.7
Adjustment financial expense ratio (%)	3.6	2.8	2.9	6.2
Loan loss provision expense ratio (%)	1.9	0.8	1.0	1.8
Adjusted personnel expense ratio (%)	5.8	6.9	5.8	10.5
Adjusted administrative expense ratio (%)	2.7	5.4	4.8	8.4
Adjusted operating expense ratio (%)	10.5	12.2	10.6	19.1
Adjustment expense ratio (%)	0.7	0.6	0.5	1.8

(continued)

TABLE 8.6	Comparative Financial Results (*Cont'd*)			
	K-Rep Bank 12/31/2003	**K-Rep Bank 12/31/2002**	**Average for Africa large microfinance institutions 12/31/2002**	**Average for all microfinance institutions 12/31/2002**
Efficiency and productivity indicators				
Adjusted operating expense/loan portfolio (%)	15.0	19.0	21.4	29.4
Adjusted personnel expense/loan portfolio (%)	8.4	10.6	11.3	16.1
Cost per borrower ($)	63	72	69	142
Productivity				
Borrowers per staff member	172	199	138	121
Loan officer productivity (number of loan clients per loan officer)	388.0	421	447	284
Voluntary savers per staff member	237	42	324	34
Personnel allocation ratio (%)	44.3	47.2	34.4	48.3
Risk and liquidity				
Share of portfolio at risk > 30 days (%)	6.7	2.3	2.1	2.8
Share of portfolio at risk > 90 days (%)	5.5	1.1	1.4	1.5
Risk coverage[a]	0.4	0.8	0.7	1.3
Nonearning liquid assets as a share of total assets (%)	9.8	5.6	7.6	8.6

a. Ratio loan loss reserves to outstanding balances of loans in arrears over 30 days.

BIBLIOGRAPHY

Market Intelligence. 2003. *Market Intelligence Banking Survey.* [www.mi.co.ke/index.asp].

9

Reducing Poverty through Free Primary Education
Learning from the Experiences of Kenya, Lesotho, Malawi, and Uganda

ROGER AVENSTRUP

During the 1990s many countries—including Kenya, Lesotho, Malawi, and Uganda—eliminated primary school fees in order to provide their people with free primary education. The results were dramatic: by reducing the direct costs to households, all four countries increased enrollments by sizable margins. The challenge these countries now face is to reform their educational systems to accommodate the increase in enrollments so that schools can provide good-quality primary education to all.

The 1990 Jomtien Conference and the Move toward Universal Primary Education

Although some movement toward universal primary education occurred before 1990, the Education for All conference sponsored by the United Nations Educational,

Roger Avenstrup can be contacted at Ravenstrup@hotmail.com. The author thanks Xiaoyan Liang and Søren Nellemann for their assistance. The case study was developed on the basis of documentation and interviews with the political, executive, and administrative levels of the ministries responsible for basic education in the four countries and with representatives of donor agencies in each country, and through video conferences.

227

Scientific, and Cultural Organization (UNESCO) and held in Jomtien, Thailand, in 1990 was the impetus for spurring policy development and implementation on a wider scale. Policymakers attending the conference reached the conclusion that the goal of universal basic education could be reached only by making primary education free (that is, eliminating compulsory school fees).

The Jomtien conference confirmed that universal primary education is one of the most beneficial interventions for reducing poverty. By providing pupils with literacy and numeracy, life skills, and a basic general knowledge of health, nutrition, and society, universal primary education lays a foundation for skills training and further education. By increasing knowledge of health and family life, universal primary education empowers women to reduce the burden of care provision, thereby improving their possibilities for employment. Primary education also empowers children who would otherwise be engaged as child workers or be socially marginalized (such as street kids). Most important, universal primary education helps break the cycle of poverty by creating a new generation that is functionally literate and numerate.

In the wake of the Jomtien conference, it became evident that a major constraint on universal primary education in Sub-Saharan Africa was the cost of schooling, which poor families could not afford. The direct costs of primary education could include school fees, parent-paid supplements to teacher salaries, textbooks, materials, examinations, uniforms, meals, sports and cultural activities, and contributions requested by local schools. These costs were high even before policies introduced as part of structural adjustment programs forced poor families to shoulder a larger share of them. In addition to the direct costs of schooling, households bear an indirect cost: the lost value of children's work at home, in the fields, fishing, or in family or other businesses.

Poor families in Sub-Saharan Africa have had to decide which child—if any—is their best investment in education.[1] Poor parents are willing to invest their children's time in education if they think they will gain something useful from their investment. However, they need to be convinced that their children have access to good-quality education—relevant knowledge and skills taught well in a conducive learning environment. If they are not convinced that their children are getting an appropriate education, they lose confidence in the system and pull their children out.

Similarities and Differences in the Educational Systems and Resources of the Four Countries

The educational systems in Kenya, Lesotho, Malawi, and Uganda share several key features. In all four countries free primary education was a central issue in the political discussions that led to multiparty elections or the transition to multiparty democracy. In Kenya, Lesotho, and Malawi, free primary education was the key election issue on which the new governments came into power. In Uganda free primary education has been a central issue in presidential elections.

All four countries have, or have had until recently, high poverty rates, high illiteracy rates, and low enrollment and completion rates (table 9.1). All face great challenges in improving conditions in remote areas, where poverty is worst and access to education is limited. All were heavily centralized and burdened by a cumbersome bureaucracy, all lacked fiscal discipline, and all provided too few resources to primary education relative to other education sub-sectors, especially tertiary education.

TABLE 9.1	Poverty Indicators in Kenya, Lesotho, Malawi, and Uganda, 2002			
	Kenya	**Lesotho**	**Malawi**	**Uganda**
Share of population living on less than $1 a day (%)	23	43	42	24
Share of population undernourished (%)	22	18	25	23
Fertility rate	4.3	4.3	6.1	6.1
Infant mortality rate (per 1,000 live births)	78.0	91.0	114.0	83.0
Under-5 mortality rate (per 1,000)	120.0	132.0	183.0	141.0
Life expectancy (years)	46	38	38	43
Illiteracy rate (% ages 15+)	16.7	16.1	38.2	32.0
Female illiteracy rate (% ages 15+)	22.7	6.1	51.3	42.0

Source: UNDP 2003; UNESCO Institute for Statistics; UNICEF 2003b; World Bank 2003d.

GDP and Foreign Debt Obligations

Economic indicators in the four countries differ widely (table 9.2).[2] Malawi, the poorest of the four countries, is constrained by both very low per capita GDP ($570) and a very high ratio of foreign debt to GDP (88 percent). Uganda, with much higher per capita GDP ($1,490) and a much lower ratio of foreign debt to GDP (21 percent), is better able to fund free primary education. Lesotho has a relatively high share of foreign debt to GDP (51 percent), but it has the highest per capita GDP of the four countries ($2,420).

Gross Enrollment Rates

The starting points for free primary education in each country were also different. In Kenya, Lesotho, and Uganda, enrollment and completion rates rose in the late 1980s but declined in the 1990s. In Kenya the gross enrollment rate rose from 50 percent in 1963 to 115 percent in 1987 before dropping to 85 percent in 1995. In 1990–91 the net enrollment rate fell to 73 percent in Lesotho and 50 percent in Malawi. The decline was due largely to civil unrest, drought, and the drop in household income caused by falling prices for agricultural exports, unemployment, and devaluations, all of which led to rising prices.

TABLE 9.2	Economic Profiles of Kenya, Lesotho, Malawi, and Uganda, 2000			
	Kenya	Lesotho	Malawi	Uganda
Primary school enrollment before introduction of free primary education (percentage of total)	68.5 (2002)	68.0 (1999)	60.0 (1993)	63.0 (1996)
Population (millions)	30.7	2.0	11.0	22.8
Population density (people per square kilometer)	53	58	109	118
GDP (billions of dollars)	11.4	0.8	1.7	5.7
GDP per capita (US dollars)	347	493	165	253
Foreign debt (billions of dollars)	4.4	0.4	1.5	1.2
Foreign debt as share of GDP	39	51	88	21
Foreign aid per capita (US dollars)	14.7	26.2	38.1	34.0

Source: World Bank 2003d; UNDP 2003; UNESCO Institute of Statistics.

Although weakened by structural adjustment programs and other factors, some of the organizational structures for education (directorates for teacher education, educational management information systems) were in place in Kenya, Lesotho, and Uganda. In contrast, Malawi lacked many of these structures.

The Role of Religious Institutions

Christian denominations have influence on the educational system in all four countries, but in different ways and to varying degrees. In Malawi government-assisted schools and unassisted private schools were merged into the same category, and the government took over all financing of both types of institutions. The situation was most difficult in Lesotho, where 90 percent of the schools are owned by several different denominations. The government paid teachers' salaries and covered the cost of some materials, but it had little say in running the schools. Free primary education meant that proprietors would lose income from parents, school committees would have a greater say in running the schools, and the government would gain more control over the system.

Providing Universal Primary Education

Before 1990 very few educational systems in Sub-Saharan Africa targeted education for all—or had the financial resources to do so. Instead, they provided services targeted mostly toward urban middle-class pupils. Educational systems were bureaucratic; curricula were oriented toward the urban middle class; teacher training programs were long; support and professional development was limited; development and provision of textbooks was slow; and gender, regional, and social inequities were large.

Malawi was the first of these four countries to start working toward universal primary education, abolishing school fees grade by grade beginning in 1991. The policy was not strongly enforced, however. Enrollments did not rise as much as policymakers had hoped because local authorities demanded that parents contribute to special funds, such as sports and development funds, and they insisted on making school uniforms mandatory. The funds collected were not always accountable.

Because the policy was controversial, it was not widely and openly discussed until the 1994 election campaign, when it became a key issue. Immediately after the election, the president himself announced the introduction of free primary education for all grades. One of the first actions of the new government was the convening of a national stakeholder conference on free primary education in May 1994. Free primary education was launched for all grades in September 1994.

Kenya had a longstanding policy that education should be provided by the government, and the 2001 Student's Act stated that the government should provide free and compulsory education. Only in 2002, however, when the newly elected government adopted free primary education as its core tenet, was such a program possible. It became a reality in 2003.

Although the Lesotho Constitution states that primary education should be free and compulsory, fees were high and enrollments low. The minister of education was about to introduce universal primary education in 1993 when political instability made the step impossible. Church control of the education system and an unstable political environment prevented the government from exercising clear leadership on the issue. After political stability was restored through new elections, the new prime minister, who was the former minister of education, championed the cause, announcing in April 1999 that primary education would be free. The ministry had only eight months to develop policy and plan implementation.

In Uganda a universal primary education policy was in place as early as 1987, a Policy Review Commission had been created, and an education white paper had been written, but the question of how to implement universal primary education remained open. Unrest, lack of resources, lack of a focus on primary education, and political constraints on how far policy implementation could go prevented turning the policy into reality. The president wrote the program into a government manifesto in December 1996. Given the short interval before implementation, the template for universal primary education had to be developed as an emergency plan.

In all four countries there was acknowledgment of the need for free primary education, but political opposition—and in some cases political instability—prevented full implementation until the issue was championed at the highest level and supported by a democratically elected majority party. In all four countries the adoption of universal free primary education was triggered by political demand rather than by rational planning processes. In each case the trigger event was a dynamic, top-level political initiative that left very little time for planning, forcing countries to adopt a "ready, fire, aim" approach. In addition, unreliable statistics and the unpredictability of educational reform processes made it extremely difficult to come up with accurate projections of needs and responses.

In some countries there was little time even to negotiate with stakeholders. Malawi held a two-day National Policy Symposium and launched a mass media campaign to mobilize the public. Uganda used radio spots to communicate with the public, but consultation was insufficient. Learning from both countries, Lesotho used the traditional form of community consultation (*pitsos*) to negotiate the policy widely, in addition to using the mass media. In Kenya a stakeholder forum was created to forge strong ownership. It set up a task force and reported to the government.

In all four countries the political opposition and skeptics among education professionals cast doubt on the proposal and attempted to weaken the social contract between the government and the people. The main criticisms included questions about the financial sustainability of free primary education given the limits of the country's resources, concerns about the lack of adequate planning, and condemnation of the government's failure to move rapidly enough to provide what it promised. People with vested interests in the former system exploited policy gaps and potential ambiguities. In Uganda, for example, some local politicians told parents not to send lunch with their children and then criticized the government for not providing school lunches. In Lesotho school owners do not openly disagree with free primary education, but they complain that their possibilities for raising funds for additional school activities are now severely limited. In all four countries quality issues were raised in the political discussion.

Among education professionals, skepticism stemmed largely from concerns over declines in quality (soaring pupil-to-teacher, pupil-to-textbook, and pupil-to-classroom ratios) and the need to field teachers and paraprofessionals trained through short courses. The lack of administrative capacity to deal with the changes is a professional as much as a political issue.

Mobilizing Budget Support

All four countries have had to deal with implementing free primary education starting in the middle of a budget year or with a change of government, and thus without sufficient extra budgets. Mobilizing the funding needed was possible only because of top political backing that empowered the ministries of education—and other ministries—to adjust their budgets to meet the demand.

The launching of free primary education revealed just how poorly prepared the educational systems had been to provide education for all, despite longstanding policy rhetoric. It showed that primary education had been given far too little priority in education budgeting and far too little attention by education administrations, and that structural changes, capacity development, and major changes in organizational culture and attitude at all levels were needed.

Attracting Donor Support

It was apparent from the outset that free primary education would need support from donors or lending agencies if it were to succeed. However, in each country some international agencies were skeptical or reluctant and joined in the initial criticism about lack of planning, the decline in quality, the lack of capacity, and the near impossibility that the programs could be sustained. When one institution (such as the United Nations Children's Fund [UNICEF], Ireland Aid, the Department for International Development, or the World Bank) followed the government's lead and made interim arrangements, others soon followed.

Developing the Entire Education Sector

Policymakers in all four countries acknowledge that universal primary education can be sustainable only if it is part of a whole-sector approach to developing the educational system. All of the countries started with primary education and are now in the process of looking at the whole sector. Plans are already being made on how to meet the increase in the demand for postprimary education by providing increased skills training and formal secondary education.

Differences in Coverage

In all four countries the government is responsible for covering the costs of facilities, textbooks, materials, and salaries. All have set targets and devised strategies to reduce the pupil-to-classroom, pupil-to-teacher, and pupil-to-textbook ratios. All allow private schools to exist side by side with the public system, but schools are not permitted to participate in the free primary education system if they raise fees from parents.

In Lesotho the government reimburses schools directly for book rental fees, stationery, building maintenance, and meals, with the money paid directly to the schools. Teachers' salaries, materials, and other inputs covered by the government are paid only to schools that agree not to demand fees from parents. In principle, churches wishing to raise fees from parents can opt out of the free primary education system. However, few schools could afford to do so.

In Kenya the government provides per capita grants to schools. Feeding programs are provided only in the arid and semi-arid areas.

Malawi abolished all forms of fees, and it made school uniforms optional. The government pays for facilities, teachers, textbooks, and materials.

In Uganda the government first agreed to provide free primary education for up to four children per family in the form of a capitation grant to the school. In families that included both boys and girls, at least two of the four children had to be girls, and children with special educational needs were given priority over other children.[3] Fifty percent of educational spending was to be spent on instructional materials; 30 percent on extracurricular activities, such as sports and culture; 15 percent on maintenance and utilities; and 5 percent on administration. In 2003 the government expanded the policy to include all children, and it made school uniforms optional.

Responding to the Overwhelming Public Response to Universal Primary Education: Dealing with Access Shock

In all four countries the sudden large influx of pupils led to "access shock": overcrowded classrooms; double and triple shifts; acute shortages of teachers, textbooks, and materials; and large numbers of over-age pupils who should have been taking adult education classes instead of sitting beside 6- to 13-year-olds. In Lesotho, Malawi, and Uganda, the public response was far greater than anticipated or than the system could comfortably handle. Grade 1 enrollment in Lesotho rose 75 percent in the first year, from 67,777 to 118,843—16 percent more than the ministry had projected—increasing overall primary education enrollment 11 percent. In Malawi enrollment rose 68 percent, from just under 2 million in 1993 to 3.2 million in 1994, the first year of full free primary education, yielding a gross enrollment rate of 108 percent. Enrollment increased 68 percent in Uganda as well, rising from 3.4 to 5.7 million in one year, bringing the gross enrollment rate to 123 percent.

The increase in Kenya was much more modest. Although policymakers had projected an increase of 25 percent, enrollment rose by just 22 percent, from 5.9 to 7.2 million, yielding a gross enrollment rate of 104 percent. The Ministry of Education believes it underestimated constraining factors, such as distance to school and the drift toward private schools.

Increasing the Number of Textbooks and Teachers

Lending and donor agencies made some provision for the immediate procurement of textbooks and materials, but their efforts were inadequate to meet the need. To recruit new teachers, distance teacher education programs were put in place as quickly as possible. In Lesotho and Uganda paraprofessionals were also trained. The number of teachers increased rapidly, but lack of experience in dealing with human resource limitations, high academic entry requirements, lack of flexibility at the training institutions, inefficient curriculum coverage, and poor quality assurance created many difficulties in developing programs appropriate to the task. In Malawi some teachers trained by a private distance education college in South Africa were so poorly prepared that they had to be retrained. There was insufficient shared knowledge to use different approaches for training teachers—for example, taking in low-level entry teachers and training them on the job to teach successive grades year by year, starting with grade 1, as some projects did successfully.

Changing the Teaching Paradigm to Reflect Education for All

The paradigm of teaching has to change to one that is appropriate for education for all—that is, a system in which all social groups and environments are represented and classes include pupils of various abilities, including pupils with special educational needs, as indicated by the 1994 Salamanca Declaration on inclusive education. Teachers also need to be trained to teach large classes, or multigrade classes in small schools, and mixed age groups of adult classes in primary schools.

Although former approaches are being adapted through the introduction of new methodologies, very few national teacher education systems in Sub-Saharan Africa have been completely redesigned on the basis of a paradigm of inclusive education for all.

Building New Classrooms

To meet the need for additional classrooms, lending and donor agencies expedited procurement and contracting. However, inadequate local building capacity and quality control, as well as the need to complete construction before the rainy season, meant that not enough good-quality classrooms were built. Lesotho purchased tents as temporary classrooms, using military helicopters to transport the tents and school equipment to remote areas.

All four countries want communities to be more involved in school management and see involvement in construction as an opportunity for this. Without proper training of the community and local craftspeople, however, the results may not be cost effective, as the experience of Uganda shows. Mobilizing and training the community to perform skilled functions, not just manual labor tasks, takes time and resources and yields medium- to long-term rather than immediate payoffs.

Kenya and Lesotho are currently learning from the experience of district-based support to primary education in Tanzania that more substantial, long-lasting community involvement is necessary. In Malawi the current government finds it politically awkward to support community mobilization for construction because it objected to citizens performing unpaid manual labor for the government while it was the minority party.

Dealing with the Effects of HIV/AIDS

The greatest short- to medium-term challenge in all four countries is managing the impact of HIV/AIDS. Recent impact studies are providing better knowledge of the problem and revealing that both the complexity and the scale of impact are greater than first believed. In Lesotho 51 percent of females between the ages of 15 and 24 are HIV-positive, and the country is on the verge of negative population growth. In Malawi average life expectancy is down to 38 years.

Many issues are immediate. Provisions need to be made for dealing with the loss of teachers who die of AIDS or who are absent from classrooms because they are ill or need to care for sick family members. The financial impact of the increase in sick leave and pensions needs to be absorbed. Programs need to be created to deal with the increasing number of orphans, who are at risk of not receiving an education, a risk that is particularly high for girls. All pupils and teachers need to receive effective HIV/AIDS education that teaches them how to avoid contracting HIV and how to provide support for those who are infected.[4] Responding to problems caused by HIV/AIDS requires improved planning and greater administrative and managerial efficiency to meet the challenge posed by the decline in human resources at a time when capacity is already stretched.

Responding to Other Challenges

In all four countries other reforms occurred concurrently with free primary education or are about to be implemented, causing other changes in education administration to be put on hold. All four countries were in the process of revising their curricula, for example. Providing large numbers of additional textbooks based on the old curricula was costly, given that new books based on the new curricula would be needed shortly. Development of the new curricula was problematic, too, as the process began before free primary education was introduced and did not reflect the new paradigm of education for all. Uganda is already drafting its revised curricula, and Lesotho will soon begin doing so. The introduction of local languages, a necessary reform in Kenya, Malawi, and Uganda, represents another challenge.

Reforms outside the education sector include civil service reforms, local government reforms and decentralization, Poverty Reduction Strategy Papers, and Medium-Term Expenditure Frameworks. Although these reforms are intended to ultimately improve transparency, accountability, and efficiency and make strategies more pro-poor, they have exacerbated uncertainty and increased the administrative burden during a period of extreme flux and overstretched administrative capacity. One of the stabilizing factors for the education sector has been the fact that the Poverty Reduction Strategy Papers and Medium-Term Expenditure Frameworks protect funds for basic education and, together with a sectorwide program, make it easier to channel donor funding to the sector. The Heavily Indebted Poor Countries (HIPC) Initiative has been very important for ensuring that primary education gets as much funding as possible from the national budget, but education ministries are still dependent on strong advocacy for education in the ministry of finance for smooth day-to-day running.

What Has Happened to Education Outcomes?

Major improvements in education outcomes have occurred in all four countries: as a result of increased access, more children are in school and more children are staying in school (table 9.3).

Enrollment Is Up

Enrollment rose 240 percent over six years in Uganda, 78 percent over eight years in Malawi, 15 percent over three years in Lesotho, and 14 percent in one year in Kenya. Free primary education is having a positive effect on the poor, who are much better represented than they had been. In Uganda, for example, enrollment of the poorest quintile is almost on a par with that of the richest.

Confidence in Government and the Education System Has Increased

Free primary education has increased public trust in government and the education system, and it has freed up private resources that had been spent on primary education.[5] According to the 2002 Domestic Household Survey of Malawi, 79 percent of respondents felt that their children were learning more than they had before free primary education was introduced (84 percent of the lowest income quintile and 66 percent of the highest quintile), 65 percent felt that teaching had improved, and 82 percent felt that the quality of infrastructure and the supply of textbooks had improved. These results suggest that education has improved, but not necessarily that the quality of education is satisfactory. The challenge of improving quality is a major concern in all four countries.

Cooperation between Line Ministries Is Closer

In addition to raising educational access, the provision of free primary education has forced education ministries in all four countries to make changes in their structure, organization, organizational culture, administration, and finance. Line ministries now work more closely together,

TABLE 9.3 Education Outcomes in Kenya, Lesotho, Malawi, and Uganda Before and After Introduction of Free Primary Education

	Kenya		Lesotho		Malawi		Uganda	
	2002	2003	1999	2001/02	1993	2001	1996	2002
Number of pupils	6,314,600	6,917,553	364,951	418,668	1,795,451	3,187,835	3,068,625	7,354,153
Percent female	49.5 (2000)	49.7	51.6	50.2	47.2	48.6	46.3	49.4
Number of teachers	197,331	178,037	8,225	8,762	26,333	53,444	81,564	139,484
Pupil-to-teacher ratio	32	38.9	44.4	47.8	68	60	37.6	52.7
Number of classrooms	186,000	191,088	5,618	6,544	17,471	31,989	45,115	69,990
Pupil-to-classroom ratio	34	36	65	64	103	100	68	105
Share of national budget to education	35	39	24	28[a]	11.4	24.6	16.4[b]	23.5
Education budget ($ millions)	361.15	(est) 419.61	82.84	113.93[a]	50	(rec.) 59	164.4	272.3
Primary education budget as share of total education budget (%)	54.4	56.7	36[c]	40[c]	49	56	65.6	66.5

a. 2003.
b. 1998/99.
c. Includes secondary education.
Source: National education statistics; UNESCO Institute for Statistics.

reflecting the fact that free primary education is not only an education sector issue but involves players from many sectors. Cooperation among donors, and between donors and ministries, has also increased, a natural result of sharing the same goals and agreeing to be task- rather than status-oriented.

Many Challenges Remain

The reforms have produced some unintended and unforeseen negative consequences. Quality issues are of concern in all four countries. Some indications suggest that overcrowding in classrooms is pushing out pupils with special needs, an issue that needs further research. Survival rates (the percentage of a cohort of children enrolled in the first grade expected to reach each successive grade) have also been affected: in Uganda, for example, the survival rate has dropped to 37 percent, down from 59 percent before the introduction of free primary education. The extent of other possible negative outcomes, such as teacher stress and burn-out, as reflected in absenteeism or physical violence, will be revealed only by additional research.

Improving completion rates. To increase primary school completion rates, especially on-time completion, policymakers need to recognize why they are low and craft policies that respond accordingly. In rural areas of Kenya, early marriage accounts for 12 percent of dropouts (17 percent in urban areas), school being "uninteresting" accounts for 12 percent (4 percent in urban areas), and examination failure accounts for 10 percent (5 percent in rural areas). Before free primary education was introduced, costs were a major constraint throughout the country, accounting for 30 percent of dropouts in rural areas and 34 percent in urban areas. In Malawi 26 percent of primary school dropouts leave school because of lack of money, 28 percent because they need to work, 43.5 percent because they "had enough school," 17.6 percent because of disability or illness, and 14 percent because they failed or had to repeat a grade (Malawi National Statistics Office 2003). Despite free primary education, costs are a factor for 55 percent of dropouts in Uganda. Twelve percent of pupils drop out because they need to work, 25 percent because they "had enough school," 13 percent because of pregnancy or early marriage, 10 percent because of disability or illness, and 10 percent because they failed or needed to repeat a grade (Uganda Ministry of Education and Sports 2003). The completion rate in Lesotho in 2002 was 77 percent.

Poor quality was not cited as a reason for dropping out in any of the surveys, but some of the reasons classified as "pupil-related," such as failure, "had enough," and disability or illness, may rather be problems arising from poor quality. The fact that in Malawi a third of nonattenders did not attend school at all because of lack of interest may also suggest a problem of quality. These statistics show that school systems are failing to include and educate all pupils.[6]

Reaching more poor and marginalized children. It will take time to make free primary education universal. The top priority is to extend delivery to the most remote areas and to the poorest and most marginalized households, most of which are located in rural areas. The domestic household survey in Malawi revealed that families continue to pay for primary education: 80 percent of households pay for school materials, 70 percent pay for uniforms, 60 percent pay for school development funds, and 33 percent pay for meals at school. The almost 18 percent gap in school attendance between the lowest and highest income quintiles suggests that the direct cost of primary education remains an obstacle for the very poor.

Formal schooling is a resource-intensive mode of education that reaches some social groups more easily than others. Different types of intervention are needed to reach different categories of marginalized children. Uganda provides evening schools and mobile schools as complementary opportunities for primary education. It also offers a basic education program for the urban poor. In Lesotho special measures are needed to reach herd boys in the mountains.

Complementary approaches to primary schooling designed to reach pupils who never entered or who dropped out of school are being piloted and extended in all four countries, with the strong support of NGOs and international organizations such as UNICEF. Alternative basic education programs can complement the formal system and feed into the development of parallel modes of primary education within the umbrella of universal primary education, developing systems that are more suited to the great diversity of African contexts and the varying life circumstances of children.[7]

Improving planning and strengthening legislation. In all four countries planning is improving as a result of increased capacity and experience. Better planning is helping to improve financial projections of what the ultimate cost of free universal primary education will be. The challenge is to make these projections as accurate as possible and use them to obtain the predicted funds necessary to reach free universal primary education by 2015. Both UNESCO and the World Bank have provided the countries with improved financial projection models.

All four countries are discovering the implications of gaps in, or lack of, enabling legislation or regulatory frameworks. Education acts that include free and compulsory primary education for all are needed, as are amendments to existing legislation and regulations that deal with the implications of education for all.

Secrets of Success: Key Factors in Implementing Free Primary Education

What factors appear to facilitate the successful implementation of free primary education?

Top-level Leadership

Where free primary education is a radical departure from the existing system, top-level political leadership in which the president or prime minister takes a leading role, commitment, and stability are needed. A strong consensus and backing are needed at the cabinet level, and the minister of education needs to work closely with the administration. Strong political leadership, commitment, and drive are key factors in overcoming donor reluctance.

The Social Contract

Top-level leaders need to be in close touch with the electorate in order to thwart opposition to or reluctance about free primary education at the political level as well as from within the administration itself. In all four countries, where the social contract between top political leaders and the people has been strong, the result has been dynamic. Stakeholder involvement is also a key factor, since many decisions directly affect parents, teachers, administrators, and others with vested interests. Conflict can be reduced by negotiating tradeoffs and making the terms of free primary education clear to all stakeholders.

Institutional Innovation

Institutional innovation supported by strong and flexible institutions is critical, but it has been very hard to achieve because of conservatism, entrenched attitudes, and the time it takes for innovation to take hold. In Lesotho neither the university nor the teacher training college could be used to train managers or paraprofessional teachers; these tasks were contracted out to the Institute of Management. In Malawi, where four key institutions (the Institute of Education, the Centre for Educational Research and Training, the Institute of Management, and the Directorate of Planning) were already weakened by staff and financing shortfalls, interim programs had to be mobilized through the Ministry of Education. In Uganda the revision of the primary curriculum that had been under way proved not to be viable for universal primary education, and external consultants are now helping the government revise it.

Provision of free primary education is a process that must proceed quickly. If existing institutions and structures cannot change rapidly enough, the onus is on the ministry to make ad hoc arrangements for dealing with what amounts to an emergency situation in the short term. Some processes of institutional development were accelerated to meet the challenge of providing free primary education. In Uganda, for example, an Instructional Materials Unit and a Classroom Construction Unit were established to meet demand, and the Inspectorate was transformed into a standards agency.

In all four countries the process within the ministry has depended on a special task force functioning as an innovation enclave, with subgroups performing specific tasks. These units have demonstrated the greatest degree of institutional innovation. In Kenya special monitoring teams at all levels track progress and problems from headquarters to the local level in order to identify new challenges. Over time there is a need to review such interim structures to determine what is needed over the longer term.

Schools are the backbone institutions of the education system, but innovation at the local level has been insufficient, either because the systems have been too centralized or because of institutional conservatism. Some innovation is taking place, however. All four countries have adopted multigrade teaching in small schools in order to facilitate teacher redeployment. Kenya is also using multigrade classrooms to teach adults. In Uganda the Girls' Education Movement, a project funded by the Forum for African Women Educationalists, mobilizes school-going girls to get their nonattending female peers to come to school. In order to ensure transparency and accountability to the community, Uganda posts information about the disbursement of public funds for primary education on notice boards in schools. All four coun-

tries have increased school attendance by allowing local synchroniza-
tion of the school year with agricultural or fishing cycles, so that pupils
do not have to miss school when they are needed by their families.

Capacity

Two kinds of capacity are needed to provide free primary education.
The first is capacity to deal with the sheer increase in volume and the
pace of that increase. The second is the capacity to develop the new
skills and attitudes needed to implement free education for all and to
initiate decentralization. Motivation and commitment underlie capacity. Without the commitment to do what is needed and the willingness to devote oneself to the task, capacity remains latent. In Malawi,
in particular, malaise in the bureaucracy is negatively affecting capacity.
All four countries have a core group of committed and capable individuals, but widespread institutional capacity is lacking. Capacity-
building programs are now in place in all four countries.

Learning from Experience

The suddenness with which free primary education was launched left
little time for learning from experience and experimentation. Some
countries did have ongoing projects that could be built on, however.
In Kenya the school audit process, which was already under way, provided a foundation for the educational management information system unit, and the Strengthening Primary Education Project (SPRED),
an in-service training program for teachers, provided a model that could
be applied throughout the country. In Malawi the Mathematics and Science Teacher Education Program (MASTEP) provided a model for
teacher development that could be adopted nationwide, and the Education Methods and Advisory Services project provided the foundation
for a teacher development unit.

Three of the countries learned from others when planning their own
transitions. Ugandan officials visited Malawi, the first of the four
countries to implement free primary education; Lesotho officials visited Uganda and Malawi; and Kenyan officials visited Uganda and
Tanzania.[8] Learning also took place through information sharing at
subregional and international conferences and through exchanges of
documentation. After a study visit to Asia, officials in Lesotho adapted
the idea of outsourcing school catering, using the community instead of

commercial caterers to provide school meals.[9] Learning from the experience of others is possible, but adapting programs to the national context is critical.

External Catalysts

Despite the efforts of international agencies and international agreements, the catalyst for change came from inside the four countries, not from outside.[10] External technical assistance supported the change rather than serving as a catalyst. At the national level, donor and lending agencies that took the lead in supporting free primary education acted as catalysts for the donor community as a whole.

Financial Security

Free primary education is possible only when there is cabinet-level and parliamentary agreement about budget allocations to education, particularly to primary education.[11] In addition, the education desk in the Ministry of Finance must have a strong advocate for education, especially for free universal primary education, so that the sector's needs are met despite demands from other sectors. Medium-Term Economic Frameworks, Poverty Reduction Strategy Papers, HIPC debt relief, and a protected envelope for primary education are all needed, given the doubtful prospects for self-sustainability in the medium term. Long-term donor support as well as economic reforms and changes in the global economy will be needed if universal primary education is to be sustainable. Much more intensive support will be needed if universal primary completion is to be reached by 2015.

Decentralization

Implementing free primary education has promoted local development. Building schools has necessitated or stimulated other infrastructural development, such as building roads, water systems, and health facilities. Moving funds directly to schools has tested the ability of local authorities and communities to handle funds. Where communities have been involved in school construction and school management, noticeable improvements have been made.

These changes do not necessarily reflect structural decentralization, since decisionmaking need not be decentralized to involve communities in construction. Free primary education can be a lever for decentralization, but decentralization need not be a lever for free primary education. Whatever the degree of decentralization, free primary education works best when there is a centrally directed or triggered process and strong local ownership.

Communication

Good communication and participation strategies have been widely used and are essential to the process. The use of both mass media and traditional leaders is critical. Poor communication has forced the government to redouble its efforts. All four countries are learning about the need for improvement in this area.

Other Factors

In all four countries the public response to free primary education has been overwhelming, but obstacles to school attendance remain. Although uniforms are no longer compulsory, some parents keep their children at home to avoid the stigma of not being able to afford a uniform. Parents are still expected to provide their children with exercise books and pens, and schools still raise funds for social, cultural, and sporting activities. Demands from schools for contributions are creeping back in, even when the ministry has stated that they should not be requested or must be negotiated first with the community.

Free primary education in Africa is not entirely free: households continue to bear some of the expense.[12] The very poor—such as dispossessed AIDS orphans in urban slums or rural areas, who are not able to contribute anything toward their education—are therefore often excluded from the system. Only completely free education provided in a supportive environment can reach such marginalized groups.

Is Free Primary Education Sustainable?

Is free universal primary education sustainable? The question is framed inappropriately for a rights-based issue, and it is an unproductive way of structuring the debate. Instead, the debate needs to reformulate the question as: "Under what circumstances will free universal primary education be sustainable, and who has responsibility for creating those circumstances?" The discussion would then lead to an appraisal of what sort of national and global society can sustain free universal primary education. Is a disinterested Weberian-style bureaucracy needed? Is managerial efficiency critical? Does the distribution of wealth and power within a country need to be more equitable? Is democracy needed? If so, what sort of democracy? What kind of economy is needed to support free universal primary education—a growth economy, a controlled economy, a liberal economy? What kind of budget allocation is needed across sectors? What level of human resources is needed? Are changes in the global economy required? Is debt relief in developing countries critical to reach free universal primary education? Are pro-poor trade agreements needed? Should protectionist tariff barriers and subsidies be removed?

The governments and people of developing countries can take responsibility only up to a certain level; beyond that, the sustainability of free universal primary education in the developing world is the responsibility of the international community. Developing countries and the international community must each accept their share of responsibility if all the children of Africa are to have good, equitable, free basic education.

Innovative solutions are needed to meet the challenges of providing free universal basic education, particularly given the devastating changes wrought by HIV/AIDS. Ways of thinking that may have been applicable before the pandemic may no longer be useful. Some measures are already being taken, such as bringing back retired teachers and extending the retirement age. Some schools are finding their own solutions to problems. In Kenya, for example, some schools have established day care centers to allow girls entrusted with the care of babies to still be able to attend school.[13]

Lessons

In trying to elicit lessons learned from the experiences in Kenya, Lesotho, Malawi, and Uganda, it is important to recognize that conditions in these countries have changed radically since the early or mid-1990s, when free primary education was initiated. What seemed like the answer to reaching primary education at the time is now at best only one of several strategies needed if universal primary education is to be reached. Policymakers in other countries can nevertheless draw several lessons from these countries' experiences:

■ *Providing free primary education is doable.* Even under difficult circumstances it is possible to implement free primary education. Political, bureaucratic, and professional opposition or reluctance are likely, but free primary education can be achieved even in countries with limited resources.

■ *The decision to provide free primary education is political.* Providing free primary education is primarily a political phenomenon linked to democratization. To succeed, visionary leadership and wide stakeholder consensus are needed. Once free primary education is announced, implementation cannot await other democratization processes, such as local government reform or decentralization. Once begun, it is nonreversible, provided that the social contract with the electorate is kept and funding is sufficient.

■ *Education for all requires a new paradigm of education.* If free primary education is to mean *education* for all and not just attendance at school, the change in the educational paradigm has to be taken seriously from the start. Education for all means that teaching, materials, and assessment have to meet the learning needs of a wide range of mixed-ability, inclusive classes. At the outset and throughout the process, issues of quality need more emphasis, and they take more time to solve than simply relieving parents of the burden of school fees. Given that it takes at least six years of good primary education to establish literacy and numeracy, universal completion with acceptable levels of learning achievement rather than universal access should be the goal.

■ *Decisionmakers can learn from experience.* Although detailed planning is not possible when the period between the pronouncement and the launch of free primary education is short, it is possible to develop overall strategies and to be prepared for flexible action as the process unfolds. Creating "emergency" measures to deal with implementation at the beginning of the process can be helpful, but such measures are difficult to sustain over time. Important lessons from experience include clarifying the scope of free primary education, conducting extensive and intensive stakeholder consultations, specifying everyone's roles, finding ways of dealing with or sidelining intractable institutions until they can be reformed, and working with donors who are willing to lead the way.[14] Learning from the experience of others is possible, but creative adaptation to national context is essential.

■ *Intersector strategies are needed to reach universal primary education.*
HIV/AIDS, which is reducing the supply of teachers and administrators and cutting household income, represents the greatest threat to reaching universal primary education. In the
short- to medium-term, educational systems will need innovative
approaches to human resource development to compensate for
the impact of HIV/AIDS on the teaching profession.[15] Contain-
ment of the HIV/AIDS pandemic alone will not solve the problem
of reaching universal primary education, however. Rising birth
rates will continue to increase the demand for schooling, putting
pressure on already overstretched resources. Making primary education free is only part of the solution to reaching universal primary education. A combination of intersector strategies that deal
with food security, health care, and care of orphans is needed.

■ *Phasing in free primary education grade by grade is easier than
introducing it throughout the system simultaneously—but it still
creates problems.* Policymakers need to be aware of the tradeoffs
between introducing free primary education one grade at a time
(stepped implementation) and adopting a "big bang" approach.
Stepped implementation is slower than the simultaneous
approach, but it gives policymakers time to plan, budget, build
schools, obtain materials, and hire teachers. The experience of
Lesotho reveals the problems with the stepped approach, however. To take advantage of free education, some parents enrolled
children in primary school early (since preschool is not free).
Others held children back to avoid paying fees in the next grade.
In addition, dropouts returned to school and adults enrolled in
large numbers. These inflated enrollments caused bulges in the
system in the fee-free grades. The big bang approach is harder to
manage than the stepped approach, but it provides quick results
and does not create such a big bulge moving through the system.

■ *Innovative solutions are needed to ensure quality and access.* The supply of infrastructure, textbooks, materials, and teachers needs
to be increased rapidly to accommodate the huge increases in
enrollment. Innovative and interim approaches that ensure
good learning are needed in all areas. A variety of complementary educational opportunities is needed to reach very poor people, marginalized groups, and dropouts. Without such measures,
a new generation of dropouts will perpetuate the vicious cycle of
illiteracy.

■ *Implementing universal primary education takes time.* Although Malawi started implementing universal primary education in 1991, it still has a long way to go. The starting point in Kenya and Uganda was much higher, and they are closer to reaching the goal. Lesotho will need at least six years to complete the process. External factors, including the national economy; the support of the international community; the impact of HIV/AIDS; foreign debt, foreign trade conditions, and tariffs; and the state of the global economy all affect the achievement and sustainability of education for all.

■ *The goal of education for all needs to be clearly defined.* Education for all can mean many things. It can mean universal attendance at school, universal completion of primary education (as called for in the Millennium Development Goals), or universal completion of primary education with optimal achievement. Policymakers need to clarify which goal they are seeking in order to estimate the human and financial resources required and the changes to be made if the goal is to be reached by 2015.

■ *Reaching universal primary education is not enough to break the cycle of poverty.* Removing the burden of paying for education increases the number of poor children who attend school, helping to break the poverty cycle. Free primary education must therefore be supported nationally and internationally until the returns to households and the national economy are large enough so that international support is no longer needed. However, achieving universal primary education is not enough to break the cycle of poverty on its own. Improved health services and nutrition are needed to mitigate the impact of HIV/AIDS and preserve human resources for the development of the country. Further, only changes to the unjust conditions of the global economy can create the circumstances in which the cycle of poverty can finally be broken by the widespread employment of a labor force well prepared for training by good-quality basic education.

BIBLIOGRAPHY

Abagi, O., and G. Odipo. 1997. "Efficiency of Primary Education in Kenya: Situational Analysis and Implications for Educational Reform." Discussion Paper 004/97. Institute of Policy Analysis and Research, Nairobi.

Ablo, E., and R. Reinikka. 1998. "Do Budgets Really Matter? Evidence from Public Spending on Education and Health in Uganda." Policy Research Working Paper 1926. World Bank, Washington, D.C.

Bah-Layla, Ibrahima. 2003. "Implementing EFA: Lessons Emerging from the Devel-
    opment of a Civil Society Capacity Building Program in Sub-Saharan Africa."
    United Nations Educational, Scientific and Cultural Organization, Paris.
Bennell, P., and E. Kadzamira. 2002. "The Impact of the Aids Epidemic on Pri-
    mary and Secondary School Teachers and University Staff in Malawi." Uni-
    versity of Sussex, Brighton, U.K.
Cohen, D. 1999. "The HIV Epidemic and the Education Sector in Sub-Saharan
    Africa." Issue Paper 32. United Nations Development Program, New York.
Dachi, H., and R. Garrett. 2003. "Child Labour and Its Impact on Children's Access
    to and Participation in Primary Education. A Case Study from Tanzania." Edu-
    cational Paper 48. Department for International Development, London.
Dattra-Mitra, J. 2001. *Uganda—Country Assistance Evaluation: Policy, Participation,
    People.* World Bank Operations Evaluation Study, World Bank, Washington, D.C.
Deininger, K. 2000. "Does the Cost of Schooling Affect Enrollment by the Poor?
    Universal Primary Education in Uganda." World Bank, Washington, D.C.
Deolalikar, A. 1999. "Primary and Secondary Education in Kenya: A Sector
    Review." Human Development Sector Unit, Eastern Africa Region, World
    Bank, Washington, D.C.
Gay, John. 2000. *Poverty and Livelihoods in Lesotho, 2000: More Than a Mapping
    Exercise.* Maseru, Lesotho: Sechaba Consultants.
Kadzamira, E., D. Banda, A. Kamlongera, and N. Swainson. 2001. *The Impact of
    HIV/AIDS on Primary and Secondary Schooling in Malawi: Developing a Compre-
    hensive Strategic Response.* Zomba, Malawi: Centre for Educational Research and
    Training.
Kenya Ministry of Education, Science, and Technology. 2001. "Education Statisti-
    cal Booklet." Nairobi.
Leach, F., V. Fiscian, E. Kadzamira, E. Lemani, and P. Machakanja. 2003. "An
    Investigative Study of the Abuse of Girls in African Schools." Educational Paper
    54. Department for International Development, London.
Lesotho Ministry of Education. 1997. "Education Sector Development Plan
    1998/99–2000/2001." Maseru.
———. 1998. "Education Statistics 1998." Maseru.
———. 1999. "Education for All. The Year 2000 Assessment Report of Lesotho."
    Maseru.
———. 1999. "Policy Guidelines on Free Primary Education (FPE)." Maseru.
———. 1999. "1999 Poverty Assessment Education Component." Draft. Sechaba
    Consultants/Ministry of Education, Maseru.
———. 1999. "The Public Sector Improvement and Reform Program." Maseru.
———. 2000. "Know about the Free Primary Education Program in Lesotho."
    Maseru.
———. 2000. "Strategic Plan for the Implementation of Free Primary Education
    2000–2006." Draft. Maseru.
———. 2001. "The Free Primary Education Program." Maseru.
———. 2003. "Impact Assessment of HIV/AIDS on the Education Sector in
    Lesotho." Maseru.
———. 2003. "Education Statistics Bulletin, 1998–2002." Ministry of Education
    and Training, Maseru.

Liang, X. 2001. "Uganda Secondary Education: Coverage, Equity and Efficiency."
World Bank, Washington, D.C.

Mackinnon, J., and Renikka, R. 2000. "Lessons from Uganda on Strategies to Fight
Poverty." Policy Research Working Paper 2440. World Bank, Washington, D.C.

Malawi Ministry of Education, Science and Technology. 1993. "Basic Education
Statistics." Lilongwe.

———. 1993. "Economic Report." Lilongwe.

———. 1997–2001. "Budget Expenditure Documents." Lilongwe.

———. 2001. "Basic Education Statistics." Lilongwe.

———. 2002. "Poverty Reduction Strategy Paper." Lilongwe.

———. 2002. "Primary Curriculum an Assessment Reform." Malawi Primary Education Needs Identification Workshop Report. Lilongwe.

Malawi Ministry of Education, Sports and Culture and UNICEF (United Nations
Children's Fund). 1998. *Free Primary Education: The Malawi Experience 1994–
1998: A Policy Analysis.* Lilongwe.

Malawi National Statistics Office. 2003. "Malawi Domestic Household Survey
EdData Survey 2002." Zomba.

Mingat, A. 2000. "Magnitude of Social Disparities in Primary Education in Africa:
Gender, Geographical Location, and Family Income in the Context of EFA."
Draft. World Bank, Washington, D.C.

———. 2003. "Magnitude of Social Disparities in Primary Education in Africa.
Gender, Geographical Location and Family Income in the Context of EFA."
World Bank, Washington, D.C.

———. 2003. "Management of Education Systems in Sub-Saharan African
Countries. A Diagnostic and Ways Toward Improvement in the Context of the
EFA-FTI." World Bank, Washington, D.C.

Mingat, A., R. Rakotomalala, and J.-P. Tan. 2002. "Financing Education for All by
2015: Simulations for 33 African Countries." World Bank Africa Region Working Paper. World Bank, Washington, D.C.

Murphy, P. 2003. "Education, Educators and Financing Modalities: Reflections on
Experience in Uganda." Draft. World Bank, Washington, D.C.

Murphy, Paud, Carla Bertoncino, and Lianquin Wang. 2002. "Achieving Universal
Primary Education in Uganda: The 'Big Bang' Approach." Newsletter. World
Bank, Washington, D.C.

Patrinos, H., and D. Ariasingham. 1997. *Decentralization of Education: Demand-side
Financing.* Washington, D.C.: World Bank.

PNoWB (Parliamentary Network on the World Bank). 2003. Parliamentarians'
Implementation Watch. Concept Note. [www.pnowb.org/html/index.php?
module=htmlpages&func=display&pid=24].

Probyn, J., J. Makawa, and S. Orr. 1999. "Malawi Primary Community School Project: Social Impact Study." Kadale Consultants, Lilongwe, Malawi.

Psacharopoulos, G., and H. Patrinos. 2002. "Returns to Investment in Education:
A Further Update." Policy Research Working Paper 2881. World Bank, Education Sector Unit, Latin America and the Caribbean Region, Washington, D.C.

Roberts-Schweizer, E., A. Markov, and A. Tretyakov. 2002. "Achieving Education
for All Goals. School Grant Schemes." Draft. World Bank, Washington, D.C.

Uganda Ministry of Education and Sports. 1998. "Education Strategic Investment
Plan 1998–2003." Kampala.

———. 1998. "Guidelines on Policy, Roles and Responsibilities of Stakeholders in the Implementation of Universal Primary Education (UPE)." Kampala.

———. 2000. "Education For All: The Year 2000 Assessment. Report of Uganda." Kampala.

———. 2000. "National Strategy for Girls' Education in Uganda." Kampala.

———. 2002. "Education Sector Fact File." Kampala.

———. 2002. "Eighth Education Sector Review, Final Aide Memoire." Kampala.

———. 2003. "Technical Note on Primary Repetition, Survival, and Completion Rates before and after Universal Primary Education (UPE) in Uganda." Kampala.

UNDP (United Nations Development Programme). 2003. *Human Development Report 2003: Millennium Development Goals—A Compact among Nations to End Human Poverty.* New York: Oxford University Press.

UNESCO (United Nations Educational, Scientific and Cultural Organization). 2000. *The Dakar Framework for Action.* Paris.

———. 2002. "Children in Difficult Circumstances. Strengthening Partnerships to Combat HIV/AIDS and Discrimination." Paris.

———. 2002. *Education For All: Is the World on Track?* EFA Global Monitoring Report 2002. Paris.

———. "Documentary Resources." [www.unesco.org/unesdi/index.php/eng].

———. "Education for All." [www.unesco.org/education/efa].

———. "Education for All by 2015." [portal.unesco.org/education].

———. "Education for All News." [www.unesco.org/education/efa/index.shtml].

UNESCO Institute for Statistics. Education statistics. [www.uis.unesco.org/].

UNICEF (United Nations Children's Fund). 2003a. "HIV/AIDS and Orphans in Lesotho." New York.

———. 2003. *State of the World's Children 2003: Child Participation.* New York.

———. "Information by Country." [www.unicef.org/infobycountry/index.html].

Verspoor, Adriaan, Angel Mattimore, and Patrick Watt. 2001. *A Chance to Learn. Knowledge and Finance for Education in Sub-Saharan Africa.* African Region Human Development Series. Washington, D.C.: World Bank.

World Bank. 1998. "Lesotho–Second Education Sector Development Project." Project Information Document. Washington, D.C.

———. 1998. "Malawi–Second Social Action Fund Project." Project Appraisal Document. Washington, D.C.

———. 1999. "Lesotho: Public Expenditure and Budget Management Review." Southern Africa Macroeconomic Unit 1, Africa Region, Washington, D.C.

———. 1999. "Lesotho–Second Education Sector Development Project." Project Appraisal Document. Washington, D.C.

———. 1999. "World Bank Mission to Lesotho Education Sector: Public Expenditure Review." Aide Memoire. Washington, D.C.

———. 2002. "Uganda–Public Expenditure Review: Report on the Progress and Challenges of Budget Reforms." Economic Report. Washington, D.C.

———. 2002. *World Development Report 2003.* New York: Oxford University Press.

———. 2003a. "Kenya–Free Primary Education Support Project, Vol. 1 of 1." Project Appraisal Document. Washington, D.C.

———. 2003b. "Lesotho–Second Education Sector Development Project (Phase 02), Vol. 1 of 1." Project Appraisal Document. Washington, D.C.

————. 2003c. "Supporting Sound Policies with Adequate Appropriate Financing."
Washington, D.C.
————. 2003d. *World Development Indicators 2003*. Washington, D.C.
————. 2004. "Strengthening the Foundation of Education and Training in Kenya:
Opportunities and Challenges in Primary and General Secondary Education."
Sector Report. Washington, D.C.
————. "The World Bank Group in Sub-Saharan Africa." [lnweb18.worldbank.org/
AFR/afr.nsf.].

10

Improving Water and Sanitation Services in Rural Areas
Lessons Learned from Ghana, Lesotho, and South Africa

JON LANE

Water, sanitation, and hygiene are essential for achieving the Millennium Development Goals—and hence for eradicating global poverty.[1] This case study contributes to the learning process on scaling up poverty reduction by describing and analyzing three programs on rural water and sanitation in Africa: the national rural water sector reform in Ghana, the national sanitation program in Lesotho, and the national water and sanitation program in South Africa.

These three programs have achieved, or have the potential to achieve, development results on a national scale that exceed the average rates of progress for Sub-Saharan Africa. The lessons from these programs are useful for policymakers around the world. None of the programs is perfect, but all demonstrate good work on a large scale. They show that strong and sustained political leadership augmented by clear legislation, devolution of authority allied

Jon Lane can be contacted at jonlane@africa-online.net. The author gratefully acknowledges Elizabeth Kleemeier, Mike Muller, and Ian Pearson, who wrote the Water and Sanitation Program's Blue Gold field notes, which form the principal sources for the case, and John Dawson, who provided editorial help. The author also thanks Piers Cross of the Water and Sanitation Program, Africa, and Louise Fox and Robert Liebenthal of the World Bank.

257

to community empowerment, and carefully targeted donor support can achieve poverty reduction on a significant scale by improving rural water and sanitation services.

The State of Rural Water and Sanitation in Ghana, Lesotho, and South Africa

Water and sanitation services in rural areas of Africa were very poor in the early 1980s. Coverage rates were typically 20 to 40 percent for water and 10 to 30 percent for sanitation. Most African societies were agrarian, but rural services of all sorts were underdeveloped. Viewing the provision of basic services, such as water and sanitation, as the duty of the government, most African countries established large, centrally managed water supply programs. These programs used conventional engineering solutions that resulted in infrastructure that was beyond the people's capability to maintain. Maintenance was a problem because governments funded and undertook maintenance centrally. They provided water free of charge to people connected to the service. As the economies of many African countries declined, however, budgets were reduced, water infrastructure fell into disrepair, and users were unable or unwilling to maintain it themselves. New projects were delayed and sanitation was neglected. The concepts of community management, human development, human rights, and empowerment of the poorest people were not commonly applied within the water sector (box 10.1).

Ghana: A Government-controlled System That Was Not Coping

The rural water sector in Ghana was typical of those in many African countries. The Ghana Water and Sewerage Corporation (GWSC), a state company under the Ministry of Works and Housing, was responsible for both urban and rural water supply and sewerage for a population of some 15 million people. Most of GWSC's staff and resources, however, were devoted to the urban sector, with just two or three staff working on rural services. As a result, donors and nongovernmental organizations wanting to work in rural water and sanitation found themselves setting up large regional projects that were almost inde-

BOX 10.1	**Important New Concepts in Water and Sanitation Development: Community Management, Human Development, Human Rights, and Empowerment**

Through community management, poor people own and manage their resources and services, including drinking water and sanitation. Development practitioners around the world are increasingly accepting community management as a broadly applicable and large-scale process, not simply a small-scale project method.

Human development is people making their own decisions about their lives rather than passively accepting the choices made by others. It relates closely to the exercise of people's rights and responsibilities.

The recognition of water as a human right is increasingly enshrined in declarations and conventions on human rights. The UN Committee on Economic, Cultural and Social Rights has stated that "the human right to water entitles everyone to sufficient, affordable, physically accessible, safe and acceptable water for personal and domestic uses" (UN Committee General Comment #15, November 2002).

Empowering the poorest people enables them to make social, political, and economic decisions. This is achieved by listening to the people and respecting their knowledge, social structures, institutions, and leadership; paying special attention to the needs of women, marginalized and indigenous people, and the poorest members of a community; and ensuring that governments and support agencies participate in the people's agendas and are accountable to the people, not vice versa.

pendent of the government, both in their policies and in their implementation.

GWSC was responsible for maintaining more than 8,000 rural point sources, mostly hand pumps, and more than 200 piped schemes in small towns. But while GWSC was responsible for maintenance and repair, it did little of either, partly because it focused its attention on urban rather than rural services, and partly because revenue collected from rural users covered only a fraction of the maintenance costs. Consequently, both hand pumps and piped systems suffered frequent breakdowns and supply interruptions. As these problems worsened, Ghanaian politicians became increasingly concerned about the water and sanitation sector.

Lesotho: A Sanitation Problem

Lesotho is much smaller than Ghana or South Africa, with a population of about 2 million people, 90 percent of whom live in rural areas. In the early 1980s Lesotho had many water- and sanitation-related health problems. Rural water supply was being addressed, but work on sanitation had barely begun: only 15 percent of the rural population had any sort of sanitation, while the remainder used open defecation. Increasing population density and the declining number of trees led to high demand for latrines. This combination of health and physical factors motivated the government and donors to take an interest in improving sanitation.

South Africa: Racially Divided Services

In South Africa, a country of some 40 million people in 1994, the situation was complex. Before 1994 the country had been governed in accordance with racist apartheid principles. Responsibility for water supply and sanitation was fragmented, allocated to local governments in 4 provinces and 10 nominally autonomous homelands, resulting in very different levels of service. The overall statistics masked extreme contrast between different sectors of society. In most of the white-ruled local areas, standards were equal to those in industrial countries. In black rural areas there were often no services at all; in black urban areas service was mixed. This situation was exacerbated by the lack of coherent national policies, guidelines, or support structures. In anticipation of people's expectations preparatory work began in many areas, including water and sanitation, during the years leading up to the democratic change of 1994.

Taking Decisive Action to Improve Water and Sanitation

These three cases were chosen because their political and professional leaders took decisive action to improve water and sanitation, reducing poverty significantly and generating lessons applicable elsewhere.

Ghana: A Major Change in Both Policy and Structure

By the mid-1980s the government of Ghana faced a dilemma regarding water. On the one hand, it regarded water as a social good, so it did not want to impose cost recovery on consumers. On the other hand, it could not afford the capital and operating costs needed to equitably provide water and sanitation. The unintended consequence was that poor people lacked water, while rich people enjoyed cheap water.

Prompted by GWSC's concerns about operating costs, the government made a one-time increase in water tariffs in 1986, raising them tenfold. People complained, but they paid, creating a cross-subsidy of poor people by rich people. Meanwhile, the government monitored the innovations associated with the International Drinking Water Supply and Sanitation Decade (1981–90) and established a stakeholder group to adopt the best practices from the decade.

This led to a broad, consultative process of policy development during the early 1990s (box 10.2). In this process the Ghanaian people and agencies raised many issues, then debated and resolved them with support from external agencies, notably the World Bank and the Water and Sanitation Program. This process resulted in a draft sector strategy that was discussed and refined by representatives from line ministries, local government, the private sector, donors, and civil society. This broad participation gave all groups a voice in the reform process. The policy discussions also drew on the experiences of pilot projects already under way. The Water and Sanitation Program worked with the

BOX 10.2	Chronology of the National Rural Water Sector Program in Ghana
1965	The Water Act, which governs the role of the Ghana Water and Sewerage Corporation, is passed.
1986	The government raises water tariffs tenfold.
1991–92	The national water policy is drafted.
1992–93	The policy is refined through a series of strategy planning workshops.
1994	The First Community Water and Sanitation Project (CWSP-1) begins.
1998	Creation of the Community Water and Sanitation Agency.
1999	CWSP-1 ends.
2000	Reforms and decentralization are completed.

government to test community-managed hand pumps, the international NGO WaterAid tested community management of whole projects, and Catholic organizations experimented with community cash contributions.

Once the national policy for rural water supply, sanitation, and hygiene education was finalized, it was implemented as a pilot project in the Volta region, supported by the United Nations Development Programme (UNDP) and the Dutch government. It was then scaled up as the First Community Water and Sanitation Project (CWSP-1), a $20 million World Bank–supported program managed by the newly formed Community Water and Sanitation Division of GWSC. CWSP-1 implemented the new policy in 26 of Ghana's 110 districts. When it ended in 1999, the national policy was enacted across the whole country.

The Community Water and Sanitation Agency (CWSA) was created from GWSC in stages. First, the functions related to rural community water supplies were placed in a separate division within GWSC, facilitating better monitoring of donors' grants for water and sanitation for poor people. Later, in 1998, that division was made into an independent agency and renamed the Community Water and Sanitation Agency. CWSA adopted a fundamentally different approach from GWSC: coordinating and facilitating—not implementing—community-managed water supplies. Whereas GWSC had had a poor reputation among communities, CWSA immediately started to establish a good reputation as it encouraged communities' sense of ownership.

At the same time CWSA was created, the government devolved certain core responsibilities from the national level to districts and communities. The district assemblies, an important tier of elected local government, became responsible for processing and prioritizing community applications for water supplies, awarding contracts for hand-dug wells and latrine construction, and running a latrine subsidy program. In order to be eligible for assistance, communities had to establish gender-balanced water and sanitation committees, complete plans detailing how they would manage their systems, and contribute 5 percent of capital costs in cash. In line with the new national policy, communities also had to pay all operational and maintenance costs. The final element of the strategy was unprecedented private sector provision of goods and services, covering borehole drilling, operations and maintenance, latrine construction, and community mobilization. This mobilization is carried out by partner organizations that are sometimes described as NGOs but actually function as commercial organizations, working to precise contracts and timescales.

By 2000 the reforms were complete and CWSA had settled into its role of helping the district assemblies implement the national community water and sanitation program. CWSA also formulates strategies, standards, and guidelines for the sector; coordinates the work of NGOs and donors; and encourages private sector activity in water and sanitation. The communities have primary responsibility for managing their water and sanitation services, while small-scale private sector firms are active in such areas as repairs and spare parts supply.

In sanitation the district assemblies start by subcontracting hygiene promotion to the same partner organizations responsible for community mobilization. The district assemblies respond to demand by providing subsidized latrine slabs, vent pipes, and fly screens on request, paying for the materials with donor funds provided through CWSA. CWSA broadcasts advertisements and jingles on local radio stations to complement the promotional work.

Traditionally, Ghanaians do not talk about latrines, and behavior change takes a long time. It is hardly surprising, therefore, that progress in promoting sanitation and hygiene has lagged behind that of water supply. Until recently, progress was also apparently hampered by the World Bank's stipulation that more than half the households in a community had to request latrines before the district assembly could start to supply them, a guideline that has now been relaxed.

The national government in Ghana plays a crucial role in developing policy but is not involved in implementation. The Ministry of Works and Housing (the parent ministry of CWSA) sets overall policy for the sector (and is trying to change its name to include "Water" to emphasize its importance). This ministry sees poverty reduction and the achievement of the water and sanitation Millennium Development Goals as vital parts of government policy. Water is a part of the portfolio of the Ministry of Local Government and Rural Development, which supports district assemblies and tries to mediate between district assemblies and line ministries such as the Ministry of Works and Housing. The Ministry of Finance does not yet give water and sanitation sufficient priority in the eyes of the line ministries, as indicated by the low percentage allocation of funds to water and sanitation in the Ghana Poverty Reduction Strategy Paper.

Lesotho: Consistent Policies Achieving Long-term Results in Sanitation

The national sanitation program in Lesotho is much older than the programs in Ghana or South Africa. By 1980 Lesotho already had a national water supply program, but professionals working in the sector identified a gap in sanitation, initially in urban infrastructure and subsequently in rural areas. After a series of technical studies by various international organizations, in the early 1980s the government initiated a two-part national sanitation improvement program covering the urban and rural sectors of Lesotho (box 10.3).

From the beginning, the sanitation program was carried out by government organizations, specifically by Urban and Rural Sanitation Improvement teams. These teams acted within the government's regular program of public sector development work. The two teams were designed to create the minimum necessary number of permanent government posts, complemented by a larger number of short-term, donor-funded posts to start the program and engage and train the private sector. This is exactly what happened: donor funding was phased out as planned, and local private sector organizations remain active in sanitation.

In both the urban and the rural work, pilot projects were launched before scaling the work up to the full national program. The pilot projects enabled ideas to be tested locally before being applied nationally, and informed the design of the full-scale work that followed.

The rural sanitation program adopted a consistent set of principles. It ensured proper institutional arrangements at the national and district

---

BOX 10.3	Chronology of the National Rural Sanitation Program in Lesotho

1980	The Urban Sanitation Improvement Team starts work on a project basis.
1983	The Rural Sanitation Improvement Team initiates its pilot phase.
1984	The Urban Sanitation Improvement Team becomes a permanent government department within the Ministry of the Interior.
1987	The rural pilot phase ends and the National Rural Sanitation Program begins within the Ministry of Health.

levels, involved communities in planning and management, and prioritized the government's efforts on education and promotion. It insisted on full cost recovery from users: the government did not subsidize latrine costs. It promoted use of the small-scale private sector to build latrines and itself trained latrine builders. Each of these principles is well known to professionals in the sanitation sector. In Lesotho they have all been put into practice together, consistently, and for a long time—a combination that may be unique in Africa.

From the start the Lesotho program adopted the ventilated improved pit latrine, suitably adapted to local conditions, construction techniques, and preferences. This decision had an important effect on the nature of the program. While sanitation programs typically begin with a strong technical bias, due to the need to test a range of technologies and select one or more to use, the Lesotho program was always more concerned with broader social issues such as community participation, health and hygiene promotion, and finance.

The government put most of its own effort into promoting sanitation and training sanitation professionals. The media promoted latrine use through printed matter, radio, slide presentations, and videos. Most of these efforts targeted potential latrine owners. The use of radio has been particularly strong and has resulted in a significant take-up of improved sanitation in terms of behavior and construction of latrines. The use of two key messages (improved health and improved status) in the promotion program appears to have increased its impact. From the beginning the design of the program aimed to prevent the ventilated improved pit latrine from being perceived as a poor person's latrine. Middle-income people were deliberately targeted in promotions, as they could easily buy latrines without direct subsidies.

The private sector, in the form of small contractors who build latrines, has been involved in the program since the beginning. Trained by the Rural Sanitation Improvement Team, contractors make a living building unsubsidized latrines for householders—a benchmark of sustainability for which many sanitation programs strive (box 10.4).

South Africa: Turning the Right to Water into a Reality

A complete change in rural water and sanitation in South Africa was triggered by the political change from apartheid to inclusive democracy in 1994. The country's population was then just under 40 million people, of whom an estimated 15 million (12 million of them in rural

BOX 10.4	A Latrine Builder's Story

A quarter of the trained latrine builders in Lesotho are women, including Mrs. Mateboho Monnanyane of Tsime, Butha-Buthe District. She pursues latrine building full time, actively marketing her skills by traveling from house to house or visiting local traditional leaders in neighboring towns and villages and explaining the importance of having a latrine. The resulting demand has been so great that she has trained five other people, four of them women, as latrine builders in the same area.

Mateboho's background as a village health worker was a logical starting point for becoming a latrine builder. She works for everyone's health, especially that of children. "I want to make an impression on the village," she says. "There is competition when I go to other villages, but people ask me [to build their latrines] because I have a good reputation. That is my work."

Source: Evans, Pollard, and Narayan-Parker 1990.

areas) lacked access to a basic water supply and 20 million lacked basic sanitation. Water—though not yet sanitation—was one of the people's top concerns, and expectations were high that the new democratic government would deliver equitable water services quickly.

In 1994 the new government made the Department of Water Affairs and Forestry (DWAF) responsible for ensuring that all South Africans had equitable access to water supply and sanitation. DWAF had previously been a technical organization focused on water resources and forestry management. Its historically apolitical character was an asset in approaching its new task, as was the involvement of progressive activists who moved into this sector of government. After consulting a range of interested parties, DWAF produced a policy on community water supply and sanitation in November 1994. This policy provided the foundation for the legislative and regulatory framework (subsequently enacted in the Water Services Act of 1997) governing the water sector and the national water and sanitation program (box 10.5). The policy recognized that local governments would eventually take responsibility for service provision. It also referred to the basic rights of access to water and to an environment that is not harmful to health or well-being (box 10.6). Both decentralization of supply and the right to water were formally stated in the country's new Constitution in 1996.

BOX 10.5	Chronology of the National Water and Sanitation Program in South Africa
1994	First democratic elections are held; a water sector policy paper is drafted.
1995	The Reconstruction and Development Programme begins.
1996	The new Constitution of the Republic of South Africa is approved.
1997	The Water Services Act is passed.
1998–2000	Various local government acts concerning water and sanitation are passed.
1999	The free basic water policy is promulgated.
2003	A strategic framework for water is developed.

In 1994 the government knew that it must quickly start work to meet the high demand for rural development, including water supply and sanitation. It launched the top-priority Reconstruction and Development Programme (RDP), from which $340 million was allocated to DWAF for water and sanitation. Since the decentralized institutional framework for water and sanitation was not ready, DWAF itself took the lead and used RDP funds to scale up its work rapidly. It involved various organizations, including water boards, NGOs (notably the Mvula Trust), some transitional local government bodies, and private sector companies, as partners in delivery. At the project level community-based project steering committees were set up and provided with guidelines by DWAF on the implementation and maintenance of their projects. Between 1994 and 2003 new water services were constructed for 9 million people, making the program one of the largest and most rapid service provision efforts in Africa.

During the late 1990s local government reform culminated in democratically elected local municipalities throughout the country. These municipalities are now responsible for implementing rural water and sanitation services, and local politicians are becoming actively involved. DWAF is changing its role from an implementer to a facilitator and regulator. The change will take some time, as many municipalities are still weak, but the Ministry of Finance has demonstrated leadership by

BOX 10.6	Equity of Access and the Free Basic Water Policy in South Africa

Under the 1994 policy the government funded the capital costs of water and sanitation infrastructure while users covered operations and maintenance costs—a financial division that applies in many other countries. Toward the end of the 1990s it became clear that the high operation and maintenance costs of many schemes meant that poorer people could not afford the charges and were therefore not benefiting from the new water and sanitation services. In response the government developed a free basic water policy. This policy, which is a more sophisticated version of a concept adopted by many other African countries in the early postcolonial era, encourages water services authorities to provide households with the first 6,000 liters a month free of charge. Operation and maintenance costs are intended to be covered by a combination of a rising block tariff above that consumption level and a subsidy from the national budget to the local government specifically for basic service provision.

The free basic water policy is controversial. On the one hand, it sends a powerful political message and aims to ensure that people's right of access to a basic water supply—and hence to the health and social benefits arising from it—is not limited by affordability. On the other hand, its critics argue that it has weakened poor people's sense of ownership, increased their dependency on the government, and reduced the accountability of water service providers to users who do not pay.

What impact does the free basic water policy have on the national economy? The subsidy needed from the national budget is known; the health and economic benefits of the water are not immediately quantifiable but are almost certainly much larger, suggesting that the policy benefits the national economy.

projecting future budgets showing DWAF's smaller role and local government's larger one. As for the private sector, whose involvement is a contentious topic in South Africa, it is deeply involved in research, design, manufacturing, and even social mobilization and training, but it is involved only minimally as a water service provider.

In South Africa the right to basic sanitation—and to receive hygiene education—is constitutionally enshrined alongside the right to water. However, as in many other countries, sanitation lagged behind water supply. This was partly because the communities themselves had always strongly prioritized water supply and partly because there was not a good system for promoting sanitation at the community level. In 2000

South Africa experienced a dangerous outbreak of cholera, which provided an important stimulus for addressing the country's slow rate of progress in sanitation. Latrine construction programs were given high priority. To ensure longer-term attention to sanitation, the government designated DWAF as the lead agency in sanitation. DWAF now provides strong political leadership for sanitation and hygiene promotion and has created a dedicated sanitation program to implement the work.

Other African Examples

Several other countries in Africa have made progress in improving rural water and sanitation services. Uganda's water and sanitation sector has been reformed in accordance with its overall poverty eradication plans. The government itself has actively led the reform process, with wide participation from donors and other stakeholders. The reforms include decentralization, increased local private sector participation, recovery of operation and maintenance costs, and subsidy for domestic latrines. A corresponding 15-year investment plan, financed partly by debt relief funds, is logically leading toward a sectorwide approach.

In Benin the government and donors have adopted a national rural water and sanitation strategy. The main features of the plan are community management of water services, decentralization from national to local government, variable levels of service in accordance with demand and affordability, and private sector provision of goods and services. In Mozambique a pioneering program of peri-urban sanitation served more than 1.3 million people in a country that was just emerging from decades of destructive civil war. In Burkina Faso sanitation in both urban and rural areas has been addressed systematically using innovative ideas such as cross-subsidies from water supply tariffs.

How Well Did the National Programs Work?

All three countries reduced poverty by increasing the provision of water and sanitation services to the rural poor (box 10.7). Until recently, rural water and sanitation coverage in Ghana was below the average for Sub-Saharan Africa; coverage is now being extended at a rate of about 200,000 people—more than 1 percent of the population—a year and accelerating. The government and other observers believe that good progress is being made. CWSA is now fully established and functioning, with the active support of several bilateral support agencies, the

BOX 10.7	How Comprehensive Is Rural Water and Sanitation Coverage in Ghana, Lesotho, and South Africa?

The Millennium Development Goals and the World Summit on Sustainable Development goals seek to halve the proportion of people who lack water and sanitation between 1990 and 2015. All three governments have committed themselves to these goals. The South African government has gone further, setting its own more ambitious goals to provide water for all by 2008 and sanitation for all by 2010.

Coverage figures for 1990 are difficult to produce because some countries changed their criteria for measurement while others used different baseline years. But current best estimates, collated from various in-country sources and the WHO/UNICEF Joint Monitoring Programme, indicate that coverage has increased in all three countries (see table).

Rural water and sanitation coverage in Ghana, Lesotho, and South Africa (percent)

Country	1980	1990	2000	2008 target	2015 target
Rural water coverage					
Ghana	30	35	41	–	68
South Africa	–	39	63	100	100
Sub-Saharan Africa average	35	40	45	–	70
Rural sanitation coverage					
Ghana	–	15	28	–	68
South Africa	–	24	44	100	100
Lesotho	15	–	55	–	66
Sub-Saharan Africa average	–	46	42	–	73

– Indicates data not available.
Source: WHO and UNICEF 2004.

European Union, and the World Bank. It intends to move to a sector-wide approach in which all donors pool their resources to support a single national program rather than separate projects. CWSA's projections, based on the current level of work and the reforms envisioned, indicate that the Millennium Development Goals for water will be achieved. Attaining the Millennium Development Goals for sanitation will be more difficult.

In Lesotho tens of thousands of new ventilated improved pit latrines have been built in rural areas, and a similar number of pit latrines has been upgraded to ventilated improved pit latrines. Sanitation coverage has risen from 15 percent to more than 50 percent in rural areas in 20 years. The rural sanitation program remains active within the Ministry of Health. Lesotho is reaping the benefits of its long engagement in sanitation development, and is on track to achieve the Millennium Development Goal for sanitation (it has already achieved the Millennium Development Goal for water).

In less than 10 years, South Africa has constructed water supply schemes designed to serve more than 9 million people—more than 20 percent of the population—helping redress the social inequity of the past. The program is continuing to extend rural water coverage at the rate of 1 million people a year. Decentralization is proceeding, and DWAF is changing its function from implementation to support and regulation. Sanitation, while still lagging behind water, is receiving much more attention than it did. DWAF expects to achieve its own targets in advance of the Millennium Development Goals.

Health and Social Impact

Water-related diseases are the single largest cause of human sickness and death in the world—and they affect poor people disproportionately. Therefore, the main impact of water and sanitation on human development is improving health. Studies from around the world have shown that provision of safe water and basic sanitation accompanied by hygiene promotion can reduce the incidence of diarrheal diseases by as much as 25 percent (Cairncross 1999; Esrey and others 1990). Better sanitation also provides greater privacy, convenience, safety, and dignity—qualities that are particularly important for women.

Rural water and sanitation programs promote access to assets and services. They also advance social development through their community management systems, which enable people to work together equitably for their own development. The water sector contains many examples of innovative and successful community management.

Only a few studies have been conducted on the health and social impacts of water and sanitation programs in Ghana, Lesotho, and South Africa. Research in Lesotho suggests that the incidence of sanitation-related diseases has fallen significantly in areas where water and sanitation projects have been implemented. These findings are typical of those from around the world indicating that the health impact derives from the combination of improved hygiene, sanitation, and water supply.

Empowerment of and accountability to the poor have been extremely important features in both the Ghana and Lesotho programs. In South Africa the national program has been centrally led, and the free basic water policy arguably reduces empowerment of poorer people because the water service providers are more accountable to their paymaster (the national government) than to their users. The government disputes this argument, but at least one independent survey (Palmer Development Group 2000) seems to confirm that the relationship between the public and the water service provider changes for the worse when users stop paying for water. Accountability must then be exercised through the ballot box.

Economic Impact

Around the world poor people place a high priority on drinking water and, to a lesser degree, sanitation. Considerable evidence suggests that improved water and sanitation generate substantial economic benefits, mainly by saving time and energy. Fetching a family's basic water requirement can be both time consuming and physically exhausting—and the burden falls disproportionately on women and children. Seeking privacy for open defecation forces many women to wake up an hour early every day of their lives. Being ill with a water-related disease, or caring for an ill family member, also consumes much time and money. The time and energy saved by improved water supply and sanitation can be used in economically productive or educational activities. Water and sanitation programs also contribute to economic development by creating jobs, although the impact is relatively modest as the number of permanent jobs created is small at the community level. These economic factors make a strong case for governments to intervene in water and sanitation through regulation or investment.

Few rigorous studies of the economic impact of improved water and sanitation have been conducted in Ghana, Lesotho, or South Africa. In Lesotho latrines are built by local private sector builders; people with latrine construction skills have a direct economic incentive to promote improved sanitation. In South Africa job creation is a stated benefit of the national water and sanitation program, and DWAF monitors the number of jobs created by it.

How Much Do the Programs Cost?

Most countries include expenditures on water and sanitation under other general headings, such as health. National expenditure figures on water and sanitation are not therefore generally available.[2] It is possible to estimate costs from individual programs, however. Those costs suggest that each of the three countries has chosen a program that is appropriate given its economic situation (box 10.8).

BOX 10.8 **Creating Water and Sanitation Programs That Are Well Suited to the National Economic Context**

The rural water and sanitation program in Ghana was implemented against a background of generally steady national economic growth. Growth has not benefited CWSA's program directly, however, because the Ministry of Finance has not allocated more money from the government budget to it. CWSA has benefited indirectly because donors have put more money into the country, including CWSA. About 90 percent of CWSA's investment, training, and consultancy budget comes from donors, with 10 percent coming from the central government and from a small but innovative cross-subsidy from urban water tariffs.

In Lesotho the macroeconomic climate has always been difficult. The sanitation program was designed to minimize the drain on national economic resources by avoiding subsidies to household latrines, generating demand through promotional work, and encouraging the private sector to meet demand on a commercial basis. This strategy has worked well, and successive governments have found the cost acceptable, as illustrated by its continued use after 20 years. Mainstreaming the sanitation budget into the district health budgets has caused it to compete with curative work, which many district-level decisionmakers view as a higher priority.

The national economy of South Africa is stronger than those of most African countries, with per capita GDP that is an order of magnitude higher than that of Ghana or Lesotho. Given its economic strength, the post-1994 government chose to construct water supply systems at comparatively high capital and operating costs. This strategy relies on both the continuing strength of the national economy and the continuing willingness of national politicians, who have many other pressing needs to fund. In other African countries both of these factors caused problems, and many water services collapsed in the 1970s and 1980s. The current government in South Africa is confident that its water services will not face similar problems.

In Ghana CWSP-1 supplied water to more than 300,000 people at a direct cost of $26 per person. This unit cost doubles to $50 if the indirect costs of institutional capacity building are included. These costs are fairly typical of other African countries.

The Lesotho sanitation program includes no subsidy for latrine construction; each household pays for the construction of its own latrine by a private sector builder. In rural areas a latrine costs about one month's salary, although people can reduce the cost by collecting and using local materials for building.

The well-documented South African national program supplies water at an average capital cost of about $90 per person. Many of its schemes use relatively high, engineering-driven design standards and technologies that may be difficult for local governments to maintain and too expensive for users to fund. An alternative approach would have been to involve communities in choosing service levels and to build systems that the communities themselves could afford and maintain. This has not happened, mainly because the Constitution states that water must be available within 200 meters of every person's house, which in scattered rural populations dictates high-cost technologies such as piped systems rather than simpler and less expensive technologies such as hand pumps and wells, as used elsewhere in Africa. Civil servants have questioned the use of high-cost technologies that follows from the 200 meter rule, but South African politicians are committed to the current policy.

How Are Costs Recovered?

Recovering the costs of water and sanitation services is an important issue for governments around the world that want to achieve the water and sanitation Millennium Development Goals. While it is easy to argue that investments in water and sanitation more than pay for themselves in improved health and saved time, those benefits are intangible; governments want to ensure that actual costs will be covered. Cost recovery is also important for the sustainability of water and sanitation services.

In Ghana the official policy specifies that communities and local governments each must pay 5 percent of capital costs (box 10.9). The balance of 90 percent comes from CWSA's (largely donor-funded) budget. In Lesotho households cover 100 percent of the capital costs for sanitation. In South Africa the government provides 100 percent of capital costs for both water and sanitation. These are markedly different policies.

BOX 10.9	What Do Ghanaians Think about Their Water and Sanitation Services?

In 2000 CWSA commissioned a beneficiary assessment in communities in which water facilities had been improved under CWSP-1. The report describes the people's own views about their improved water and sanitation services.

■ More than 90 percent of respondents were satisfied with the location, quantity, and quality of the water they received.

■ Almost all respondents—97 percent—used the improved water source and did not feel that poverty had constrained their access to improved water.

■ About 92 percent of respondents had contributed to capital costs and 85 percent were contributing to operation and maintenance costs. The vast majority felt that the principle of payment was fair and intended to continue paying.

■ More than 80 percent of respondents had adopted improved hygiene practices, such as keeping water in a clean container and washing their hands after using the latrine and before cooking.

■ Only about 20 percent of respondents constructed new latrines, although almost 70 percent were aware of the sanitation component of the program.

■ More than 90 percent of water and sanitation committees had received training, opened bank accounts, and held regular meetings. Women played active and influential roles on these committees.

■ Latrine builders, well diggers, mechanics, and health workers all received training through the program. Sixty percent of latrine builders dropped out due to lack of demand for latrines.

Source: Baah 2000.

Ghana's policy, in which the community contribution is intended to generate a sense of ownership, is typical of many countries. The policy seems sensible enough, but some observers view the rigid application of the policy as reflecting directives from the World Bank. Moreover, the policy may discriminate against the poorest people. Lesotho's policy was innovative 20 years ago and remains cutting edge even today. It seems likely that many other countries will need to adopt this policy in order to achieve the Millennium Development Goal for sanitation. Even this policy is not faultless, however, because the poorest households have been unable or reluctant to construct latrines. Some NGOs have offered subsidies to such households in the rural areas, and the government itself may soon do so. South Africa's policy, in which the government covers all costs, is unusual among poorer countries but typical of middle-income countries.

Like many poor countries, Ghana and Lesotho require users to cover operation and maintenance costs. In Ghana each community fixes the tariff based on CWSA guidelines circulated by the local government. The decisions of the communities are endorsed by the water and sanitation development boards of each community and approved by the local government. In South Africa the basic level of water and sanitation service is free to users, while higher levels are charged to them; the balance of operation and maintenance costs is covered by a subsidy from the national budget.

In practice, application of these policies is more flexible than the policies themselves appear. For example, in Ghana poor people are often identified at the community level and exempted from paying (a form of community-managed cross-subsidy). In Lesotho the government subsidizes the emptying of latrine pits. In South Africa evidence is mounting that many users are not paying even for higher levels of service, suggesting that the national subsidy is covering most of the operation and maintenance costs. Only in a few richer or better-managed South African municipalities do enough people pay the higher tariffs to achieve full operation and maintenance cost recovery from users.[3]

Integrating Improved Hygiene, Sanitation, and Water

In recent years it has become clear that greater health benefits accrue from the combination of improvements to hygiene, sanitation, and water supply than from the provision of water alone. Integration of the three activities is therefore vital for achieving poverty reduction through water and sanitation. Professionals working on the national program in Lesotho were particularly aware of the fact that this integration must underpin any national water and sanitation program. Hygiene promotion played a particularly important role in generating demand for improved sanitation. In Ghana and South Africa the slower spread of sanitation has been identified as a problem.

Putting Sound Principles into Practice

Learning and experimentation have not been central features of these national water and sanitation programs. The main source of learning and experimentation has been the use of pilot projects, which Ghana and Lesotho have used to test new ideas.

The strength of all three programs has been in consistently putting sound principles into practice. The Lesotho program put into practice a complete set of policy ideas that were comparatively new in the 1980s, but its main characteristic has been in applying those ideas. The South Africa program is also based on a strongly articulated set of political beliefs, not on innovations for their own sake.

Key Factors for Successful Implementation

Several factors are critical to the successful implementation of a nation-wide water and sanitation program.

Strong Political Leadership

The commitment of political leaders has been a strong factor in the success of all three national programs. In Ghana the national mood in the 1980s favored reform and innovation. The rural water sector reform fits well with the other changes in the country's political economy, although its immediate drivers were more pragmatic considerations. Rural water had been neglected, and the sector as a whole was stuck in a downward spiral of inadequate cost recovery and poor service. Politicians made the decision to reverse that trend by increasing tariffs, seeking grants and loans, and separating the rural from the urban sector. Successive governments of different parties have all seen water and sanitation as important contributors to social and economic development, and reform of the sector has not been used as a political issue.

In South Africa the whole concept of the national water and sanitation program derived from national politics. After the apartheid era ended, the new government was elected on the promise of "a better life for all." There was a strong political commitment to service delivery programs; the national water and sanitation program was part of a shared vision of a nation in which people would have opportunities to develop their skills and use them productively, working for an income from which they could meet their basic needs. Successive ministers of water have provided energetic and determined leadership to the sector (box 10.10). The water program is one of the government's most popular achievements, reinforcing politicians' enthusiasm for it. Local political leaders also play an active role, setting budget priorities and

BOX 10.10	Kader Asmal, South Africa's Water Rights Advocate

Professor Kader Asmal is a lawyer and educator by profession—and a veteran of the struggle against apartheid. Before South Africa's democratic change in 1994, he was instrumental in drafting the Bill of Rights on which the new Constitution was based, a document including the human right to water. President Nelson Mandela appointed him Minister for Water Affairs and Forestry, a post that he held from 1994 until 1999.

Minister Asmal provided vigorous political leadership to the National Water and Sanitation Program in South Africa. At a time when many other issues competed for attention, he championed the cause of water and sanitation at the cabinet level within the government and obtained substantial financial allocations for the water sector. He galvanized his own department and other sector players into action, driven by his passionate belief in the people's right to water.

In 2000 Minister Asmal received the prestigious Stockholm Water Prize in recognition of his leadership of the South African national program. He saw the award as a "celebration of the democratic gains in South Africa that have enabled us to carry out the far-reaching changes to our body politic."

Source: Personal communication to the author, April 2000.

service delivery standards and approving projects, and they have a positive effect on the success of the program.

In Lesotho politicians played a different, though still important, leadership role. The original impetus for the sanitation program came from sector professionals and external agencies, which stressed the importance of fitting their work into the mainstream government structure. Recognizing this, for many years politicians have allocated significant sums to sanitation through the government's regular budget.

In all three countries the government's priority to water and sanitation has not flagged over time. Even when different political parties have been elected, as in Ghana, the impetus for water and sanitation work has been maintained. This long-term commitment has underpinned the success of all three programs. It is important because water and sanitation expansion, and especially hygiene promotion, are activities that must be sustained over a long period in order to achieve success.

Clear Legislation

Legislation has played an important role in improving water and sanitation services in the three countries, especially in South Africa, whose 1996 Constitution includes extensive social, economic, and environmental rights, including the right to basic water and sanitation. South Africa's National Rural Water Supply and Sanitation Program became not just a short-term activity conducted by DWAF, but an integral element of the nationally legislated human rights program. An independent Constitutional Court holds the government accountable for adherence to the Constitution, a document complemented by successive acts of Parliament clearly stating the policies and their applications. Every organization involved in the water program in South Africa knows its role.

Ghana also has clear laws, notably various acts of Parliament dating from 1988 to 1998 that define the policies and roles of most sector agencies. Local government is the subject of a recent bill. By defining district assemblies' roles and responsibilities, it will help them recruit higher-caliber staff and implement the National Water and Sanitation Program more effectively.

In Lesotho the legal framework evolved as the sanitation program progressed from the pilot stage to a nationwide operation, notably through the formation of the National Rural Sanitation Program in 1987. This evolving legal framework gave legitimacy to the sanitation program's position as a regular part of the public sector's work.

Decentralization to Local Government

The devolution of authority from national to local government is a governance trend that has been widely adopted in developing countries in recent years. Its merits include increased accountability to the people and flexibility to tailor development work to meet local needs. Other sectors, such as health, have pioneered this devolution. In the water sector all three countries have applied this devolution of authority and recognized many positive benefits, although they have also encountered problems.

The two main problems have been the long time needed to build up the expertise of local government organizations to fulfill their new role (which may cause a temporary reduction in coverage rates) and their natural inclination to revert to supply-driven centralized approaches and technologies. In Ghana, for example, the devolution process has wisely been slowed to a pace below what donors would have liked by the government, while CWSA still has to implement water programs on behalf of many local governments as a temporary measure. In South Africa a significant proportion of local governments are not yet ready to take on their legal obligations for water and sanitation, mainly because they lack the financial and operational capacity.

The successful transfer of power to local government depends on strong support from a powerful central agency. This is precisely CWSA's role in Ghana. While it was the implementing agency in the early stages, it now principally helps and supports local governments as they take on this work. In South Africa DWAF is following a similar path, handing over responsibility for implementation to local governments as it takes on a regulatory and support role. In Lesotho the devolution to local government took place at the start of the program, with district sanitation teams taking the main role in implementing the program, supported by the Rural Sanitation Improvement Team.

Strong Communities, Civil Society, and the Media

National governments have taken the leadership role. However, communities themselves, local civil society organizations, and the mass media have also played important roles.

Community management principles have been important in Ghana and Lesotho and in a few aspects (notably sanitation) of the South African program. They are crucial to the sustainability of water and sanitation services. Communities cannot manage their water and sanitation services in a vacuum; they need long-term technical and professional support from intermediary organizations. In Ghana and Lesotho this role is largely filled by small-scale private-sector companies, whose role has not been well documented or acknowledged. In South Africa government agencies provide this support.

Civil society organizations are particularly active in South Africa. Many human rights organizations were influential in the debates that led to the constitutional right to water; some have even taken cases of water disconnections to the Constitutional Court, where they have prevailed on behalf of water users. NGOs, notably the Mvula Trust, also work in water service delivery in South Africa. The Trust was influential in both drafting and implementing policy, particularly in the sanitation sector. The South African media have also played an important role in ensuring public scrutiny and transparency of the water program.

In Ghana the media provide lively coverage of water issues, relating mainly to private sector participation in the urban water sector. They have reported some progress in rural areas in water, and less in sanitation. They believe that their role is to communicate people's views to politicians. For their part, politicians feel that the media are often careless or negative in their coverage.

Ghanaian NGOs were initially helpful and constructive in their contributions to the policy debate. Recently, however, CWSA has perceived them as antagonistic toward possible private sector participation, apparently as a result of influence from international social justice and antiglobalization organizations.

In Lesotho the sanitation program was wholly implemented by the government; NGOs played only a minor role. The media were important in promoting hygiene, which generated demand for sanitation.

Active Support from Donors

Donors have played different supporting roles in the three countries. In Ghana they have played a secondary role in policymaking but have been vital in financing the water and sanitation sector. Several bilateral and multilateral donors had been active in the water sector for years and recognized the weaknesses of the centralized government–run implementation and maintenance system. The new policy process was therefore one for which most donors felt empathy. These donors continue to provide the vast majority of funds for CWSA's capital investments, and this dependence on external finance seems likely to continue for many years. This pattern is typical for a low-income country.

The role of the World Bank in the Ghana program attracts a range of comments. On the one hand, the Bank has made loans available and supported sector reforms and decentralization. On the other hand, some sector players in Ghana have the impression that the Bank is stipulating certain conditions (fixed percentage contributions to capital costs, minimum proportion of people demanding latrines in a community, private sector involvement) before it will grant loans. The Bank denies any such conditionality, but there is a feeling in Ghana that it has a disproportionate influence over sector policies.

In Lesotho donors were instrumental in starting the national sanitation program, but they worked with the government to design the program specifically to avoid financial dependence on them in the long term. Initially, they supplied expert personnel, who helped develop the program in close cooperation with national staff within government and handed over all management responsibilities to government staff. Donors also provided funds to develop the national program as a whole, in particular to train private sector players to build latrines.

In South Africa donors have had little influence on the policy process and have provided only a small percentage of the funding for the national program. The South African government appreciates their support, but the program is overwhelmingly a South African one and would have progressed almost as quickly without external support. This pattern is typical of a middle-income country.

Problems to Address

In all three countries problems need to be solved in order to achieve the water and sanitation Millennium Development Goals and hence eliminate poverty:

- The main institutional concerns in Ghana and South Africa relate to local government. It is difficult to delegate operational responsibility for water services in the poorest areas of a country from a relatively well-resourced national department to often weak local governments. Since this institutional change is regarded as a central feature in the national programs, it is vital that it be implemented successfully. The success of the process will be measured only by the sustainability of services over the long term.
- The main financial concerns are different in each case. Ghana is typical of many low-income countries in that the achievement of the Millennium Development Goals will depend on continuing external financial support. South Africa is a richer country and does not need external support, but there is concern about the financial sustainability of water supplies when users do not pay for service. This reliance on funding from general taxation depends on the strength of the national economy and politicians' continued commitment to the program.
- The biggest remaining technical and financial problem in Lesotho is emptying latrine pits. All latrine pits eventually fill up; a sustainable sanitation system must be able to empty the pits economically. The only viable technology used today is conventional

suction tankers, a relatively expensive method that is subsidized out of the national budget. Many other countries (including South Africa) are beginning to encounter the problem of pit emptying; Lesotho has already encountered the problem because its national sanitation program is comparatively old.

Lessons

National programs in Ghana, Lesotho, and South Africa have improved water and sanitation. Several general conclusions can be drawn from their experiences:

- Top-level political commitment to water and sanitation, sustained consistently over a long time period, is critical to the success of national sector programs.
- Clear legislation is necessary to give guidance and confidence to all agencies working in the sector to determine their own policies and plans and to advance their activities as quickly and as well as they can.
- Devolution of authority from the national level to local governments and communities improves the accountability of water and sanitation programs. Local governments need professional support from strong, central, public sector organizations in order to implement their work programs effectively.
- The involvement of a wide range of local institutions—social, economic, civil society, and media—empowers communities and stimulates development at the local level.

Sensitive, flexible, and country-specific support by donors can accelerate progress in the water and sanitation sector.

BIBLIOGRAPHY

Baah, K. 2000. "Beneficiary Assessment Study of the First Community Water and Sanitation Project." Government of Uganda, Community Water and Sanitation Agency, Accra.

Cairncross, S. 1999. "Measuring the Health Impact of Water and Sanitation." WELL Technical Brief 10. WELL, University of Loughborough, U.K.

Daniels, D. L., S. N. Cousens, L. N. Makoae, and R. Feachem. 1990. "A Case-Control Study of the Impact of Improved Sanitation on Diarrhoea Morbidity in Lesotho." *Bulletin of the World Health Organization* 68(4): 455–63.

Department of Water Affairs and Forestry. 2003. *Water is Life, Sanitation is Dignity: Strategic Framework for Water Services.* Government of South Africa.

Esrey, S., J. B. Potash, L. Roberts, and C. Shiff. 1990. "Health Benefits from Improvements in Water Supply and Sanitation: Survey and Analysis of the Literature on Selected Diseases." WASH (Water, Sanitation, and Hygiene) Technical Report 66. United States Agency for International Development, Washington, D.C.

Evans, P., R. Pollard, and D. Narayan-Parker. 1990. "Rural Sanitation in Lesotho: From Pilot Project to National Programme." UNDP/World Bank Water and Sanitation Program and PROWWESS Discussion Paper 3.

Kleemeier, E. 2002. "Rural Water Sector Reform in Ghana: A Major Change in Policy and Structure." Blue Gold Field Note 2. Water and Sanitation Program, World Bank, Washington, D.C.

Mphuthi, S., and others. 2003. "Mid-Term Review of the Water Services Sector Support Programme." Department of Water Affairs and Forestry, Government of South Africa.

Muller, M. 2002. "The National Water and Sanitation Programme in South Africa: Turning the Right to Water into Reality." Blue Gold Field Note 8. Water and Sanitation Program, World Bank, Washington, D.C.

Palmer Development Group. 2000. "PPP and the Poor in Water and Sanitation: Case Study on Durban." Water, Engineering and Development Centre, Loughborough University, U.K.

Pearson, I. 2002. "The National Sanitation Programme in Lesotho: How Political Leadership Achieved Long-Term Results." Blue Gold Field Note 5. Water and Sanitation Program, World Bank, Washington, D.C.

Wakeman, W., and T. Hart. 2001. "Implementation Completion Report on the [First] Community Water and Sanitation Project." Report 21785. World Bank, Washington, D.C.

WHO (World Health Organization) and UNICEF (United Nations Children's Fund). "Joint Monitoring Programme for Water Supply and Sanitation." [www.wssinfo.org].

World Bank. 2004. "Water Supply and Sanitation in Poverty Reduction Strategy Papers." Water and Sanitation Program, Africa Region, Washington, D.C.

11

Defeating Riverblindness
Thirty Years of Success in Africa

JESSE B. BUMP, BRUCE BENTON,

AZODOGA SÉKÉTÉLI,

BERNHARD H. LIESE,

AND CHRISTINA NOVINSKEY

Over the past 30 years, riverblindness (onchocerciasis)—a scourge that had long afflicted most of Sub-Saharan Africa—has been eliminated from large parts of the continent through the efforts of a large international partnership. This partnership has defeated the disease in most of West Africa and is making rapid progress in the remaining endemic countries in Central and Eastern Africa.

Thirty countries are infested, from Senegal to Ethiopia in the north and from Angola to Malawi in the south. Before control programs began, tens of millions of people were infected and hundreds of thousands suffered from the worst symptom, total blindness.

Riverblindness control began in 1974 in West Africa as a large regional project (box 11.1). At the time the only available approach was vector control—treating the breeding sites of disease-transmitting flies with larvicides. Earlier control attempts dating to the 1950s had shown that

Jesse B. Bump can be contacted at jbump@worldbank.org, Bruce Benton at Bbenton@worldbank.org, Azodoga Sékétéli at seketelia@oncho.oms.bf, and Bernhard H. Liese at Bliese@worldbank.org. The authors gratefully acknowledge the research assistance of Katherine Allen, and the expert technical assistance of George Callen in preparing the graphics and the PowerPoint presentation.

BOX 11.1	**Chronology of Riverblindness Control in Sub-Saharan Africa**

1968	At an expert meeting in Tunis, participants agree that riverblindness should be controlled regionally.
1970	United Nations Development Programme (UNDP) funds a World Health Organization (WHO) team to prepare a regional strategy for West Africa.
1972	The World Bank convenes a meeting in London of the Food and Agriculture Organization of the United Nations (FAO), UNDP, and WHO, which jointly sponsor Phase I of the riverblindness partnership, dividing roles along lines of expertise.
1974	Phase I is launched.
1978	The program is extended into southern Côte d'Ivoire to prevent reinvasion of blackflies.
1981	Rotational larvicide is introduced as a viable solution to resistance.
Mid-1980s	Currency fluctuations create a $35 million shortfall in the program trust fund.
1986	The program expands farther west and south.
1987	Ivermectin is approved for human use.
1988–95	Drug delivery strategies are developed and tested.
1994	A plan is formed to transfer and devolve post–Phase I surveillance and activities to participating country governments.
1995	Emphasis is placed on community-directed treatment methods.
1995–present	TDR studies continue to evaluate and optimize methods.
1996	Phase II, covering 19 more countries, is launched, with the establishment of the first four projects.
1997	Distribution projects total 29.
2000	Distribution projects total 63.
2002	Phase I ends; riverblindness is eliminated as a public health and socioeconomic problem in large parts of West Africa.
2003	Phase II projects total 107.
Present	Phase II continues to extend the drug distribution network to the remaining 19 endemic countries and to foster delivery of a wide variety of health interventions. By 2010 Phases I and II will have protected some 150 million people.

riverblindness is transmitted on a regional scale. The first projects had been small, and the savanna was consistently reinfested. Accordingly, the West African phase of the program was planned as a regional initiative to overcome the epidemiological factors that had undermined village-level efforts. The program systematically expanded over its first few years to achieve full coverage of several river systems in seven countries. But even this ambitious start was not sufficient; the program subsequently doubled in size and was expanded to cover 11 countries. Vector control was the primary strategy in West Africa, supplemented by drug distribution beginning in the late 1980s and early 1990s.

In 1996 Phase II of the program was launched to cover 19 more countries—the remainder of infested Africa. Phase II is based on distributing Mectizan (ivermectin). Merck & Co., which developed the drug in the 1980s, now donates the medicine on an unlimited basis to control riverblindness.

Phase II represents a much more conventional scaling up story than Phase I. Mectizan is distributed by communities themselves, trained and supported by the riverblindness partners, which include international agencies, participating national governments, nongovernmental development organizations (NGDOs), donor countries, and, of course, the communities themselves.

Phase II was tested and validated on a local basis and has been scaled up by continually launching more projects. From modest beginnings in 1996, the program was funding 107 projects by the end of 2003. These projects delivered more than 35 million treatments in 2003 alone. As of April 2004, six more projects were established; by 2007 another nine projects will be launched, bringing the number of people reached to 65 million. By 2010, when Phase II ends, 150 million people are projected to be protected in all 30 countries under both phases of the project (box 11.2).

The distribution network is also being tested to deliver other health interventions. This possibility opens the door to further scaling up to help control other diseases in the riverblindness areas, which are almost exclusively remote, rural, and poor. Most of the people living in these areas are not reached by other programs, and some are not reached by the national governments themselves.

What Is Riverblindness and How Is It Controlled?

Onchocerciasis, or "oncho," is known as riverblindness because it is prevalent around fast-flowing rivers and causes blindness. The disease

BOX 11.2	**Thirty Years of Achievement in Fighting Riverblindness**
1975	Ten million people are protected; 10,000 kilometers of rivers are treated, covering 660,000 square kilometers in seven countries.
1979–80	Twenty million people are protected; 40,000 kilometers of rivers are treated, covering 780,000 square kilometers in eight countries.
1989–90	Thirty million people are protected; 50,000 kilometers of rivers are treated, covering 1.3 million square kilometers in 11 countries. Aerial spraying is fully scaled up.
	Large-scale Mectizan distribution begins, with 60,000 people treated.
1994	Thirty-five million people are protected; 2 million people are treated with Mectizan. Larviciding continues.
2001	Phase II establishes community-directed drug distribution networks in 16 countries.
2002	Sixty-six million people are protected, 40 million in Phase I and 26 million in Phase II. Phase I ends. Six hundred thousand cases of blindness are prevented, and 18 million children are spared the risk of riverblindness. Twenty-five million hectares of land are freed for resettlement and cultivation, which will feed an estimated 17 million additional people. Phase II treats 26 million people with Mectizan.
2003	Seventy-five million people are protected. Thirty-five million people are treated in 68,000 communities in the Phase II area; more than 160,000 community distributors and 18,000 health workers are trained or retrained.
2007	One hundred and five million people are projected to be protected, including 65 million treated with Mectizan in 100,000 communities in 16 Phase II countries.
2010	One hundred and fifty million people are projected to be protected in all 30 countries under both phases of the project. Phase II ends.

causes unrelenting itching, physical scars from the constant scratching, depigmentation and thickening of the skin, reduction of vision, and eventually blindness. More than 99 percent of all cases of riverblindness occur in Africa.

Riverblindness is a parasitic disease caused by worms. As adults these worms can measure nearly a meter long and live in coiled mating pairs in nodules under the skin. Reproducing adult females spawn about 2,000 immature worms every day. These tiny juvenile worms migrate throughout the skin and eyes, causing the various symptoms of the disease. While they are damaging, these immature worms cannot mature to adulthood without the blackfly, their intermediate host. Flies ingest immature worms when they bite infected people. As the worms live in the fly, they mature sexually over the course of a week. If the fly bites a human, the maturing worm will grow to adulthood inside the human body. Upon finding mating partners, the adults become encapsulated and produce more immature worms, completing the transmission cycle.

Riverblindness control is complicated by the 15-year lifespan of the adult worm. Adult females also remain fertile throughout most of their long lives. Although the immature worms live in the skin for only about two years, their numbers are continually refreshed as long as adult females are alive in the body. Therefore, even with instant and complete transmission control, the disease would not die out naturally for 15 years (the lifespan of adult worms). In practical terms, this means that attempts to eliminate the disease must last at least 20 years.

Phase I of the program in West Africa attacked the disease by killing the larvae of the flies that transmit the worms. It depended on killing these immature flies over a long enough period that the adult parasites in human hosts would all die out. Once the reproducing adult worms were eliminated, biting flies would no longer ingest any parasites, and the transmission cycle would be broken. The key to this approach lay in reducing the fly population for 15 years to stop transmission and then sustaining the achievement with follow-up surveillance to prevent recrudescence. As Phase I moved into infested areas of West Africa in several stages, more than 30 years of control have been required to fully eliminate the public health problem posed by riverblindness.

When ivermectin was developed and then donated by Merck, the program adopted a second strategy, implemented in West Africa in the late 1980s and early 1990s. This strategy formed the basis for Phase II (figure 11.1).

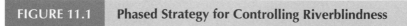

FIGURE 11.1   **Phased Strategy for Controlling Riverblindness**

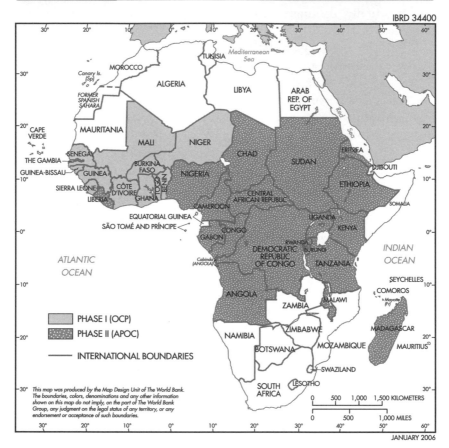

Phase II of the program, in the remainder of endemic Sub-Saharan Africa, is based on ivermectin distribution; vector control is not possible in these areas because forest cover precludes West African–style aerial spraying. This method aims to disrupt transmission by a different mechanism. The drug is effective against only the juvenile parasites, killing 95 percent with a single dose. The adult worms continue to live, churning out offspring. However, because it is the juvenile parasites that cause the disease, ivermectin immediately relieves symptoms and allows the body to begin healing itself. Doses of the drug are required only once a year, but they must be taken for as long as any adult worms are still alive—up to 15 years. By killing almost all the immature worms, ivermectin also dramatically lowers the chance of parasite ingestion by biting flies. To affect transmission, it is therefore necessary to treat a high share of people who have the disease in a given community, because if only a few people take the drug, flies will continue to transmit parasites ingested from others.

The Devastating Socioeconomic Toll of Riverblindness

The consequences of infection are severe. Infected people face physical disability and social stigma that can reduce the quality of life. The unbearable itching and blindness hinder individuals' contributions to their own well-being and undermine the emotional and economic health of the household and community (box 11.3). Consequently, riverblindness—which predominantly affects poor people in remote areas—has a direct link to poverty.

Before World War II little was known about the relationship between riverblindness and poverty in Africa. The disease was neglected by colonial administrations because it did not threaten their interests, as it affected the poorest of the poor, living in the most remote rural areas.

BOX 11.3	The Human Face of Riverblindness: A Nigerian Woman's Daily Torment

The rashes first appeared when I was six years old. That was when the itching began. At school I couldn't concentrate because of the incessant itching. The children in class used to laugh at me, so I stopped going to school when I was nine. I married in 1989. My father arranged the marriage; my husband didn't see me before we got married. When we met and he saw my skin, he was very angry. I lived with him for a few months and became pregnant. Then my skin got worse. Despite the pregnancy, he sent me home to my parents. From the time I left until the birth of my baby, I had no support from my husband, no money for me or my baby. You can see from my skin that I am always scratching. It affects the amount of attention that I can give to my children. I can hardly sleep at night. I feel weak from the pain and nuisance that is always there. What can I do?

—Agnes, a Nigerian mother, 1995

Following treatment with ivermectin, Agnes' symptoms disappeared. She has since reconciled with her husband.

When scientists began to investigate riverblindness in the endemic villages and districts of West Africa, they made astonishing and disturbing discoveries. They found that more than 60 percent of the savanna population carried the parasite, and 10 percent of the adult population and half of males over age 40 were blind. Thirty percent of people were visually impaired, and early signs of riverblindness were common among children.

Eventually, scientists discovered the huge socioeconomic consequences of the high infection rates they had found. As village blindness reached epidemic proportions, it left too few able-bodied people to tend fields. Food shortages and economic collapse forced residents to abandon homelands in fertile river valleys. Moving to highlands and forested areas offered some protection from further infection, but it forced farmers to struggle with poor soil and water shortages on overcrowded lands. Eventually, riverblindness pushed prosperous communities into poverty. Armed with this new knowledge about its economic impact, development agencies made the disease a new priority.

A Vision Takes Shape

The roots of the program and the partnership to defeat riverblindness as a public health problem in Africa can be traced back to the 1940s, but a comprehensive plan was not formulated until 1968. The riverblindness problem was evaluated at a meeting in Tunis sponsored by the government of France through the West African Epidemic Disease Control Organization in the former French areas (OCCGE), the World Health Organization (WHO), and the United States Agency for International Development (USAID). Participating experts agreed that it was both technically feasible and desirable to control riverblindness in the Volta River Basin of West Africa, the region with the highest blindness rates.

Funded by the United Nations Development Programme (UNDP), a team of WHO scientists and consultants began to lay the technical groundwork for a major regional initiative to defeat riverblindness in 1970. By 1972 the international development community was mobilizing to fight the disease (box 11.4). In 1974 the affected countries, the World Bank, and three UN agencies (WHO, the Food and Agriculture Organization of the United Nations [FAO], and UNDP) launched an unprecedented partnership to defeat riverblindness.

BOX 11.4	Robert McNamara's Vision for Controlling Riverblindness

During a 1972 visit to Upper Volta (now Burkina Faso) and Mali, World Bank President Robert McNamara saw shattered villages and fallow fields, a then-common feature of regions with endemic riverblindness. He saw chains of blind people led by small boys whose vision had not yet been extinguished by the scourge. After meeting scientific experts, he was quickly convinced that it was possible to control the disease. It was estimated that a program to control the disease would cost $120 million over 20 years at the 1973 exchange rate.

About a month after his visit to West Africa, McNamara convened a meeting in London with counterparts from WHO, UNDP, and FAO. Together they agreed to jointly sponsor the program and form its steering committee. Annual meetings would assemble the governing body, to be composed of all donors, participating countries, the World Bank, and the three UN agency sponsors.

"Nothing like that had ever been done before," McNamara later recalled. "We [the World Bank and three UN agencies] brought together a group of interested parties—both the nations of the infected areas and potential donors. It was a very tight organization. It never did develop a big bureaucracy, and we were able to get the commitments for long-term financial support from various governments."

The riverblindness program has funded two distinct phases: the Onchocerciasis Control Program (OCP) between 1974 and 2002 (Phase I) (figure 11.2) and the African Programme for Onchocerciasis Control (APOC) between 1996 and 2010 (Phase II). Phase I had a dual mandate: to eliminate riverblindness as a public heath problem and as an obstacle to socioeconomic development. Phase II also seeks to eliminate riverblindness as a public health problem, but East and Central Africa do not have the same socioeconomic development needs as West Africa did in Phase I. The effects of riverblindness are different in East and Central Africa because the strain of parasite prevalent outside the savanna belt is less likely to be blinding but has a greater impact on the skin. The stigma and disability due to these dermatologic effects is difficult to quantify, but humanitarian reasons alone were more than sufficient to justify the expense of control. The labor lost due to itching runs in the millions of person-years

Phase I (OCP) in 1974

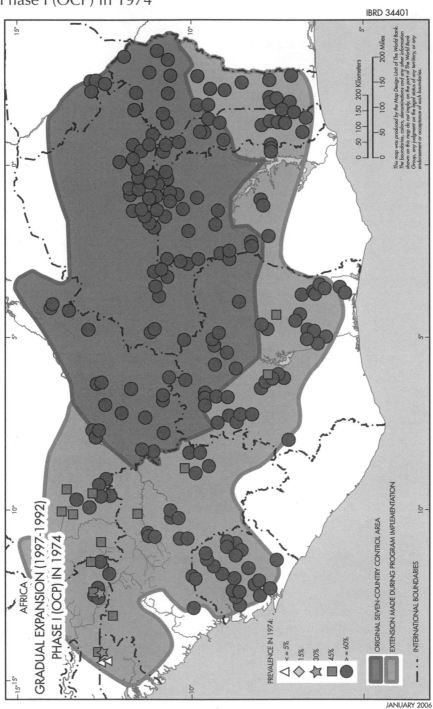

Source: Onchocerciasis Coordination Unit, World Bank

Phase I (OCP) in 2002

IBRD 34402

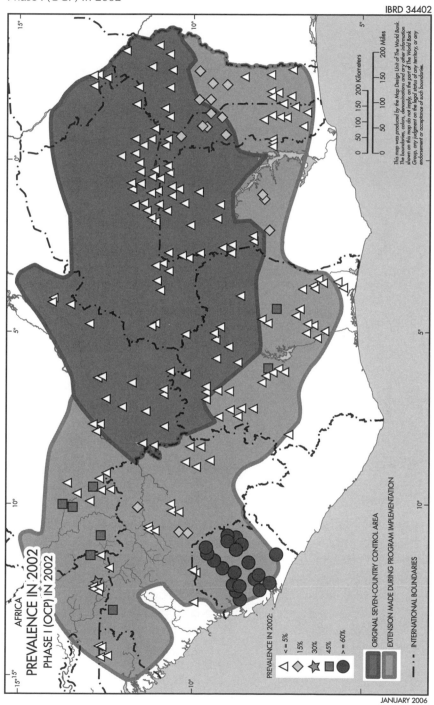

AFRICA
PREVALENCE IN 2002
PHASE I (OCP) IN 2002

PREVALENCE IN 2002:
◁ <= 5%
◇ 15%
☆ 30%
■ 45%
● >= 60%

ORIGINAL SEVEN-COUNTRY CONTROL AREA

EXTENSION MADE DURING PROGRAM IMPLEMENTATION

— ·· — INTERNATIONAL BOUNDARIES

This map was produced by the Map Design Unit of The World Bank.
The boundaries, colors, denominations and any other information
shown on this map do not imply, on the part of The World Bank
Group, any judgment on the legal status of any territory, or any
endorsement or acceptance of such boundaries.

0 50 100 150 200 Kilometers
0   50   100   150   200 Miles

JANUARY 2006

every year; this labor is added back into rural economies as the disease is brought under control.

By the end of Phase I, the riverblindness program had covered 1.3 million square kilometers of land in 11 countries, protecting 40 million people at risk. Based on the lessons learned, Phase II was launched in the mid-1990s to defeat the disease in the continent's 19 remaining endemic countries.

Phase I: Controlling Riverblindness in West Africa

For sheer magnitude and duration, the campaign to defeat riverblindness is unique. The program spans 30 countries across Africa, embracing a comprehensive approach to eliminate the disease as a public health problem. Remarkably, seven of the nine original donors have been with the campaign steadily over three decades. Such a long-term commitment has been crucial, since it takes up to 20 years to interrupt the disease's transmission.

Since blackflies migrate across international borders, the affected governments and international experts were convinced that only a regional program could control riverblindness. Phase I therefore targeted seven West African countries (Benin, Burkina Faso, Côte d'Ivoire, Ghana, Mali, Niger, and Togo). With the collaboration and political commitment of these nations, control operations were discussed and planned. As the primary method of control, aircraft would spray environmentally safe larvicides around fast-flowing rivers, the breeding grounds of the intermediate host of the disease, the blackfly.

Containing the Blackfly through Vector Control

Initially, vector control operations covered 660,000 square kilometers in seven countries—an area believed to be large enough to contain the blackfly vector. However, in May 1975, after three months of successful operations, many migrant blackflies from untreated watercourses reappeared, threatening to reintroduce the disease into the program area. "We were really very, very worried," recalls Dr. Azodoga Sékétéli, who has been involved in technical operations for the program since 1976. "After investigations, we found the flies were coming from up to 600 kilometers away from the area we were treating." In response, the program extended operations to another four West African countries—Guinea, Guinea-Bissau, Senegal, and Sierra Leone (figure 11.2). The program area increased geographic coverage to 1.3 million square kilometers, enabling the campaign to increase the number of people protected from 10 million to 30 million.

The program's experts, who formulated the so-called long-term strategy, fully recognized that extension of control operations had two purposes. The first was to halt reinvasion of infected blackflies into the central area and make the program sufficiently comprehensive to eliminate the disease throughout much of West Africa. The second was to nearly double the number of at-risk people protected from the disease, thereby greatly enhancing the welfare of a high proportion of West Africa's rural villages. (Figure 11.2 shows the program's effect on disease prevalence.) In light of this opportunity to protect many more people, the program expanded beyond what was required to stop reinvasion in the original area.

This large initial effort is not typical of a scaling-up operation, but the ecology of the target disease demanded an extensive initial scope. Some issues must be addressed on a regional basis; sometimes a large approach can work where a local one has failed. Riverblindness is one of many epidemic diseases that is best addressed comprehensively.

Size limitation—leading to reinvasion—was not the only problem faced in Phase I. In 1980, while the campaign was struggling with reinvasion, blackflies began to develop a genetic resistance to previously lethal doses of the only larvicide available to the program. "That was really bad for all of us," recalls Dr. Sékétéli. "To have such resistance plus the reinvasion phenomenon looked like a disaster."

Through intensive scientific research and experiments, program scientists kept fighting the resistance and exploring the potential for new larvicides. The result: an innovative strategy to use seven different larvicides in rotation. Because each larvicide is used for only a few weeks at a time, the fly population does not have a chance to develop resistance before facing a different insecticide. Their various compositions and modes of action are sufficiently different to prevent cross-resistance as well. This strategy, which addressed several parameters and met ecological standards, successfully eliminated resistance within the fly population. It has now become the standard model for vector control. This aspect of the program is directly applicable to other programs involving insect management.

Expanding operations to fight reinvasion and developing new larvicides to overcome resistance involved huge new expenses. Ultimately, donors' commitment carried the day. "Donors appreciated our ability to give them scientific explanations of the problems," says Dr. Sékétéli. "Their continued commitment and understanding was crucial to us. They always responded positively and increased the budget for operational research accordingly." Bruce Benton, who manages the World Bank's Onchocerciasis Coordination Unit, adds, "If the Bank had been the executing agency, the response may have been different. I think our ability to speak to donors on their own level generated trust and confidence that we could overcome these crises."

The expensive effort to develop new larvicides began in the early 1980s and lasted for many years. In the mid-1980s, when this effort was in full swing, international currency markets delivered a crushing blow to the program. The U.S. dollar–denominated trust fund plummeted in value, while the program's obligations increased thanks to the soaring French franc and Japanese yen. In a little more than two years, these shifts, coupled with the increased cost of combating resistance, created a shortfall of $35 million.

With the campaign in jeopardy, the World Bank set out to visit as many donors as possible to solicit more support. Building on its role as a fellow donor that was prepared to reinvest in the program, the Bank convinced other partners to follow suit. "The donors' willingness to increase support shows their commitment to the program, but it also demonstrates why it's so important to maintain good donor relations," says Benton. "If we had just called them up out of the blue, they might not have been so receptive. But because we had involved them all along, keeping them informed and trying to meet their own priorities, I think they had a greater sense of ownership over the program. What was at stake was the survival of their program too. The series of crises that could have brought the program down demonstrated two things: overall commitment by the various partners and the importance of clearly delineated roles. WHO staff could go ahead and address problems on the ground, including resistance and implementing the long-term strategy, while the Bank could talk to donors and say, 'We've got a problem, but it's not insurmountable. It's something we think we can address.'"

Political instability also threatened the program. Two major conflicts could have derailed the campaign's work in Phase I, but the success of operations had increased awareness of the disease and its devastating socioeconomic impact. As a result, the program director was able to prevail on heads of state to allow operations to continue uninterrupted. When the program began, regional aerial operations were based in Ghana. When Ghana closed its borders during the 1978–79 revolution, the entire campaign was jeopardized. Togo's president, Gnassingbe Eyadema, whose parents had suffered from riverblindness, appreciated the importance of continued larvicidal spraying and offered a new base for operations in Kara, Togo. By 1982 all air operations had moved from Ghana to Togo, where they remain today. A few years later, in 1985, the program was again threatened when Burkina Faso and Mali closed their borders as a result of the conflict between the two countries. Following an appeal by the program, the countries made exceptions for the campaign, allowing aircraft to continue larvicidal spraying.

A New Drug and New Possibilities: Using Ivermectin to Control Riverblindness

Rotational spraying was defeating transmission, but the strategy did nothing to relieve the symptoms of those already afflicted. By the late 1970s Merck & Co.'s Mectizan (ivermectin) was shown to be effective against the juvenile worms that cause the disease's symptoms. Following slow and expensive drug development and safety trials, ivermectin was finally registered in 1987. Under treatment, the unbearable itching quickly subsides, the skin heals, and the sight is saved as long as a patient is not yet completely blinded.

Since ivermectin does not kill adult worms, an infected person must typically take the drug every 6 to 12 months for 20 years to interrupt transmission. A community must obtain 65 percent therapeutic coverage to interrupt disease transmission.

Most people with the disease, however, live in rural areas, which are often beyond the reach of national health services. Sustaining a drug coverage threshold long enough to interrupt transmission therefore represented a daunting challenge. Recognizing the importance of the drug—and the inability of the riverblindness partnership to afford it—in 1987 Merck & Co. generously agreed to donate it, free of charge, for as long as necessary (box 11.5). The drug—effective, safe, and now free—presented the opportunity to control riverblindness in far-flung areas in which the use of expensive larvicides was not practical. Most blackfly breeding areas outside West Africa are also covered by foliage, which precluded Phase I's strategy of aerial larviciding.

The program first used ivermectin only in highly endemic areas, where the risk of blindness was greatest. As it became clear that iver-

| BOX 11.5 | **Using a Veterinary Drug to Control a Human Disease: How Merck & Co. Decided to Donate Mectizan to Fight Riverblindness** |

The Mectizan Donation Program resulted from the convergence of several unique factors. Ivermectin was initially tested and subsequently developed as a broad-spectrum antiparasitic veterinary drug. In the veterinary market, ivermectin was one of Merck's biggest successes ever. The animal formulation of the drug is extensively used in cattle, sheep, and other farm animals, as well as in dogs as protection against heartworm.

Ivermectin was not developed for human use because there is no need for it in the countries where most drugs are sold. But some of Merck's scientific staff had experience in the areas of Africa affected by riverblindness and realized its potential for use against the disease. Much of the subsequent testing for this purpose was done in Ghana at a program-affiliated research center, with the cooperation of Merck scientists, who often conducted research on their own time.

When it became clear that the drug would be useful, Merck management initially considered selling it at a reduced price. However, at the time, no one knew how good the drug was, and there was disappointment that it was not able to kill adult worms. Accordingly, donors decided against paying for it. In the meantime, Merck management and some of the Merck scientists who had worked on the drug's development began to discuss the possibility of donating the drug. Merck was faced with the lack of a buyer and saw an opportunity to make a significant impact on public heath. Many research scientists felt that the drug should be donated, since none of the people afflicted with the disease could afford to buy it and the donor countries would not, but the need was clear.

In 1987 Merck announced that it would donate the drug on an unlimited basis, its financial stability enabling it to make such a large and long-term commitment. The lack of a human need in paying markets proved helpful, since Merck did not have to be concerned about donated ivermectin being smuggled into countries and undermining legitimate sales.

This experience was unusual. The lack of a commercial market generally means that no research is conducted and no drugs developed. Where drugs have been developed, drug companies face many problems in giving them away in some countries and charging for them in others—as the struggle to supply free or inexpensive HIV/AIDS drugs to developing countries has shown. The riverblindness program was fortunate to find a drug with no other human applications—and a drug company that was willing to donate it on a large scale.

mectin was well tolerated—both physically and culturally—the partnership scaled up treatment. In 1989–90, the first years of scaling up ivermectin treatments, the partnership provided doses to 60,000 people. The scaling-up process continued, reaching 2 million people in 1994 over much of the Phase I territory. The combination of aerial spraying and ivermectin distribution allowed for complete coverage, prompt alleviation of symptoms, permanent interruption of transmission, and a defined end-point for the partnership based on the lifespan of the adult worm. By 2002 the partnership had lowered the prevalence rate of infection and virtually stopped transmission within 10 of the 11 West African countries where it operated.[1]

Planning for other programs that require pharmaceuticals cannot assume that the manufacturer will donate the drugs. However, this experience shows what can be achieved with donated drugs, and it may prove useful in publicizing the opportunity available to other pharmaceutical companies considering philanthropic initiatives of their own.

Phase II: Scaling Up to Control Riverblindness Throughout Africa

The introduction of ivermectin presented challenges and opportunities that became catalysts for scaling up at all levels. It transformed the program from a technologically driven categorical health initiative to a community-directed process of treatment and empowerment, focused on riverblindness, of course, but applicable to other diseases as well. Not only did this grassroots approach contribute to high population coverage and empower communities to take charge of their own health; it also planted the seeds of sustainability—absolutely vital for a disease that must be treated for at least 20 years to interrupt transmission.

With the drug challenge solved thanks to Merck & Co., the program had to find a cost-effective and feasible way to distribute ivermectin in remote areas of Africa where the disease was endemic. Many vaccines, immunizations, and vitamins are inexpensive or free but go unused because they never reach those who need them. In 1990 the program began full-scale distribution in extension areas—to the south and west of the original core area in West Africa—using mobile teams in jeeps plus local health staff support.

In this first step toward scaling up, paid local health professionals called communities to a central location for dosing. In more than 30 river basins, therapeutic coverage averaged about 65 percent in 1987, rising to more than 70 percent by 1995. Using trained health staff at the local level was expensive, however. The program considered various cost-recovery schemes, to no avail.

The answer to the high cost of mobile teams arrived indirectly. Invariably, when drugs were distributed some villagers were away—hunting, working, or traveling. In response, once it became clear that ivermectin's safety profile allowed unsupervised dosing, the program authorized the mobile teams to leave doses for absent community members.

In the second step toward scaling up, national health services combined with local health staff to distribute the drug through a community-based distribution approach. This approach had several advantages over the mobile teams—particularly higher coverage and benefits at a lower cost. But even community-based methods proved too expensive, because some remote areas required high daily stipends and travel costs for supervising staff. After evaluating community-based methods, the program decided that the key to effective, replicable, and inexpensive distribution was to scale up again to "community-directed treatment," a strategy that enabled communities to take charge of distribution—and ultimately their own health (boxes 11.6

BOX 11.6	**How Do Community-directed Treatments Compare with Treatments Provided by Regular Health Services?**

In 1994–96 the riverblindness partnership and the UNDP/World Bank/WHO Special Program for Research and Training in Tropical Diseases (TDR) jointly compared drug delivery methods used by health services with those used by communities in five countries. Health service providers determine the steps and schedule, as well as the design and implementation. In community-directed treatment systems, after training and support, the community itself decides how to organize treatment for its members, including selecting the drug distributor, determining the timing and method of drug collection and distribution, and reporting to local health providers. Thus, the role of the community changes from being solely the recipient of services within the guidelines and limits set by out-

BOX 11.6	How Do Community-directed Treatments Compare with Treatments Provided by Regular Health Services? (*Cont'd*)

side providers to a position of prominence as the lead stakeholder and decisionmaker in community-level health services.

Conducted in Cameroon, Ghana, Mali, Nigeria, and Uganda, the study showed that community-directed treatment offered several important advantages:

- Less work for local health providers.
- Better treatment and geographical coverage.
- Stronger ability to adapt the drug distribution and treatment program as the communities' needs and requirements change.
- A greater sense of commitment to and ownership of the program, which in turn promotes sustainability and the possibility of eventual integration into the local health system.

The study concluded that community-directed treatment with ivermectin was feasible and effective in a wide range of geographical and cultural settings in Africa and likely to be replicable in other communities where riverblindness was endemic. It recommended that this approach become a principal method for riverblindness control in Africa.

Community-directed treatment overwhelmingly exceeds the treatment coverage rates of regular health services in Ghana and Kenya (see figure). It produces therapeutic coverage well over the 65 percent threshold necessary for long-term riverblindness elimination.

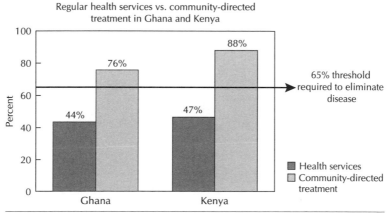

Regular health services vs. community-directed treatment in Ghana and Kenya

65% threshold required to eliminate disease

■ Health services
□ Community-directed treatment

Source: TDR.

and 11.7). The decision represented a major turning point for the riverblindness program.

The program adopted community-directed treatment for Phase I in 1995. Under this approach each community collectively appointed a local drug distributor from within its village. This person, who became the contact between the community and health care services, received supplies of ivermectin annually. NGDOs and public health workers trained and supervised community drug distributors, who then ensured that medicine was dosed properly and delivered to those who needed it. Communities themselves determined what compensation, if any, the drug distributor received.

Training and communication between the distributors and their trainers (NGDOs and health workers) have been essential for maintaining the quality and responsiveness of services, and open channels of communication between the ministries of health, NGDOs, and health workers have facilitated field operations. Overall, the close links established between the partners have facilitated greater ownership, innovation, and treatment coverage.

Emboldened by the remarkable success of Phase I—and empowered by Merck & Co.'s donation of free drugs and the feasibility and efficacy of community-directed treatment—the program embarked on a broader and more ambitious mission for Phase II (box 11.7). Together the same sponsoring agencies, most of the same donors, and 19 new participating countries joined forces to defeat the disease throughout Africa.[2]

Community-directed treatment enabled the campaign to dramatically scale up operations. The program has already established a drug distribution network in 16 of the 19 Phase II countries. Reaching the most remote rural areas, this network reliably delivers annual doses of medicine where national health services are weak or nonexistent. In 2003 alone 35 million people in 68,000 communities were treated—doubling the coverage provided in 2001 (table 11.1). More than 160,000 community distributors and 18,000 health workers were trained or retrained in 2003. By 2010 the riverblindness program will protect 150 million people.

Phase II faces many difficulties, including a lack of health infrastructure in many affected areas (box 11.8). As everywhere else in the world, trained nurses and doctors in many African countries prefer to work in urban areas. Meanwhile, the number of doctors and nurses has been decreasing in Africa because of death and illness caused by HIV/AIDS. To strengthen capacity, partner NGDOs are

| BOX 11.7 | Scaling Up Riverblindness Control in Nigeria |

Nigeria, Africa's most populous country, provides a good example of scaling up along a variety of dimensions—number of projects, population treated, therapeutic coverage achieved, and number of community drug distributors trained.

Scale-up of riverblindness projects in Nigeria

Year	Approved projects, new	Phase II projects total	Population treated	Therapeutic treatment coverage (%)	Trained community drug distributors
1995	pre-Phase II	–	4,237,982	20	–
1996	4	4	5,901,961	66	na
1997	5	9	8,617,602	70	na
1998	8	17	9,000,000	77	4,884
1999	8	25	13,180,987	86	37,663
2000	1	26	na	64	49,352
2001	0	26	16,586,354	75	56,797
2002	1	27	18,552,844	75	58,384

–is not applicable
na is not available
Source: African Programme for Onchocerciasis Control.

At the inception of Phase II, Nigeria was the world's most heavily endemic country, representing almost 40 percent of all riverblindness cases. A serious public health problem in 26 of 30 Nigerian states, riverblindness was estimated to put more than 30 million people at risk. Although Nigeria was not a Phase I country, treatment with ivermectin began, as both a humanitarian mission and a cross-border initiative, under the auspices of Phase I in 1989. Cross-border community-initiated ivermectin treatment also brought relief to six communities in Cameroon: by 1995 roughly 4.2 million people had been treated for riverblindness, mainly through NGDO programs. These results achieved only a 20 percent therapeutic coverage rate, however—far below the 65 percent required to interrupt transmission.

In 1997, with Nigeria officially participating in Phase II, the riverblindness partnership implemented four principal projects in the country using community-directed treatment with ivermectin. Since then it has treated almost 20 million people a year, trained tens of thousands of community drug distributors, and surpassed the threshold in therapeutic treatment coverage needed to halt transmission. Overall community-directed treatment activities in 2002 included an average geographical coverage of 95 percent and an average therapeutic coverage of 75 percent, with 18.5 million people treated. Moreover, many projects in Nigeria have added other health interventions to community-directed treatment for riverblindness, including treatment for lymphatic filariasis, vitamin A deficiency, schistosomiasis, and guinea worm, as well as primary eye care and cataract identification.

TABLE 11.1	Scaling Up Phase II, 1996–2003								
	1996	1997	1998	1999	2000	2001	2002	2003	Total
Community-directed projects approved	4	25	16	12	6	6	11	27	107
Annual treatments (millions of people)	7.9	10.5	14.1	17.0	22.0	24.5	28.0	35.0	159
Geographic coverage (%)[a]	69.6	69.6	73.6	75.5	82.6	83.3	87.7	88.1	–
Therapeutic coverage (%)[b]	51.2	52.7	54.2	55.7	59.7	60.8	64.5	74.0	–

–is not applicable
a. Percentage of area treated per total area at risk.
b. Percentage of people covered per total population.
Source: WHO 2003e.

training health service staff to take more responsibility for training drug distributors.

Empowered health service staff and local communities play an increasingly important role in Phase II operations. Strengthening capacity is a central feature of the program's sustainability plans. All projects are launched with program management, technical assistance from Phase II's NGDO partners, and financial assistance from donors. For the first five years of each project, 75 percent of costs are paid by the Phase II Trust Fund, with participating countries and NGDOs contributing the remaining 25 percent in cash or in kind. Projects making progress toward sustainability become eligible for an additional three years of international financing at a greatly reduced level.

The program is building capacity where needed in national governments, health services, local NGDOs, and communities. By 2010, when international financing for all projects will cease, the countries themselves will bear responsibility for distributing ivermectin and supporting the community distribution network.

Unlike more linear, health service-based distribution systems, community-directed treatment endorses active community participation, which improves drug access while creating a sense of responsibility and ownership. Communities often hold the position of drug distributor in high esteem. Many community drug distributors, in fact, feel honor-bound to give their time freely for the benefit of the whole community. Moreover, through the process of creating extensive net-

BOX 11.8	**Building Capacity Where Health Services Are Weakest**

The paucity of trained health staff in riverblindness-endemic countries, particularly in remote rural areas, presented a tough challenge to maximizing coverage rates and eliminating riverblindness as a public health problem. How to distribute drugs when national health systems had inadequate access to rural populations, the main target group? Accordingly, the program directed research toward operational efficiency. Thus far, community-directed treatment has proven to be one of the most successful methods of distribution for developing countries in Africa, planting seeds for the long-term sustainability of ivermectin distribution (see figure).

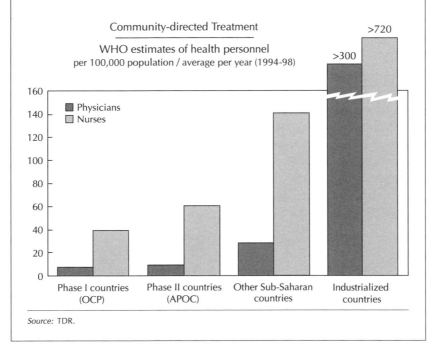

Community-directed Treatment

WHO estimates of health personnel
per 100,000 population / average per year (1994-98)

Source: TDR.

works of community drug distributors, the program has strengthened many of the weakest ministries of health, and several international partner NGDOs have worked to build capacity among local NGDOs. With support from the partnership, community-directed treatment stresses ownership by communities, grassroots viability, empowerment, and self-reliance.

Community-directed treatment has empowered Africans to successfully fight riverblindness in their own villages, relieving suffering, boosting productivity, and slowing transmission across the entire region. The approach provides hope, and it empowers communities to help themselves or seek the partnerships that allow them to do so. It allows them to play a large role in determining their own health outcomes and future.

How Much Did the Program Cost?

The riverblindness partnership is set to complete its second and final phase by 2010. The total budget for the two phases will amount to about $735 million in donor financing, primarily for larviciding and entomological evaluation. Other costs have included administration, ivermectin delivery, training, research and development, and extensive meetings aimed at ensuring transparency within the wide-ranging partnership. The annual cost of protecting one person was well under $1 a year in Phase I. The target cost per treatment is about $0.15 for the end of Phase II.

The economic rate of return for Phase I—the result of an increase in labor and arable land made available by the program—was 20 percent. Labor was calculated based on the 20 years of productive labor per person formerly lost to the disease—8 years of blindness and 12 years of reduced life expectancy. The increased benefits from land assumed a conservative resettlement rate and the increased agricultural production that would occur in the new lands minus the production forgone in the abandoned areas. Normally, a 10 percent rate of return for World Bank projects in the "productive sector" (excluding social projects such as education and health) is considered a success. By 2010 the economic rate of return for Phase II is expected to reach 17 percent.

Expanding the Program to Cover Other Health Problems

What began as a categorical disease program has broadened into an ideal entry point for providing health care to tens of thousands of people living in remote communities in Africa—most of them not reached by other programs and many not reached by national health services. The community-directed distribution network can provide primary health care to the poorest of the poor through simple, once or twice a year interventions by nonmedical staff. In some areas, additional activities have been tested and planned; in other areas, communities themselves have taken spontaneous action. In some cases communities chose to distribute other externally provided drugs using the same distributor and distribution method. In other cases ivermectin distributors obtained supplies on their own from district health centers and then provided them to community members.

Participating countries, donors, and the partnership's governing board have all endorsed the integration of community-directed treatment into existing health systems through other health interventions. Some countries, such as Uganda, have begun reorganizing their rural health services to use the community-based network as a national strategy. Communities within the 30 African countries, along with NGDOs such as Helen Keller International and Global 2000, have begun distributing other medications, including vitamin A to prevent malnutrition, pediatric blindness, and death; Praziquantel to control schistosomiasis; ivermectin and albendazole to halt the transmission of lymphatic filariasis; bed nets to prevent malaria; and condoms to prevent HIV/AIDS and promote reproductive health.

Distributing other drugs along with ivermectin can also boost acceptance. Because ivermectin brings immediate relief from the maddening itching of riverblindness, patients want to take it. Demand for the drug and compliance with the drug regime are therefore high among affected communities. The dramatic, immediate effect of ivermectin demonstrates to patients the value of pharmaceuticals in general. Establishing a positive attitude toward appropriate drugs is essential for ensuring the acceptance of important interventions that do not act as quickly or in ways as obvious to patients. Vitamin A, for instance, can reduce under-five child mortality by 25 to 35 percent, but its effect is not immediate, making the link between the drug and its effects harder for patients to appreciate. Codistributing vitamins along with ivermectin helps boost acceptance.

Results from a pilot study in Nigeria on the codistribution of ivermectin and vitamin A have shown the potential of the drug distribution network. Helen Keller International, a Phase II partner, teamed up with the Micronutrient Initiative to promote vitamin A distribution, working through the national health service's district facilities. Coverage was disappointingly low, ranging from zero in some areas to 30 percent in others. Once Helen Keller International began distributing the capsules through the Phase II network, coverage jumped to an average 80 percent. WHO is halfway through a three-year, multicountry study to evaluate this wider potential to deliver new health interventions in the poorest areas of Africa.

The community network established for riverblindness control has enormous potential, but it is necessary to clarify what it can be expected to do and what remains out of reach. No one would argue that this program—or any other—is a replacement for a functioning primary health care system. However, riverblindness areas are typically so poorly served that it has been necessary to construct an intermediary system.

With this system in place, the natural question becomes: what can be done through it? Some other interventions are already being tried (figure 11.3), but there are limits. Some vaccines may not be appropriate for community distribution, because they are too time- and temperature-sensitive or need to be administered by trained personnel.

FIGURE 11.3   **Scaling Up for Additional Interventions**

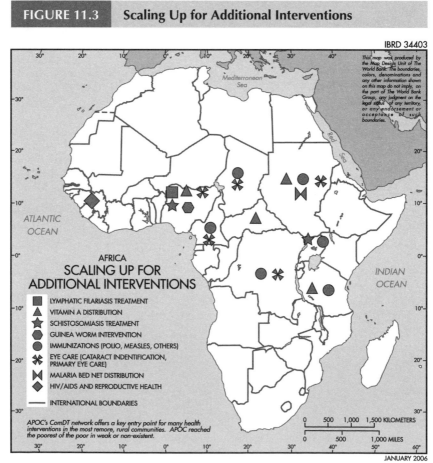

Source: Onchocerciasis Coordination Unit, World Bank.

In contrast, antimalarial bed nets or tsetse traps to prevent sleeping sickness could be distributed through the system. Some drugs, such as azithromycin for trachoma, which is donated by Pfizer, or albendazole for lymphatic filariasis, which is donated by GlaxoSmithKline, could also be safely distributed through community networks. A WHO/TDR study is now under way to evaluate the feasibility of handling complicated interventions such as tuberculosis and home management of malaria through Phase II projects. The first data are expected by 2005.

The riverblindness partnership does not expect to fully address many diseases, but the partnership can pursue aspects of disease control and health promotion to offer partial solutions when complete answers are out of reach. Insecticide-treated bed net distribution, for example, is an important step in preventing malaria.

The fundamental tension between the appeal of delivering more interventions and the danger of overwhelming the distribution system has long been acknowledged. Both the World Bank and WHO have sponsored studies on the issue, many executed by TDR. One study showed that community distributors were already involved in a wide range of health care activities (WHO 2003c). Often the person selected by the community for riverblindness work is the same person chosen for other externally driven health activities, including National Immunization Day work and the polio eradication campaign.

A second TDR study showed that involvement in additional activities was actually beneficial. In general, more activities correlated with better coverage rates and improvements in other key indicators. A third study, which compared the effectiveness of distribution through Phase II community projects with that of school-based programs, found that communities achieved much better coverage (Ndyomugyenyi and others 2004).

While these studies have been progressing, governments have begun advocating wider use of the Phase II system. Guinea is working with its Phase II projects to distribute condoms and HIV/AIDS educational materials. The current optimism may or may not be borne out by future experiences, but it is supported by both scientific studies and field experiences. Much remains to be seen, but there is good reason for a hopeful outlook.

Lessons

Over 30 years the riverblindness program has continually scaled up to cover more territory, reach more people, and push back a devastating disease. As a result of its efforts, riverblindness has been defeated throughout the program area in West Africa, except where operations were delayed by conflict in Sierra Leone. Operations continue there and in the Phase II area, with the goal of eliminating the public health problem posed by the disease throughout Africa by 2010.

Several lessons emerge from the partnership's three decades of operations.

Establishing a Broad Partnership and Defining Each Partner's Role

Continuity and stability among international partners have tremendous benefits, offer valuable synergies, and provide the longevity required to deal with even the most intractable problems.

In addition to its broad geographic scope and long duration, the riverblindness partnership has benefited from the breadth of its membership. More than 80 partners are involved—including 26 donors, 30 African countries, a major pharmaceutical firm (Merck & Co.), and 12 major NGDOs—and tens of thousands of local communities are served. This broad coalition, with its mix of different "corporate cultures," is complex to maintain, but it has created synergies that have yielded enormous advantages (box 11.9). By and large, the partnership's constituents have collaborated remarkably well and have pulled the campaign forward toward its well-defined objectives.

BOX 11.9   Seven Lessons about Partnership

1. Wide-ranging partnerships can have distinct synergies.
2. Given the mix of "corporate cultures," wide-ranging partnerships are complex to form and maintain.
3. Program proactivity and service to the partner constituencies are essential in holding a large coalition together.
4. The perception of transparency is necessary to instill trust.
5. All constituents need to enjoy distinct benefits, since altruism is an inadequate basis for long-term sustainability.
6. Trust enhances equity of participation.
7. Clearly delineated roles and responsibilities are critical for reaping comparative advantages.

An international agreement clearly delineated roles for all parties. Each UN agency relies on its comparative advantage and reputation to develop the program and maintain high standards of operation and treatment. WHO, the executing agency, handles all operations, as well as all technical and scientific matters. The World Bank generates interest among donors and participating country governments and manages donor relations, and UNDP focuses on postcontrol development. FAO applied its agricultural expertise to the many fertile valleys in West Africa once they had been freed of disease.

WHO has flourished in its role as the executing agency. Freed of fundraising obligations and able to count on the Bank's convening power, it has been able to concentrate on the scientific and technical matters in which it is proficient. Handling the disease control aspects is exactly what WHO is intended to do and is best at. In cooperation with other partners, WHO fulfills this role without distraction.

The World Bank's well-defined role has been advantageous for the partnership. Since it is a donor and fiscal agent, the Bank has been able to approach other donors as an equal. Because WHO is the executing agency, the Bank avoids the conflict of interest inherent in advocating on behalf of its own program. Moreover, recognizing that altruism is not the sole motivating factor for involvement, the Bank has worked hard to address the priorities and needs of each donor. This attention to donor relations has built trust and goodwill, creating a sense of ownership among the partners that has helped the campaign weather its crises. It has required that the Bank meet with each donor at least once a year on a one-on-one basis, and that it be prepared to answer questions, address problems, and be attentive to each donor's needs and concerns. The result has been the mobilization of $700 million in donor financing since 1974—an unprecedented level of long-term support for a multidonor program.

The World Bank recognized that the unusually long duration inherent in riverblindness control would require a major effort to recruit new donors. By the mid-1990s, the program had tripled the number of donors from the original nine in 1974. This served the program well by ensuring continuity in financing, as support from individual donors varied over time as a result of changes in governments, shifting aid priorities, economic recessions, and donor fatigue. Despite inconsistent participation by some donors during the 1980s and 1990s, the program did not incur financial shortfalls. Between 1985 and

2000 new donors were enlisted from the Far East, the Middle East, and Northern, Western, and Central Europe.

NGDOs have been key partners in Phase II. Individually, some NGDOs had been working on riverblindness for a long time. Sight-Savers International (originally the British Empire Society for the Blind) has been active in Ghana and Northern Nigeria since the 1950s, surveying the disease and then providing rehabilitative services. Over the past two decades, more and more NGDOs have been providing eye care and other services in riverblindness areas. Even before Phase II began, many NGDOs were distributing ivermectin on their own. Within the riverblindness partnership, these NGDOs offer essential experience and expertise in community mobilization, training, and other areas crucial to achieving high coverage rates in drug distribution. At the same time, these partners have benefited from inclusion in Phase II, which provides them with external financing, scientific expertise, and a forum for coordinating activities continentwide.

The partnership has benefited tremendously from Merck & Co.'s donation of ivermectin—and the company has been well served by its participation in Phase II. However generous, the donation would mean little without a distribution system. Other partners in Phase II provide that mechanism, maximizing the effectiveness of Merck & Co.'s contribution. The initial donation helped boost morale among senior Merck scientists; as Phase II has progressed, the humanitarian benefit has become a major source of pride and employee satisfaction companywide. In an industry frequently blamed for the high cost of drugs and shortcomings in the health care system, Merck has found that the Mectizan Donation Program has been an important factor in recruiting top researchers by reassuring them about the company's corporate citizenship.

By the 1980s the program had an international reputation as one of the most successful health programs since smallpox eradication. It brought high visibility to a disease that might otherwise have been overlooked and attracted resources to defeat it. African health ministers became aware of the disease and were consistently involved in the program, meeting frequently, exchanging views, and putting subtle pressure on one another to achieve as much progress as possible. In this way the program provided a forum for participating countries to collectively take action, learn from one another, and defeat the disease. In Phase II participating countries have taken on a large role in coordinating other partners' activities, collecting and synthesizing data, storing Mectizan, and often operating jointly with NGDOs.

The broad partnership pioneered by the riverblindness programs stands as a ready model for other large programs. Through clearly defined roles and explicit governance rules, the riverblindness program has been able to address a complex problem for three decades. The partnership attained stability by delivering benefits to each constituent, allowing the partnership as a whole to endure. Other programs addressing integrated issues, such as health and development or industry and the environment, could consider similar partnerships.

Funding Ongoing Research

Consistent operational research investments can pay large dividends when they are needed most. Having a research mechanism in place allows anticipated issues to be addressed ahead of time and is invaluable for reacting quickly to unforeseen problems.

The ability of the campaign to adapt from aerial spraying to community-directed treatment with ivermectin was made possible only through ongoing research. The program now invests at least 10 percent of its budget in operational research, which is considered the minimum amount necessary. Continued research has led to the development of Rapid Epidemiological Mapping of Onchocerciasis, a technique vital to rapid mapping and accelerating the scaling-up process. Social development research has led to greater understanding of local conditions and the most effective method of treatment.

Flexibility and Community-directed Approval

Flexibility is essential. Over three decades the program maintained riverblindness control by adapting strategies as circumstances changed. From a vertical, categorical vector-control program to community distribution and now community mobilization, each approach has helped the program advance the ultimate goal of improving health while dealing with changing circumstances and maximizing technological innovations.

The community-directed approach can be scaled up further for use in non-onchocerciasis areas of Africa—and perhaps other regions as well. It can also be adapted to deliver other health interventions.

BIBLIOGRAPHY

Amazigo, U. V., E. Nnoruka, C. Maduka, J. Bump, B. Benton, and A. Sékétéli. 2004. "Ivermectin (Mectizan) Improves Skin Condition and Self-esteem of Females with Onchocerciasis: A Report of Two Case Studies." *Annals of Tropical Medicine and Parasitology* 98(5): 533–37.

Amazigo, U. V., W. R. Brieger, M. Katabarwa, O. Akogun, M. Ntep, B. Boatin, J. N'Doyo, M. Noma, and A. Sékétéli. 2002. "The Challenges of Community-directed Treatment with Ivermectin (CDTI) of the African Programme for Onchocerciasis Control (APOC)." *Annals of Tropical Medicine and Parasitology* 96(1): 41–58.

Amazigo, U. V., O. M. Obono, K. Y. Dadzie, J. Remme, J. Jiya, R. Ndyomugyenyi, J.-B. Roungou, M. Noma, and A. Sékétéli. 2002. "Monitoring Community-directed Treatment Programmes for Sustainability: Lessons from the African Programme for Onchocerciasis Control (APOC)." *Annals of Tropical Medicine and Parasitology* 96(1): 75–92.

Benton, B. 1998. "The Economic Impact of Onchocerciasis Control through the African Program for Onchocerciasis Control: An Overview." *Annals of Tropical Medicine and Parasitology* 92(1): 33–39.

Benton, B., J. Bump, A. Sékétéli, and B. Liese. 2002. "Partnership and Promise: Evolution of the African River-blindness Campaigns." *Annals of Tropical Medicine and Parasitology* 96(1): 5–14.

Benton, B., and E. D. Skinner. 1991. "Cost-benefits of Onchocerciasis Control." *Acta Leidensia* 59(1–2): 405–11.

Clemmons, L., U. V. Amazigo, A.-C. Bissek, M. Noma, U. Oyene, U. Ekpo, J. Msuya-Mpanju, S. Katenga, and A. Sékétéli. 2002. "Gender Issues in the Community-directed Treatment with Ivermectin (CDTI) of the African Programme for Onchocerciasis Control (APOC)." *Annals of Tropical Medicine and Parasitology* 96(1): 59–74.

Homeida, M., E. Braide, E. Elhassan, U. V. Amazigo, B. Liese, B. Benton, M. Noma, D. Etya'alé, K. Y. Dadzie, O. U. Kale, and A. Sékétéli. 2002. "APOC's Strategy of Community-directed Treatment with Ivermectin (CDTI) and Its Potential for Providing Additional Health Services to the Poorest Populations." *Annals of Tropical Medicine and Parasitology* 96(1): 93–104.

Hougard, L., A. Yaméogo, A. Sékétéli, B. Boatin, and K. Y. Dadzie. 1997. "Twenty-two Years of Blackfly Control in the Onchocerciasis Control Programme in West Africa." *Parasitology Today* 13(11): 425–30.

Liese, B., N. Blanchet, and G. Dussault. 2003. "The Human Resource Crisis in Health Services in Sub-Saharan Africa." Background paper for *World Development Report 2004*. World Bank, Washington, D.C.

Liese, B., P. S. Sachdeva, and D. G. Cochrane. 1991. "Organizing and Managing Tropical Disease Control Programs: Lessons for Success." Technical Paper 159. World Bank, Washington, D.C.

Merck & Co., Inc. 2002. *Enabling Access to Health: Mectizan for Onchocerciasis and Lymphatic Filariasis.* Whitehouse Station, N.J.: MSD.

Molyneux, D. H. 1995. "Onchocerciasis Control in West Africa: Current Status and Future of the Onchocerciasis Control Programme." *Parasitology Today* 11(11): 399–402.

Molyneux, D. H., and J. B. Davies. 1997. "Onchocerciasis Control: Moving Toward the Millennium." *Parasitology Today* 13(11): 418–25.

Ndyomugyenyi, R., E. Tukesiga, D. W. Buttner, and R. Garms. 2004. "The Impact of Ivermectin Treatment Alone and When in Parallel with Simulium Neavei Elimination on Onchocerciasis in Uganda." *Tropical Medicine and International Health* 9(8): 882–86.

Nigeria Department of Primary Health Care and Disease Control, Ministry of Health and Social Services. 1996. *Revised National Plan of Action for Control of Onchocerciasis (River Blindness) in Nigeria 1997–2001.* Lagos.

Remme, J. H. F. 1995. "The African Programme for Onchocerciasis Control: Preparing to Launch." *Parasitology Today* 11(11): 403–06.

Sékétéli, A., G. Adeoye, A. Eyamba, E. Nnoruka, P. Drameh, U. V. Amazigo, M. Noma, F. Agboton, Y. Aholou, O. O. Kale, and K. Y. Dadzie. 2002. "The Achievements and Challenges of the African Programme for Onchocerciasis Control (APOC)." *Annals of Tropical Medicine and Parasitology* 96(1): 15–28.

WHO (World Health Organization). 1984. "Proposal for a Long-term Strategy, Joint Programme Committee, Fifth Session. Niamey, Niger." Document JPC 5.7. Onchocerciasis Control Programme, Ouagadougou, Burkina Faso.

———. 1985. "Plan of Operations for the Third Financial Phase (1986–1991), Joint Programme Committee, Sixth Session. Geneva, Switzerland." Document JPC 6.6. Onchocerciasis Control Programme, Ouagadougou, Burkina Faso.

———. 1996. *Community Directed Treatment with Ivermectin: Report of a Multi-Country Study.* United Nations Development Programme/World Bank/World Health Organization Special Programme for Research and Training in Tropical Diseases in collaboration with OCP and APOC, Geneva.

———. 1997. *Tropical Disease Research, Progress 1995–96, Thirteenth Programme Report.* United Nations Development Programme/World Bank/World Health Organization Special Programme for Research and Training in Tropical Diseases, Geneva.

———. 1999. *Progress Report, Joint Action Forum, Fifth Session. The Hague, The Netherlands.* Document JAF 5.2. African Programme for Onchocerciasis Control, Ouagadougou, Burkina Faso.

———. 2001. *Empowering Partnerships and Communities: APOC and the Fight to Rid Africa of River Blindness.* Ouagadougou, Burkina Faso: World Health Organization/APOC.

———. 2002. *Progress Report, Joint Action Forum, Eighth Session. Ouagadougou, Burkina Faso.* Document JAF 8.4. African Programme for Onchocerciasis Control, Ouagadougou, Burkina Faso.

———. 2002. *Success in Africa: The Onchocerciasis Control Programme in West Africa, 1974–2002.* Geneva.

———. 2003a. *Consideration of National Onchocerciasis Control Plans and Project Proposals Approved in 2003, Joint Action Forum, Ninth Session. Gattineau, Canada.* Document JAF 9.7. African Programme for Onchocerciasis Control, Ouagadougou, Burkina Faso.

———. 2003b. *Implementation and Sustainability of Community-Directed Treatment of Onchocerciasis with Ivermectin.* Document TDR/IDE/RP/CDTI/00.1. WHO/TDR, Geneva.

———. 2003c. *The Involvement of Community-Directed Distributors of Ivermectin in Other Health and Development Activities.* Document TDR/IDE/CDDI/03.1. Geneva.

———. 2003d. *Plan of Action and Budget for 2004, Joint Action Forum, Ninth Session. Gattineau, Canada.* Document JAF 9.6. African Programme for Onchocerciasis Control, Ouagadougou, Burkina Faso.

———. 2003e. *Progress Report, Joint Action Forum, Ninth Session. Gattineau, Canada.* Document JAF 9.5. African Programme for Onchocerciasis Control, Ouagadougou, Burkina Faso.

12

Using Social Investment Funds in Africa
Scaling Up Poverty Reduction in Malawi and Zambia

WIM H. ALBERTS, JOHN T. MILIMO,
AND COLIN WILSHAW

During the 1990s Malawi and Zambia were hit hard by economic, political, and institutional crises. In both countries social investment funds, designed to finance community-selected development projects, empowered poor people and helped protect them from macroeconomic shocks.

The bottom-up approach to community development that the social investment funds adopted enabled communities to manage their own projects, including project funds. Communities themselves built or rehabilitated roads and bridges, schools, health facilities, boreholes, water points, and latrines. The improvements made real

Wim H. Alberts can be contacted at Walberts@worldbank.org, and John T. Milimo at jtmilimo@yahoo.co.uk. The case study was prepared under the leadership of Wim Alberts and Nginya Mungai Lenneiye. The individual case study on the Social Action Funds in Malawi was prepared by Colin Wilshaw, and the individual case study on the Social Investment Funds in Zambia was prepared by John T. Milimo. The final synthesis paper was prepared by Wim H. Alberts with inputs from John T. Milimo and Colin Wilshaw. The preparation of the MASAF/ZAMSIF case study benefited greatly from feedback and input from an advisory group, including Louise Fox, Hope Philips-Volker, Robert Liebenthal, Cosmas B. Mambo, and Sam Kakhobwe. The staffs of MASAF and ZAMSIF provided valuable input. This chapter is dedicated to the memory of Colin Wilshaw, who unfortunately did not live to see its completion.

319

differences in people's lives—and they did so more cost-effectively than government, the private sector, or donor-financed initiatives. The funds have clearly demonstrated the ability of communities with limited literacy, numeracy, and exposure to formal systems to deliver certain kinds of infrastructure and services more effectively than top-down centralized systems.

The Difficult Circumstances Facing Malawi and Zambia in the 1980s and 1990s

Malawi and Zambia faced tumultuous circumstances in the 1980s and 1990s, simultaneously confronting three types of crises:

- *Economic crisis.* Like most African countries, Malawi and Zambia experienced falling economic growth rates, adverse terms of trade, rising international indebtedness, and growing poverty during the 1980s. These developments led to tough economic adjustments, including public expenditure cuts, tax reform, trade liberalization, parastatal reform, and privatization, especially in agriculture. The measures adversely affected employment, incomes, and the delivery of public education and health, causing poverty to increase well into the 1990s.
- *Institutional crisis.* Declining public expenditure and growing political patronage had devastating effects for public services during the 1970s and 1980s. In both Malawi and Zambia the state became less able to deliver services to poor people—and less committed to doing so. Like other one-party states, the governments favored strong centralization and top-down approaches, leaving little if any role for community-driven initiatives. Local governments were appointed by central authorities, not elected; service ministries were controlled from capital cities and poorly coordinated locally. Communities were recipients of services, not participants in their delivery.
- *Political crisis.* The economic crises in Malawi and Zambia were associated with growing public disillusionment with the one-party state. Expenditure cuts and parastatal reform undermined the patronage systems that had developed since independence and fueled public discontent with poor services and rising unemployment. Trade reform made it difficult for inexperi-

enced, debt-financed African-owned businesses to compete. The independence leaders—Hastings Banda in Malawi, Kenneth Kaunda in Zambia—were still ruling as the 1990s dawned, after more than a quarter century in power. When their countries became multiparty democracies (in 1991 in Zambia, in 1994 in Malawi), the new governments had unambiguous, grassroots-driven mandates to address poverty.

Poor people in Malawi and Zambia face daily problems. Severe food shortages force many people to eat only one meal a day—or even every other day. Access to education is very limited; health services, water, sanitation, shelter, and clothing are inadequate; and vulnerable social groups (orphans, the disabled, the elderly) experience discrimination and neglect. Unemployment rates have increased, per capita calorie intake has dropped, and per capita GDP has fallen in the 1990s. Morbidity and mortality rates have increased, largely as a result of HIV/AIDS, reducing life expectancy from 50 in Zambia and 44 in Malawi in 1980, to 37 and 38, respectively, in 2002.

A New Approach to Reducing Poverty

Following the move to multiparty democracies, perspectives on poverty and the approach to community development changed. Policymakers looked beyond the traditional measure of income poverty to one that also embraced basic needs and human capabilities. The development focus shifted from the top-down approach to a bottom-up approach that gave communities the opportunity and power to make choices and to participate more fully in their own development.

The governments of Malawi and Zambia adopted several measures and programs aimed at addressing poverty. Establishment of the Social Recovery Project (SRP) in Zambia in 1991 (box 12.1) and the Malawi Social Action Fund (MASAF) in 1995 (box 12.2) were integral parts of the new policies.

In Malawi the government embarked on a comprehensive Poverty Alleviation Program that focused on free primary education and community projects funded by the country's social investment fund. In Zambia, where the accelerated pace of liberalization and structural adjustment programs had won wide acceptance (Seshamani 2002), poverty and the poor came into sharper focus. The SRP was intended

| BOX 12.1 | Chronology of Zambia's Social Investment Funds |

1991–95	SRP I, with a budget of $20 million, seeks to address poverty by financing community projects for socioeconomic infrastructure and strengthening communities' ability to improve their lives through self-help.
1995–2000	SRP II, with a budget of $30 million, increases the emphasis on training poor communities and empowering them to participate in the program.
2000–10	The Zambia Social Investment Fund (ZAMSIF), with budgets of $65 million for 2000–05 and $61 million for 2006–10, is designed to support the government's two main strategic objectives: decentralization and empowering local authorities.

Source: World Bank, Staff Appraisal Reports SRP I (1991) and SRP II (1995), and Project Appraisal Document ZAMSIF (2000).

to protect the poor from the macroeconomic crisis during the structural adjustment program.

The social investment funds sought to rehabilitate and expand small-scale social and economic infrastructure in order to help ensure adequate provision of services to the poor. The governments needed

| BOX 12.2 | Chronology of the Malawi Social Action Fund (MASAF) |

1995–2001	MASAF 1, with a budget of $56 million, finances self-help community subprojects for socioeconomic infrastructure and transfers cash to vulnerable groups through public works programs.
1998–2003	MASAF 2, with a budget of $66 million, introduces risk management and social assistance projects for vulnerable groups.
2003–15	MASAF 3, with a budget of $240 million over 12 years, aims to empower communities and make them accountable. The loan covers three phases: 2003–06, with a budget of $60 million; 2006–11, with a budget of $100 million; and 2011–15, with a budget of $80 million.

Source: World Bank Staff Appraisal Report MASAF I (1995) and Project Appraisal Documents MASAF II (1998) and MASAF III (2003).

quick and highly visible interventions to reduce discontent and make structural adjustment more palatable (Frigenti, Harth, and Huque 1998) and recognized that their own line ministries largely lacked the capacity to provide targeted support at the community level. The social investment funds filled this institutional gap, with the understanding that their operations would have to coincide with the larger policy framework as well as with sector policies.

Zambia's first social investment fund, SRP I—also the first in Africa—began in 1991. It initially focused on addressing the social impact of the economic crisis by opening a new funding channel for social services and by generating employment. By 1995 both SRP and MASAF, which drew on the Zambian experience, were starting to address community empowerment and the support needed from district governments.

SRP I was followed in 1995 by SRP II, which introduced a capacity-building element to strengthen linkages between project activities and line ministries at all levels. SRP II had four aims:

- To support the government's poverty reduction program by financing community initiatives and capacity building.
- To finance community initiatives that help the poor and vulnerable meet their own needs.
- To improve the capacity of communities and government staff to plan, assess, manage, and maintain investment projects.
- To enhance the capacity of Zambian institutions to collect and analyze poverty data.

Zambia's third social investment fund, ZAMSIF, was begun in 2000. It has three aims:

- To achieve sustainable improved availability and use of good-quality basic social services by beneficiary communities and specific vulnerable groups.
- To build capacity for improved local governance.
- To strengthen capacity to provide timely information on poverty and social conditions and facilitate its use in policymaking.

ZAMSIF is structured as an Adaptable Program Loan, with a budget of $126 million over 10 years. The program's design includes an implicit exit strategy.

MASAF 1 was piloted between July 1995 and May 1996, then scaled up between May 1996 and December 2001. MASAF 2 further expanded the scope of MASAF 1. It had four objectives:

- To promote community-driven development by having communities participate in all project processes.
- To address the need to develop socioeconomic infrastructure.
- To support safety net programs by creating temporary employment for the poor and financing initiatives to assist the most vulnerable (orphans, street children, people with disabilities, the elderly, and people with HIV/AIDS).
- To enhance the in-country capacity to identify, prioritize, and implement projects by training stakeholders at the community, district, and national levels.

MASAF 3 was designed to empower communities and make them accountable. The program supports institutional changes at the community, district, and national levels. It also works to enhance development management capacities, thereby strengthening the phased implementation of the decentralization program. The fund's objectives are the following:

- To improve communities' access to and utilization of social and economic services.
- To transfer cash income to the poor by having them construct or rehabilitate community assets.
- To improve the quality of life for the most vulnerable.
- To increase poor communities' access to savings and investment opportunities.
- To strengthen the capacities of communities and local governments for local governance and improved management of development.

MASAF 3 is structured as an Adaptable Program Loan, with a budget of $240 million over 12 years.

What Impact Have Social Investment Funds Had?

Throughout Malawi and Zambia the results of the social investment funds are visible. Building and rehabilitating roads and bridges, schools, health facilities, boreholes, water points, and latrines have changed the lives of individuals, community groups, and communities in both countries.

As beneficiary assessments have shown, the social investment funds have improved beneficiaries' lives by increasing their access to and utilization of social services and assets and raising their quality. Many community members have also taken advantage of economic opportunities arising from the improvement in infrastructure. Social safety nets in targeted areas have made a difference to many poor households.

Analysis of the household impact of SRP projects in Zambia confirms that the funds are making a difference.[1] School attendance and household education expenditures rose significantly in households participating in education projects financed by SRP. Health projects increased child vaccinations and the use of primary health facilities. Moreover, community participation proved superior to alternative efforts with similar objectives, particularly in rural areas.

Impact evaluation of the social funds also confirms the positive effects they are having.[2] It shows that education projects increased enrollments and improved the quality of education, health projects increased access to and the quality of health facilities, and water projects improved access to and the quality of drinking water (table 12.1).

In Malawi social investment funds have provided almost 100,000 desks and built or rehabilitated almost 4,300 classrooms. In Zambia communities now have 8,400 new latrines and more than 1,200 new water points.[3]

The impact evaluations also confirm that social investment funds do reach the poor. Poor districts receive more per capita than wealthier districts, and the very poorest districts receive funding shares that exceed their shares of the population. As social investment funds have improved their geographic targeting over time, benefits have become concentrated among the poor. These results show that demand-driven mechanisms are indeed capable of reaching poor areas and poor households.

Social investment funds are also reaching the poor in a cost-effective manner, as cost comparisons with comparable interventions by government line ministries or donor-financed implementing agencies (against similar design standards) show. The construction of a standard school block with two classrooms under MASAF was 37 percent less expensive than under projects sponsored by either the British Department for International Development (DfID) or the government

TABLE 12.1	Education, Health, Water, and Sanitation Outputs of the Social Investment Funds in Malawi and Zambia (Number of Facilities Built or Rehabilitated)					

Outputs	MASAF 1	MASAF 2	MASAF total	SRP I	SRP II	ZAMSIF mid 2004	Zambia total
Classrooms	3,240	1,037	4,277	1,365	1,711	1,400	4,476
Teachers' houses	987	517	1,504	434	753	850	2,037
School offices	53	30	83	72	0	213	285
Desks provided	62,708	34,025	96,733	0	0	22,500	22,500
Health centers	47	15	62	58	22	114	196
Wards and maternity	3	2	5	10	28	185	223
Water points (wells, bore-holes, piped)	1,717	3,591	5,308	379	171	690	1,240
Latrines	4,855	2,964	7,819	1,657	2,437	4,300	8,394
Roads (kilometers)	5,145	5,802	10,947	4	0	38	42
Bridges and culverts	n.a.	n.a.	880	0	0	260	260

Source: MASAF 3 PAD and SRP I & II Completion Reports, ZAMSIF 2002 Annual Report and ZAMSIF Report to the National Steering Committee, 2001.

building department, and 57 percent less expensive than projects funded by the Danish International Development Agency (Danida) (World Bank Project Appraisal Document for MASAF III, 36). Pit latrines built under MASAF were 71 percent less expensive than those built under DfID and 53 percent less expensive than those built by the government building department. Boreholes under MASAF were 27 percent less expensive than those built under DfID and Danida and 50 percent less expensive than those built by the government. Bridges built under MASAF were 24 percent less expensive than those built by the National Roads Authority.

As for SRP/ZAMSIF, a cost-effectiveness evaluation revealed that community-based classroom block construction under the program was 55 percent less expensive than construction performed by private sector contractors (Chase and Sherburne-Benz 2001). Staff housing was 58 percent less expensive, pit latrines 44 percent less expensive, and boreholes 7 percent less expensive than those built by the private sector. These findings suggest that communities in Malawi and Zambia can construct assets that are more cost-effective than those built under government, private sector, or donor-financed initiatives.

MASAF and SRP/ZAMSIF investments in small-scale social and economic infrastructure increased access and utilization of services and produced gains in basic welfare—increased enrollments, improved health of infants and children, and increased availability of safe water and sanitation services—all at a time when overall income poverty levels were rising. The conclusion from the impact and cost-effectiveness evaluations is clear: social investment funds in Malawi and Zambia have improved people's lives, and they have done it more cost-effectively than other organizations.

Impact on Education

School infrastructure improvements have been a major thrust of both social investment funds, with about two-thirds of all investment going to education. The beneficiary assessments and impact evaluations indicate that the education interventions have increased enrollments, improved the quality of school infrastructure, and dramatically reduced travel distances for students. As a result of the funds, students sit at new desks rather than on dirt floors. They have more and better classrooms, brighter and cleaner learning environments, and sanitary facilities. For their part, teachers have better housing and higher morale. As the beneficiary assessment comments, "A few respondents noted that the school had become the pride of the community. One of the schools reported a halt to the exodus of teachers, who, prior to the completion of the project, were leaving the school. An influx of both teachers and students who were now being attracted by the good condition currently prevailing at the renovated school was reported in these communities" (World Bank Staff Appraisal Report for SRP II 1995, 16).

The impact evaluations found that a rise in staffing generally accompanies improvements in infrastructure (Chase and Sherburne-Benz 2001). A beneficiary assessment of MASAF reveals that in all

45 schools sampled, increased enrollments—of more than 50 percent in some cases—were attributed to the MASAF investments. Learning conditions had also improved. Students who had once sat under trees or in classrooms with leaking roofs and windows that let in cold air, dust, and rain now sat at desks in comfortable, well-built classrooms. The impact evaluations show that schools that received social investment funds have more teachers, more desks, better electricity and safe water, and fewer students per toilet facility than those that did not (Chase and Sherburne-Benz 2001). Good classrooms, good teacher housing, and desks have boosted the morale of both students and teachers, which is improving class performance. The SRP impact evaluation reveals higher educational attainment as well.

Access to learning has also been facilitated by better road infrastructure and the building of bridges, which have not only reduced travel distances but also made getting to school less hazardous. As a beneficiary notes, "The community [is no longer worried] about the children's education being affected when the river is flooded" (ZAMSIF News 2002, 3).

Impact on Health

Health interventions have improved the quality of infrastructure and services; increased access to medical equipment (delivery kits, sterilizers, thermometers, baby scales, medical trolleys, furniture, and other equipment); improved physical conditions, increasing the number of medical rooms and improving access to water and sanitation (although often not to electricity); reduced the distance to health facilities; and reduced congestion—a big boon to women, who are generally the ones who take sick members of their families to the clinic.[4] Health facilities aided by the social investment funds often attract more and better qualified medical staff, and social investment fund facilities are open longer hours.

These improvements usually lead to higher utilization of services at the facilities, and greater use of health services often leads to improvements in immunization, family planning, and other health practices. Construction and rehabilitation of health facilities is generally accompanied by health education efforts from the health personnel, which improves hygienic practices and habits.

Social investment funds also increased the number of patients, especially at maternity and child health clinics; helped provide greater privacy at health institutions; and improved the availability of water, functioning ventilated improved pit latrines, and shelter for relatives who look after the sick. The beneficiary assessments of both countries report that beneficiaries perceive that the health status of the population at large has risen and child mortality rates have declined.

Health sector outputs in ZAMSIF and MASAF differ to some extent. Much of the health center, clinic, and ward construction in Zambia took place under SRP. Since ZAMSIF's inception the focus has been on the construction and rehabilitation of medical wards, maternity wards, and shelters for visiting relatives. In contrast, MASAF II health interventions have focused mainly on building new centers; very little rehabilitation work was carried out under MASAF.

Impact on Water and Sanitation

Social fund investments in water and sanitation have improved access to safe water, making life easier for people—especially women—and reducing the incidence of water-related diseases. The sinking of boreholes and wells and the construction of water points and latrines have increased the supply of safe potable water and good sanitary facilities. Better access to potable water has reduced morbidity rates, causing the incidence of water-related diseases to fall 74 percent in communities assisted by MASAF water projects. Educating health officials in Malawi about sanitation practices has helped communities there reduce the incidence of cholera and diarrhea (box 12.3). The building

---

| BOX 12.3 | Changing People's Lives in Malawi |

Reports from the ground suggest that social investment funds are having real effects on people's lives. According to one beneficiary, "There have been diarrhea and cholera cases because people were collecting water from the Shire River. These diseases have now been reduced because of water from the MASAF project. The diseases have also been reduced because there are health officials who come to advise us on hygiene" (*MASAF News* 2002).

In the village of Kwitanda, in central Malawi, the building of the Kwitanda Health Center has brought relief to pregnant women, who previously had to walk more than eight kilometers for prenatal checkups. According to the village headwoman, many women ignored the checkup. The result was frequent miscarriages and sometimes even deaths (*MASAF News* 2002).

of latrines, the sinking of boreholes, and the provision of good health facilities have increased health and sanitation in schools.

Impact on Economic Infrastructure

Construction, rehabilitation, and maintenance of economic infrastructure in rural and peri-urban areas have been major thrusts of MASAF's community subprojects and the public works program. Almost 14,000 kilometers of mainly rural access roads and 668 bridges were built through the public works program, and 212 bridges were built through a community subproject funded by MASAF 2. Other infrastructure projects include rainwater harvesting structures and natural resource management. Some 4,500 hectares of land have been planted with trees.

By comparison, ZAMSIF's involvement in the construction and rehabilitation of economic infrastructure has been more limited. Its main outputs have been the rehabilitation of 54 culverts. It also built or rehabilitated a small number of roads, bridges, and irrigation facilities. Under SRP beneficiaries built seven markets.

Improvements in economic infrastructure have increased access to markets and social services, reduced time spent on household chores such as fetching water, created new venues for generating income, reduced transport costs, and improved communication. Irrigation subprojects have enabled community members, especially women, to grow vegetables, which puts money in their pockets and improves the health status of their families. The public works program in MASAF focuses on forestation and tree-planting activities, helping to restore the environment, which has been destroyed by tree cutting. At the individual household and community levels, successful forestation and tree-planting subprojects have generated income from the sale and management of forest products.

Economic infrastructure improvements in rural and peri-urban areas have greatly facilitated socioeconomic activities. In rural areas bridges and roads are vital to the lives of the people who use them. Access to social services as well as to economic opportunities and necessities depend on these infrastructure links (box 12.4).

The public works program in MASAF helps reduce the impact of poverty at both the individual and community levels. The social safety net relieves poverty through cash transfers to beneficiaries employed in public works projects. Some 390 public works program projects

BOX 12.4	Building Bridges, Transforming Lives

Building a single four-span bridge—at a cost of less than $10,000—has transformed people's lives in Malawi. "No more lives will be lost, including those of school children crossing the flooded river," notes one beneficiary. "Traveling problems have been alleviated and business boosted between Emzizini and the Ekwendeni trading centers," notes another. "Much greater access to schools has been created. . . . Acute health problems are more easily referred to the mission hospital on the other side of the river. [Before the bridge was built] many patients died in the rainy season due to lack of access."

Source: MASAF News 2001.

have been supported, more than 51 million employment days created, and more than $4 million paid out in wages to 338,983 beneficiaries, 48 percent of them women.

The cash transfer not only brings relief from immediate hunger but often acts as a buffer against individual (idiosyncratic) and communitywide (covariate) risks or shocks, making beneficiaries less vulnerable. The social safety net increases beneficiaries' economic stability, improves their nutritional status by increasing their intake of nutrients, and in some cases allows them to acquire assets. The public works program extends the benefits of the economic infrastructure to project beneficiary communities and helps sustain those benefits through its maintenance program.

Social and Institutional Scaling Up

For empowerment to be sustainable, an appropriate institutional framework needs to be in place (Davis 2004). Building the capacities of district-level administrations is critical to the institutional scaling-up process.

The social investment funds have built capacities at the community, district, and, in the case of Zambia, provincial levels of government. Efforts to empower communities are an integral part of the social scaling-up process. Capacities to plan and manage community-level development processes are being enhanced. The funds are both developing beneficiaries' skills and increasing their ability to work together and organize themselves.

Social Scaling Up

The empowerment of communities focuses on community participation in prioritizing needs, identifying projects, requesting funding for projects, selecting project committees, and organizing community contributions for the project. These empowerment activities instill a sense of responsibility for and ownership of the project in the beneficiary community. This social scaling-up process empowers community members and strengthens the community's social capital. It helps communities maintain and undertake other development activities.

The social investment funds have made a point of imparting skills to beneficiary communities. Participating communities, especially project management committees, have acquired skills in simple bookkeeping, project and financial management, and procurement, as well as such technical skills as repairing and maintaining boreholes, windlasses, and buildings.

Community members as well as district staff have also acquired an improved awareness of development issues. Cash and in-kind contributions toward project implementation have instilled a deep sense of self-reliance, which has helped reduce dependency on the government or donors. Empowering communities has improved the technical quality of the new or rehabilitated infrastructure, improved project management, and improved communities' ability to identify, plan, and manage their local development process.

Institutional Scaling Up

MASAF and SRP/ZAMSIF have contributed to the decentralization process by supporting the deconcentration of the central government rather than by devolving central government authority to local levels.[5] In Malawi the decentralization policy was introduced in 1998, although local government elections did not begin until 2000. MASAF supported the work of district executive committees made up of central government employees working in the districts under the supervision of central ministry agencies. In Zambia the decentralization policy has not yet been implemented, but ZAMSIF has made significant efforts to facilitate the devolution of administrative and financial responsibilities to stakeholders at the district level.

MASAF 1 and 2 and SRP I and II operated largely without formal linkages to local governments; most of the working arrangements between social investment fund staff and district staff were ad hoc. Coordination between fund staff and the District Assembly (in Malawi) and the District Development Coordinating Committees (in Zambia) was weak. Project funds for community subprojects are channeled directly to communities (bypassing districts), which manage and account for them through their project committees. In MASAF 3 and ZAMSIF more concerted efforts are being made to empower local government capacities and help establish institutional frameworks that promote local development and accountability.

Both social investment funds have evolved from community-oriented organizations that largely bypassed local government to local development organizations that empower communities and help strengthen the local institutional framework. In ZAMSIF, a capacity building ladder supports the progressive scaling up of local government capacity. It calls for providing more funding and more responsibility to the district administrations as their capacity grows (table 12.2).

The capacity-building ladder reflects a new, phased approach to developing local government capacities, an approach that helps ensure

TABLE 12.2	Capacity-building Ladder for Scaling Up Local Government Capacity
Level	**Demonstrated capacity**
1	Facilitates community access to funding.
2	Facilitates participatory identification processes, monitors and evaluates community projects, implements District Investment Fund projects, and accounts for project funds.
3	Adopts a district development and poverty reduction strategy, shows that community-based projects reach those targeted by the strategy, and demonstrates design and financial management skills.
4	Demonstrates continued satisfactory performance in all phases of the community project cycle, including approval of funding for community projects (but not disbursements).
5	Demonstrates consistent good performance for more than one year, maintains a basic poverty information system, and shows evidence of some district planning.

Source: World Bank Project Appraisal Document for ZAMSIF 2000.

that expectations about district capacities by both communities and the central government are realistic. The phased approach provides an opportunity to build checks and balances into the capacity development process, and it facilitates monitoring and evaluation of how capacities are being developed and applied.

ZAMSIF and MASAF have played important roles in decentralizing financial management. Since their inception community project funds have been handled by beneficiary communities through their project committees. This process has instilled financial discipline and encouraged communities to plan for the resources they have at hand. It has also enhanced their self-confidence and reduced their spirit of dependence.

The success of social investment funds may convince the central government that districts have the capacity to manage resources if sufficiently transparent rules are in place addressing fiduciary issues and if there is technical support from the central government.

Key Factors for Scaling Up

Successful scaling up of a social investment fund depends on several key factors, including such important examples as political commitment and support, external catalysts, autonomous management, learning and innovation, partnership and collaboration, and direct funding.

Political Commitment and Support

Both MASAF and ZAMSIF have benefited from strong political commitment and support from their respective governments. The political commitment and support is evident in four areas:

- Placement of the social investment funds under high-profile ministries.
- The central role of the social investment funds in poverty alleviation programs.
- The collaboration between government and civil society on poverty reduction.
- The fight against corruption.

Both social investment funds are under very high-profile government ministries. MASAF was established under the aegis of the Office of the President and Cabinet, with its budget to Parliament presented through the Department of Economic Planning and Development. ZAMSIF is situated in the Ministry of Finance and National Planning. It has sometimes been perceived as one of many donor-assisted development programs that has been operating in the country since the downturn in the economy. In contrast, MASAF is perceived as a special government agency that has been one of the main instruments of poverty reduction in Malawi.

The placement of the social investment funds under high-profile ministries has helped preserve their autonomy and to some extent protected them from unwarranted interference from politicians and other ministries. The status of each fund has helped it maintain a high degree of political neutrality. Both social investment funds are respected by all political parties. (This does not mean that efforts have not been made to politicize the funds. On numerous occasions members of Parliament in Malawi have tried to influence project selection and awards.)

The status of MASAF may have hurt implementation at the district level. The MASAF community subproject was initially perceived as "a World Bank project" and its staff as "better-off NGO types." This image affected their relationship with line ministry officials, who resented being asked to do MASAF work. A recent evaluation suggests that despite their perceptions of MASAF, however, district staff were actively involved in project appraisal, facilitation, monitoring, and supervision.

ZAMSIF experienced similar problems at the district level, though for different reasons. The district staff had been alienated by what was perceived as the top-down manner of the SRP. District staff also considered SRP work as not their own. Much of ZAMSIF's work through the District Investment Fund can be seen as breaking down barriers raised by the SRP approach by developing a closer working relationship with the district staff, facilitating capacity building, and bridging the communication gap between district staff and communities.

The government's political commitment and support is evident in the central role of the social investment funds in poverty alleviation programs. MASAF's objectives were in line with the 1995 Poverty Alleviation Program and the 1998 Malawi Poverty Reduction Strategy Paper. MASAF 3 is including the Millennium Development Goals in its objectives.

In Zambia the SRP objectives were in line with the National Poverty Reduction Strategy formulated in 1998. That strategy assessed and analyzed the causes of poverty and identified the structural transformations needed to address it. Two years later the initiative was translated into the National Poverty Reduction Action Plan, which spelled out the kinds of strategies and actions that needed to be taken to reduce poverty. In recent years the government participated in the Poverty Reduction Strategy Paper process, which addresses the various social and economic sectors in which improvement is needed if poverty is to be reduced.

Autonomous Management

Although located in perhaps the most powerful agencies of their respective governments, MASAF and SRP/ZAMSIF have, since the beginning, operated autonomously. The results have been both positive and negative. On the positive side the funds have functioned without excessive bureaucracy or interference from government ministries, making them efficient. Over the years both funds have developed strong fiduciary reputations, based on stringent and transparent financial management systems, procurement and disbursement procedures, and reporting requirements. Detailed operational manuals have guided their work at the central, district, and community levels.

The funds have also been able to recruit highly qualified professionals for their management and operations. Personnel are recruited on a contract basis, and contracting, selection, and payment procedures are not restricted by bureaucratic civil service requirements. The planning and management culture is largely results oriented, with concrete output targets and benchmarks. The quality of the staff and of the administrative and management systems has made the funds efficient, effective, accountable, and transparent organizations, allowing them to operate in institutionally weak environments.

Autonomous management has the added advantage of flexibility in planning and management. Flexibility is a key mindset in all areas of implementation, which MASAF and SRP/ZAMSIF have used to improve their structure, functions, and operational procedures to great effect. SRP/ZAMSIF demonstrated flexibility in resolving the weaknesses and irregularities confronting collaboration with NGO partners in the Community Investment Fund. The recent restructuring of the ZAMSIF project was greatly facilitated by the willingness of the management team to change course. MASAF demonstrated flexibility in many instances and at crucial stages of its development. Revising, at communities' request, the subproject tranche structure to accelerate the pace of implementation, for example, showed a willingness to listen to communities and to examine the rigidity of the fund's procedures. This flexibility is essential in any scaling-up exercise.

On the negative side, the autonomous management structure and style have meant that other government ministries and departments have often looked at the social investment funds as separate entities with which they cooperate only if financial or other benefits can be derived from the association.

In the initial phases of the social investment funds, much emphasis was put on quick response and disbursement. A social investment fund portfolio review carried out by the World Bank's Quality Assurance Group noted that "the pressure for action has overwhelmed all other objectives, while the emphasis on results has often been interpreted in quantitative terms. Part of the reason for this was the prevailing view that social investment funds were temporary mechanisms that would self-destruct once the emergency was over, and the disbursement schedule and the number of projects implemented would determine their success" (Frigenti, Harth, and Huque 1998, 25).

The second generation of both social investment funds has shifted away from emergency funding toward more sustainable development. The shift was facilitated by institutional innovations and changes in the funds' organizational characteristics. In Zambia, for instance, the fund is evolving from a funding mechanism to a change agent focusing on capacity building. In both countries the funds are centralized organizations with regard to technical and financial management and decentralized organizations in terms of their operations. Both have grown into complex institutions that face continuous organizational, personnel management, and communication challenges. Management often needs to deal with the conflict between quick turnaround and the pressure to disburse on the one hand and the need to invest time and resources in order to ensure sustainability.

Learning and Innovation

The social investment funds in Malawi and Zambia are learning organizations that continually change, learn, and innovate to meet their internal and external demands. They nurture innovation and make conscious efforts to expand their capacities to create the desired impact.

Since their inception the funds have benefited from the experience of other social investment funds. The initial design of SRP I drew heavily on experience in Latin America, particularly Bolivia. World Bank staff involved in the early days of SRP had previously worked with social investment funds in Latin America. The initial design of MASAF drew heavily on SRP I. Yet innovative characteristics were introduced right from the start to adapt the social investment fund to local conditions in both countries.

From the beginning the funds' managers have adopted innovative concepts, including direct funding to communities (unheard of at the time), community decisionmaking, and participatory processes. In introducing these concepts and managing their operations, managers have been quick to adjust in order to optimize their operations and investments. Beneficiary assessments and impact evaluations take place regularly. The recommendations of these reviews have guided the adjustment of the organizational structure as well as operational policies and procedures. They have also strongly influenced the evolution of the social investment funds, which began as community infrastructure organizations and became change agents for local development.

Partnerships with Donors

When SRP was founded it joined the European Union–funded Micro-Projects Program to form the Micro-Projects Unit. SRP and the Micro-Projects Unit worked closely together, since they had similar objectives and followed the same procedures. Although the two programs separated in 2000, they continue to collaborate at the operational level.

ZAMSIF has also developed partnerships with development agencies that have similar approaches and objectives. These include SNV Netherlands, which is working in Western and Northwestern Provinces; GTZ, which is working in Southern Province; and the Development Cooperation of Ireland, which is working in Northern and Luapula Provinces. These agencies share common visions about community participation, capacity building, and decentralization. Each partnership is established through a memorandum of understanding that details the roles and responsibilities of each partner. These partnerships greatly facilitate the capacity-building efforts of ZAMSIF at both the community and the district levels.

MASAF's partnerships with donors are more recent, but they are significant. Initially, other donors, particularly the European Union, were reluctant to work with MASAF, which they viewed as a competitor in development. Recently, informal technical cooperation and information exchanges between MASAF and the European Union have taken place. The most recent involvement is with DfID. In September 2000 the government of Malawi endorsed a national safety net strategy developed jointly with donors and representatives of other stakeholders. The strategy includes free or subsidized agricultural inputs, access to employment, supplementary programs, and direct cash transfers. DfID's response to that strategy has been to provide MASAF's public works program with £4.9 million in financing. A second partnership with DfID falls under the Malawi Emergency Drought Recovery Project, supported by the International Development Association, which provides $8 million to support expansion of the public works programs and essential social investments and services.

Both social investment funds have received strong technical and financial support from the World Bank and other donor partners, including the European Union and DfID. Without this support the social investment funds could not have had the coverage or impact they did—and might not have existed at all. In the current environment in Malawi and Zambia, the social investment funds are reliable partners for a lending institution such as the World Bank or for grant-providing donors such as the European Union and DfID.

Both MASAF and SRP/ZAMSIF have excellent track records as effective lending instruments that disburse funds well, are effective and efficient, and to a large extent have the desired impact. In the otherwise weak institutional environments of both countries, social investment funds are a welcome alternative for addressing poverty. It is not surprising therefore that both governments have made the funds integral parts of their poverty reduction programs and that the Bank has included them in their Country Assistance Strategies.

Partnerships with Nongovernmental and Community-based Organizations

Both social investment funds work closely with nongovernmental organizations and community-based organizations, the main implementers of subprojects. Under MASAF, NGOs are not commissioned to implement community subprojects or public works program projects. Community-based organizations implement most sponsored projects. Sponsored projects were established under MASAF 2 to bridge the gap created by the failure of MASAF 1 to reach out to vulnerable and marginalized groups who had not benefited from MASAF funding. The community-based organizations are close to beneficiaries, familiar with the vulnerable populations, and well-positioned to identify and help them. Sponsored projects have been successful largely because of the capacity building with NGOs and community-based organizations.

In Zambia collaboration with NGOs has developed over time. In the early days of SRP, church organizations and NGOs were invited to help implement subprojects. Early beneficiary assessments discovered weaknesses and irregularities in the practices of NGOs, however, with some disempowering rather than empowering communities (by making all decisions themselves), misrepresenting funding sources, and claiming ownership of supported projects and subsequent benefits. ZAMSIF has addressed these problems, and collaboration between ZAMSIF and NGOs/community-based organizations has improved.

Challenges in Moving Forward

Several challenges are likely to be encountered in scaling up social investment funds:

- *Ensuring the sustainability of subprojects.* By design social investment funds do not have responsibility for delivering services once the infrastructure subprojects have been handed over to the implementing partner; delivery of the service is the responsibility of the implementing partner, in many cases a government ministry, NGO, or faith-based organization. Because covering the recurrent costs of services can be a problem for resource- and revenue-constrained ministries, delivery of services can be interrupted or halted.
- *Ensuring the sustainability of institutional arrangements.* The sustainability of institutional arrangements at the district and community levels depends on the development of local government capacity and the implementation of a decentralization framework. If the institutional arrangements are not adequate, sustainability is guaranteed only during the life of a project.
- *Ensuring the sustainability of capacity-building efforts.* The empowerment of communities and the strengthening of capacities of district staff may not be sustainable in the absence of decentralization and an appropriate institutional framework. The capacity-building efforts at the district level are sometimes constrained

because of high staff turnover; lack of incentives, transport, and infrastructure; and inadequate follow-up.

- *Improving pro-poor targeting.* The social investment funds have produced pro-poor outcomes, but targeting of subprojects could nevertheless be improved. In community-level subprojects the most vulnerable often have insufficient voice in identifying and planning projects. In district-level subprojects the linkages and accountabilities between the districts and the communities are not always clear. Better use of local poverty assessments, poverty mapping, and district situation analyses could inform participatory planning and implementation.
- *Increasing efficiency.* For social investment funds to become sustainable agents for development, their cost of doing business needs to be lower than alternative public service delivery modes. Overhead costs therefore need to be reduced.
- *Addressing community priorities.* The subproject menu does not always cover the highest priorities of the communities concerned. Income-generating activities feature regularly as a top priority for beneficiaries. The extent to which these needs can be met by the social investment funds is limited.
- *Improving coordination with sector ministries.* Lack of adequate coordination with sector ministries is a concern in both countries, at the central as well as the local levels. Sector concerns and priorities need to be better integrated into the project cycle and delivery of the social investment fund and the financing of the service.
- *Integrating social investment funds with local governments.* To scale up to cover a larger range of local services, the social investment fund approach has to forge better links with local governments instead of remaining a stand-alone financial intermediary.
- *Obtaining administrative, technical, and financial support.* In both countries the governments face the challenge of backing up their verbal political support with administrative, technical, and financial support.
- *Implementing decentralization policies.* More concerted efforts are needed to implement the decentralization policies that have been approved in Malawi and Zambia. Without the devolution of administrative, political, and financial responsibilities to the local level, the institutional environment for district administrations will not be conducive to community-led development.

■ *Empowering communities and local governments, decentralizing,
ensuring accountability and transparency, and learning by doing.*
The absence of any one of these pillars for scaling up a social
investment fund makes it difficult for a social investment fund
to reach its full potential for reducing poverty.

BIBLIOGRAPHY

Centre for Social Research, Malawi, Institute of Development Studies, UK; and Nor-
wegian Institute for Urban and Regional Research. 2003. "Poverty Reduction
During Democratic Transition: The Malawi Social Action Fund 1996–2001, An
Independent Review." Lilongwe.

Chase, Rob, and Lynne Sherburne-Benz. 2001. "Household Effects of African
Community Initiatives: Evaluating the Impact of the Zambia Social Fund."
Johns Hopkins University School for Advanced International Studies and
World Bank, Washington, D.C.

Davis, Deborah, 2004. "Scaling-Up Action Research Project, Phase One: Lessons
from Six Case Studies," paper presented at the CDD Scaling Up Action
Research Workshop at the World Bank, Washington, D.C.

Frigenti, Laura, Alberto Harth, and Rumana Huque. 1998. "Local Solutions to
Regional Problems: The Growth of Social Funds and Public Works and
Employment Projects in Sub-Saharan Africa." World Bank, Washington, D.C.

MASAF News. 2001. Vol. 4, no. 1.

———. 2002. Vol. 5, no. 1.

Seshamani, Vankatesh. 2002. *Poverty Reduction and Water Access in Zambia.* Lusaka,
Zambia: WaterAid.

World Bank. Project documents for Zambia Social Investment Fund and Malawi
Social Action Fund. Various dates. Washington, D.C.

World Bank, Quality Assurance Group. 1997. "Review of Social Fund Portfolio."
Washington, D.C.

ZAMSIF News. December 2002.

———. September 2003.

13

Turning the Tide
How Openness and Leadership Stemmed the Spread of HIV/AIDS in Uganda

NARATHIUS ASINGWIRE
AND SWIZEN KYOMUHENDO

As a low-income country just emerging from violent conflict, Uganda was hit hard by the HIV/AIDS epidemic in the 1980s and 1990s (box 13.1). The response by the government was swift and forceful. Through an extraordinary level of commitment and leadership by high-ranking officials, including the president, and the implementation of a variety of innovative policies, the country turned the tide of the disease. Astute leadership and well-designed programs reduced the prevalence of HIV/AIDS in the general population and caused a massive decline in prevalence rates among pregnant women. The fight is far from over—more needs to be done to reduce the disproportionate

Narathius Asingwire is head of the Social Work and Social Administration Department, Makerere University, Kampala; he can be contacted at nasingwire@ss.mak.ac.ug. Swizen Kyomuhendo is lecturer in the Social Work and Social Administration Department, Makerere University, Kampala; he can be contacted at swizen@ss.mak.ac.ug. The authors were supported by John Rwomushana, a director of research and policy development at the Uganda AIDS Commission, particularly in developing the analytical framework; he can be contacted at johnrwomushana@ yahoo.com. The authors gratefully acknowledge the help of Peter Okwero of the World Bank, Uganda Country Office, for reviewing the report and providing background material, and Richard Ssewakiryanga of the Ministry of Finance for assisting with coordination of the case study.

| BOX 13.1 | **Chronology of HIV/AIDS-related Events in Uganda** |

1982	The first AIDS case in Uganda is diagnosed.
1986	Uganda's minister of health stuns his colleagues by bringing up the subject of AIDS before the World Health Organization Assembly.
	The Ministry of Health establishes the first AIDS control program.
	The first information, education, and communication campaigns begin.
1988	A national survey is conducted to assess the magnitude of the epidemic.
1989	Philly Lutaaya, a renowned Ugandan musician, publicly announces that he is HIV-positive, making discussion of the disease more acceptable.
1990	The AIDS Information Centre is established in Kampala.
1991	The first national AIDS conference is held.
1992	The Uganda AIDS Commission is established, under the Office of the President.
	Uganda develops a multisector AIDS control approach.
	Uganda adopts a peer education approach to AIDS education, targeting students and out-of-school youth.
	The AIDS epidemic reaches a peak, with hard-hit areas, especially urban sites, registering prevalence rates of more than 30 percent.
1993	The second national AIDS conference is held.
	The Uganda AIDS Commission coordinates the development of the first multisector national operational plan.
1994	Uganda borrows $75 million from the World Bank.
1995	HIV prevalence rate declines among women attending prenatal clinics.
1996	Vaccine trials are initiated following thorough consultations with all key stakeholders.
1997	A five-year national operation plan, the National Strategic Framework 1997, is developed.
1998	The Drug Access Initiative for antiretroviral drugs is established.
1999	The Ministry of Health develops a national health policy.

BOX 13.1	Chronology of Reform in Uganda, 1986–2001 (*Cont'd*)

2000	The National Strategic Framework 1997 is revised to produce the National Strategic Framework 2000/01–2005/06.
	The government integrates HIV/AIDS into the Poverty Eradication Action Plan, its overarching strategy for development.
2001	Uganda's financial commitment to HIV/AIDS quadruples, reaching $2.7 billion.
	The Uganda AIDS Control Program is established with a $50 million loan from the World Bank.
2002	Fifty million male condoms and 110,000 female condoms are distributed in the first six months of the year.
2003	Voluntary counseling and testing and condom policies and guidelines are developed.
2004	The revised National Strategic Framework for HIV/AIDS Activities 2000/01–05/06 is published.
	Free access to antiretroviral therapy is announced. Not fully implemented yet.

share of orphans, adolescent girls, and young people with HIV/AIDS, for example—but the results so far have been impressive.

Uganda's experience serves as a model for other developing countries. It shows what strong commitment, openness in addressing HIV/AIDS, effective policy implementation, and good relations with development partners can do to reduce infection rates in a country with limited resources.

The Rapid Spread of HIV/AIDS in Uganda

HIV/AIDS spread rapidly in Uganda, quickly reaching epidemic proportions. Within five years of the first diagnoses in 1982, 6 to 8 percent of the population was infected (figure 13.1). By mid 1991, 9 percent of the population and 20 percent of people ages 15 to 49 were infected; in urban areas a stunning 24 to 36 percent of women seeking prenatal care at major hospitals tested positive for HIV (ACP records of 1992) (figure 13.2).

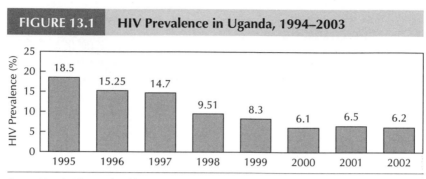

FIGURE 13.1 **HIV Prevalence in Uganda, 1994–2003**

Source: Uganda Ministry of Health, National Surveillance Reports.

Available data suggest that the prevalence of HIV has been declining significantly in Uganda since 1992. Figure 13.1 indicates that HIV prevalence has declined among antenatal clinic attendees. Overall, the estimated prevalence rate of HIV among antenatal attendees nationally was 6.2 percent in 2003, compared to 6.5 percent in 2002 and 6.1 percent in 2001 (MoH-STD/ACP 2003). Despite the precipitous decline, HIV/AIDS continues to threaten Uganda's economic progress and the future of its children.

The Government and Civil Society Respond

The fight against HIV/AIDS was initially hampered by misinformation and misconception about the disease, negative cultural beliefs and

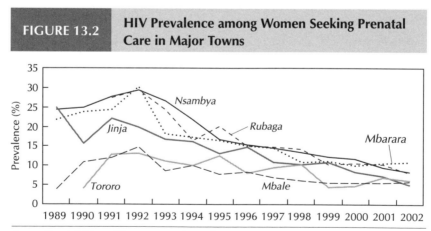

FIGURE 13.2 **HIV Prevalence among Women Seeking Prenatal Care in Major Towns**

Source: Uganda Ministry of Finance, National Surveillance Reports.

practices, resistance to changing sexual behavior, and stigmatization of people infected with or affected by the disease. Popularly known as "slim" because of its emaciating effect, the disease appeared at a time when there was a paucity of scientific knowledge about the disease in Africa. The early symptoms of the disease—general malaise and sporadic fever, followed several months later by diarrhea, weight loss, and skin rash and discoloration, frequently accompanied by sexually transmitted diseases (STDs) and tuberculosis—convinced many Ugandans that the disease was caused by witchcraft and ancestor revenge. Because many of the people with the disease were affluent traders, the belief that the disease was a curse or retribution for illicit business practices became common.

The Government's Response

The government's first response to the HIV/AIDS epidemic, in the early 1980s, was largely ad hoc and slow. Failure to act allowed the epidemic to spread rapidly. Then, in May 1986, Dr. Ruhakana Rugunda, the new Minister of Health, publicly announced to a World Health Organization (WHO) Assembly in Geneva, "Fellow delegates, I have to inform you that we have a problem with AIDS in Uganda, and we would like the support of the international community in dealing with it." Other delegates, especially those from Africa, were stunned by the simplicity and openness of this announcement concerning a disease then largely associated with homosexuality and drug use.

A few months after Dr. Rugunda's announcement, the government established the National Commission for the Prevention of AIDS. In October 1986, in collaboration with WHO, it launched the AIDS Control Program in the Ministry of Health. During its first four years the AIDS Control Program made substantial progress in epidemiology, surveillance, health and HIV/AIDS education, and blood transfusion services, meeting weekly under the chairmanship of President Yoweri Museveni. It organized an extensive program of seminars and training, introduced HIV/AIDS education into school curricula beginning in the late primary grades, and encouraged political leaders from the president down to become active advocates for HIV/AIDS prevention. Building on the demands of a population now clamoring for a voice in civic affairs, President Museveni called for a massive public information campaign about HIV/AIDS, opening the issue up for public debate with the aim of building broad consensus on how to proceed and whom to engage.

Getting the Message Out

Key to the government's strategy was a massive information, education, and communication campaign, which initially focused on increasing awareness of HIV/AIDS and later on effecting behavior change. Early on the government used the mass media and distributed leaflets, posters, and booklets advocating abstinence, mutual faithfulness, and condom use as the main methods of prevention. Eventually, these campaigns reached even the hardest to reach communities, including transient groups.

Uganda also used traditional means of communication. "Early in the mornings, when we were waking up, there was the drum," recalls Dr. Elizabeth Madra, manager of the AIDS Control Program. "Here, traditionally, when there was an invasion . . . the drum was the one to warn. The drum was a sign of danger."

For the next several years President Museveni toured extensively throughout the country, his charisma attracting large crowds at rallies. Wherever he went, the president opened or closed his remarks by talking about HIV/AIDS. Frequently alluding to African proverbs or stories, his messages combined fear with knowledge about how to prevent the disease and exhortations about morality, national pride, and patriotic duty.

Civil Society and Traditional Healers Join the Fight

In 1987 the AIDS Support Organization (TASO) was founded as the first indigenous African organization focused on living with, rather than dying from, AIDS. TASO helped combat stigma and ignorance and bring discussion of HIV/AIDS into the public domain.

Many of the founders of TASO were HIV positive or had a close family member with HIV/AIDS, a unifying experience that made them particularly sensitive to stigma, discrimination, and the need for care, support, and quality of life. Led by Dr. Noerine Kaleeba and 15 colleagues, TASO expanded to become the largest AIDS support organization in Uganda.

More headway in national response to the epidemic was made in 1989, when the renowned Ugandan musician Philly Lutaaya announced that he was HIV positive. His announcement set the stage for people with HIV to publicly give "personal testimonies" about their experiences. It also led to the foundation of the Philly Lutaaya

Initiative and the involvement of people with HIV/AIDS in public education activities. Lutaaya's hauntingly beautiful song "Alone" became the anthem of AIDS volunteers in many parts of Africa.

One of the objectives of the initiative was to provide different target groups with opportunities to assess, analyze, consult, and take appropriate action to prevent or manage HIV/AIDS and STDs. It spurred the establishment of more organizations, including the National Community of Women Living with HIV/AIDS (NACWOLA) and the National Guidance and Empowerment Network of Positive People (NGEN+), which attracted members in almost every district of Uganda. Through their national umbrella organization (the National People Living with HIV/AIDS Forum) these agencies have since developed mechanisms for networking. Participation of people with HIV/AIDS in prevention activities represents a best practice in Uganda's efforts to combat the disease.

Another innovation was the formation of partnerships with traditional healers. Under the partnership forged in 1992—the Traditional and Modern Health Practitioners Together against AIDS (THETA)—modern and traditional practitioners work together to provide counseling on and care of such issues as nutrition and treatment of opportunistic infections. THETA is currently operating in 10 districts in Uganda.

Building Capacity and Training Leaders at the District Level

Between 1987 and 1992 the Ministry of Health developed the capacities of a variety of players, including local leaders, health workers, lower-level political leaders, county and subcounty chiefs, and extension workers. The training enabled local leaders to launch HIV/AIDS campaigns in their districts, which then encouraged action at the subcounty, parish, and grassroots levels. This district-focused response was gradually consolidated and intensified.

Targeting Young People

In 1992 the government initiated a peer education approach to HIV/AIDS education, targeting mainly students in secondary and tertiary institutions as well as out-of-school youth. The Ministry of Health and the AIDS Control Program, the United Nations Children's Fund (UNICEF), the Ministry of Education, nongovernmental organizations, community-based organizations, and government departments of social services implemented the approach.

The results are reflected in significant behavior change among young people. The age at first sexual encounter has risen, condom use has increased, the number of sexual partners has fallen, and marriage age has risen.

In an effort to reach more young people, the Straight Talk Foundation created *Straight Talk,* a newspaper providing candid information to help young people develop healthy life skills. Since 1993, when *Straight Talk* hit the streets and schools, it has been joined by *Young Talk* and *Teacher Talk.* A fourth publication, *Parent Talk,* will be launched shortly.

Developing a National Approach to HIV/AIDS

Initially, the Ministry of Health was responsible for coordinating the AIDS Control Program activities carried out by various organizations in Uganda. Because coordination was being handled by the health sector, however, the epidemic continued to be addressed almost exclusively as a health problem. As a result, the response by other organizations in the public and private sectors was inadequate.

Policymakers realized that the impact of the epidemic went beyond health, cutting across all aspects of individual, family, community, and national life. To have the impact it desired across sectors, the government adopted a multisector AIDS control strategy. In 1990 it asked a national task force, working with international agencies, to work out modalities for the new approach. Following the task force's recommendations, in 1992 the government created the Uganda AIDS Commission and developed a national multisector approach for dealing with HIV/AIDS. The strategy called for the involvement of all parties, individually or collectively, to fight the epidemic within their mandates and capacities. Other line ministries implemented the AIDS Control Project by incorporating it into their work plans.

To provide an appropriate environment in which to operationalize the multisector approach, in 1993 the Uganda AIDS Commission developed national AIDS control policy proposals. The proposals addressed 34 key issues in five thematic areas: preventing HIV infection, caring for people infected with or affected by HIV/AIDS, mitigating impact, conducting research, and building capacity for more effective action against HIV/AIDS (UAC 1996).

In the decade that followed, Uganda moved to combat HIV/AIDS in many ways. On the prevention front, it successfully mobilized the political and administrative system, launched a mass information and education campaign at the grassroots level, established health education networks in every district, introduced peer education in postprimary and tertiary institutions, developed a training module on behavior process, promoted condoms, and established networks of people with HIV/AIDS. On the control front, it established and expanded voluntary counseling and testing, improved blood screening, controlled opportunistic infections and STDs, and worked to develop a vaccine that prevents mother-to-child transmission.

The Cornerstone of Uganda's Prevention Plan: ABC

The prevention model pioneered in Uganda—known as ABC (Abstinence, Be faithful, use a Condom)—is the cornerstone of its strategy. The program initially met with opposition from various religious and cultural groups, which viewed the distribution of condoms as immoral. Commitment from Uganda's top leadership was strong, however, and the model was implemented aggressively.

The results of the campaign have been impressive. Awareness of HIV/AIDS is now universal in Uganda, in both rural and urban districts. In addition, the level of knowledge about the disease is high (survey respondents could cite at least two prevention interventions) in more than 90 percent of urban and about 80 percent of rural districts (Uganda Ministry of Health 2001b, 2002b).

The program has also had success changing behavior. The age of first sexual encounter rose from 14 in 1989 to more than 16 in 2001. Condom use with nonregular partners during the last sexual encounter rose, particularly in urban areas. Condom use has rapidly been rising from 7 percent in 1989 to about 60 percent in 2000 in most urban areas. The increase in condom use has been prompted not only by attempts to persuade people to adopt safer sex practices but also by the distribution of 50 million male condoms and 110,000 female condoms during the first six months of 2002, with special emphasis on high-risk groups.

Treating People with HIV/AIDS

Antiretroviral therapy (ART)—the use of a combination of medications that delay HIV replication and the deterioration of the immune system—was first introduced in Uganda in 1992, through clinical trials initiated by the Joint Clinical Research Center. It was integrated into the Ministry of Health's National Program for Comprehensive HIV/AIDS

Care and Support in 2001, after the pilot phase of the Drug Access Initiative demonstrated that it was possible to provide antiretroviral therapy even in resource-poor countries such as Uganda. Support for providing antiretroviral therapy has come from the World Bank's Multicountry AIDS Program; the Global Fund for AIDS, Tuberculosis and Malaria; and the Presidential Emergency Plan for AIDS Relief.

The public sector ART program was officially launched in June 2004 with drugs for treating 2,700 adults that were procured under the World Bank–funded Uganda AIDS Control Project. The drugs have been distributed to 26 health facilities, including all of the 11 regional referral hospitals. To facilitate the program, 381 doctors, 63 clinical officers, 238 nurses and midwives, 200 laboratory staff, 1,000 counselors, and 60 nursing assistants were trained in HIV/AIDS management including ART, and 96 trainers, 330 supervisors, and 390 community volunteers were trained for home-based care.

Most of the people receiving antiretroviral therapy are adults. Two-thirds of people on free therapy are female, while the majority of people on paid therapy are male. A small number of children have been started on highly active antiretroviral therapy: 160 of 2,100 sick children in Mildmay and 30 of 900 in Mulago. Plans are under way to procure syrup formulations for children under five. Antiretroviral therapy is being used to prevent mother-to-child transmission in 35 districts. The Prevention of Mother to Child Transmission program runs parallel with the national ART program.

Since 2004 Uganda has been offering free antiretroviral therapy throughout the country to all in need. Between 2004 and 2009 more than 40,000 people are expected to benefit from the antiretroviral program funded by the Global Fund for AIDS, Tuberculosis and Malaria (Kamya 2003).

Government and donors are faced with difficult choices about who will have access to ART. It is estimated that to provide ART to the over 150,000 Ugandans who need it, Uganda will need $100 million per year over the next few years, increasing to more than $131 million in 2012. Vulnerable groups such as rural populations, orphans and vulnerable children, internally displaced people, and others continue to face troublesome barriers to ART access.

Providing Voluntary Counseling and Testing

HIV testing began in the late 1980s in Uganda, when policymakers recognized the threat the disease posed to human livelihood. At that time there was an acute shortage of HIV testing facilities, and counseling was rarely provided. Most testing was done at the national blood bank on people claiming to be potential blood donors and seeking to find out their HIV status before donating blood (Kaleeba and others 2000).

In 1990 the AIDS Information Centre was established in Kampala.[1] It provided voluntary and anonymous testing for a fee. Counseling was eventually added to the testing program. Over the years voluntary counseling and testing (VCT) services have been expanded to cover more districts. The service is highly subsidized; clients pay a nominal fee. Since the VCT sites have been overwhelmed by excessive demand, the AIDS Information Centre is trying other options of dealing with this problem, including creation of more indirect sites, in which case some health units (both government and NGO) have been considered as delivery points of VCT services. The other option is that of the mobile van for VCT.

Screening the Nation's Blood Supply

The government significantly increased the capacity of blood screening services between 1986 and 1999, raising the proportion of blood screened from 25 to 70 percent. By 2003 the goal of reducing the risk of blood-borne HIV transmission from 2–4 percent to 1–2 percent by 2005/06 had been substantially achieved. The current risk of donated prescreened blood being infected with HIV is 2.1 percent (UAC 2004).

Providing Home-based Care

Home-based care interventions in Uganda have been implemented mostly by NGOs, which have piloted programs in 11 districts. NGOs have developed a training manual for health workers, monitoring and evaluation tools, and support supervision tools. Links between home-based care and palliative care interventions are being strengthened to enhance the quality of care.

Volunteers and health workers visit people who are bedridden, housebound, elderly, or neglected, irrespective of social status, to diagnose and treat HIV/AIDS. They determine whether patients need referrals to health centers. Enhancing this approach improves the quality of care for people with HIV/AIDS while considerably reducing costs and hospital bed occupancy rates (UNDP 2002). The strategy is based on

the premise that people in communities have the capacity to understand and handle their problems and the willingness to help each other.

Participating in Regional and Global Initiatives

Participation in international forums and declarations helped
Uganda respond to the epidemic early and develop appropriate
strategies. Several of its policies were guided by the WHO strategic
plan for 1985/86. Uganda has participated in the Great Lakes Initiative on HIV/AIDS, the African First Ladies HIV/AIDS Initiative, and the
Eastern African National Networks of AIDS Service Organizations.
Today Uganda subscribes to the shared program framework of the
"three ones"—one national coordinating authority, one national
strategic framework for HIV/AIDS action, and one national monitoring and evaluation framework.

What Have These Efforts Achieved?

In less than two decades Uganda has changed the face of HIV/AIDS
in the country. It has helped prevent Ugandans from contracting
HIV/AIDS and improved the lives of people already infected. Specific
accomplishments include the following:

- HIV prevalence declined dramatically among women seeking
  prenatal care at clinics. The data available suggest that the prevalence of HIV has been declining significantly in Uganda since
  1992; most recent estimates put the prevalence rate of HIV infection at 6.2 percent (Uganda Ministry of Health 2003b).
- HIV prevalence at STD clinics declined. Among patients in Kampala, prevalence declined from 44 percent in 1989 to 29 percent
  in 1998.
- Condom use skyrocketed, rising from 7 percent in 1989 to
  about 60 percent in 2000 in most urban areas.
- Free antiretroviral therapy is now available at all major health
  facilities in Uganda.
- The management of STDs and care and support interventions
  that require a continuum of comprehensive care has improved
  as a result of the availability of drugs for treating opportunistic
  infections.
- Human resources are in place at the national, district, and operational levels.

■ Palliative care centers have been established for the terminally ill.
■ The capacity of the Uganda Virus Research Institute, the national blood screening program, and the Joint Clinical Research Center has been vastly increased.

What Accounts for Uganda's Success?

What accounts for the phenomenal success of Uganda's national strategy to combat HIV/AIDS? From the beginning the strategy received very strong political commitment from the top. Government officials, especially President Museveni, were remarkably open in addressing the problem—something that had never been seen in Africa, where sex was not openly discussed. Uganda launched a massive information, communication, and education campaign that led to public debates; it made active efforts to mitigate the stigma associated with the disease; and it established a broad range of partnerships, including partnerships with all of Uganda's main faith communities. Early on it approached HIV/AIDS as a threat to development, not just a health problem. All of these factors worked together to produce extraordinary outcomes.

Commitment, Openness, and the Political Economy for Change

During the late 1980s, when taboos against public discussion of sex were pervasive in Uganda, President Museveni openly discussed the risky behaviors that lead to HIV/AIDS. Despite opposition from some groups, including cultural and religious institutions, the president and key members of the government persisted, demonstrating considerable political courage. The boldness and openness displayed by government and many community religious leaders paved the way, albeit gradually, for a more open and candid national response to HIV/AIDS by the general public.

Openness was critical in three areas:

■ Sensitizing local communities to accept the fact that HIV/AIDS exists but can be controlled.
■ Mobilizing the international community to support Uganda in fighting the epidemic.
■ Enabling government, politicians, and civil society to give HIV/AIDS the importance it deserved if development was to remain on course.

The support and commitment of the country's leadership have encouraged spontaneous and positive responses from people within and outside Uganda. Political commitment at the center has helped mobilize financial and technical support from donors and establish a multisector approach that reaches communities throughout the country.

This policy environment enabled the government to formulate effective national policies. The National Overarching Policy on AIDS provides the overall policy and planning environment through which the National Strategic Framework is delivered. It includes policies on orphans and other vulnerable children, condoms, HIV/AIDS and the world of work, antiretroviral therapy, and other issues.

The key guide to policy is the National Strategic Framework 2000/1–05/06. The National Strategic Framework complements and is subordinate to key policies and development planning frameworks for fighting poverty in Uganda. These include Vision 2025, the 2001 and 2004 Poverty Eradication Action Plans, the National Health Policy, the Local Government Act of 1997, and the Plan for the Modernization of Agriculture 2000. The government's 2000 decision to integrate HIV/AIDS issues into the Poverty Eradication Action Plan, Uganda's overarching national strategy for national development, reflects the depth of its commitment to fighting HIV/AIDS.

Ugandan authorities formulated and implemented policies and programs in a nonconfrontational way. Every player—the government, the private sector, civil society, and faith communities—was encouraged to join the fight against HIV/AIDS and to contribute in a manner consistent with its basic values and beliefs and reflecting its comparative advantages. Particular care was taken to prevent actors from expressing strong, undocumented views about condoms. Every constituency was given space, in a nonthreatening way that gradually allowed consensus to form.

Institutional Innovation

Under Uganda's multisector approach, institutions outside the health sector incorporate aspects of HIV/AIDS control or prevention in their plans. Planning cuts across sectors and includes efforts by the Ministries of Health, Education, Agriculture, Finance and Planning, Public Service, Water, and Gender, Labour and Social Development:

- ■ The Directorate of Education is carrying out community sensitization on HIV/AIDS, targeting in-school youth.

- The Directorate of Community Services in the Ministry of Gender, Labour and Social Development is implementing community sensitization on HIV/AIDS, counseling for families affected by HIV/AIDS, and arbitration procedures for use in inheritance disputes among relatives of people who die of AIDS.
- The Directorate of Agriculture is ensuring food security for people infected with or affected by HIV/AIDS.
- The Directorate of Finance and Planning is ensuring that financial proposals are approved by district councils and funds released to carry out HIV/AIDS work.
- Top coordinators in the districts are coordinating and managing HIV/AIDS activities.

Strengthening coordination of HIV/AIDS activities. A 2001 review of the Uganda AIDS Commission recommended strengthening coordination at the national level. A new coordination structure, the Uganda HIV/AIDS Partnership, was developed and operationalized. The structure includes four components: the Partnership Committee, the Partnership Forum, self-coordinating entities, and the Partnership Fund. The structure provides formal and representative coordination and information-sharing forums for all stakeholders, with the goal of strengthening overall coordination by the Uganda AIDS Commission (figures 13.3 and 13.4).

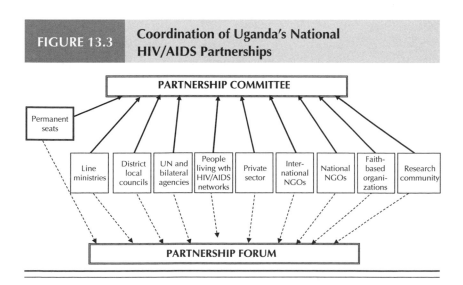

FIGURE 13.3 **Coordination of Uganda's National HIV/AIDS Partnerships**

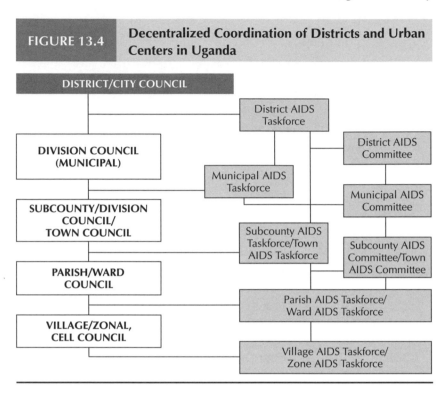

FIGURE 13.4 Decentralized Coordination of Districts and Urban Centers in Uganda

The Partnership Committee, chaired by the Uganda AIDS Commission, is the working group. It is made up of 15 representatives of self-coordinating entities. The self-coordinating entities are forums for institutions, clustered into government line ministries, decentralized governments, the UN and bilateral partners, networks of people with HIV/AIDS, the private sector, international NGOs, Ugandan NGOs, faith-based organizations, the research community, and the media. The Partnership Committee meets monthly and serves as the policy coordinating core unit for both the Partnership Forum and the self-coordinating entities. The Partnership Forum, which meets once a year, is a larger forum consisting of all members of the self-coordinating entities. The first Partnership Forum met during the Third National AIDS Conference in October 2002.

Working with local governments and urban authorities, the Uganda AIDS Commission developed guidelines for district HIV/AIDS coordination, with both technical and political coordination bodies for HIV/AIDS activities. The coordination mechanism for the districts is similar to that of the Uganda AIDS Commission partnership and enhances existing structures.

Uganda now has a well-defined coordination structure, implemented at the central level through a broad and inclusive coordination mechanism that brings together different constituencies to push for policy development, reform, and implementation of actions to combat HIV/AIDS. The Partnership Fund supports the coordination activities of the self-coordinating entities. At the district level HIV/AIDS "focal people" have been appointed, and discussions about the institutionalization of their positions are at an advanced stage. District HIV/AIDS coordination committees have been formed under the World Bank's Multicountry AIDS and Integrated District AIDS Model programs. District guidelines, developed by the Uganda AIDS Commission and approved by the Uganda Local Authorities Association, have been circulated and are being used. Some training in the use of the guidelines has also been carried out.

The Uganda AIDS Commission has also established a monitoring and evaluation subcommittee that is a standing committee within the partnership structure. The subcommittee's membership is drawn from a cross-section of agencies, including funding agencies, government, and civil society.

Mainstreaming HIV/AIDS into other development activities. HIV/AIDS is now included in the Poverty Eradication Action Plan, the principal guide to developmental activities in Uganda. The plan requires all sectors and areas of government to treat HIV/AIDS as a cross-cutting issue and to mainstream it within their sector plans. The Plan for Modernization of Agriculture, which addresses key elements of the National Strategic Framework for HIV/AIDS, is part of the government's broader strategy for implementing the Poverty Eradication Action Plan. Universal Primary Education provides a framework for mitigating the psychosocial effects of HIV/AIDS experienced by orphans and other vulnerable children. Schools provide a favorable environment for channeling HIV/AIDS messages to young people.

Preparing new institutional initiatives. A memorandum of understanding on strengthening information sharing and increasing the sense of mutual accountability between the Uganda AIDS Commission and the self-coordinating entities, research organizations, districts, and other key players has been drafted and is awaiting signing. A proposal to create an HIV/AIDS think tank focusing on planning, coordination, and resource mobilization is being discussed.

Donor Support

Uganda's frankness in discussing HIV/AIDS has generated immense goodwill and positive response from international development institutions and donors. Development partners contributed $171 million for HIV/AIDS services and activities between 1986 and 1998. Estimates for 2000/01–05/06 indicate that excluding the cost of antiretroviral therapy and drugs for treating opportunistic infections, the cost of treating HIV/AIDS will reach $130 million—equivalent to the entire annual health budget. Much of this funding will come from donors.

Donor activities. Uganda's international development partners—multilateral agencies, bilateral agencies, and other international humanitarian organizations—are engaged in funding projects; allocating financial resources, including resources for education and prevention; introducing new concepts to guide design; improving service delivery structures; organizing service delivery at the grassroots level; supporting orphans and widows; and training.

The Deutsche Gesellschaft für Technische Zusammenarbeit is promoting and providing condoms, providing mother-to-child transmission services, and encouraging behavioral change. The Africa Youth Alliance is promoting behavioral change and providing youth-friendly services. Compassion International provides support to orphans and vulnerable children. Other NGOs reach out to additional groups, such as refugees.

Other donors, including the French and U.S. governments and the Global Fund for AIDS, Tuberculosis and Malaria, have funded or are funding antitretroviral therapy programs. Their efforts have reduced the annual cost of treatment from about $12,000 in 1996 to $400 in 2000 and $28 in 2004 (UAC 2004).

Shortcomings of donor funding. Donor funding has helped Uganda finance its HIV/AIDS activities. However, it has meant that most programs are project oriented and therefore close when funds run out. Networking, developing communities' own resources, and empowering individuals and families have enabled people and communities to fill some of the gap (AMREF-Uganda 2001).

Negotiations for funding and programming usually take a long time, but once funds become available they are usually disbursed immediately. This undermines normal planning, the rational allocation of resources, equity, and in some cases program implementation (Adupa 2003).

Allocating and disbursing donor funds. A variety of vertical funding mechanisms for allocation, disbursement, and accountability are in place. Many line ministries have strategic plans, and most have HIV/AIDS operational plans developed primarily to access funds. Some districts have strategic and operational plans for accessing funds from the AIDS Control Program.

The need for more support. Including donor budgetary support, financial commitments to HIV/AIDS activities by the Ugandan central government increased fourfold in 2001, rising from about half a million US$ in 2000/01 to about US$15 million in 2001/02. Despite the increase, the figure represents only about $0.06 per capita, or 0.5 percent of the total budgetary allocation for 2001/02.[2]

Major additional financial resources have become available in the past two years with the creation of the Global Fund for AIDS, Tuberculosis and Malaria; World Bank Multicountry AIDS Program grants; and the Presidential Emergency Plan for AIDS Relief. Uganda has been actively trying to benefit from these resources.

Learning and Experimentation: Expanding What Works

Uganda first piloted voluntary counseling and testing services, then expanded the services when it learned that they are effective in changing behavior, particularly when people diagnosed with HIV join post-test clubs (AIC 2001). In one national survey (UNICEF 2003), over 28.9 percent of study participants had ever taken an HIV test and many more (78.8 percent) are willing to test. Today 51 of Uganda's 56 districts offer voluntary counseling and testing. Home-based care has also expanded as a result of its success.

Decentralization

Decentralization was introduced gradually in Uganda. Political decentralization occurred in 1986, followed by administrative decentralization in 1993 and fiscal decentralization in 1995. Budgetary transfers to districts increased from 11 percent of the national budget in 1995/96 to 20 percent in 2000/01 and 34 percent in 2002/03, as the Local Government Act of 1997 gave local authorities responsibility for delivering almost all services within their districts. The challenge for government was to increase spending on priority areas through the districts while ensuring that the funds disbursed reached the intended beneficiaries.

To ensure that they do, the central government requires districts to prepare budget paper frameworks, from which the district development
plan and annual budget are prepared. Funds are then disbursed in
line with the development plan and budget.

Decentralization has spurred HIV/AIDS interventions at lower levels
of government. The HIV/AIDS District Response Initiative is a strategy
for scaling up community-based responses to HIV/AIDS, executed by
UNICEF's Uganda Country Program in 31 focus districts (UNICEF
2003). The initiative aims to develop communities' capacities to assess
their HIV/AIDS situation and take concrete actions to address specific
problems. It also aims to build partnerships between duty-bearers
(local governments and service providers) and rights-holders (key
social groups), to open avenues for skills and knowledge development
and transfer both horizontally and vertically (UNICEF 2003).

The Uganda AIDS Control Program project, financed by the World
Bank, is promoting and supporting community-led HIV/AIDS initiatives to mobilize and organize communities to respond to HIV/
AIDS by developing relevant subprojects. The initiatives are sponsored
by civil service organizations, NGOs, faith-based organizations,
community-based organizations, private sector organizations, and
networks of people living with HIV/AIDS.

Communication and Sensitization

Twenty years ago most Ugandans knew little about HIV/AIDS. Today,
as the result of a massive information campaign, Ugandans understand how the disease is contracted, how it is spread, and how it can be
prevented. Openness has enabled leaders and organizations, including
those from faith communities, to launch public information campaigns and establish care and treatment facilities.

Public information campaigns have gradually shifted from messages of fear and recrimination to messages of hope, comfort, and dignity, which serve to motivate people to seek testing and adopt less
risky behaviors. Openness means that people can more easily access
treatment, and it empowers them to translate information into action.

The nature and level of sensitization about HIV/AIDS achieved in
the national response represents a landmark in Uganda. By openly
addressing the problem of HIV/AIDS, government leaders opened
up discussion of sexuality, breaking a long-held taboo. Two decades
ago Uganda was a society in which social and cultural norms made it

impossible to talk about sexuality. Today HIV/AIDS is openly discussed on the airwaves, and parents and teachers talk about the disease with children. The fact that condom use is now publicly demonstrated using penis models in public gatherings represents a sea change in acceptance.

This extraordinary openness in discussing HIV/AIDS helped make Uganda's approach a success. People in the field were also savvy about adjusting the emphasis of the message, variously focusing on abstinence, faithfulness to a sexual partner, or condom use, depending on the target group.

Heads of teacher training institutions and education managers at the district levels have been trained to participate in the fight against HIV/AIDS. The Ministry of Education produces draft communication guidelines on HIV/AIDS to be used by primary school teachers to educate children about the disease. In collaboration with the Uganda AIDS Commission and the Ministry of Health's information, education, and communication unit, the Ministry of Education developed draft assembly messages for all government schools. The messages are part of the Presidential Initiative on AIDS Strategy for Communications to the Youth, an initiative that arose from the president's call for a communications strategy to improve HIV prevention support to young people.

Surveillance and Research

HIV/AIDS surveillance began in Uganda in the late 1980s, after a control unit on AIDS and STDs was established in the Ministry of Health. Surveillance was based largely on STD prevalence studies and data from women attending prenatal clinics in the hardest-hit districts. Over time surveillance sites have been expanded to cover most parts of the country. Twenty sentinel sites are currently based in hospital prenatal clinics, and there is one STD referral clinic with an HIV surveillance focus.

The sentinel surveillance protocol involves testing blood samples taken as part of normal care of patients visiting prenatal and STD clinics. In addition to anonymous HIV screening, the STD/AIDS Control Program Unit in the Ministry of Health conducts other routine activities, including behavioral surveillance, AIDS case reporting, syndromic reporting of STDs, and tuberculosis reporting. It publishes its findings in annual reports.

Since 1997 Uganda has been participating in vaccine development and trials. It has worked closely with the United Nations Joint Programme on HIV/AIDS on developing and evaluating a vaccine and on reviewing the ethical and legal issues related to vaccine development.

Uganda has also conducted two studies on mother-to-child transmission, the Petra Studies and the Nevirapine Studies. The Medical Research Council program, based at the Uganda Virus Research Institute, has been implementing cohort studies in Masaka and Sembabule. Cohort data are generated from serological and census surveys.

Involving People with HIV/AIDS

Several associations of people with HIV/AIDS are now operating in Uganda, with members from almost every district. The groups perform drama shows and give testimonies about HIV/AIDS, raising awareness and the perception of risk. Dozens of HIV-positive members of the Philly Lutaaya Initiative have been trained to talk about their experience living with HIV/AIDS. They speak at schools and community gatherings and give radio, newspaper, and television interviews.

Participation in prevention activities by people with HIV/AIDS is a best practice that has helped Uganda prevent infection. Once condemned to die without dignity, people with HIV/AIDS have provided a new perspective on the reality of the disease. They have helped establish empathy, tolerance, and acceptance, making it easier for all people to work together in the fight against HIV/AIDS.

A national forum has been formed to bring together all networks, associations, support groups, and individuals living with HIV/AIDS in Uganda. The aim is to share information and experience and to increase coordination and involvement in all HIV/AIDS activities, especially policy issues, in order to increase the influence of people with HIV/AIDS on Uganda's responses.

Lessons

Developing countries—and industrial ones—can learn much from Ugandans' success in slowing the HIV/AIDS epidemic and moderating its impact:

■ Openness, advocacy, and publicity at all levels of government can have an enormous impact on people's lives. Widespread sensitization about HIV/AIDS has made all Ugandans aware of the risk of HIV/AIDS. Behavioral change interventions need to be scaled up, however, to increase their impact.

- Open parent-child, peer, and community discussion of HIV/AIDS is critical. Frank discussion of the disease by the president and other high-ranking officials helped reduce stigma, isolation, and discrimination; increase knowledge; and change behavior in Uganda.
- ABC works—but it is not enough. Uganda complemented the ABC program with other, locally initiated responses. Together these approaches have significantly reduced the prevalence of HIV/AIDS.
- Allowing actors endorsing a variety of approaches to participate in the fight against HIV/AIDS increases the scope for dealing with the problem.
- Establishing partnerships with a wide variety of groups is an effective way of promoting prevention. Partnerships between the government and traditional healers and all of the country's major faith groups helped educate Ugandans about HIV/AIDS.
- Involving people with HIV/AIDS in prevention activities is effective in combating the disease.
- The existence of voluntary counseling and testing services can stimulate people to get tested for HIV and to adopt appropriate behavioral changes. It also increases activism. Most of the members of Uganda's community-based groups, which play a leading role in community outreach, sensitization, and care, are members of post-test clubs.
- Making antiretroviral therapy accessible to all in need can help reduce the sense of hopelessness engulfing many communities, particularly in poor districts hard hit by the disease.

BIBLIOGRAPHY

Adupa, R. L. 2003. "Planning, Resource Mobilization and Resource Management." In *Mid Term Review of the National Strategic Framework for HIV/AIDS Activities in Uganda 2000/01–2005/06*. Uganda AIDS Commission, Kampala.

AIC (AIDS Information Centre). 2001. "Information Booklet for Provision of Quality Integrated VCT, STD, FP, TB and PTC/PLI Services." Kampala.

AMREF-Uganda (African Medical and Research Foundation). 2001. "Inventory of Agencies with HIV/AIDS Activities and HIV/AIDS Interventions in Uganda: A Review of Actors, Interventions, Achievements and Constraints Relating to the HIV/AIDS Challenge in Uganda." AMREF-Uganda, Uganda AIDS Commission Secretariat. [www.aidsuganda.org/pdf/hiv_agencies_inventory.pdf].

Barnett, T., and P. Blaikie. 1992. *AIDS in Africa: Its Present and Future Impact.* London: Belhaven Press.

Bazeyo, K. W. 2003. "Coordination and Institutional Arrangements." In *Mid Term Review of the National Strategic Framework for HIV/AIDS Activities in Uganda 2000/01–2005/06.* Uganda AIDS Commission, Kampala.

Directorate of Water Development. 2003. "A Draft National Operation and Maintenance Framework for Rural Water Supplies." Kampala.

Green, E. C. 1998. "Report on the Situation of AIDS and the Role of IEC in Uganda." USAID/World Learning, Washington, D.C.

Kagimu, M., and E. Marum. 1996. "Review of AIDS Prevention and Control Activities in Uganda." Uganda AIDS Commission, Kampala.

Kaleeba N., D. Kalinaki, J. Namulondo, and G. Williams. 2000. *Open Secret: People Facing Up to HIV and AIDS in Uganda.* Strategies for Hope 15. London: ActionAid.

Kamya, M. 2003. "Care and Treatment." In *Mid Term Review of the National Strategic Framework for HIV/AIDS Activities in Uganda 2000/01–2005/06.* Uganda AIDS Commission, Kampala.

Kayita, J., and J. B. Kyakulaga. 1997. "HIV/AIDS Status Report." Uganda AIDS Commission, Kampala.

Kifuko, B. M. 2003. "Monitoring and Evaluation." In *Mid Term Review of the National Strategic Framework for HIV/AIDS Activities in Uganda 2000/01–2005/06.* Uganda AIDS Commission, Kampala.

Kiirya, S. 1999. "A Baseline Study on Sexual and Reproductive Knowledge, Attitudes and Practices of Muslim Adolescents." Uganda Muslim Supreme Council, United Nations Population Fund, Kampala.

Kiirya, S., R. Sewakiryanga, and E. Were. 2000. "HIV Infected, Uninfected and Unaware Persons: Awareness, Perceptions, Practices and Inhibitors of Positive Living in Uganda." United Nations Population Fund, Ministry of Finance, Planning and Economic Development, Makerere Institute of Social Research, National Community of Women Living with HIV/AIDS in Uganda, Kampala.

Konde-Lule, J. 2003. "Prevention and Behaviour Change." In *Mid Term Review of the National Strategic Framework for HIV/AIDS Activities in Uganda 2000/01–2005/06.* Uganda AIDS Commission, Kampala.

Kyomuhendo, S. 2003. "Psychosocial Support, Protection and Human Rights." In *Mid Term Review of the National Strategic Framework for HIV/AIDS Activities in Uganda 2000/01–2005/06.* Uganda AIDS Commission, Kampala.

Kyomuhendo, S., and N. Asingwire. 2003. "The ABC Model: Prevention Practices in Uganda's Response to HIV/AIDS." Abstract 1098843 and Presentation at the 13th International Conference on AIDS and STIs in Africa, September 21–26, Nairobi, Kenya.

Lyons, M. 1996. "Summative Evaluation of Prevention and Control Project." USAID/World Learning, Washington, D.C.

Levy, Brian D., and Sahr John Kpundeh, eds. 2004. *Building State Capacity in Africa: New Approaches, Emerging Lessons.* Washington D.C.: World Bank.

Ntozi, J. P. M., and G. G. Turyasingura. 2000. "Adolescent Sexual and Reproductive Health Study in Uganda." Institute of Statistics and Applied Economics; Program for Enhancing Adolescent Reproductive Life; Ministry of Labour, Gender and Social Development; and United Nations Population Fund. Kampala.

TASO (The AIDS Support Organization). 2002. *The Uganda AIDS Support Organization: Annual Report.* Kampala.

———. 2002. "The Uganda AIDS Support Organization: Positive Attitude, Caring Services." *Newsletter* 10(1). Kampala.

UAC (Uganda AIDS Commission). 1996. *National AIDS Control Policy Proposals.* Kampala.

———. 2000. *The National Strategic Framework for HIV/AIDS Activities in Uganda 2000/01–2005/06.* Kampala.

———. 2001. "The Uganda AIDS Control Project (UACP): Project Updates June 2001." Kampala.

———. 2002. "Guidelines for District HIV/AIDS Coordination." Kampala.

———. 2002. "The Monitoring and Evaluation Plan of the Expanded National Response on HIV/AIDS in Uganda 2000/02–2005/06." Kampala.

———. 2002. "Third National AIDS Conference (NAC) Report." Kampala.

———. 2003. "Follow-Up to the Declaration of Commitment on HIV/AIDS (UNGASS)." Uganda Country Report. Kampala.

———. 2003. "Mainstreaming HIV/AIDS Issues into the Poverty Eradication Action Plan (PEAP)." Uganda HIV/AIDS Partnership, Kampala.

———. 2003. "The Overarching HIV/AIDS Policy." Kampala.

———. 2004. *The National Strategic Framework for HIV/AIDS Activities in Uganda 2003/04–2005/06.* Kampala.

UBOS (Uganda Bureau of Statistics). 2002. "Uganda Population and Housing Census." Provisional results. Intersoft Business Services Ltd., Kampala.

Uganda Ministry of Finance, Planning and Economic Development. 2001. "Poverty Eradication Action Plan (PEAP), 2001–2003." Kampala.

———. 2002. "Uganda Participatory Poverty Assessment Process: Deepening the Understanding of Poverty." Second Participatory Poverty Assessment Report. Kampala.

———. 2003. "Background to the Budget, Financial Year 2003/04." Kampala.

———. 2003. "Uganda Poverty Status Report: Achievements and Points for the PEAP Revision." Kampala.

———. 2004. "Reducing Poverty Sustaining Growth, from Conflict to Sustained Growth and Deep Reductions in Poverty." Kampala.

Uganda Ministry of Health. 1996. *Results of the Population Based KABP Survey on HIV/AIDS and STDs in Four Districts in Uganda.* STD/AIDS Control Programme, Kampala.

———. 1997. "HIV/AIDS Surveillance Report 1997." STD/AIDS Control Programme, Kampala.

———. 1999. "HIV/AIDS Surveillance Report 1999." STD/AIDS Control Programme, Kampala.

———. 2000. "Health Sector Strategic Plan 2000/01–2004/05." Kampala.

———. 2000. "HIV/AIDS Surveillance Report 2000." STD/AIDS Control Programme, Kampala.

———. 2001a. "Annual Health Sector Performance Report." Kampala.

———. 2001b. "HIV/AIDS Surveillance Report 2001." STD/AIDS Control Programme, Kampala.

———. 2001c. "Policy Guidelines on Feeding of Infants and Young Children in the Context of HIV/AIDS." Kampala.

———. 2002a. "2001/2002 Annual Health Sector Performance Report." Kampala.

———. 2002b. "HIV/AIDS Surveillance Report 2002." STD/AIDS Control Programme, Kampala.

———. 2002c. "Prevention of Mother to Child Transmission of HIV: Annual Report." STD/AIDS Control Programme, Kampala.

———. 2003a. "Antiretroviral Treatment Policy for Uganda." Kampala.

———. 2003b. "Ministry of Health Statistical Abstracts." Kampala.

UNAIDS (United Nations Joint Programme on HIV/AIDS). 1999. "Global Estimates of the HIV/AIDS Epidemic as of December 1999." Geneva.

———. 1999. "Knowledge Is Power: Voluntary HIV Counseling and Testing in Uganda." UNAIDS Case Study, Best Practice Collection. Geneva.

———. 2001. "Reaching Out, Scaling Up: Eight Case Studies of Home and Community Care for and by People with HIV/AIDS." UNAIDS Case Study, Best Practice Collection. Geneva.

UNDP (United Nations Development Programme). 2002. *Uganda Human Development Report: The Challenge of HIV/AIDS—Maintaining the Momentum of Success.* Kampala.

UNICEF (United Nations Children's Fund). 2000. "Situational Analysis Update 2000." Uganda Country Programme, Kampala.

———. 2003. "The District Response Initiative on HIV/AIDS in Uganda—Action Research: National Synthesis Report." Kampala.

Interviews and Personal Communication

Director General, Uganda AIDS Commission

Head, HIV/AIDS Cluster, UNICEF, Uganda

Director, National AIDS Documentation and Information Centre, Uganda AIDS Commission

Senior Presidential Advisor, HIV/AIDS, Office of the President

Chairperson, National People Living with HIV/AIDS Forum Board

Program Manager, Sexually Transmitted Infection/AIDS Control Program, Ministry of Health

Former Chairman, the Uganda AIDS Commission (1995–97)

Minister of Health (1986)

Ag. Admn. General, Administrator General's Office, Ministry of Justice

Coordinator, National Community of Women Living with HIV/AIDS

Commissioner, Gender and Community Development, Ministry of Gender, Labour and Social Development

Program Director, Models of Learning Program, World Vision

Executive Director, AIDS Information Centre

Country Director, Orphans and Vulnerable Children Programme, Association Francois-Xavia Bagnoud

Director, Multiservice support for people living with HIV/AIDS, orphans and
  vulnerable children and affected families, Kitovu Mobile
Focal Point Officer HIV/AIDS, Inter-Religious Council, Catholic Secretariat
Capacity Building Officer, National Forum of People Living with HIV/AIDS
Executive Director, National Council for Children
Chairperson, Uganda Network of AIDS Service Organisations
Head, National Documentation and Information Centre, Uganda AIDS Com-
  mission
Project Coordinator, Community-led HIV/AIDS Initiatives, Uganda AIDS Control
  Project
Director, Policy and Research, Uganda AIDS Commission

Notes

Chapter One

1. The July 2004 agreement by the United States and the European Union (EU) to remove agricultural export subsidies and reduce other farm subsidies and the WTO panel decision against cotton subsidies in the United States and the EU in September 2004 suggest that there is some progress on these trade issues.

2. Easterly (2003) reports that between 1980 and 2000 the World Bank gave Kenya 21 adjustment loans, despite clear evidence of the problems of the Moi government. According to him, the Bank provided aid to support identical agricultural policy reforms five separate times.

3. Interestingly, key developing country demands—including addressing the special needs of the least developed countries, dealing with developing country debt problems, and ensuring access to medicine—were not given verifiable targets and left vague (see UNDP 2003).

4. See the Millennium Challenge Corporation Web site at www.mca.gov/; the Millennium Challenge Account Update of June 3, 2002, at www.usaid.gov/press/releases/2002/fs_mca.html; and *East African* (2004).

5. This characterization of institutions is from Dani Rodrik.

6. Two important exceptions were Botswana and Mauritius, both of which recorded consistently strong economic performance since the 1960s.

7. The dilemma of a political imperative toward regime survival based on the economically irrational use of resources for patronage at the expense of fostering a dynamic process of economic growth that could supply the wherewithal for state building was also a central theme in the work of such political scientists as

371

William Reno (1998), Jean-François Bayart (1993), and Robert Jackson and Carl Rosberg (1982).

8. For an excellent summary of the problems of the state-led development approach adopted by African states after independence, see Rapley (2002).

9. See for example chapter 10.

10. This contrasts with the East Asian experience, in which democratic forms are less common and accountability takes other forms.

Chapter Two

1. In 1986 Uganda had different militia controlling different parts of Kampala and the country—such as FEDEMU, UFM, NRF, UNLA.

2. Under the governments of Idi Amin (1971–79), Milton Obote II (1980–85), and Tito Okello Lutwa (1985–86), a soldier could confiscate a person's house, shop, car, or factory with impunity.

3. The World Bank, for example, said in its 1992 *Project Completion Report, First Economic Recovery Credit* that government "practically abandoned the stabilization components of the Economic Recovery Program in 1987/88 and 1988/89" (World Bank 1992, p. 12). Yet the Bank and the IMF remained involved in the country.

4. In 1987 government tax revenues represented only 5 percent of GDP. The government placed a high priority on improving revenue mobilization in order to increase state spending. It improved tax administration and diversified sources of revenue by imposing import taxes and other indirect taxes on fuel, beer, and tobacco. Despite these efforts, most government revenue came from foreign donors, as grants increased from 1.7 percent of GDP in 1987 to 7.2 percent in 1992.

5. Collier and Dollar (1998) offer an interesting analysis of the contribution of foreign aid to policy orientation and economic growth in Uganda.

6. Brig. Jim Muhwezi, interview, July 2003.

7. Empirical research suggests that such investment is robustly and positively correlated with the rate of economic growth (Reinikka and Svensson 2001).

8. Critics of the plan argued that the devaluation would reduce the purchasing power of money wages. The National Resistance Council passed a resolution in 1989 asking the government not to devalue the shilling. In September 1989 President Museveni organized a seminar on the exchange rate, attended by bureaucrats, donors, politicians, academics, and businesspeople. Tumusiime-Mutebile presented a paper extolling the virtues of foreign exchange liberalization. The seminar went beyond the expectations of all stakeholders and called for legalization of the black market (Mamdani 1989; Henstridge and Kasekende 2001).

9. Scarcities of basic consumer goods had been a major impediment to improving welfare because commodities like soap, sugar, salt, and kerosene were unavailable.

10. Keith Muhakanizi, interview, October 16, 2003.

11. The treasury bill interest rate averaged 17 percent in the last half of 2003, while commercial bank rates averaged 25 percent. See Bank of Uganda Monthly Economic and Financial Indicators on the Bank of Uganda Web site.

12. Keith Muhakanizi, interview, October 15, 2003.

13. Further analysis of the data is exploring the impact of increased access to social services on the livelihoods of the poor, which is not captured in household expenditure data.

14. Budget Speech, June 12, 2003.

15. Keith Muhakanizi, interview, October 15, 2003. The figure for 2001 is 80 percent of the funds released reach the intended beneficiaries.

16. Keith Muhakanizi, interview, October 15, 2003.

17. President Museveni, meeting with journalists, December 31, 2003.

18. DHS Surveys (www.measuredhs.com/data/indicators).

Chapter Three

1. Statistics in this section draw predominantly on Obidegwu 2003; Republic of Rwanda (2002, 2003); United Kingdom, Department for International Development (2003); and World Bank (2003).

Chapter Five

1. Most of the historical data are drawn from Jaffee 1995.

2. The Horticulture Crop Development Authority estimates total fresh horticultural exports at Ksh 26.7 billion in 2002 and Ksh 28.8 billion in 2003, which would put total exports above $400 million after including processed pineapple products. There appear to be some anomalies in these data, however. Figures 5.1 and 5.2 try to correct these anomalies.

3. FAOSTAT database (www.fao.org).

4. Smallholders' share of the two main export crops, coffee and tea, increased from virtually zero in 1955 to 40 percent for coffee and 70 percent for tea in 1980. Smallholders participated through a highly successful contract farming arrangement for tea that involved 230,000 farmers by 1990 (Swamy 1994).

5. Growth in tea production has been significant, if slower, but it has been partially offset by falling prices.

6. The average Kenyan household has a lot more than four people, but most farmers and laborers probably have working spouses. Most farmers, and some laborers, also have other sources of income, so the horticulture industry cannot claim to be supporting all of these people.

7. Minot and Ngigi (as reported in Gabre-Madhin and Minot 2003) report much higher returns for French beans. The figures presented here are still higher than the income estimates of McCulloch and Ota (2002).

8. Note that this does not include the value of household labor, much more of which is required for horticulture. Horticulture is also riskier, as yields are more susceptible to disease and poor weather, and postharvest losses are higher due to the greater perishability of the product.

9. Humphrey, McCulloch, and Ota (2004) show that current growth in the sector adds far more jobs than might feasibly be obtained by shifting more production to smallholders. Their findings imply that the primary emphasis should be on the continued growth of the sector. Indeed, some observers argue that

smallholder production is actually less labor intensive, so that a shift in their favor would reduce the level of employment.

10. The total poverty line for Nairobi appears to be high, so it is not clear whether the level of poverty among packhouse workers is actually higher (as suggested by the total poverty line) or lower (as indicated by food poverty) than that of horticulture smallholders.

11. A maximum of two additional hours of work is permitted.

12. While the cost of urban living is certainly higher, it would not offset such a gap.

13. Alleged circumvention of existing foreign exchange controls was another important motivation (Jaffee 1995).

14. Medium and large-scale outgrowers accounted for 29 percent of export vegetables and 14 percent of export fruit, with the remainder accounted for by farms leased or owned by export companies (44 percent of vegetables and only 1 percent of fruit) (Jaffee 2003).

15. An estimated 10,000 smallholders are involved in producing avocados for export.

16. This section is based on Jaffee and Bintein (1996).

17. Some of the sprayers were selling the chemicals and then using inadequate dosages, which increased resistance of the bean rust disease to the chemicals in use.

18. While Kenya has until January 2005 to comply with European Union traceability requirements, in practice compliance has already been required by buyers for the leading European supermarkets.

Chapter Six

1. One of the results of competition in the mobile telecommunications sector is the elusiveness of accurate figures on the subscribers, which are regarded as competitive intelligence. The figures shown here are from the Office of the Secretary of State for New Technologies.

2. For a comprehensive brief on the telecommunications environment in Botswana, Mauritania, and Tanzania, see "Telecoms Country Report," published by the World Markets Research Centre. The latest information, however, is as of February 4, 2003.

Chapter Eight

1. Savings are collected and loans disbursed at weekly meetings. Two members of each *watanos* are eligible for loans in the first month, two more the second month, and the remainder the third month. (This loan disbursement pattern may be altered to meet specific circumstances.) Each member pays a membership fee and buys a passbook for a total of $3.70. Each borrower pays 1.5 percent of the loan amount to cover the application fee (1 percent) and insurance (0.5 percent). All member savings are deposited into a group savings account at a commercial bank, with a credit officer and two members serving as cosignatories. These savings serve as an additional guarantee against loan default but are withdrawn only as a last resort.

2. K-Rep had required collateral security in the form of savings equivalent to 10 percent of each *chikolo* loan and 20 percent of each *juhudi* loan. In January

1998 it changed the loan guarantee amount for new clients to 5 percent of the loan amount, incrementally rising to 20 percent for loans of $862 and higher.

3. In Kenya only financial institutions licensed by the Central Bank of Kenya can mobilize deposits from the public. K-Rep's mobilization of "forced savings" from its customers as guarantees of their loans was not considered deposit-taking, since the funds were not lent.

4. K-Rep had nine board members at the time of transformation from an NGO to a microfinance commercial bank. The chairman (a respected diplomat) and the managing director were founding members of K-Rep. The other board members included a politician, a founding member of the Institute of Certified Public Accountants of Kenya, two academicians/researchers, an entrepreneur skilled in consulting on leadership and governance, and a businessman.

5. By law K-Rep the NGO was not permitted to own any part of a commercial bank.

6. The minimum capital requirement at that time was $2.5 million, but there was a proposal to increase it to $6.3 million over the next two years.

7. Market Intelligence 2003.

8. Each individual in a group has his or her own account, with all group member accounts electronically linked to each other to cover group guarantees.

9. This account encourages parents and guardians to open up savings accounts for their children. A minimum balance of $6 is required to open the account, which earns interest as long as a balance of $60 is maintained.

10. Both inflation and Treasury bill rates fluctuated during the early 2000s. The rate on 90-day Treasury bills fell from 13 percent in 1999 to 1.6 percent in 2003.

Chapter Nine

1. In most countries, that choice has tended to be boys first (investment in girls takes the form of marriage). In contrast, in Lesotho boys have been sent to work in the mines in South Africa or as herd boys, and girls have benefited more from schooling. The gender equity Gini coefficient in Lesotho in 1990–91 was 1.21 in favor of girls.

2. Differences between social and cultural contexts within each country are as great as those among the four countries. This case study concentrates on the cross-country differences.

3. Many parents simply ignored the fact that free primary education was initially for just four children per family and sent more than four children to school.

4. Uganda has done more than most African countries in providing effective HIV/AIDS education. Its efforts appear to have helped slow the spread of the disease.

5. In Lesotho free primary education has freed up $6 (in the mountain regions) to $23 (in urban regions) a year per household. No studies have been conducted on how poor households are using the money or how they are compensating for the loss of labor at home.

6. Social and systemic factors are not mutually exclusive: dissatisfaction with schooling lowers motivation to stick it out when personal circumstances are difficult.

7. Ethiopia is going farthest in providing alternative basic education schools. Its programs are being studied as a model for primary education as a whole.

8. Policymakers visiting Tanzania benefited from observing the way in which the community was mobilized and involved in school and teacher development in the District-Based Support to Primary Education program. The use of preregistration in October to help plan for the succeeding year was another important lesson learned from Tanzania's experience.

9. In some cases, communities have begun growing food to meet the needs of the school catering program.

10. An exception was the role played by Ireland Aid (then Irish Aid) in Lesotho, which created an environment for negotiation between government and proprietors, with whom Ireland had strong previous links through churches.

11. The potential of using the Forum for African Parliamentarians in Education has yet to be fully explored.

12. Households headed by single women tend to spend a greater share of their domestic income on the education of children than do households headed by men, even though their income is usually lower.

13. Whether early childhood education should be promoted and if so how needs to be researched in the light of the HIV/AIDS pandemic. Providing early childhood education would reduce primary school dropout and repetition rates by freeing girls from the responsibility of caring for preschool-age children.

14. The international community has pledged support to achieving the Millennium Development Goals and buffering the impact of HIV/AIDS.

15. The potential of using literate community members as classroom assistants has not been adequately explored in Africa.

Chapter Ten

1. Strictly speaking, drinking water is the subject of one of the Millennium Development Goals, while sanitation is the subject of a goal set by the World Summit on Sustainable Development. This case follows normal custom in describing both as Millennium Development Goals.

2. One study estimates expenditure on water and sanitation in Ethiopia, Kenya, and Uganda as ranging from 0.5 to 1.0 percent of GDP (World Bank 2004). South Africa has a policy of allocating 0.75 percent of its GDP to water and sanitation; the actual allocation has reached 0.4–0.5 percent.

3. The Mvula Trust estimates that cost recovery occurs in 10–20 percent of municipalities.

Chapter Eleven

1. Benin, Burkina Faso, Côte d'Ivoire, Ghana, Guinea, Guinea-Bissau, Mali, Niger, Senegal, and Togo. Operations that had been interrupted in Sierra Leone due to a decade-long civil war are now resuming.

2. Phase II countries include Angola, Burundi, Cameroon, Central African Republic, Chad, the Democratic Republic of Congo, the Republic of Congo, Equatorial Guinea, Ethiopia, the Gabon, Kenya, Liberia, Malawi, Mozambique, Nigeria, Rwanda, Sudan, Tanzania, and Uganda.

Chapter Twelve

1. Evaluation of the impact of the Zambia social investment fund was carried out by the World Bank in collaboration with the government of Zambia as part of a 2000 study of social funds. The evaluation used a nationally representative household survey, oversampling in areas where the fund was active. Applying propensity and pipeline match techniques to control for community self-selection, the study evaluated the household impacts of rehabilitating and constructing schools and health posts (Chase and Sherburne-Benz 2001).

2. The independent review of poverty reduction during the democratic transition in Malawi was carried out between 2001 and 2003 by a consortium of research groups from Malawi, Norway, and the United Kingdom. The review included discussions with key informants, consultations with stakeholders, and in-depth research on key issues, using both quantitative and qualitative techniques

3. The differences in the achievements of the two funds revealed in table 12.1 can be explained by the different levels of financial resources. Although MASAF was established four years after the Zambia fund, it has received more than twice the financial resources. MASAF 1 used almost three times the financial resources as SRP I, and the budget for MASAF 2 was more than twice as large as the budget for SRP II. The budgets for the first phases of MASAF 3 and ZAMSIF I are of similar magnitudes.

4. SRP clinics were not found to perform better than other clinics in terms of the availability of essential drugs and supplies.

5. *Deconcentration* refers to the representation of central line ministries at the local level; *devolution* refers to transferring administrative, political, and financial authority to local governments, where elected bodies may or may not have jurisdiction over these local government representatives. Devolution is typically carried out as part of a public sector reform process, with central governments in the driver seat. Social investment funds do not engage in these top-down public sector reform processes. In recent years, however, the funds have accumulated significant experience preparing the ground for the devolution process by strengthening the capacities of local government, establishing efficient local development mechanisms, and forging accountability links between communities and local government, as they have in Malawi and Zambia.

Chapter Thirteen

1. The center was funded by the U.S. Agency for International Development (USAID), which worked with the Ministry of Health, the Nakasero Blood Bank, the Uganda Virus Research Institute, the World Health Organization, the AIDS Support Organization, and other institutions (UNAIDS 1999a).

2. As Uganda mainstreams HIV/AIDS spending, it will become increasingly difficult to disaggregate commitments for HIV/AIDS from sector commitments.

Index

Eco-Audit

Environmental Benefits Statement

The World Bank is committed to preserving endangered forests and natural resources. We have chosen to print *Attacking Africa's Poverty: Experience from the Ground* on 30% post-consumer recycled fiber paper, processed chlorine free. The World Bank has formally agreed to follow the recommended standards for paper usage set by the Green Press Initiative—a nonprofit program supporting publishers in using fiber that is not sourced from endangered forests. For more information, visit www.greenpressinitiative.org.

The printing of these books on recycled paper saved the following:

Trees*	Solid Waste	Water	Net Greenhouse Gases	Electricity
18	843	7,646	1,656	3,075
*40' in height and 6-8" in diameter	Pounds	Gallons	Pounds	KWH